The Learned and the Lewed

Bartlett Jere Whiting   (Photograph by Linda Sundwall)

The Learned and the Lewed

Studies in Chaucer and Medieval Literature

Edited by
Larry D. Benson

Harvard University Press, Cambridge, Massachusetts 1974

Written for
Bartlett Jere Whiting
by his students

Editorial Note

Since medieval literature was the intended theme for this fifth volume of Harvard English Studies, B. J. Whiting's colleagues thought it appropriate that this issue be used to honor our department's most distinguished teacher of medieval literature on the occasion of his seventieth birthday.

A work containing contributions from all of Mr. Whiting's friends and colleagues would have created great problems of space, as it would have run to several volumes. Even one containing only contributions from his students would have been far too long, for his teaching has affected almost every student in the College and the Graduate School for more than forty years. It was therefore decided to limit contributions to those students for whose doctoral theses Mr. Whiting had served as reader. This has the advantage of showing the great range of subjects and critical approaches of his doctoral students. We hope it does not obscure the fact that those whose works appear in this volume are but a small percentage of his many friends, students, and colleagues who would have liked to demonstrate their affection in this way. For a time we thought of calling this volume *Chaucer and His Friends,* since most of his students develop the conviction that Mr. Whiting *is* Chaucer, and all are his friends eager to pay him honor and wish him well on this, his seventieth birthday.

L. D. B.

Contents

The Learned and the Lewed

DAVID STAINES

Bartlett Jere Whiting

The Learned and the Lewed: Studies in Chaucer and Medieval Literature, dedicated to B. J. Whiting by his students, the fifth volume of *Harvard English Studies,* is focused on the literary world of Chaucer and his contemporaries. The unity of the volume lies not in the subject matter of the individual essays, but in the teacher and scholar who inspires them. All of the contributors wrote their doctoral dissertations under the direction of Bartlett Jere Whiting, Gurney Professor of English Literature at Harvard University. The dissertations found encouragement and inspiration in Whiting's scholarly scrutiny and careful criticism. These new essays express the homage and respect, "lered other lewed," which Whiting's students feel toward their teacher and friend. The authors of these studies profited not only from Whiting's teaching at Harvard and his many scholarly books, but also from his continued interest in their academic careers, his unending assistance with their scholarly questions (his study in Widener Library remains a reservoir for questioning letters from former students now far from the wealth of Widener), and the example he offers as a model of fine teaching, excellent scholarship, and humane understanding. The twenty-seven contributions attest to the fact that Whiting stands as a continuing inspiration

1

to these students who journeyed into medieval literature under his guidance and influence.

The center of Whiting's teaching is his undergraduate Chaucer course; the center of his scholarship is the figure of Geoffrey Chaucer, the man Whiting once described as "our sanest and most tolerant man of letters." At the beginning of his Chaucer course, Whiting customarily outlines its history, which turns into an account of his own involvement with the course. For nearly half a century, Whiting and the Chaucer course have been a distinguished union in the curriculum of Harvard's English Department and a continuation of a tradition which looks back to George Lyman Kittredge and Francis James Child.

In 1923, his junior year at Harvard College, Whiting enrolled in the Chaucer course, conducted by Fred N. Robinson and Kittredge. At that time the course was called English 1, since it had been one of the four courses Child, the first Professor of English at Harvard, offered; Child met the class at nine o'clock on Mondays, Wednesdays, and Fridays. On the same days, Child also offered English 2 (Shakespeare) at ten o'clock, English 3 (Anglo-Saxon) at eleven o'clock, and English 4 (Middle English) at noon. Child offered only one other course, English 5 (Advanced Composition), which he gave from time to time on Tuesday afternoons. When Whiting joined the teaching staff of the Chaucer course in 1929 as Assistant to Robinson and John Livingston Lowes, the course was still English 1. Because of revised numerical designations, the course soon became English 15; later it grew to be English 115. In 1970, further changes made it English 1150. When Whiting divided the course into a two-year study of Chaucer, the number grew only to English 1151, or, as he comments, "Inflation slowed down and it registered merely a one-digit raise." Finally, in 1972, further revisions returned it to English 115, "In a bold fight against inflation, the course rolled back to 115." Whiting's account of the history of the course fails to diminish its stature as a classic course in the Harvard tradition, a continuation of the methodology of Kittredge and Child.

Bartlett Whiting was born in East Northport, Maine, in 1904. His education and his academic career in Cambridge have never changed the ironic humor and casual self-deprecation which he brought with him from his more rural background. When he came to Harvard College as a freshman in the fall of 1921, he entered Standish Hall. The second arrival of the three occupants of D-42, he saw that the first arrival had hung a sign from the cord of a drop light, "This room reserved for J. Belfort Keogh." As his mocking response to this novel way of writing a name, he attached a similar sign in his room with the name "B. Jere Whiting." Harvard's first taste of Whiting satire introduced the employment of his middle name by which his post-Maine friends have come to know him. Four years later, he received his A.B. degree and left for Europe on a Sheldon Fellowship. He returned the following year and joined the Harvard faculty as an English tutor. He received his A.M. degree in 1928 and four years later he obtained his doctorate.

Kittredge began his career as a student of Child; in parallel fashion, Whiting began his career as Kittredge's student. Like Kittredge, he became a friend and a colleague of his teacher and mentor. In his preface to the fifteenth edition of Kittredge's *Chaucer and His Poetry,* Whiting observed, "Kittredge's reverence and affection for Child were intense and lasting . . . His feeling for his master was admirably expressed in his answer to a student who asked why a passage in Shakespeare was explained in one way by Kittredge and in another by an editor, 'Because *he* did not have Mr. Child to tell him what was right.' " The respect Whiting noted in Kittredge's relationship to Child is the respect he himself has always shown to his own master. Kittredge was named the first Gurney Professor of English Literature in 1917. It was fitting that Whiting was named Gurney Professor of English Literature in 1967. Thus after the chair had been occupied by Fred N. Robinson, Hyder Rollins, and Douglas Bush, the honor fell on one of Kittredge's most eminent students.

In the Chaucer course, Whiting is the worthy successor to Kittredge. His description of Kittredge's lecture style is an accurate description of his own style: "He did not give set lectures, but read aloud with dramatic vigor, pausing for explanatory and interpretative comments which might be as short as a sentence or take as long as fifteen minutes. Except when reading he would stride to and fro across the platform, a truly peripatetic teacher.

His comments were clear and beautifully expressed, touched on every aspect of the text, and explained what the author meant to himself and to his original audience." Whiting always tells his opening classes that "the purpose of the course in Chaucer is to enable you to get some of the understanding of Chaucer which a contemporary of Chaucer would have received, had he known Chaucer's works." He wants students "to acquire something of the ability to understand Chaucer which his own audience had intuitively." To this effect, he emulates Kittredge by reading the text aloud in a manner which suggests a medieval minstrel or a literary poet reciting to his audience. More accurately, as he himself suggests in his lectures, he addresses his class as Chaucer may have addressed his audience. Whiting does become Chaucer — the wit of the fourteenth-century poet finds a modern parallel in the Maine humor of his twentieth-century scholar.

In presenting a colorful and dramatic introduction to Chaucer and his world, Whiting always remains a dedicated and demanding teacher. He insists that students know Chaucer's language before they begin a study of his writings. Thus he begins the course with a series of lectures on Middle English grammar. Though students often find such a beginning difficult to accept as the introduction to a literature course, they always come to see that their teacher is correct in emphasizing the necessity of mastering the language as a prelude to mastering the literature. Even the most antigrammatical students cannot resent the study of grammar when they listen to Whiting's seeming apology, "Grammar is one of those seven-letter four-letter words. It is almost indecent to mention it."

When his analysis of the grammar draws to a close, Whiting begins to read the text. His method is the method of medieval instruction: text and gloss. The tone of the course is always scholarly, though Whiting never finds scholarship and humor antithetical. He offers most undergraduates their first experience of studying a single author in depth. In my seven years as Assistant in the course, I have listened to the laments of not a few students who sigh aloud, at the outset, about the seemingly slow pace of the course or the detailed manner of reading the text; never have I encountered a single student who, by the end of the course, feels any regret for its strict nature. Other courses teach the necessity of a close reading of texts; Whiting's Chaucer course teaches this precept and offers a year-long practical application. By the end of the spring term, students have a thorough under-standing of one author and his writings; in addition, they come to see the wealth of literature and life that stands behind this pan-oramic introduction to fourteenth-century England.

Every student of the Chaucer course will have his or her favorite moments in their memories of Whiting's dramatic ex-position of the text. For some, it will be the account of the eagle sighting the House of Fame and Whiting's modern analogues; for others, it will be Whiting's analysis of fourteenth-century housing problems as seen in the *Troilus* or his account of the events of the Hundred Years' War or his half-hearted attempt to answer the Pardoner's "bad press." Others will remember his long explanations of the text, his delight in recounting the fable that prompts the Wife's question, "Who peyntede the leon, tel me who?," or the reference to Chichevache or Niobe or the many, many proper names that demand his attention. Each scholarly background, always filled with humorous commentary, is complemented by more serious explanations of the text, for example, the history of sworn brotherhood or the classification of the wars in the portrait of the Knight. Finally, there are the many moments when the learned scholar uses humor to reveal the folly of inadequate scholarly investigation. In his discussion of *Sir Thopas,* Whiting describes the work of "Mr. Manly and Miss Winstanley" in their attempts to find a single historical fig-ure whom Chaucer burlesques in the character of Thopas. This done, Whiting announces to the class that his own efforts have been crowned with even greater success than theirs, for he has almost certainly discovered a historical figure whose career is more closely parallel to Thopas' story. This figure, after captur-ing Ghent, swore an oath on a pheasant that he would undertake a crusade and that he, supported by God, would challenge the three-headed sultan (i.e., the ruler of three fortified cities) and his god Termagaunt to single combat in order to determine the future of Christianity and Islam: winner take all. As a result of his oath, he collected a great deal of money, which he kept for himself; indeed, he never intended to crusade. At one time he had been an ally of the English; later he turned to the French and incurred the consequent wrath of the English. In addition, we know the names of no less than thirty of his mistresses and at least sixteen of his bastard sons and daughters. Except for one small detail, we can be certain that in this historical figure we have the original and opposite of Thopas and the butt of Chaucer's satire. The figure is Philip of Burgundy, jestingly called Philip the Good. Lastly, Whiting reports, there is one small detail, namely, the date, which may be an apparent obstacle in the identification: Philip swore his oath in 1453.

Whiting has a humility which veils an underlying kindness and a wit which hides a sense of vulnerability. As a teacher, he is always encouraging while simultaneously withholding encouragement. He shares Chaucer's ironic perception of the glories and the incongruities of human existence. He is effective in the classroom because he draws out the student on a given subject, not by parading his own brilliance, but by showing the complexity of Chaucer. Under the benign but critical eye of their master, his students may come to sympathize with Geffray's plight:

> For when thy labour doon al ys,
> And hast mad alle thy rekenynges,
> In stede of reste and newe thynges,
> Thou goost hom to thy hous anoon;
> And, also domb as any stoon,
> Thou sittest at another book
> Tyl fully daswed ys thy look.

The brilliance and erudition of Whiting never face complete exposure. Like "a man of gret auctorite," though his presence is always felt, Whiting, the master, never appears.

Though the Chaucer course stands preeminent among Whiting's teaching, there is no aspect of medieval English literature which has not been studied in one of his many other medieval courses. Whiting's more recent students tend to forget that he offered "Introduction to Old English" and "*Beowulf:* An Introduction to English Heroic Legend" for many years before he began to center his teaching almost exclusively on the Middle English period; indeed, his first official teaching was as Assistant in the Anglo-Saxon course. He frequently offers his exhaustive survey, "English Literature from the Norman Conquest to 1500, excluding Chaucer." The detailed study of Chaucer in his under-graduate course finds an extension in his similarly close reading of "Middle Scots Poetry from Barbour to Lindsay." His many graduate students always remember with fondness his Monday afternoon seminars. To each meeting, Whiting arrives armed with his text, the file cards containing the students' names, and two cigars. Whether the topic is "Middle English Verse Ro-mances" or "Medieval English Drama" or "Chaucer," the sem-inar always lasts about four hours. Whiting seems to time the seminar according to the duration of his two cigars, always dif-ferent brands, which he smokes in the course of the meeting; a brief pause at Leavitt and Peirce is his necessary prelude to the seminar. Whatever the content of the seminar, the meeting reaches its natural conclusion simultaneously with the expiration of the second cigar. During the afternoon, Whiting listens pa-tiently and attentively to the papers or reports, interrupting only to offer suggestions for further thoughts or to inject moments of humor to relieve an especially monotonous or long-winded reader. At the conclusion of each paper, he makes detailed and penetrating remarks that present clarifications and improvements to be incorporated before the later submission of the paper. An air of gentle wit, complemented by a genuine interest in the ma-terial and a sincere desire to share knowledge, pervades his seminars.

Whiting's illustrious teaching career is paralleled by an equally significant career as scholar. The bibliography of his scholarly endeavors compiled by McKay Sundwall, my immediate pre-decessor as Assistant in the Chaucer course, is evidence of the range and diversity of his publications. Even before his academic research introduced him to the world of scholarly publications, Whiting was already an inventive commentator; during his high school years, he contributed brief articles to philatelic journals. His more scholarly writings reveal an incomparable familiarity with all of medieval literature as well as the literature, both En-glish and American, of more recent times. His latest volume, the monumental *Proverbs, Sentences, and Proverbial Phrases from English Writings Mainly before 1500,* involved a reading of the entire corpus of Old and Middle English literature both published and unpublished; this achievement stands as the definitive work in its field.

Aside from his teaching and his scholarly writings, Whiting has given much of his time to the administrative side of education. He served as Chairman of the English Department in the years 1947–1952 and 1963–1965; he has also been the head of the graduate program in English and has served on numerous departmental and university committees. He has been a Fellow of Lowell House, where he has enjoyed a long and warm association; indeed, he has been a member of the Lowell House Senior Common Room since the House began in 1931. Whiting has also brought his dedication and his genial wit to many learned societies. He is a member of the Modern Language Association of America and its American Dialect Society; he has been active in the Association's Chaucer section; he has also served on the Executive Council of the Association. He is a former Director of the American Council of Learned Societies. Most notable is his long and distinguished relationship with the Mediaeval Academy of America. He was Assistant Editor of *Speculum* (1936–1947); he has been a member of the Executive Council since 1938 and a Fellow of the Academy since 1948; he is now President of the Fellows. Since 1947, he has been Delegate of the Mediaeval Academy to the American Council of Learned Societies; his annual reports on the proceedings of the Council, delivered with a wit of Chaucerian scope in its disproportion to the seriousness of the described events, have become its unofficial history so that the first fourteen were published under the collective title, *Respectfully Submitted*.

In all his endeavors, Whiting is assisted by his wife, Helen Wescott Whiting. They first met in Maine when they entered the same freshman class at Belfast High School in 1917. When he came to Harvard College, his future wife went to Wheaton College in Norton, Massachusetts. When the Sheldon Fellowship took him to Europe, Helen Wescott came to Radcliffe where she obtained her Master's degree in Romance Languages in 1926. They were married in 1928. In addition to her own distinguished career as a teacher and later as Chief Cataloguer at Harvard's Peabody Museum of Archaeology and Ethnology, Helen Whiting always assists her husband in his search for proverbial lore. It is fitting that the reference work, *Proverbs, Sentences, and Proverbial Phrases from English Writings Mainly before 1500,* is the product of the academic collaboration of B. J. and Helen Whiting. To many students, the Whitings are a constant source of encouragement and friendship.

In concluding his description of Kittredge, Whiting offered a final statement which the contributors agree is a description of the man to whom these essays are dedicated:

> What endeared him to his students was not so much his erudition as his willingness to share it, his infinite patience with their first attempts at scholarship, and his aid in furthering their careers. If he was aware of personal conflict between research and teaching, it was resolved in favor of teaching. His writings are a noble monument, and yet he could have varied Child's remark, "I should have been more of a producer, if I had not spent about half my life in helping people."

LEGER BROSNAHAN

Now (This), Now (That) and *BD* 646

Now by the fire, now at table, line 646 of Chaucer's *Book of the Duchess,* seems to give some readers trouble. Translators appear uncertain of both its meaning and reference, and what seems to be its only purely critical evaluation to date finds it wanting. But when the line is read — with the critical assistance of B. J. Whiting's recent and definitive collection of early English proverbs — as a drastic form of a common proverb illustrating instability and recurring regularly in descriptions of Fortune and given its closest grammatical reference and its homeliest meaning, it becomes perfectly appropriate in its context, though unusual in its content and arguable as to the precise image it conjures.

The line occurs in the Man in Black's tirade against Fortune:

> She ys th'envyouse charite
> That ys ay fals, and semeth wel,
> So turneth she hyr false whel
> Aboute, for hyt ys nothyng stable,
> *Now by the fire, now at table;*
> For many oon hath she thus yblent. [1]

1. *BD* 642–647. All references to Chaucer's works are to *The Works of Geoffrey Chaucer,* ed. F. N. Robinson, 2nd ed. (Boston: Houghton Mifflin, 1957).

It was shown by Kittredge to have been drawn from a passage
of rather similar spirit in *Le Jugement dou Roy de Behaingne* by
Machaut,[2] in which the deserted lover is lamenting the incon-
stancy of his former lady:

> Dame, il me samble
> Qu'une chose qui se part et assamble
> En pluseurs lieus, et avec c'elle tramble
> Et n'arreste ne que fueille de tramble
>   Et n'est estable
> Eins est toudis changant et variable,
> *Puis ci, puis la, or au feu, a la table,*
>   (var. ore a(au E) table EKJ)
> Et puis ailleurs, c'est chose moult doubtable,
>   Car nullement
> On ne la puet avoir seürement:
> C'est droitement li gieus d'enchantement,
> Que ce qu'on cuide avoir certeinnement,
>   On ne l'a mie.
> Einsi est il, dame, quoy que nuls die,
> De ma dame qui se change et varie. [3]

A reading of the line — still probably the best to date —
was made by Fr. Klaeber, who classified its images under "Haus-
halte" in *Das Bild bei Chaucer*[4] and glossed it with a proverb
still quite alive in German: "Now *by the fire,* now *at table* (un-
beständig, bald hier, bald dort, — so geht es bei der Fortune
her)," and the line was translated, quite differently and curiously, by John S. P. Tatlock and Percy MacKaye: "She is the
envious charity that is ever false, and seems goodly; so she turns
her false wheel about, now to one side the hall, now at the other,
for it is never steadfast," [5] and by Frank Ernest Hill:

> She is an envious charity
> That ever is false, though it look well;
> So turneth she her fickle wheel

    2. "Guillaume de Machaut and the Book of the Duchess," *PMLA,* 30
(1915), 12.
    3. *Oeuvres de Guillaume de Machant,* ed. Ernest Hoepffner, I (Paris,
1908), 97–98, ll. 1068–82.
    4. Berlin, 1893, p. 94.
    5. *The Complete Poetical Works of Geoffrey Chaucer* (New York:
Macmillan, 1912), p. 325.

> About, and it is no wise stable,
> But now by the fire, now by the table;
> Full many a one she blinds this way. [6]

The line seems, however, to have escaped direct critical evaluation until very recently, when it was glossed: "This uninspired
line, which seems to serve only to complete the couplet, is translated directly from the *Roy de Behaingne*, l. 1074." [7]

This last judgment, tentative as it is, seems questionable for a
number of reasons. First, the rhyme is one relatively easy to find
in English and hardly likely to motivate the otherwise pointless
borrowing of an entire line. Second, though weak full lines which
seem so motivated can surely be found in Chaucer,[8] they are
rare when compared with weak second half-lines (or parts of
second half-lines),[9] and *BD* 646 seems full of content when
compared with either. Third, the judgment draws into question
the inspiration of Machaut as well as Chaucer, since the line
occurs in both poets in very similar contexts. In Machaut, however, the phrase in question is clearly an extension or elaboration of the basic proverb *Puis ci, puis la* for instability, as
Klaeber interpreted Chaucer's borrowing of the elaboration
alone. The problem with Chaucer's line, for both translator and
critic, seems to be failure to recognize the line as a proverb and
its appropriateness to a description of the instability of Fortune,

6. *The Canterbury Tales. The Prologue and Four Tales with the Book
of the Duchess and Six Lyrics* (New York: Longmans, Green, 1930), p.
167.
7. A. C. Baugh, ed., *Chaucer's Major Poetry* (New York: Appleton-
Century-Crofts, 1963), p. 15, n. 646.
8. See *BD* 514: But at the last, to sayn ryght soth; 698: And bethenke
me every del; 989: And, soth to seyne, therwythal; 1194: So at the laste,
soth to sayne; 1221: So at the laste, soth to seyn.
9. See *BD* 35: as I gesse; 98: by my trowthe; 113: or in what wise;
141: on alle thyng; 147: hit ys no nay; 159: ne noght elles; 227: for
bote ne bale; 248: ryght now, as blyve; 275: and therwith even; 280:
withoute drede; 303: y trowe; 349: and other thyng; 364: So at the
laste; 466: by my trowthe; 550: as wys God helpe me soo; 591: by my
trouthe; 657: ywys; 687: y trowe trewly; 722: for trewely; 746: al hooly;
820: withoute doute; 832: ryght as hirselve; 1073: withoute drede; 1080:
so have I reste; 1090: soth to say; 1099: be my trouthe; 1119: so have
I joye; 1148: leve hyt wel; 1197: trewely; 1321: as I yow telle. Cf. J. A.
Burrow, *Ricardian Poetry* (New Haven: Yale University Press, 1971),
pp. 12–23.

or doubt about the grammatical reference and intended image of
the line, or some combination of these.

The proverb elaborated here and its common associations
have remained less than highly visible in collections of proverbs
until the publication of Whiting's collection of early English
proverbs, where it is for the first time thoroughly illustrated at
N 179 *Now (this) now (that)*.[10] Earlier notices of this proverb
have been very few and scattered and have afforded little opportunity to appreciate the history, frequency (particularly in
Chaucer), or variety of forms of the expression.[11] The richness
of Whiting's collection, with over sixty examples of this proverb
from c. 1000 to 1556, allows a view of the whole history of the
proverb in early English, its rise to a peak of popularity in the
late fourteenth and fifteenth centuries, and its apparent decline
after 1500, which would at least in part explain its absence from
standard collections of later periods of English and its relative
obscurity in modern times.[12] The sixty-two collected examples
include only one before c. 1300 and thirteen after 1500. A
similar rise and fall of frequency, apparently peaking about
1380–1386, can also be traced in Chaucer's use of the proverb.[13]

The wealth of examples now collected also illustrates the wide

10. B. J. Whiting with the collaboration of Helen Wescott Whiting,
*Proverbs, Sentences, and Proverbial Phrases from English Writings
Mainly before 1500* (Cambridge, Mass.: Harvard University Press,
1968), pp. 434–436.

11. See Willibald Haeckel, *Das Sprichwort bei Chaucer*, Erlanger Beiträge zur Englischen Philologie, 8 (Erlangen, 1890), 50, 66; Klaeber, pp.
47, 94; W. W. Skeat, *Early English Proverbs* (Oxford, 1910), p. 91; B. J.
Whiting, *Proverbs in the Earlier English Drama*, Harvard Studies in
Comparative Literature, 14 (Cambridge, Mass.: Harvard University
Press, 1938), 19, 87–88, 299; B. J. Whiting, "Proverbs and Proverbial
Sayings from Scottish Writing before 1600," *Mediaeval Studies*, 13
(1951), 87–164, *Now* and *World;* John Heywood, *A Dialogue of Pro-
verbs*, ed. Rudolph E. Habenicht (Berkeley: University of California
Press, 1963), pp. 140, 210.

12. See G. L. Apperson, *English Proverbs and Proverbial Phrases:
A Historical Dictionary* (London: J. M. Dent, 1929); M. P. Tilley, *A
Dictionary of the Proverbs in England in the Sixteenth and Seventeenth
Centuries* (Ann Arbor: University of Michigan Press, 1950); *The Oxford
Dictionary of English Proverbs*, 3d ed., rev. F. P. Wilson (Oxford: Ox-
ford University Press, 1970).

13. 1369–1370 — *BD* 646: Now by the fire, now at table. 1372–1380
— *HF* 896–903: And y adoun gan loken thoo,/And beheld feldes and
playnes,/And now hilles, and now mountaynes,/Now valeyes, now

variety of contrasts that could be brought to flesh out the *this-that* in the formula *Now (this) now (that)*. Just as proverbial expressions of totality, such as *the rich and the poor, the high and the low, the long and the short,* have been literarily extended even as far as *the bald and the curly-headed,* these expressions of instability heavily favor such popular contrasts as *up-down, here-there, hot-cold, well-woe* but allow, especially as literary elaborations of one of these more popular forms of the proverb, practically any kind of opposition: *high-low, above-under, ebb-flow; in-out, to-fro, near-far; warm-cool, chill-heat, red-pale; good-bad, laugh-weep, pleasure-pain, full-hungry.*[14] The search for originality in these elaborations of the proverb seems to send writers further and further afield, yielding such drastic oppositions as *now waverand wynd, now weit; now sande, now clay; now lef, now thef; now gouins gay, now brats laid in pres; now cled in gold, dissolvit now in as; now with his love, now in his colde grave; now in the crope, now doun in the breres; now by the fire, now at table.*[15] Though these literary extensions of the

---

forestes,/And now unnethes grete bestes;/Now ryveres, now citees,/ Now tounes, and now grete trees,/Now shippes seyllynge in the see; 947: And beren hym now up, now doun. *Anel* 55: But throng now her, now ther, among hem bothe; 194: She sent him now to londe, now to shippe. 1380–1386 — *Bo* V Pr6 271–273: ne he ne entrechaungith nat, so as thou wenest, the stoundes of foreknowynge, as now this, now that. *TC* I.186–187: Byholding ay the ladies of the town,/Now here, now there; II.197: Now here, now ther, he hunted hem so faste; II.698: Now was hire herte warm, now was it cold; II.810–811: Than slepeth hope, and after drede awaketh;/Now hoot, now cold; III.94–95: Goodly abaist, and now hise hewes rede,/Now pale; IV.239–240: Right as the wylde bole bygynneth springe,/Now her, now ther, idarted to the herte; IV.460–461: But kanstow playen raket, to and fro,/Nettle in, dok out, now this, now that, Pandare? V.454–455: Now this, now that, so faste ymagenynge; V.1118: Now was his herte dul, now was it light. *LGW* 2419–20: The se, by nyghte, as any torche it brende/For wod, and possith hym now up, now doun. 1387–1392 — *CT* I (A) 1532–35: Now in the crope, now doun in the breres,/Now up, now doun, as boket in a welle./Right as the Friday, soothly for to telle,/Now it shyneth, now it reyneth faste; I (A) 2777–79: What is this world? what asketh men to have?/Now with his love, now in his colde grave/Allone, withouten any compaignye; *Fort* 2: As wele or wo, now povre and now honour.

14. Collectively, these oppositions are rimed, assonanced, or neither in about the proportion 1 : 2 : 8.

15. For this tendency to join innovative literary elaborations with traditional popular proverbs cf. Burrow, pp. 130–141.

popular proverb become increasingly remote or "metaphysical" in their oppositions, *or au feu, a la table* is explicitly linked with *Puis ci, puis la* in Machaut, and the connection of the two phrases was apparently clear enough to Chaucer's audience to allow him to use *Now by the fire, now at table* in the absence of a more common form of the proverb such as *Now here, now there*. It was probably no more mystifying than such modern proverbial allusions as *a stitch in time, a burnt child,* or *spilt milk,* occurring as it does in a context of fortune before an audience for whom the popular forms of the proverb were common property.

This connection of the proverb with fortune is also made clear by Whiting's collection. All the examples, of course, indicate instability, but a clear majority refer to the instability of fortune, and fifteen, even in their short citation forms, make explicit mention of fortune, chance, or this world as subject to fortune. This close association of the proverb with fortune, illustrated by *BD* 646, reaches back as far as classical Latin literature,[16] and as Patch notes: "This lady Fortune is so changeable that her variations are to all intents and purposes instantaneous; hence most appropriately the rhetorical formula 'now — now' is often used in describing her or her activities. This device, or the conception which prompts it, naturally gives rise to considerable use of contrast and antithesis, even without the particular formula; and this in turn leads to the adoption of paradoxes to express the particular distaste the author in question feels at Fortune's fickleness." [17]

The position of *Now by the fire, now at table* in its context seems to permit a variety of possible grammatical references. The most remote would be back to *She* (Fortune) in line 642, but the distance makes it awkward and most unlikely. A reference back to *Aboute* in line 645 seems much more natural and was apparently accepted by Tatlock and MacKaye and Hill. This reading, however, raises serious problems, since it converts the wheel of Fortune into a vehicle, or at least a hoop, carrying Fortune or being rolled about by her from one place to another.

16. See Howard R. Patch, *The Goddess Fortuna in Mediaeval Literature* (Cambridge, Mass.: Harvard University Press, 1927), pp. 10–12.
17. *Ibid.*, pp. 55–56.

Such a reading cannot be rejected out of hand, because there is some evidence of the concept of the wheel of Fortune as a vehicle.[18] The *Roman de la Rose* contains one isolated and difficult reference to the wheel of Fortune, "Puis va tant roant par sa sale,/Qu'ele entre en la partie sale,/Feible, decrevee e crolant,/O toute sa roe volant," which has been so interpreted.[19] Moreover, Chaucer, in a single and singular reference, writes, "Tempest thee noght al croked to redresse,/In trust of hir that turneth as a bal," [20] suggesting a not too different image. These references, however, remain so rare, isolated, and atypical in the history of the wheel of Fortune, and among the numerous references to the wheel of Fortune in Chaucer and in the *Roman de la Rose,* that this reading of *BD* 646 seems strained at least. All such readings also seem to make an excessively literal identification of Fortune or her wheel with all aspects of the objects with which they are compared, while the writers were more probably associating Fortune or her wheel with only a single aspect of the objects, such as circular motion or instability. A grammatical reference back only to the immediately preceding phrase *nothyng stable* seems the most natural, avoids the difficulties just mentioned, and leaves the line a simple extension of the idea of instability, as in Machaut, rather than the literal beginning and end of a route traveled by the wheel.

This restricted and figurative rather than literal reading still leaves the question of the intended image in the line. If read as here suggested, the *fire* and *table* would not represent the limits of a trip made by a rolling wheel but the limits of some continual oscillation or cycle, and the great majority of oppositions found in this proverb refer to such common oscillations and cycles as *day-night, rain-shine, ebb-flow, hot-cold, well-sick, living-dead, full-hungry,* the common experiences and daily rounds of men. Probably nothing more complicated need be looked for in *BD* 646 than the normal thrice-daily round from cooking place to

18. *Ibid.,* p. 169.
19. Guillaume de Lorris and Jean de Meun, *Le Roman de la Rose,* ed. Ernest Langlois, II (Paris, 1920), 285. ll. 6145–48. See S. L. Galpin, "Fortune's Wheel in the *Roman de la Rose,*" *PMLA,* 24 (1909), 340–341, but cf. Harry W. Robbins, trans., *The Romance of the Rose* (New York: E. P. Dutton, 1962), p. 128, ll. 143–146.
20. *Truth* 8–9.

eating place. Since the phrase in question is rather clearly a literary extension of a popular proverb, it is not surprising that a search for other, perhaps slightly different forms of the extension, which might make it clearer, has produced nothing closer than a sententious expression of Montaigne, but one which seems very close to the spirit of the line Chaucer borrowed from Machaut: "Manger, boire, dormir . . . : nous rouons sans cesse en ce cercle." [21]

21. Quoted in an interesting context in R. Grandsaignes d'Hauterive, *Dictionnaire d'Ancien Français* (Paris: Librairie Larousse, 1947), p. 519: "*roër* I. v., dev. ROUER. Sign. aussi (XIIIᵉ–XVIᵉ s.) 1° Tourner, tournoyer: *Manger, boire, dormir. . . : nous rouons sans cesse en ce cercle.* (XVIᵉ s., Montaigne.) — 2° Rouler, faire rouler. — 3° Circuler, rôder: *Il alloit ça et la rouant par les isles.* (XVIᵉ s., Amyot.) || ETYM. *Rotare*, tourner comme une roue. — V."

ALFRED DAVID

How Marcia Lost Her Skin:
A Note on Chaucer's Mythology

The following note offers a new solution to a minor Chaucerian puzzle and identifies a humble French source for Chaucer's knowledge of a well-known classical myth. The inquiry, which involves the difficulties several French scribes experienced with a strange word, goes through some intricacies in order to establish a small fact; nevertheless, it raises some significant questions about the use of mythology by medieval poets and about some recent critical interpretations of their practice in this matter.

Among the musicians at the House of Fame, Chaucer sees

> Marcia that loste her skyn,
> Bothe in face, body, and chyn,
> For that she wolde envien, loo!
> To pipen bet than Appolloo. (1229–32)

The reference is to Apollo's flaying of the satyr Marsyas after beating him in their musical contest. Chaucer's curious notion that Marsyas was female has been explained as a misunderstanding of the Italian form *Marsia* (derived from the Latin accusative of Marsyas), which occurs both in Dante's *Paradiso*

19

and Boccaccio's *Teseida*.[1] The passage from Dante was fresh in Chaucer's mind when he wrote of "Marcia" because he had imitated it only some two hundred lines before in the invocation to the third book of the *House of Fame*. It is Dante's invocation of Apollo:

> Entra nel petto mio, e spira tue
> Sì come quando Marsïa traesti
> De la vagina de le membra sue! (I.19–21)

Chaucer encountered the same form of the name in the *Teseida* where Egeo provides Teseo with

> un bello scudo e di molto valore,
> nel qual vedeasi Marsia sonando,
> sé con Appollo nel sonar provando. (XI.62)

For anyone accustomed to regard "Marcia" as a woman's name (as in "Marcia Catoun," one of the ladies in the ballade from the Prologue to the *Legend of Good Women*), the mistake seems a natural one. A problem remains, however. If Chaucer supposed that the "Marsia" in these Italian passages was female, where did he learn the details of her story, namely that she had "loste her skyn/ . . . For that she wolde envien, loo!/To pipen bet than Appolloo?" It would seem impossible for Chaucer to have understood Dante's and Boccaccio's allusions, much less to have reconstructed the story by putting them together, if he had not already been familiar with the myth from some other source. The obvious source would have been the *Metamorphoses,* "thyn oune bok," as the Eagle calls it (712), referring his pupil to Ovid's description of the House of Fame. F. N. Robinson, therefore, concludes his note on *Marcia:* "Elements from Ovid's account (Met., vi, 382 ff.) seem to be combined here with those from Dante." [2] But if Chaucer did use the account in the *Meta-*

---

1. Skeat first attributed the error to Chaucer's misunderstanding of the name in the *Paradiso, Complete Works,* 2nd ed. (Oxford: Clarendon Press, 1900), III, 269–270. R. A. Pratt suggests that the mistake would have been confirmed by the identical form of the name in the *Teseida,* "Conjectures Regarding Chaucer's Manuscript of the *Teseida,*" *Studies in Philology,* 43 (1945), 756–757.

2. *The Works of Geoffrey Chaucer,* 2nd ed. (Boston: Houghton Mifflin, 1957), p. 785. All citations from Chaucer are from this edition.

morphoses, a still more puzzling question arises. How could anyone who had read the story in Ovid be in any doubt as to the sex
of Apollo's victim? To be sure, the only mention of the satyr's
name is a reference to the river into which he was transformed:
"Marsya nomen habet" (*Marsya* is an alternate Latin nomina-
tive as well as the normal accusative). All the same, the preceding passage leaves absolutely no question that this "Marsya" was
male. Ovid's first mention of him, "satyri" (383), is in the
masculine genitive. After his death his brother satyrs, "satyri
fratres," mourn him, "illum" (392-393). On similar grounds,
Professor Pratt argues that Chaucer's manuscript of the *Teseida*
did not contain Boccaccio's mythological gloss, for the story of
Marsyas told in the gloss would have removed any misunderstanding based on the text that the "Marsia" on Teseo's shield
was female.[3] But would not any version of the Marsyas story,
wherever Chaucer may have come across it, have made it clear
at some point that the satyr was male?

The answer to this objection lies in the variant readings of an
interpolation in the *Roman de la Rose* that among other mythological matters relates the story of Marsyas and Apollo. The
interpolation occurs in many manuscripts of the *Roman,* both
early and late. Langlois in the notes to his edition provides a text
of the passage edited from eight manuscripts for which he prints
variants.[4] His note indicates that he found the interpolation in
other manuscripts as well, though he does not specify how many.
I have seen it myself in a number of other manuscripts, some
of which were classified by Langlois and some that were not.[5]
Chaucer must have known the passage and must have known
it from a particular group of manuscripts in which Marsyas
undergoes a grammatical sex transformation; for the only completely satisfactory explanation of the error in the *House of
Fame* is that the satyr had already changed sex in his source.
This metamorphosis, as shall be demonstrated, did take place
in one family of French manuscripts. The allusions in Dante
and Boccaccio might well have confirmed the mistake in Chau-

3. Pratt, "Conjectures," 756-757.
4. *Le Roman de la Rose,* Société des Anciens Textes Français (Paris:
Firmin-Didot, 1921), III, 305-307.
5. For citations of some of these, see notes 11-13 below.

cer's mind, but are not sufficient in themselves to account for the error.

The interpolation is forty lines long. Only the last twenty-three concern the story of Marsyas, but I shall give the entire passage along with a translation, for my conclusions depend on the context in which the story is told. The story in context helps us to understand, I believe, something of the spirit in which we should read and interpret this and many other mythological allusions in the *House of Fame* and elsewhere in Chaucer. What finally matters is not how Marcia lost her skin, but the tone in which we are told about it and what that tone implies — a comic and humane attitude toward pagan mythology shared, with varying degrees of subtlety, by Jean de Meun, the unknown interpolator, and Geoffrey Chaucer.

In the *Roman* the God of Love is swearing a lengthy oath to his barons:

> Mais par sainte Venus ma mere
> E par Saturnus son vieil pere,
> Qui ja l'engendra jeune touse,
> Mais non pas de sa fame espouse; . . . (10827–30)

At this point the interpolator begins in mid-sentence by recalling Jupiter's castration of Saturn, which earlier in the *Roman* had been the subject of an amusing exchange between the lover and Reason, a scene that the interpolator obviously relished:

> Dont trestouz les enfanz manja, [6]
> Fors Jupiter, qu'il estranja
> De son regne, et tant le bati
> 4 Que jusqu'en enfer l'embati.
> Copa li ce que vous savez,
> Car maintes foiz oï l'avez,
> Mes bons peres, puis monta seur
> 8 Venus, tout fust ele sa seur,
> Et firent leur joliveté:
> De la vint ma nativeté,
> Dont je n'ai honte ne esclandre,

6. The antecedent of *dont* is *fame espouse* (10830). Because of the length and difficulty of this passage (never before translated) I append an English translation.

12   Qui bien set mon lignage entendre,
     Car onc de mieudre ne fu nus,
     Par mes trois oncles Neptunus,
     Jupiter, Pluto! par m'antain
16   Juno la vieille, que tant ain
     Que je voudroie qu'el fust arse!
     Bien l'ain tant com Phebus fist Marse,
     Que Midas aus oreilles d'asne
20   Par jugement dampne et prophane.
     Chier compera sa fole verve,
     Mar vit la buisine Minerve,
     Qu'el jeta dedenz la palu.
24   De buisiner ne li chalu,
     Pour ce que li dieu se rioient
     De ses joues qui li enfloient
     Quant el buisinoit a leur table.
28   Le satyreau tieng a coupable,
     Non pour ce que la buisine ot,
     Mais contre Phebus buisinot,
     Qu'il[7] buisinot mieuz, ce disoit,
32   Et Phebus mieuz se reprisoit;
     Si firent du roi Midas juge,
     Qui contre le satyreau juge:
     A l'arbre pendu l'escorcha
36   Phebus tout vif; tant le torcha
     Par tout une seule plaie ot,
     De par tout li sans li raiot,
     Et criot: "Las! pour quoi l'empris?
40   N'iert pas buisine en si grant pris!" [8]

7. Langlois: *Qui.* But *Qu'il,* the reading of Be, Ja, Jo, and Maz, makes clearer syntax and better sense.

8. The interpolation is a mélange, probably pieced together from the author's recollection of a number of different sources. According to Ovid (*Met.* XI.142ff.) Midas earned his ass's ears by giving the wrong decision in the contest between Pan and Apollo. Hyginus in the *Fables* (No. 191) transfers this story to the contest between Marsyas and Apollo. Fulgentius, *Mythologiarum* (III, 9) tells the same story, but in the version of the first Vatican mythographer (No. 125) Midas makes the right decision against Marsyas (for the latter see Georg H. Bode, *Scriptores rerum mythicarum latini tres* [1834; rpt. Hildesheim: Georg Oluns, 1968]). All the mythographers supply the story of Minerva's invention of the pipe and her discarding it after the gods laugh at her. Lines 35–40 are directly influenced by Ovid, "nec quicquam nisi vulnus

All of whose children he ate, except Jupiter, whom (Saturn) he
(Jupiter) drove from his kingdom and defeated him so badly that
he drove him all the way to hell. He cut off the you-know-what
because you've heard tell about it often. My good father then
mounted Venus even though she was his sister, and they performed their jollity. That's how my birth came about for which I
feel neither shame nor scandal—whoever has the good sense to
understand my ancestry—for there was never better, by my three
uncles, Neptune, Jupiter, Pluto! by my aunt old Juno, whom I
love so much that I wish she might be burned! I love her as much
as Phoebus did Marsyas, whom ass-eared Midas doomed and
condemned by his judgment. He paid dear for his foolish whim.
In an evil hour he saw Minerva's pipe, which she had thrown into
the swamp. She didn't care for piping because the gods had
laughed at her puffed-out cheeks when she played at their banquet. I blame the satyr not because he took the pipe but because
he played in competition with Phoebus, because he played better,
so he said; and Phoebus thought himself the better. They made
King Midas judge, who gave judgment against the satyr. Phoebus
flayed him alive hanging from a tree. He stripped him so that he
had one wound everywhere; everywhere the blood shot out; and
he cried: "Alas! Why did I undertake it? The pipe was not worth
so great a price!" [9]

My argument depends on lines 28 and 34 in which the interpolator's term for "satyr" clearly gave the scribes trouble. I do
not accept Langlois' reading *satyreau* as the original. Let us consider it simply one of the variants. The others, as given by Langlois, are as follows:

— 28 Be satyrien, Bâ Maz satirien, Ja sathirien He satyrain; Bê
La satyre en t. . . .
— 34 Be 1. satyrien, Maz 1. satirien, Bâ la satyrien, He 1. satyran,
Ja 1. sachenau, Bê les atirans.

The most common variant, *satyrien* (*satirien, sathirien*), is, I

---

erat; cruor undique manat" (388) and " 'a! piget, a! non est' clamabat
'tibia tanti' " (386).
9. For assistance with the translation and the interpretation of the
French variants I am indebted to my colleagues Anna G. Hatcher and
Emanuel J. Mickel.

believe, the original, not only because it is most widely distributed but because it occurs in Be, which seems to be the oldest of the manuscripts involved — Langlois attributes it to the end of the thirteenth century.[10] Moreover, it is an unusual form, not listed by Godefroy, who gives *satyreau* as a variant of *satirel:* "Satirel, *-ral, -rial, -riel, satyrel, -reau,* s. m., dimin. de satyre." [11] What exactly was a *satyrien?* The uncertainty of the scribes is evident in the variants. Was this *satyrien* male or female? Even with the definite article for a guide (and, for that matter, in a carelessly written manuscript it is not always easy to distinguish a *le* from a *la*), a number of scribes seem to have felt an ambiguity or strangeness about the form that required clarification. Perhaps "Marse" (line 18) was interpreted as feminine because it is syntactically parallel to "Juno" (16). Possibly the abrupt shifts from the satyr to Minerva (22) and back to the satyr (28) created some confusion. Whatever the reason or combination of reasons, the scribes tampered with the word and the article modifying it. Two of Langlois' scribes (and Langlois himself) went to the more familiar and decisively masculine *satyreau.* Bâ's *satirien* is masculine in 28, feminine in 34. Bê, a manuscript closely related to Be, which has *satyrien,* wrote *La satyre,* an unambiguously female satyr. In 34, either through inadvertent false division (the exemplar probably read *le satiran*) or by intent, Bê changed the meaning by writing *les atirans* (the sense becomes that Midas judged against "the conventions" or "the rules").

Bê's mistake is repeated and taken one step further by Bo, a manuscript classified by Langlois but not used by him for this passage.[12] Like Bê, Bo writes *La satire* in line 28. But he changes line 29, which in the original reads "Non pour ce que la buisine ot" ("Not because he took the pipe"), to "Non pour

10. *Les Manuscrits du Roman de la Rose* (Paris: Honoré Champion, 1910), p. 188. For the identification of the manuscripts Langlois cites, see his table of classified manuscripts, pp. 238–240.

11. *Dictionnaire de l'Ancienne Langue Française* (1892; rpt. New York: Kraus, 1961), VII, 323. British Museum Royal 20 D VII has *le satirel* (28), *la saturan* (34). National Library of Wales 5011 E has *le satirion* (28), *le sathiren* (34). Bodleian Douce 195 has *le satirain* (28, 34). British Museum Harley 4425 has *le sauterion* (28, 34). Paris, Bibl. de l'Institut 209 has *le psalteryon* (28), *le saptirion* (34).

12. Paris, B.N., fr., 2195, fol. 70ᵛ.

ce quelle businoit" ("Not because she played the pipe"). At line 34 Bo reads *les atiriens,* which appears to be a variant spelling of Bê's *les atirans.* Manuscript Bó, a close relative, has *La satire* (28), *quelle buisinoit* (29), and *les saturans* (34).[13] Bó noticed that the reading of 29, "quelle buisinoit," and the standard reading of 30, "contre Phebus buisinoit," violated the conventions of *rime riche,* and he changed line 30 to read "contre Phebus estriuoit."

Although my reconstruction of the manner in which the mistake occurred is necessarily hypothetical, I trust that the fact has been clearly established that in a subbranch of a relatively numerous family (the B group contains thirteen manuscripts in all) there exists a passage in which Apollo flays a female satyr called "Marse." Lacking a manuscript of the *Roman de la Rose* with Chaucer's personal book plate, we may be as certain as such things can ever be that he first read the story of Marsyas and Apollo in a manuscript belonging to this branch of the B family.

More significant than the establishment of the source in this case is the elimination of some other hitherto possible sources. These include Ovid and the numerous Christian moralizations of the *Metamorphoses* and other pagan myths such as the *Ovide moralisé.* It should not really surprise us that Chaucer did not know his "oune bok" as thoroughly as he sometimes leads us to believe. I do not for one moment question his close and intimate familiarity with Ovid, but I do not think that, in order to acquire his evident rapport with the Latin poet, Chaucer must have read the *Metamorphoses* from cover to cover. Very often, even when Chaucer claims to be dealing directly with a celebrated Latin writer, practically everything can be traced to the *Roman de la Rose* or some other French intermediary.[14] As with so much else in Chaucer, before searching the Roman poets, Boccaccio, or Dante, not to mention arcane medieval Latin sources, one should ask, "Does it occur in the *Roman de la Rose?*"

13. Paris, Bibl. de l'Arsenal 2988 fol. 91[r].
14. In the *Physician's Tale,* for example, Chaucer's "as telleth Titus Livius" is lifted directly from Jean de Meun's "Si con dit Titus Livius." The *Roman* is his primary source for the tale.

The point may serve as a corrective to a great deal of recent criticism that assumes a detailed knowledge not only on the part of Chaucer but on the part of his audience of a vast amount of learned Christian exegesis of classical mythology. For example, in the introduction to his book *Chaucer and the Tradition of Fame,* B. G. Koonce tells us that he is attempting "to restore to the reading of the [*House of Fame*] a background of medieval meanings, familiar enough to Chaucer's contemporary reader but almost lost to the modern, which will clarify its purpose and provide the basis for a unified interpretation." [15] When he comes to explicate the Marsyas passage, Mr. Koonce explains: "Whereas Apollo is moralized as divine wisdom (*sapientia*), Marsyas is interpreted as ignorance or folly (*insipientia*), and his contesting Apollo's wisdom is an example of vainglory." [16] For this interpretation, Mr. Koonce cites *Mythographus Vaticanus III;* Giovanni del Virgilio, *Allegorie librorum Ovidii Metamorphoseos;* the *Ovide moralisé;* and Pietro Alighieri's commentary on the *Divine Comedy.* He would not of course claim that Chaucer knew any one or all of these works directly but that they were part of the "tradition" familiar to Chaucer and his audience.

No doubt Chaucer was acquainted with the practice of giving moral and Christian interpretations to pagan mythology, but what his humble *insipientia* about "Marcia" (which Mr. Koonce, incidentally, ignores) suggests is that Chaucer was far less familiar with such literature and such interpretations than a modern scholar like Mr. Koonce. This is not to say that the interpretation is altogether off the mark. Chaucer would not have needed the exegetes to tell him that challenging the god of poetry to a musical competition is an act of vainglory. Certainly "Marcia" is an entirely appropriate figure at the court of Fame. What I feel *is* inappropriate is the solemnly didactic tone that this kind of weighty baggage introduces into a poem that is serious, to be sure, but serious in a manner that remains continually light and irreverent.

15. *Chaucer and the Tradition of Fame* (Princeton: Princeton University Press, 1966), p. 4.
    16. *Ibid.,* p. 200.

The great difference between Chaucer, Jean de Meun, and the interpolator (mediocre poet that he is) on the one hand and the third Vatican mythographer, Giovanni del Virgilio, and the rest on the other is the quality of humor. Reading the allegorizations of these learned exegetes one is never for a moment reminded that the myths they are expounding are entertaining. To Jean de Meun, to the interpolator, and to Chaucer they are a perpetual delight, a delight conveyed to their readers. These poets look upon the pagan gods and the stories about them not as lies to be redeemed by hidden allegory, but as substantial beings in an imaginary world. Jean de Meun makes the God of Love swear "par sainte Venus ma mere" as one of the Canterbury pilgrims might swear by a Catholic saint or "by my fader soule." More crudely, but with obvious pleasure, the interpolator tells how Jupiter and Venus "firent leur jolivité."

The same comic treatment of mythology can be found throughout Chaucer's works from the Cave of Morpheus in the *Book of the Duchess* to the Wife of Bath's twisted tale of King Midas. This humor informs the treatment of the gods in the *Knight's Tale;* indeed, Saturn's addressing of Venus as "My deere doghter" (I.2453) may owe something to the French passage under discussion. This is the comic spirit of Pandarus who finds mythology a storehouse of homely and humorous examples. This humor is present also in our passage. One should not become too solemn or too moral about

> Marcia that loste her skyn,
> Bothe in face, body, and chyn,
> For that she wolde envien, loo!
> To pipen bet than Appolloo.

Something about the rhymes of "skyn" and "chyn," "loo" and "Appolloo," and a phrase like "pipen bet" limits the didactic weight that the passage will bear.

There is no better interpreter of this genial spirit than B. J. Whiting, whose reading of the *House of Fame* first led me to take delight in Chaucer. I did not know then that it might lead to a career involving such studies as how Marcia lost her skin, but the pleasure remains:

Lo here, the fyn and guerdoun for travaille
Of Jove, Appollo, of Mars, of swich rascaille!
Lo here, the forme of olde clerkis speche
In poetrie, if ye hire bokes seche.

R. T. LENAGHAN

The Clerk of Venus:
Chaucer and Medieval Romance

Nearly fifty years ago Howard Rollins Patch, writing in tribute to Barrett Wendell, asked how much romance appeared in the works of the realistic Chaucer. The answer, of course, was a great deal, but the interest of his essay derives mainly from the puzzle of how to reconcile Chaucer's talent with his form and material. It is perennially surprising that so clearheaded a realist put so much energy into forms so little given to realism. To be sure, some of this surprise is a product of dubious division, either romance or realism, high or low, serious or frivolous, but even with allowance for arbitrary classification, Chaucer's variety cannot be constrained to a *via media*. He travels both the high road and the low road. It may be that, in trying to follow him, we hop always behind because of something like a dissociation of risibility. As the temporal restrictor in Patch's graceful summary implies, it is hard now to believe that there were "odd moments when he, too, held Launcelot de Lake in full great reverence." [1] Fortunately we can set the question in the terms of literary history without formulating large laws of cul-

1. Howard Rollins Patch, "Chaucer and Medieval Romance," in *Essays in Memory of Barrett Wendell* (Cambridge: Harvard University Press, 1926), p. 108.

31

tural change — what did Chaucer find so attractive in the romances? or, more strictly, what did he do with them?

My answer is that romances implied to him a narrative role as a clerk and that he accepted in the clerk's role a combination of literary and cultural offices, some old and traditional and others just coming into conscious definition.

The didacticism essential to the clerk's offices flickered in the openings of romances from Chretien's *Erec et Enide* to Caxton's preface to his edition of Malory. The subject matter of that didacticism is nicely defined in a parenthesis of no less an authority than Bercilak's lady.

> ... of alle chevalry to chose, the chef thyng alosed
> Is the lel layk of luf, the lettrure of armes. (1511–12)[2]

The game of love and the discipline of arms summarize the activities of the courteous Gawain according to another persistent investigator who may be said to have learned more about Gawain by his methods than the lady did by hers: "At his very best he is a man of war and women." [3] Arms and the woman are the song of the romancer. Chaucer, however, seems to have been listening with only one ear, because he is concerned just with the game of love when he turns to that genre.

It can hardly be said that war had gone out of style in the late fourteenth century, and it can certainly be said that the game of love was very much in style. Chaucer's selective address to romance put him in very good company. Gervase Mathew cites the tapestries of Thomas of Woodstock and shows an elite interest in love: "In 1397 among the goods of Thomas of Woodstock, Duke of Gloucester, were tapestries representing the Siege of the Castle of Love, the History of Love, Lancelot in battle, the Siege Perilous, the stories of Godfrey de Bouillon and of Charlemagne and what was apparently a *roman courtois*." [4] Edith Rickert cites a dozen French romances among the

2. *Sir Gawain and the Green Knight,* ed. J. R. R. Tolkien and E. V. Gordon, rev. Norman Davis, 2nd ed. (Oxford: Clarendon Press, 1967), p. 42.
   3. B. J. Whiting, "Gawain: His Reputation, His Courtesy, and His Appearance in Chaucer's *Squire's Tale,*" *Medieval Studies,* 9 (1947), 206.
   4. Gervase Mathew, *The Court of Richard II* (London: John Murray, 1968), pp. 49–50.

books of Richard II.[5] When Froissart presented his book of love poems to Richard II, he noted with approbation the king's sophistication; Richard read French easily and was an *afficionado* in the game of love.[6] Boccaccio uses the matter of the old romance of Floris and Blanchfleur for the vehicle of his literary aspirations as inspired and commanded by *la gentilissima donna.*

Certo grande ingiuria riceve la memoria degli amorosi giovani, pensando alla gran costanza de' loro animi, i quali in uno volere per l'amorosa forza sempre furono fermi serbandosi ferma fede, a non essere con debita ricordanza la loro fama esaltata da' versi d'alcun poeta, ma lasciata solamente ne' favolosi parlari degli ignoranti.[7]

The elevated theme deserves elevated statement, and the charge falls to the poet. It is a kind of cultural conservation, and the romance was a popular means of discharging the office. The romance, as a poem of refined sentiment, was a form for addressing issues that were important to Chaucer and his contemporaries.

The Squire's Tale, though certainly a romance, seems an uncertain text upon which to affirm this importance, because it is not clear just what issues the tale does in fact address. The Squire is invited to speak of love, demurs, and tells two parts — one of wonder and one of sentiment — of an incomplete tale, which he stops after promising "To speken of aventures and batailles" (F 659).[8] The leisured pace of the narration promises the extensive course so characteristic of the romance, but since the course is not actually run, its direction is uncertain. Still, the emphasis of each of the parts is tolerably clear. The narrative interest of the first part is in the grandeur and elegance of Cambyuskan's court, which serve to establish it as a proper

5. Edith Rickert, "King Richard II's Books," *The Library,* 4th ser., 13 (1932), 144–147.

6. Jean Froissart, *Oeuvres: Chroniques,* ed. Kervyn de Lettenhove (Brussels: Devaux, 1867–1877), XV, 167.

7. Giovanni Boccaccio, *Il Filocolo,* ed. Salvatore Battaglia (Bari: Laterza, 1938), p. 7.

8. *The Works of Geoffrey Chaucer,* ed. F. N. Robinson, 2nd ed. (Boston: Houghton Mifflin, 1957), p. 134.

setting for the marvelous gifts. This is the image of chivalric
magnificence. In the second part of the tale the narrative interest shifts to Canacee's delicate sympathy with the falcon's love-
grief and to the implicit sense of ethical exaltation that such a
sympathy and such a grief combine to create. This is the image
of *fin amour*.

All suitably elevated, such interests are proper to the romance, but as a number of commentators have observed, there
are awkwardnesses in the tale which call this clarity into question. First, of course, is the problem of coherence; then there
are intrusions of rhetoric, confusion about gentilesse, and simple
lapses of tone. These can be taken as negative characterizations
of the Squire, and it must be conceded that the layered narration of the *Canterbury Tales* invites this dramatic ironic reading.
Chaucer is surely an ironist, and ventriloquism is surely an apt
metaphor for describing irony. The problem in the *Canterbury
Tales* is that the critic's convenience quickly develops such a
potency as to become a universal solvent. All is irony and ne-
gation. The need to explain the substantive norms of the irony
requires some restraint, but defining the norms so often involves
complex historical references — like chivalric ideals and social
or military realities — that the restraint too frequently seems in-
effectual. A simpler check would be to ignore all but the clearest
invitations to extend dramatic irony and treat the discrepancies
as simple awkwardnesses reflecting more upon Chaucer than
upon the Squire. Chaucer began a romance by dwelling first on
marvels in a magnificent setting and then on a refined sentiment,
but he did not complete the tale. The various problems and his
announcement of things to come suggest that the undertaking
involved more difficulties than its attractions had promised.

However that may be — the *Knight's Tale* and *Troilus* show
that the difficulties were not insurmountable — the Franklin's response to the Squire's tale is instructive. He praises the Squire's
eloquence and infers *discrecioun* from it. Though his notion of
discrecioun makes him sound like the property-conscious Midill
Elde in *The Parlement of the Thre Ages,* he attaches it to the
larger virtue, gentilesse. So, in the Squire's romance, the Franklin sees the *colours of rhetoryk,* the marks of learning and the
indication of virtue. His response, like that of Boccaccio's *gen-*

tilissima donna, assumes that the romance is a literary genre suited to the display of learned skills, and their display testifies to the acquisition of gentilesse. As the occasion for giving the Franklin rhetorical evidence of ethical merit, the Squire's romance seemed to have developed the latent didacticism of the genre.

Under, but not faithful to, the Host's adjuration, "Straw for your gentilesse!," the Franklin follows the Squire's lead. As we read his tale, however, the dominant voice is not his but Professor Kittredge's. The marriage group is so firmly fixed in our awareness because Chaucer and Kittredge seem to work so well together. The good sense of the contract between Dorigen and Arveragus seems so clear that it is hard not to agree "to accept the solution which the Franklin offers as that which Geoffrey Chaucer the man accepted for his own part. Certainly it is a solution that does him infinite credit." [9] Yet, as we read further, doubts do appear, and since they have now received effective statement, it seems clear that there is more to the *Franklin's Tale* than the resolution of the marriage debate. Dorigen's dilemma is the narrative center, but as it passes from man to man, from Arveragus to Aurelius to the clerk of Orleans, it becomes more and more a debaters' issue and less and less a narrative crisis. The focus shifts from the adjustment of marital balances between husband and wife to the dialectical concern of the source, which is the fourth of a series of *quistioni d'amore* proposed before a courtly company in Boccaccio's *Filocolo.* Fitting his narrative materials to this context, Boccaccio draws *la dimanda* from *la novella* and so does Chaucer. The question is which of the three men has been most "fre" ("liberale"). So focused, the tale seems hardly to belong to the marriage group at all, because the point of casuistry is the argument not the issue.

Since Chaucer gives no actual debate on the question, only its announcement and the invitation to debate, the stress on the form is all the more emphatic. The story was cast in a dialectical mold to be an occasion for the display of skill and sophistication in the discipline, very like a hypothetical case on a law school examination. The doctrinal ground of both *novella* and

9. George Lyman Kittredge, "Chaucer's Discussion of Marriage," *Modern Philology,* 9 (1911–12), 467.

dimanda is the rhetorical commonplace, gentilesse, which comprehends so much of the vocabulary of secular values. Chaucer adds a further dialectical dimension to Boccaccio's *quistione* by describing the magician as a clerk. The common association of literary learning and magic is evident in Virgil's medieval reputation and justifies the change of Boccaccio's Tebano into the clerk of Orleans. Tebano is a meanly dressed, bearded man who is encountered while he is gathering herbs, but the turn Chaucer gives to the competition requires that this character be a clerk.

> Thou art a squier, and he is a knyght;
> But God forbede, for his blysful myght,
> But if a clerk koude doon a gentil dede
> As wel as any of yow, it is no drede! (F 1609–12)

All are *gentil,* but there is another commonplace topic in the social typing — the debates of clerks and knights. The *Franklin's Tale* is concerned at least as much with dialectics as with marriage, and the romance provides generic occasion and context for the expression of that concern.

Both Boccaccio and Chaucer turn the narrative to a dialectical end. In Boccaccio's expansive narration the purpose of the debating can be variously alluded to ("e il tempo utilmente e con diletto sará adoperato")[10] and implied so that it functions easily as a formal expression of the quality of life lived according to courtly ideals. Chaucer, working within a narrower compass, makes this more direct in the Franklin's response to the Squire's tale in which he moves quickly from literary-rhetorical skill to ethics, but in setting the *demand* or question in the terms of the commonplace topics, gentilesse and clerks against knights, he also attains something of Boccaccio's cumulative enhancement by drawing on a rhetorical treasury laid up over the years.

Each of the two topics has its own history, and although both lead to a discussion of social distinctions, gentilesse is more comprehensive and thus more various. It sometimes involves nothing more than manners in a very restricted sense, but sometimes it in-

10. *Filocolo,* p. 298.

volves basic ethical questions. Professor Gaylord is a helpful guide to the various texts on gentilesse.[11] Boethius, Dante, and Jean de Meun all figure in Chaucer's ken, and Boccaccio includes a parallel discussion in the Decameron. Chaucer sets himself straightforwardly in the tradition with his moral ballade on the theme of gentilesse. The debates of the clerk and the knight are to be found in a number of twelfth- and thirteenth-century Latin and French texts in which ladies debate the relative claims of clerks and knights as lovers.[12] The virtues of each are more or less predictable, but the damaging characteristic of the knight is his penchant for talk. He talks about his love affairs. The texts commonly cited are all quite a bit earlier than Chaucer — though they include the universal Jean de Meun — but the formal antithesis of clerk and knight survived in more places than in the *Franklin's Tale*. Machaut makes light of his timidity, asserting that bravery is as inappropriate for the clerk as cowardice for the knight.[13] Froissart assumes a similar antithesis when he opposes "le fait de bonne science/ Aornée de conscience" to the chances of knight errantry in the third of the *demandes* at the end of his *Tresor Amoreux*.[14]

In *The Romance of the Rose* Jean de Meun joins the two topics. Nature lectures on gentilesse:

> Noblece vient de bon courage,
> Car gentillece de lignange
> N'est pas gentillece qui vaille
> Pour quei bonté de cueur i faille (18619–22);

11. Alan T. Gaylord, "Gentilesse in Chaucer's *Troilus*," *Studies in Philology*, 61 (1964), 19–22; "Seed of Felicity: A Study of the Concepts of Nobility and *Gentilesse* in the Middle Ages and in the Works of Chaucer," Ph.D. diss., Princeton University, 1959.

12. Charles Oulmont, *Les Débats du clerc et du chevalier* (Paris: Champion, 1911); Edmond Faral, *Recherches sur les sources latines des contes et romans courtois du Moyen Age* (Paris: Champion, 1913), pp. 191–303.

13. Guillaume Machaut, "La Fonteinne amoureuse," *Oeuvres*, ed. Ernest Hoepffner, Société des Anciens Textes Français (Paris, 1921), III, 416–148.

14. Jean Froissart, *Oeuvres: Poesies*, ed. Auguste Scheler (Brussels: Devaux, 1870–1872), III, 277.

and stresses the title of the clerk to gentilesse:

> Si ront clerc plus grant avantage
> D'estre gentill, courteis e sage,
> E la raison vous en lirai,
> Que n'ont li prince ne li rei,
> Qui ne sevent de letreure; (18635–39).

Nature speaks, in a clerical voice, of neglected merit:

> Or est li tens a ce venuz
> Que li bon qui toute leur vie
> Travaillent en philosophie
> . . .
> Ne sont amé ne chier tenu.

and with a clerical antagonism:

> Prince nes prisent une pome;
> E si sont il plus gentill ome,
> Si me gart Deus d'aveir les fievres,
> Que cil qui vont chacier aus lievres,
> E que cil qui sont coustumiers
> De maindre es paterneus fumiers. (18740–52).[15]

As Jean de Meun describes it, the clerk's duty is the same as any man's, to pursue virtue; and since virtue is exemplary, others may learn from it (18847–48). The clerk's special identification, however, lies his study of virtue, and that implies a special duty to add formal to exemplary instruction. Since instruction in true gentilesse would be most required by those susceptible to notions of false gentilesse, princes were the natural, if somewhat symbolic, audience for such teaching. Chaucer accepts the clerk's duty as a poetic moralist in his moral ballade, *Gentilesse,* and some years later Henry Scogan incorporated Chaucer's poem in his own poem on the same subject to the sons of Henry IV, thus directing it to the explicit instruction of real princes.

The clerk as moralist, even the sharp-tongued moralist above,

15. Guillaume de Lorris and Jean de Meun, *Le Roman de la Rose,* ed. Ernest Langlois, SATF (Paris, 1922), IV, 236–241.

seems far removed from the clerk described by the ladies of the
Council of Remiremont:

Non noverunt fallere, neque maledicere;
Amandi periciam habent, et industriam. (72–73) [16]

Yet, since the moralist's authority sets the clerk apart from the
knight just as firmly as the lover's, the social division between
knights and clerks is reinforced by a different justification. The
source of the moralist's authority is his learning, and that learning — "the writings of old clerkes" — leads in the form of grammar and rhetoric to the qualification of the clerk as poet. When
the old clerk is Ovid or Dante, the authority is in love poetry,
and the two clerical offices are not so far apart in their basic
qualification. The specific discharge of the responsibility varied
with the poet, but Chaucer, unlike Boccaccio, was careful to
keep his concern with love vicarious or theoretical. His responsibility as "d'amours mondains Dieux en Albie" was to provide
instruction in the discipline of *fin amour,* in matters of feeling.
The literary-cultural roles of student, moralist, love poet combined in the clerk and made him as *gentil* as the knight. Chaucer
had his Franklin recognize this combination in his response to
the Squire's romance and in the narrative arrangement of his
own. In short, an elevated romance was a proper job for a clerk.

This identification of the romance narrator coincides well with
Chaucer's self-portraiture. He is the student of old clerks, of
"Virgile, Ovide, Omer, Lucan and Stace." His contemporaries
saw him as a clerk. He *was* a clerk, not a clergyman in orders
but a literary moralist, a poet, and a civil servant. Tout points
to Chaucer as an example of the kind of culture one of the increasingly numerous lay civil servants might attain.[17] The precise
nature of such a clerk's social position may be elusive or simply individual, but its general character can be imagined readily
enough. Chaucer's early training was preparation for a career in
which administrative service was combined with the more purely

16. "Das Liebesconcil," ed. G. Waitz, *Zeitschrift für Deutsches Alter-
thum,* 7 (1849), 162.
17. T. F. Tout, *Chapters in the Administrative History of Mediaeval
England* (Manchester: The University Press, 1923–1935), III, 201–202.

social and domestic services of companionship. The poems of Deschamps record the formalities and informalities of such a society. As the various agencies of governmental administration, increasingly staffed by lay officers, became more and more independent, something of a parallel development was taking place in the social position of these new clerks. A number of French scholars have pointed to the development of an early humanism; and while their primary concern is with the clerk as moralist, it seems clear that poet-clerks were instructing princes in matters of sentiment as well.[18] The romance narrator was, like Ovid, the clerk of Venus.

The Franklin's *demand* and his remarks on the Squire's performance have indicated the form of Chaucer's interest in the romance, but the internal difficulties and consequent dramatic complications of the tales impair their utility as examples of Chaucer's romances. *The Knights Tale* and *Troilus and Criseyde,* his *magna opera,* are more promising. The matter of these poems is drawn from the work of old wise clerks, and their *sentence,* a compound of Boethius and Boccaccio, is spoken from the clerk's double authority as moralist and love poet. Given the dialectical antithesis of knights and clerks, *The Knight's Tale* would seem an odd choice as a clerk's vehicle if it were not so probable that the tale antedates the pilgrimage scheme and reflects the same concerns as *Troilus and Criseyde.* The fictive, dramatic, explanation is that so perfect and *gentil* an exemplar of the knight's estate would have learned the clerk's lesson so well as to stand forth as a *gentil* synthesis.

The Knight's Tale is a carefully sculptured narrative; the stress is on ceremony, and the climax is Theseus' Boethian conclusion. The aim seems to have been to celebrate the high chivalric civilization while setting it at the same time in its mortal perspective. Sentiment is served by lovers' complaints and turned out from the narrative in the *demand,* "Yow loveres axe I now this questioun" (A 1347). The lists and temples testify to The-

---

18. Alfred Coville, *Gontier et Pierre Col et l'humanisme en France au temps de Charles VI* (Paris: Droz, 1934); Jacques Le Goff, *Les Intellectuels au Moyen Age* (Paris: Editions du Seuil, [1957]); Daniel Poirion, *Le Moyen Age II, 1300–1480,* in *Littérature française,* 16 vols., ed. Claude Pichois (Paris: Arthaud, 1971), pp. 69–105.

seus' magnificence and the tournament itself to his respect for
civilized order as the stay against armed chaos. The final sober
affirmation balances mortality and the attractions of life. Although the final speech is a didactic address of universal application, the narrower appeal of the courtly values of its context
restricts the application. The convictions that animate the tale
are very much those of a humanist instructor of princes.[19]

As comparison with the *Filostrato* shows, *Troilus and Criseyde* is also a sculptured narrative, though it is at the same
time a far more dynamic one than *The Knight's Tale*. It is a
romance of love shaped by a clear thematic intention directly
in line with the Boethian principles of Theseus' speech. Criseyde's feelings are the effective center of the poem because they
are clarified by a narrator whose sophisticated sympathies are
refined by *fin amour*. As C. S. Lewis remarked, there could be
no Criseyde without *The Romance of the Rose*. The sensitivity
of the narrator is grounded in love poetry.

> Now, lady bright, for thi benignite,
> At reverence of hem that serven the,
> Whos clerc I am, so techeth me devyse
> Som joye of that is felt in thi servyse. (*Troilus,* III.39–42)

Chaucer is trying to synthesize his two authorities as a clerk,
that of the moralist and that of the love poet. His success needs
no vindicating, but it must be conceded that it was not perfect.
As with *The Knight's Tale,* only more so, there are lapses and
stresses in *Troilus and Criseyde,* and if we no longer think of a
Christian moral forced on a pagan love story, we still are aware
of an anxiety in the resolution. The uncertainties of *The Franklin's Tale* are evident even in the *magnum opus*. Chaucer has
trouble with a most deliberately chosen vehicle, and the trouble
seems to stem from the very conflict of moral forces that is also
the poem's achievement.

19. John Reidy reached a similar conclusion from different materials
in his paper, "The Education of Chaucer's Duke Theseus," read at a
conference on "The Epic in Medieval Society" sponsored by the Department of Germanic Languages and Literatures of the University of
Michigan, April 11–14, 1973.

It seems that the romance was something Chaucer could neither take nor leave alone. He accepted the double charge of the clerk to speak of morality and of the refinements of love, and while there was nothing new in this, the role of the clerk was changing in ways that invited new combinations of the old offices. A layman could take part in all the social activities of a courtly household, or at least a part uncomplicated by a vow of chastity. Specifically, a lay clerk could more easily claim authority in the discipline of *fin amour*. In the line of the wise old poets, a clerk could qualify himself quite without sacerdotal title to speak on morality by reading the poets, and often by reading the same poets he could qualify himself to speak of love. The heart's refinement would have been as much a part of gentilesse as the traditional wisdom and, therefore, as much a part of the preceptor's responsibility. Still the two authorities and the two roles do not sit easily together. Still less easily do they sit with a clerk's administrative duties. Custom house tallies could not have seemed more *gentil* than the knight's noxious *fumiers*. Yet while the duties, activities, aspirations, and ideals of the clerk were complex and often discrepant, his role was important in the court or household society, and his literary-rhetorical capacities were vital to that role. He was a guide to the *sentence* of the old clerks and poets. He was a coach of *fin amour*. He was expert in the *matter* of the formalities and ceremonies of the court society. The romance offered Chaucer a literary, narrative, even dialectically structured role that corresponded significantly with one he took, or perhaps felt he ought to take, in the real world. The clerk's role added a literary-rhetorical articulation to a social position and function. Boccaccio testifies to the poet's importance and proclaims a vigilance over individual progress along the high road of this articulation.

Si quis autem ex his, quibus hic infunditur fervor, hec minus plene fecerit, iudicio meo laudabilis poeta non erit. Insuper, quantumcunque, urgeat animos, quibus infusus est, perraro impulsus commendabile perficit aliquid, si instrumenta, quibus meditata perfici consuevere, defecerint, ut puta grammatice precepta atque rethorice, quorum plena notitia opportuna est, esto non nulli mirabiliter materno sermone iam scripserint et per singula poesis officia peregerint. Hinc et liberalium aliarum artium et moralium atque naturalium saltem novisse principia necesse est; nec non et vocabulorum valere copia, vidisse monimenta maiorum ac etiam meminisse et hystorias nationum, et regionum orbis, marium, fluviorum et montium dispositiones.[20]

Of course there were discrepancies in the relationship of the literary and social roles of the clerk as well as correspondences, and they are social referents for Chaucer's difficulties of execution in the romances and for the ambivalence they imply. Given the intimidating weight of a pronouncement like Boccaccio's, it is easy to think of Chaucer on the low road when Brunetto Latini, speaking interestingly enough in an Aristotelian passage of *compaignie,* says of the jongleur:

> Gengleor est celui ki gengle entre les gens a ris et a gieu, et moke soi et sa feme et ses fiz et tous autres.[21]

20. Giovanni Boccaccio, *Genealogie Deorum Gentilium Libri,* ed. Vincenzo Romano (Bari: Laterza, 1951), II, 700.

21. Brunetto Latini, *Li Livres dou Tresor,* ed. Francis J. Carmody, University of California Publications in Modern Philology, No. 22 (Berkeley and Los Angeles, 1948), p. 204.

KENNETH A. BLEETH

The Image of Paradise in the *Merchant's Tale*

Almost twenty-five years ago, D. W. Robertson, Jr., noted
that the final episode of the *Merchant's Tale* recalled another
scene in a garden: "ultimately, we are back at Eve and Adam's
in medio ligni paradisi." [1] Robertson's observation, though it
may have surprised readers of *Speculum* in 1951, hardly seems
startling to us now: over the past decade or so, a number of
scholars have argued convincingly for the presence of biblical
parody in Chaucer's fabliaux. The investigation of scriptural allusion in the *Merchant's Tale* raises special problems, however.
Unlike the echoes of the Song of Songs in the *Miller's Tale* or
the Pentecostal imagery in the *Summoner's Tale,* the parallels
to Genesis noted by Robertson and others — a husband and
wife in a garden, a traitor in a fruit tree, the wife's desire for
fruit, and the opening of her husband's eyes — occur as well in
the relatively unsophisticated analogues of the *Merchant's Tale.*[2]
Thus, though we are free to speculate that Chaucer was drawn

1. "The Doctrine of Charity in Medieval Literary Gardens," *Speculum,* 26 (1951), 44.
2. Germaine Dempster, "The Merchant's Tale," *Sources and Analogues of Chaucer's Canterbury Tales,* ed. W. F. Bryan and G. Dempster
(Chicago: University of Chicago Press, 1941), pp. 341–356; Karl P.
Wentersdorf, "Chaucer's Merchant's Tale and its Irish Analogues," *Studies in Philology,* 73 (1966), 604–619.

to the Fruit Tree story because of its resemblance to the biblical
account of the Fall, we must, nevertheless, be wary of attributing undue significance to the mere sequence of events in the final
scene of the poem. If we are tempted to find there "an allegorical pattern central to Christian awareness," [3] we should recognize that the basis for this pattern is in fact the plot of a popular
folk narrative.

Such a recognition need not, however, impede our exploration of scriptural parody in the *Merchant's Tale*. We may observe — at least insofar as our knowledge of the probable
sources of the tale permits — that Chaucer has stressed some
aspects of the Fruit Tree story at the expense of others, that
he makes his own additions, and, most important, that he provides an elaborate framework for the fabliau plot which (among
other things) brings into relief its latent religious elements. Perhaps the most significant "Christian context" for the notorious
episode in January's garden is the series of references to paradise in the first part of the tale. We are prepared for the complex
comedy of the final scene by the changes rung on this image
almost from the opening lines of the poem.

We first hear of paradise from January himself. Having spent
sixty years without a wife, he now wishes to live

> under that hooly boond
> With which that first God man and womman bond.
> "Noon oother lyf," seyde he, "is worth a bene;
> For wedlok is so esy and so clene,
> That in this world it is a paradys." (1261–65) [4]

Here, as elsewhere in the tale, January's arguments are freely
embellished with Christian commonplaces. The image of marriage as a paradise occurs, for example, in *Cleanness,* where
God says of honest wedlock that "pure paradys moȝt preve no

3. Robert P. Miller, "Allegory in the Canterbury Tales," *Companion to Chaucer Studies,* ed. Beryl Rowland (Toronto: Oxford University Press, 1968), p. 283.
4. All quotations from Chaucer are from *The Works of Geoffrey Chaucer,* ed. F. N. Robinson, 2nd ed. (Boston: Houghton Mifflin, 1957).

better" (704), and in *Piers Plowman,* in Wit's speech on "trewe wedded libbing folk": "And thus was wedloke ywrouȝt . and god hym-self it made;/In erthe the heuene is . hym-self was the witnesse" (B, IX,116–17). Though January sounds orthodox enough in appropriating this traditional figure and in claiming that marriage is "clene" — or righteous — the Merchant is clearly unimpressed: "Thus seyde this olde knyght, that was so wys" (1266). Not only are January's motives for taking a wife suspect, but the Merchant's own experience of wedlock has left him incurably cynical about the clerkly ideal of marriage as a paradise on earth. It is in this disillusioned mood that he recounts God's creation of Eve (1325–29), concluding with the observation "That wyf is mannes help and his confort,/His paradys terrestre, and his disport" (1331–32). The rhyme of "confort" and "disport" will occur again, when January invites May into the private paradise which is to become the setting for his cuckolding: "Com forth, and lat us taken oure disport;/I chees thee for my wyf and my confort" (2147–48). Yet it is not only in retrospect that the Merchant's gloss on Genesis seems tinged with irony. The speech on marriage in which these lines occur includes a list of Old Testament heroines — Rebecca, Judith, Esther, and Abigail — who ostensibly provided men with helpful advice, but whose activities — at least as summarized by the Merchant — seem at best dubious examples of "good conseil." [5] In such a context, the statement that the creation of Eve proves a wife to be man's earthly paradise must be read as an "ironic assertion of the contrary" (Bronson, p. 590), a wry inversion of the inevitable antifeminist moral.

If the Merchant's misogyny is often expressed indirectly, antifeminism finds an outspoken voice in Justinus, whose conversation with January provides the next important variation on the paradise theme. Having heard that no man may "han parfite blisses two, — /This is to seye, in erthe and eek in hevene"

5. For the Biblical heroines as deceivers of men, see J. S. P. Tatlock, "Chaucer's Merchant's Tale," *Modern Philology,* 33 (1935–36), 376; B. H. Bronson, "Afterthoughts on the Merchant's Tale," *SP,* 58 (1961), 591. For a modification of this view, see Charlotte F. Otten, "Proserpine: *Liberatrix Suae Gentis,*" *Chaucer Review,* 5 (1971), 277–287.

(1638–39), the old knight states his fear that the delights of marriage will be so great as to supersede the rewards of the afterlife:

> Yet is ther so parfit felicitee
> And so greet ese and lust in mariage,
> That evere I am agast now in myn age
> That I shal lede now so myrie a lyf,
> So delicat, withouten wo and stryf,
> That I shal have myn hevene in erthe heere. (1642–47)

Taking up January's image, Justinus wittily deflates it:

> And therefore, sire — the beste reed I kan —
> Dispeire yow noght, but have in youre memorie,
> Paraunter she may be youre purgatorie!
> She may be Goddes meene and Goddes whippe;
> Thanne shal youre soule up to hevene skippe
> Swifter than dooth an arwe out of a bowe. (1668–73)

Justinus' *auctoritee* here is the Wife of Bath, whose account of the "wo that is in mariage" includes the following tribute to her fourth husband: "By God! in erthe I was his purgatorie,/For which I hope his soule be in glorie" (III.489–490). Memories of Alice's sadistic *maistrie* serve as a corrective to January's vision of marriage as an Edenic Golden Age: far from being heaven on earth, wedlock is at best purgatorial "penaunce"; and, Justinus goes on to suggest, it also offers ample opportunities for sin, in the form of that very "ese and lust" which January has gleefully been anticipating (1675–81). The argument here revolves around the distinction between marriage *ante* and *post lapsum,* the one, according to Peter Lombard, "ad officium facta in paradiso, ubi esset thorus immaculatus, et nuptiae honorabiles, ex quibus sine ardore conciperent . . . altera post peccatum ad remedium facta extra paradisum, propter illicitum motum devitandum." [6] The "remedium" of which Peter speaks is the Pauline concession to our fallen condition: limited marital inter-

---

6. *Sententiae* IV.26.2 (J. P. Migne, ed., *Patrologia Latina* CXCII, 908); cf. *ParsT* X.882.

course "to avoid fornication" (1 Cor. 7.2–6). January interprets this permission as license for unrestrained sexual indul-
gence. "It is no fors how longe that we pleye," he says to May,

> In trewe wedlok coupled be we tweye;
> And blessed be the yok that we been inne,
> For in oure actes we mowe do no synne.
> A man may do no synne with his wyf,
> Ne hurte hymselven with his owene knyf;
> For we han leve to pleye us by the lawe. (1835–41)

The spectacle of an old man frantically making up for lost time
has about it a certain grotesque pathos, reinforced here by January's thinly veiled sexual boast about his "knyf." The psychological implications of this passage, however, are firmly linked
to a moral evaluation; though January views his marriage as
paradise regained, Chaucer has provided us with a more sober
perspective on his speech, in the Parson's reminder, in his remarks on marital lechery, that "a man may sleen hymself with
his owene knyf, and make hymselve dronken of his owene tonne.
Certes, be it wyf, be it child, or any worldly thyng that he loveth
biforn God, it is his mawmet, and he is an ydolastre" (X.858-
859). The precise nature of January's idolatry becomes clear
when he takes "in armes . . . His fresshe May, his paradys, his
make" (1821-22), acting out that earlier moment when

> . . . in his herte he gan hire to manace
> That he that nyght in armes wolde hire streyne
> Harder than evere Parys dide Eleyne. (1752–54)

January's choice of a classical model for his love-making provides a fitting coda to the mordant mock-heroics of the marriage
feast: in patterning his wedding night on a notorious rape, he
exposes his vision of "paradys" as a fantasy of violent, unnatural
lust. (May's response to January's passion, though never explicitly described, is vividly suggested when the narrator, with
affected delicacy, says he dares not tell us whether she thought
her husband's embraces "paradys or helle" [1964].) The consummation of January's marriage as he envisions it will in fact
be an act of adultery, not only in its recollection of the ill-fated

abduction of Helen, but also in the sense in which the Middle Ages understood any too-ardent relations between husband and wife to be "adulterous." As Robertson observes, "to develop a *passio* in marriage, as Chaucer's Januarie seeks to do . . . is to destroy the marriage so that it becomes a vehicle for original sin rather than a remedy for it." [7]

The implications of Robertson's remark are realized in the tale not through theological exposition, but in dramatic action, as January gives substance to his obsessive fantasy of marriage as an earthly paradise by building a garden which becomes the scene for a burlesque reenactment of the Fall. The identification of January's garden with the biblical paradise is established only gradually, however. When the Merchant first describes the pleasance, he implicitly compares it to the Garden of Deduit:

> For, oute of doute, I verraily suppose
> That he that wroot the Romance of the Rose
> Ne koude of it the beautee wel devyse. (2031–33)

Robertson and, after him, John Fleming have argued convincingly that the "beau vergier" embodies an invitation to destructive self-indulgence which becomes patent in the retelling of the story of Narcissus.[8] The Lover's susceptibility to the allurements of the garden, Fleming observes, "is typical of unreasonable *adolescentia*"; as Dame Reason puts it, "folie et enfance / t'ont mis em poine et en esmoi" (2982–83).[9] Failures of judgment understandable in the youthful Amant are painful to contemplate, however, in the sixty-year-old January, who by his own admission is on his "pittes brynke" (1401). Guillaume's "ver-

7. D. W. Robertson, Jr., *A Preface to Chaucer* (Princeton: Princeton University Press, 1962), pp. 429–430. On adultery in marriage, see Jerome, *Adversus Jovinianum* I.49 (*PL* XXIII, 281); Deschamps, *Miroir de Mariage,* 5389–92, *Oeuvres,* ed. G. Raynaud (Paris, 1894), IX, 177. The story of Paris and Helen is used to warn against adultery in *The Epistle of Othea,* ed. C. F. Bühler, Early English Text Society, 264 (London: Oxford University Press, 1970), 55; cf. Robertson, *Preface,* p. 436.

8. Robertson, "Doctrine of Charity," pp. 40–43; *Preface,* pp. 91–96; John V. Fleming, *The Roman de la Rose: A Study in Allegory and Iconography* (Princeton: Princeton University Press, 1969), pp. 54–103.

9. Fleming, p. 77n. Quotations from the *Roman* are from *Le Roman de la Rose,* ed. F. Lecoy, 3 vols. (Paris: Champion, 1965–1970).

gier" had pointedly excluded Old Age (339–404); in the *Merchant's Tale,* the topography of the earlier garden is transformed to accommodate January's senile lusts. Neither the author of the *Roman,* the Merchant tells us,

> Ne Priapus ne myghte nat suffise,
> Though he be god of gardyns, for to telle
> The beautee of the gardyn and the welle,
> That stood under a laurer alwey grene. (2034–37)

For readers of the *Roman,* the "welle" would recall Guillaume's treacherous Fountain of Narcissus, which in the French poem stands "soz un pin" (4425); the point of this allusion is clarified by the reference to Priapus — another exemplum of frustrated and self-deluded lust — and by the presence of the "laurer." [10] It was to a laurel, we remember, that January had earlier compared himself in his startling assertion of sexual energy:

> Though I be hoor, I fare as dooth a tree
> That blosmeth er that fruyt ywoxen bee;
> And blosmy tree nys neither drye ne deed.
> I feele me nowhere hoor but on myn heed;
> Myn herte and alle my lymes been as grene
> As laurer thurgh the yeer is for to sene. (1461–66)

The irony of this speech extends beyond January's self-deceptions about his virility: the fruit-tree simile (the "fruit," presumably, being the children he expects from marriage) looks forward to the final episode of the poem, where May's desire for fruit is linked graphically with her lust for Damian. The passage

---

10. For the identification of the "welle" with the Fountain of Narcissus, see John Burrow, "Irony in the Merchant's Tale," *Anglia,* 75 (1957), 204; Robertson, *Preface,* p. 110; George Economou, "Januarie's Sin against Nature: The *Merchant's Tale* and the *Roman de la Rose,*" *Comparative Literature,* 17 (1965), 255–256. On medieval interpretations of Narcissus, see Robertson, *Preface,* p. 93; Louise Vinge, *The Narcissus Theme in Western Literature* (Lund: Gleerups, 1967), pp. 72–76, 91–100. Ovid's account of Priapus' attempt to rape the nymph Lotis (*Fasti* I.415–438) is recalled by Chaucer in *PF* 252–256; see Robertson, *Preface,* pp. 20–21, and Arthur Hoffman, *Ovid and the Canterbury Tales* (Philadelphia: University of Pennsylvania Press, 1966), pp. 154–156.

is also a parody of the common figure of the good man as a garden: "Holy writ [Cant. 4:12] likneþ a good man and a good womman to a fair garden ful of grene and of faire trees and of good fruyt . . . For in þat garden graffede þe grete gardener, þat is God þe fadre, whan he makeþ þe herte nesche and swete and esy as wex tempred . . . Þes þinges doþ þe Holy Gost to þe herte and makeþ it wexe al grene and bere flour and fruȝt, and he makeþ it as a paradis riȝt delitable, ful of goode trees and precious." [11] The model for the paradise of virtue within the heart is, of course, the garden of Eden: "But riȝt as God sett erþeli paradis ful of goode trees and fruyȝt, and in þe myddel sett þe tree of lif . . . Riȝt so doþ gostly to þe herte þe goode gardyner" (*Vices and Virtues,* p. 93). Inverting this "gostly" parallel, January builds a mock Eden in the image of his own lustful fantasies.

The elements of the garden which we examined in connection with the *Roman* are clearly related (as is Deduit's pleasance itself) to the biblical paradise. The evergreen laurel, emblematic of January's desire for eternal youth, is a carnal analogue of the *lignum vitae,* standing, as does the Tree of Life, beside a spring or fountain.[12] A second tree within the garden inevitably sug-

11. *The Book of Vices and Virtues,* ed. W. N. Francis, EETS 217 (London: Oxford University Press, 1942), 92–93. For this image and its popularity in the Middle Ages, see Rosemond Tuve, *Allegorical Imagery* (Princeton: Princeton University Press, 1966), pp. 22–24, 108–111.
12. The *paradisus voluptatis* was often depicted as containing a fountain, owing, perhaps, to the association of the *fluvius* (Gen. 2:10) with the *fons* (Gen. 2:6), as in Augustine, *De Genesi ad Litteram,* V.7.21–22 (*PL* XXXIV, 328). See Paul A. Underwood, "The Fountain of Life in Manuscripts of the Gospels," *Dumbarton Oaks Papers,* 5 (1950), 46–47; Robertson, *Preface,* pl. 89; Sir Frank Crisp, *Medieval Gardens* (London: John Lane, 1924), I, figs. 116–117, and compare the miniature of the *Roman* garden (Narcissus gazing into a fountain which runs into a river) in Fleming, pl. 3 and p. 93. The placement of the Tree of Life near the stream or fountain of paradise is an extremely common motif; see R. E. Kaske, "A Poem of the Cross in the Exeter Book," *Traditio,* 23 (1967), 64; also *Vices and Virtues,* pp. 95–96; Tuve, pp. 22–24 and fig. 7. For the *lignum vitae* as a source of eternal youth, see, for example, Augustine, *De Civ. Dei* XIII.20, 23, XIV.26. Though the laurel is not, to my knowledge, anywhere directly linked with the Tree of Life, Pierre Bersuire associates it with the Cross, commonly prefigured by the *lignum vitae* in medieval typology; see *Reductorium Moralis,* XII.84, *Opera Omnia* (Cologne, 1730), II, 543; *Metamorphosis Ovidiana Moraliter a Magistro Thoma Walleys* (Paris, 1509), fols. vii^v, xx^v. See also Al-

gests the *lignum scientiae boni et mali;* though the fig seems to have been the most popular candidate for the *lignum scientiae* during the Middle Ages (the tree was connected with the fig-leaves of Gen. 3:7), various other possibilities, including the pear, were proposed.[13] The pear tree appears, of course, in several versions of the cuckolding tale, but its sexual associations provide an apt link as well with the story of the Fall, since the *lignum scientiae* was sometimes regarded by medieval commentators as conveying specifically sexual knowledge.[14] In the light of this tradition, the comedy of May's "appetit" lies not only in the obvious phallic suggestions of the "smale peres grene" (2333),[15] but also in the parallel with Eve's desire for fruit, commonly associated with the promptings of fleshly delight.[16] The standard tropological account of the Fall equates

fred Kellogg, "Susannah and the *Merchant's Tale,*" *Speculum,* 25 (1960), 271–272.

13. For the fig tree as the *lignum scientiae,* see Oswald Goetz, *Der Feigenbaum in der Religiosen Kunst des Abendlandes* (Berlin: Mann, 1965), pp. 34–41. Although it would be pleasant to report a "tradition" of the pear tree as the *lignum scientiae,* a fairly thorough search of written and pictorial evidence has turned up only one certain medieval example of the association: Gonzalo de Berceo, *Vida de Sto. Domingo de Silos,* ed. Germán Arduna (Madrid: Anaya, 1968), st. 330 (p. 114). Cf., however, the scene in *Li Romanz de la Poire,* ed. Fr. Stehlich (Halle, 1881), p. 46, where the narrator eats a pear offered to him by a woman who has herself nibbled at it, and immediately feels the pangs of desire: "Des puis qu'Adans mordi la pome, / Ne fus mes tel poire trovée" (453–454).

14. J. Coppens, "L'interprétation sexuelle du péché du paradis dans la littérature patristique," *Ephemerides Theologicae Louvanienses,* 24 (1948), 402–408.

15. In the *Lydia,* a twelfth-century Latin version of the Pear Tree story, there is elaborate punning on *Pirrus* (the hero's name), *pirus,* and *pirum,* which (as Paul Olson points out, "Chaucer's Merchant and January's 'Hevene in Erthe Heere,' " *ELH,* 28 [1961], 207n), can mean both "pear" and "rod"; text and translation in *The Literary Context of Chaucer's Fabliaux,* ed. Larry D. Benson and Theodore M. Andersson (Indianapolis: Bobbs-Merrill, 1971), pp. 206–237. See also "I haue a newe gardyn," *Secular Lyrics of the XIVth and XVth Centuries,* ed. R. H. Robbins, 2nd ed. (Oxford: Clarendon Press, 1955), pp. 15–16. Bersuire (*Reductorium Moralis,* XII.120) associates pears with *luxuria;* cf. Chrétien de Troyes, *Cligés,* 6259–384, and L. Polak, "Cligés, Fénice, el l'Arbre d'Amour," *Romania,* 93 (1972), 310–316.

16. Chaucer, *ParsT* X.330–331; Deschamps, *Miroir de Mariage,* 7003–08, 7025–27; Augustine, *De Trinitate* XII.12.17 (*PL* XLII, 1007–08);

Eve's eating of the fruit and subsequent presentation of it to
Adam with the seduction of the higher reason by the *pars inferior,* an inversion of the harmonious "marriage" of reason and
sensuality which should exist within the soul.[17] In the *Merchant's
Tale,* these moral commonplaces merge with slapstick comedy:
stooping down to allow May to climb upon his back (a detail
peculiar to Chaucer's version of the story), January in effect acts
out an image of his topsy-turvy union.

The curing of January's blindness depends for its comic point
on similar inversions of Christian motifs. In Genesis, both man
and wife eat the forbidden fruit, their eyes are opened, and they
see themselves naked. As one might expect, exegetes comment
that at this moment Adam and Eve experience concupiscence
and that "their eyes are opened" to sinfulness and shame.[18] In
the *Merchant's Tale,* May's shamelessness is, if anything, increased after she has enjoyed her "fruit," while the restoration of
January's vision and the sight of his wife's "nakedness" serve
only to confirm him in his refusal to recognize the realities of his
condition: his meek acquiescence to May's outrageous explanation of what he has seen, far from demonstrating a knowledge of
good and evil, hints at a long future of pathetic "blindness" to
similar episodes.

The embittered misogyny which colors the Merchant's allusions to Genesis in the garden scene governs as well his use of
scriptural authority elsewhere in the poem. January's pastoral
invitation to his young wife, for example, is a patchwork of
phrases from Canticles:

> "Rys up, my wyf, my love, my lady free!
> The turtles voys is herd, my dowve sweete;
> The wynter is goon with alle his reynes weete.

Bersuire, *Reductorium Moralis* III.2; Coppens, pp. 406–408. Some marginal illustrations in a MS of the *Roman de la Rose* (Bibl. nat. fr. 25526,
fols. 106ᵛ, 160ʳ) show women (dressed as Beguines; cf. *Roman,* 11907ff.,
12035ff.) plucking "fruit" in the form of male genitalia.

17. In addition to Robertson, *Preface,* pp. 70, 74, and the works cited
there, see Deschamps, *Miroir de Mariage,* 6991–7039.

18. Augustine, *De Civ. Dei* XIV.17; *De Genesi ad Litteram* XI.31.40
(*PL* XXXIV, 445–446); Ambrose, *De Paradiso* VI.33 (*PL* XIV, 289).

> Com forth now, with thyne eyen columbyn!
> How fairer been thy brestes than is wyn!
> The garden is enclosed al aboute;
> Com forth, my white spouse! out of doute
> Thou hast me wounded in myn herte, O wyf!
> No spot of thee ne knew I al my lyf.
> Com forth, and lat us taken oure disport;
> I chees thee for my wyf and my confort." (2138–48)

In view of the frequency with which the Song of Songs was allegorized in the Middle Ages, it seems unlikely that Chaucer's audience could have heard January's defiantly literal use of the text as an incitement to springtime dalliance without being reminded of its spiritual glosses as well. Though a number of the traditional allegories of Canticles contribute to the satiric richness of these lines, the interpretations of the Sponsus and Sponsa as Christ and the Church, or as Christ and the human soul, seem to me less relevant to January's lyric than the equally common reading of the Song of Songs with reference to the Blessed Virgin.[19] The Marian exegesis of Canticles was available in various forms — in hymns and sequences, for example, and in vernacular poems to the Virgin; indeed, as E. T. Donaldson suggests, out of context and minus the concluding couplet, January's speech bears more than a passing resemblance to a number of Middle English religious lyrics.[20] Read at its proper place in the narrative, however, the old man's spring song stands as a telling example of what Donaldson calls "the most obvious feature of the Merchant's Tale ... its juxtaposition of the seemingly, or potentially, beautiful with the unmistakably ugly" (p. 34). January's lecherous desire for his deceptively "fresshe" May is expressed in language which recalls the ritual of devotion to an-

19. For the Marian interpretation of Canticles, see Albertus Magnus, *Biblia Mariana, Opera Omnia,* ed. A. Borgnet (Paris, 1898), XXXVII, 397–402; Henry de Lubac, *Méditation sur l'Église,* 2nd ed. (Paris: Aubier, 1953), pp. 306–315; F. J. E. Raby, *A History of Christian Latin Poetry in the Middle Ages* (Oxford: Clarendon Press, 1953), pp. 363–375.
20. "The Effect of the Merchant's Tale," in *Speaking of Chaucer* (New York: Norton, 1970), p. 44. Cf. the poems to the Virgin in *Religious Lyrics of the XVth Century,* ed. Carleton Brown (Oxford: Clarendon Press, 1939), pp. 22–78, esp. pp. 65–67.

other, truly sweet "may." [21] The exegetical tradition connecting the *hortus conclusus* with Mary's inviolate virginity lends further ironic resonance to January's invitation: the walled garden, which literally embodies his hopes for a private world of lust, is extended — by way of an association with the supreme example of womanly chastity — to include as well his fantasy of May's "spotless" purity.[22]

As I noted earlier, the Merchant first presents January's garden as a version of the pleasance in the *Roman*. We should recall, however, that the stock properties of the medieval love-garden — the wall, the gate, the fountain beneath the tree — were standard features as well of both Eden and the Marian *hortus conclusus;* a glance at Sir Frank Crisp's *Medieval Gardens* will reveal that artists rarely distinguished between the basic topography of sacred and secular paradises. In describing January's "honest" garden, Chaucer exploits the multiple associations which surrounded the elements of his setting, allowing details with amusingly incongruous meanings to blend into each other. The Garden of Deduit, for example, has its little "guichoit" (552) which Oiseuse unlocks to admit the Lover; a well-known illustration of the *Roman* shows her with key in hand, leading Amant to the locked door of the pleasance.[23] In the *Merchant's Tale,* the key and gate take on sexual overtones: the silver "clyket," which January will permit no one but himself to carry, suggests his jealous guardianship of May's sexual "gate," [24] an association made explicit in the transference of the

21. Chaucer uses the epithet "may" for the Virgin in *MLT* 851. See also *Religious Lyrics of the XIVth Century,* ed. Carleton Brown, 2nd ed. (Oxford: Clarendon Press, 1952), pp. 13–14, 74, 178; *Ludus Coventriae,* ed. K. S. Block, EETS 120 (London, 1922), 88.

22. For the connection between the *hortus conclusus* and Mary's virginity, see the works cited in n.19. Chaucer could have encountered this figural association in Jerome's *Adversus Jovinianum* (*PL* XXIII, 254); as Kellogg notes, "it would be difficult to imagine that the Marian connotations of the enclosed garden could have been far from Chaucer's mind" ("Susannah," p. 278n).

23. Crisp, II, fig. 75; Dieter Hennebo, *Gärten des Mittelalters* (Hamburg: Broschek, 1962), fig. 12. Cf. *Roman,* 2987–88.

24. Robertson suggests (*Preface,* pp. 256–257) that Chaucer's January is intended to recall the "two-faced" god Janus. He might have noted that in Ovid, Janus is a gatekeeper and is described as carrying a key (*Fasti* I.99, 125–126, 137–140, 228, 253).

invariable epithet for May to the "fresshe gardyn" (2158) and
in the sequence of the Merchant's description at lines 2045–52:

> . . . of the smale wyket
> He baar alwey of silver a clyket,
> With which, whan that hym leste, he it unshette.
> And whan he wolde paye his wyf hir dette
> In somer seson, thider wolde he go,
> And May his wyf, and no wight but they two;
> And thynges whiche that were nat doon abedde,
> He in the garden parfourned hem and spedde.

The erotic symbolism of the key is further developed when May
"counterfetes" it "pryvely" for Damian in warm wax (ironically,
the very image January had used earlier [1430] to describe his
projected dealings with young women), thus transferring sexual
lordship from husband to lover.[25]

Urged by May to "go biforn with his cliket,"

> This Damyan thanne hath opened the wyket,
> And in he stirte, and that in swich manere
> That no wight myghte it se neither yheere,
> And stille he sit under a bussh anon. (2151–55)

This little scene vividly prefigures the denouement of the tale:
again in response to signs from May, the squire climbs the tree,
waits for her to join him, "And sodeynly anon this Damyan/
Gan pullen up the smok, and in he throng" (2352–53). The
verbal parallels suggest not only a causal connection between
these two moments, but a kind of metaphorical identification as
well: given the persistent association of January's marriage and
of May herself with "paradise," Damian's entrance into the garden is equivalent to his physical act of cuckolding the old knight.
It is, of course, January's literal blindness which allows these
activities to take place; when we read, however, of January, "as

25. Compare the symbolism of the key in one of the so-called Cambridge Songs: "Veni dilectissime,/Gratam me invisere,/In languore
pereo,/Venerem desidero,/Si cum clave veneris/Mox intrare poteris."
Peter Dronke, *Medieval Latin and the Rise of the European Love-Lyric*
(Oxford: Clarendon Press, 1965), I, 274.

blynde as is a stoon" (2156), leading May into the garden
"walled al with stoon," we are forcibly reminded, again by a
verbal echo, that this train of events has its ultimate cause in the
moral blindness which would make a marriage a private preserve
for jealous lusts.

The scene just described follows directly upon January's lyric
from Canticles, and, in view of the Marian connotations of the
"gardyn enclosed," the juxtaposition suggests a further level of
meaning in the episode. The locked gate is a standard motif in
pictorial representations of the *hortus conclusus,* a feature doubtless influenced by the *porta clausa* of Ezekiel 44:1–2, a common
Old Testament type of the Virgin.[26] The gate of the *hortus conclusus,* open only to Christ at his Incarnation and Birth,[27] is
sometimes contrasted with the gate of Eden, open to Satan, and
to Adam and Eve when they leave paradise; commenting on the
two scriptural gardens, Richard of St. Lawrence writes: *"Planta-
verat quidem Dominus Deus hortum voluptatis a principio . . .*
scilicet paradisum . . . cujus usum amisimus, quia conclusus non
fuerat hortus ille . . . Aperuit Satanas ostia paradisi, de quo
quasi foetus de ventre genus humanum exivit . . . Sed ad remedium hujus mali fecit Dominus alium paradisum, scilicet Virginis
uterum . . . et ita conclusis hunc hortum, ut nulli hosti, nulli
maligno ejus pateret ingressus."[28] A passage such as this opens

26. For examples of the Marian *hortus conclusus* with locked gate
(and, in some instances, with key), see *Speculum humanae salvationis,*
ed. E. Breitenbach (Strassburg: J. H. E. Heitz, 1930), pl. 3; Crisp,
Medieval Gardens, I, figs. 10, 11, 18; Kellogg, "Susannah," fig. 3; Stanley Stewart, *The Enclosed Garden* (Madison: University of Wisconsin
Press, 1966), figs. 8, 10. Ambrose directly links the *porta clausa* and
the *hortus conclusus* in his commentary on Ezek. 44:1–2: "Quae est
haec porta, nisi Maria; ideo clausa, quia virgo? . . . Porta ergo clausa
virginitas est: et hortus clausus virginitas: et fons signatus virginitas"
(*De institutione virginis,* VII–IX, *PL* XVI, 320–321). For the
extremely common association of Mary with the *porta clausa,* see, for example,
Religious Lyrics of the XIVth Century, pp. 49–50; J. Lutz and P.
Perdrizet, *Speculum humanae salvationis* (Mulhouse: E. Meninger,
1909), II, fig. 102 (*porta clausa* with lock and key); cf. *Hymni Latini
Medii Aevi,* ed. F. J. Mone (Freiburg, 1854), II, 51.

27. See Ambrose, n. 26; Jerome, *Epistola* xlviii (*PL* XXII, 510). The
princeps of Ezek. 44:3 is commonly interpreted as Christ.

28. *De Laudibus B. Mariae Virginis,* Albertus Magnus, *Opera Omnia,*
XXXVI, 605–606. Cf. Fleming, p. 66: "The good garden of the Canticles offered fruitful possibilities for contrast with the old dangerous

up surprising comic possibilities for Damian's entrance into the walled paradise. In allowing her lover — who is earlier compared to a "naddre in bosom slye untrewe" (1786) and who hides, snakelike, under a bush — to slip through the "smale wyket," May supplies January's pleasance with its serpent and, reversing the traditional relation between the two gardens, in effect transforms the *hortus conclusus* into the *paradisus voluptatis*.

I advance this interpretation tentatively, but I believe it to be supported by several allusions in the final scene of the poem associating May with Eve and Mary. The most striking of these has been discussed at length by Bruce Rosenberg: May's desire for "fruit," in addition to linking her with Eve, recalls the legend (preserved in the "Cherry-Tree Carol" and the *Ludus Coventriae* cycle) in which the pregnant Mary asks Joseph for cherries from a tree in a garden.[29] Rosenberg suggests that the contrast between the two pregnancies — Mary's "sacred and archetypal," May's "feigned for an immoral purpose" — focuses our perception more strongly on May's guilt (pp. 266, 272); the allusion, as he sees it, provides the same sort of "implicit orientation toward a controlling set of values" that Robert Kaske finds in the echoes of the *Canticum* in the "Miller's Tale." [30] But the *Merchant's Tale* is a darker poem than the Miller's relatively good-natured narrative, and we may feel, as the tale draws to a

---

garden of Eden. Just as it was from the first paradisal *hortus* that the old Adam had been expelled, it was from the paradisal *hortus conclusus* of the Canticles — i.e., the Blessed Virgin Mary — that the new Adam, Jesus Christ, was expelled in sinless conception and miraculous parturition."

29. "The 'Cherry-Tree Carol' and the *Merchant's Tale*," *ChauR*, 5 (1971), 264–276. Surprisingly, Rosenberg doesn't mention May's rather startling expletive when she tells January of her longing for pears: "I moot dye, so soore longeth me/To eten of the smale peres grene./Help, for hir love that is of hevene queene!" (2332–34). In addition to the "Cherry-Tree Carol" analogy, the fact that we see May in a tree may be intended as a further parallel linking her with Eve and Mary. As Robert Kaske has pointed out to me, a popular illustration of the *Biblia Pauperum* shows, as one of several Old Testament prefigurations of the Annunciation, a woman in a tree — the *mulier* of Gen. 3:15 — stepping on the head of a serpent. See Ernst Guldan, *Eva und Maria* (Graz-Köln: Hermann Böhlaus, 1966), fig. 32.

30. "The *Canticum Canticorum* in the *Miller's Tale*," *SP*, 59 (1962), 497.

close, that the Merchant's misogyny has carried all before it, that, in Donaldson's words, "even those things that are generally accepted unquestioningly as valuable are ... made to seem fatally flawed ("Effect," p. 34). As innumerable medieval writers observe, it was Mary who gained for us the heavenly paradise to replace the earthly one forfeited by Eve; the *Merchant's Tale,* however, presents a vision of Eve-like deceptiveness triumphant. To be sure, the poem ends with a prayer for Christ's blessing and that of His Mother, but in this concluding couplet, "Seinte Marie" is linked with "Januarie." The incongruity of the pairing serves as a reminder that, unlike Adam's, January's "fall" is not a *felix culpa;* the image we are left with is of the old knight leading May home, kissing her and stroking her belly. In the larger world of Christian history, the love of a woman offers the possibility of redemption for fallen man; in the Merchant's parody of that world, the hero, believing only what he wants to believe, continues to live in his fool's paradise.

ROBERT LONGSWORTH

Chaucer's Clerk as Teacher

Chaucer's Clerk is a man of learning, and learned men have customarily written of him with fraternal sympathy. Whether he be measured by his preference for the bookshelf above the fiddle, by his genteel poverty, or by his Oxonian dignity, his mien and manner have endeared him to his latter-day colleagues. Rare, at any rate, is the learned Momus who has seen in Chaucer's treatment of his Clerk some glimmering of satire or of amusement. The Miller's Nicholas and the Wife of Bath's Jankyn may be fit for fun, but the pilgrim-clerk wears his gown soberly and his philosophy penuriously: both are badges of high seriousness in the Academy.

In light of this fraternal approbation, it seems curious that little attention has been given to the Clerk's prowess as a teacher. Chaucer, after all, says that he would as gladly teach as learn. If he was indeed fond of teaching, the arrangements for story-telling fixed on by the Canterbury pilgrims offered him a splendid opportunity to display his skills. If, moreover, the tale that he tells does not have the flavor of a lecture or a disputation, it nevertheless deserves some scrutiny as a repository of his pedagogical impulses, hidden though they be in the crannies of the narrative form.

By telling the story of Griselda, the Clerk certainly seeks to inculcate a lesson. In his seminal article on "Chaucer's Discussion of Marriage," G. L. Kittredge has indicated how aptly this lesson was intended for the Wife of Bath.[1] The pilgrimage is rather more public than a tutorial session, however: the teacher must reckon with an audience of other pupils as well.

In fact, the Wife of Bath is perhaps the least likely of all the pilgrims to profit by the Clerk's teaching. Her fifth husband had, by her own account, pretty well exhausted her tolerance for learning, and she has had enough of "experience" in life to have made a strong claim for professorial privilege during the long preamble to her tale. Indeed, the Clerk wisely refrains both from assailing her credentials and from offering her tutorial assistance. His tale is a pedagogical rejoinder to her argument; but it is addressed to her audience rather than to herself. The Clerk has set himself the task of refuting her without attacking her.

The lesson, both in matter and in method, is put together with admirable skill. With conspicuous graciousness, the Clerk declares his obedience to Harry Bailly's bantering injunction that he tell a tale: he exemplifies the forbearance and submissiveness that he intends to extol. He summons to his aid not St. Jerome but Petrarch. His "retorike sweete" is itself disciplined, and the tale unfolds in formal tidiness that tolerates neither digression nor decoration.

As to his method, the Clerk makes clear that he has the Wife of Bath's lesson in mind without either accepting or denying the premises of her argument, by alluding to themes that she has introduced. Moreover, where he can he pays her the tribute of approbation in such allusions. He puts into the mouth of the noble Walter's wise old vassal the charmed word *soveraynetee* with which the Wife of Bath has promulgated her doctrine of feminism: "Boweth youre nekke," the vassal urges Walter, "under that blisful yok/Of soveraynetee, noght of servyse,/Which that men clepe spousaille or wedlok" (113–115).[2] Furthermore, the noble marquis himself, when he comes to choose a wife, echoes

1. *Modern Philology,* 9 (1911–12), 435–467.
2. Citations of the text are to F. N. Robinson, ed., *The Works of Geoffrey Chaucer,* 2nd ed. (Boston: Houghton Mifflin, 1957).

the commonplace definition of gentility (cribbed from Dante) that the Wife of Bath has given to the old hag in her tale:

> "Bountee comth al of God, nat of the streen
> Of which they been engendred and ybore." (157–58) [3]

The Clerk also accepts the Wife of Bath's implicit view of marriage as a contest of wills. He is intent on teaching a moral lesson, and he chooses shrewdly to do so without questioning the Wife's formidable experience and without invoking the clerical authorities that she has defied. Indeed, in his tale as in the Wife of Bath's the woman prevails — which even allows to the Clerk the luxury of a veiled rebuttal to the Wife's assertion that "no womman of no clerk is preysed" (*Wife of Bath's Prologue,* 706):

> Though clerkes preise wommen but a lite,
> Ther kan no man in humblesse hym acquite
> As womman kan, ne kan been half so trewe
> As wommen been, but it be falle of newe. (935–938)

Griselda, whose self-abasement and fidelity provoke this praise from the Clerk, is also the agent of the moral lesson that he seeks to teach. Although her forbearance has earned for her the epithet "patient," the Clerk displays in her a more heroic and strenuous moral quality than the epithet is able to convey. For the Clerk, Griselda prevails against every hostile threat precisely because her relentless submissiveness requires a more powerful act of will than any kind of sheer willfulness, such as Walter's, requires.

Griselda's fabulous patience, then, is no shrunken virtue: the Clerk plainly intends that his students should perceive that this patience entails a heroic assertion of control over normal human impulses and desires. Indeed, the tale is at bottom a contest — nearly an enacted debate — between the will to command and the will to obey. Walter, of course, is the antagonist whose role requires the display of sheer willfulness. His assertiveness is evident from the outset, when, despite his reluctant concession to

3. Cf. *Wife of Bath's Tale,* 1117–18.

marry, he insists on the right to choose his own wife. The grounds of the contest are established in the betrothal of Walter and Griselda, when he tells her, "Be ye redy with good herte/ To al my lust" (351–352), and she replies by swearing "that nevere willyngly,/In werk ne thoght, I nyl yow disobeye" (362–363). In the contest of wills that follows, Griselda sacrifices every other human desire — for material comfort, for approbation, for the exercise of parental affection, for the receipt of filial devotion, and for marital solace — to her vow of obedience.

By thus suppressing her desires, Griselda demonstrates — at least to the Clerk's apparent satisfaction — a more disciplined "maistrie" than Walter possesses. In the end, after all, Walter implicitly concedes that her will to obey is stronger than his impulse to exact obedience or even to test her moral stamina. He does so not only by translating his mock-marriage into a celebration of their reunion, but also by becoming finally attentive to Griselda's own happiness: "Walter hire gladeth, and hire sorwe slaketh. . . . Walter hire dooth so feithfully plesaunce/That it was deyntee for to seen the cheere/Bitwixe hem two" (1107, 1111–13).

At the very end of his discourse, the Clerk draws a distinction between Walter's treatment of Griselda and God's treatment of men. Citing the Epistle of James — "God cannot be tempted with evil and he himself tempts no one, but each person is tempted . . . by his own desire" (1:13) — he insists that God's permitting man to endure adversity is done "nat for to knowe oure wyl" (1159): unlike Walter, God knows the extent of man's frailty and the power of his will. Thus, for the Clerk, God allows man to exercise his will both by undergoing suffering and by receiving it patiently. It is again characteristic of the Clerk's didactic method that he should make the distinction and at the same time use it to reinforce his lesson. Griselda's will is exemplary both of marital propriety and of Christian obedience; but Walter's motives are not exemplary of God's motives.

That the Clerk should choose as the subject of his lesson a moral issue about the nature of the human will no doubt reflects an interest among fourteenth-century moral philosophers in voluntarism. Indeed, Oxford, as the professorial seat of Duns

Scotus and William of Ockham, was virtually the contemporary
home of speculation on the subject.[4] In conveying his lesson,
however, the Clerk avoids the subtleties of the issue in order to
drive home his point that the power of the will is more evident
in submissiveness and restraint than in assertiveness.

As a teacher, then, the Clerk adroitly counterposes the authority of moral discipline to the Wife of Bath's heterodox
experience; his moral fable to her fairy tale; his intellectual control to her emotional disorder. He exalts Griselda's submissiveness by playing it off against Walter's willfulness — and, by implication, against the Wife of Bath's belief in the practical value
of assertiveness.

Moreover, the skill with which he offers his matter is equally
evident in his pedagogical manner. The story is tidy, the characters are uncomplicated, and the lesson is pointed. The Clerk
overlooks no opportunity to underline the bases of the contest
with which he deals: he repeats the word "wyl" at every handy
juncture,[5] the conflict is joined thrice (by the ostensible murder
of the two children and by the carefully staged banishment of
Griselda in favor of the mythical second wife), and the Clerk
allows himself occasionally to cluck disapprovingly over Walter's
excessive enthusiasm for his experiments. The set speeches of
Griselda — when she bids farewell to her first child, when she
replies to Walter's command that the second child be dispatched,
when she leaves his castle to return to her aged and miserable
father, and when she admonishes him to be more tender of his
second wife's feelings — are finely crafted and rhetorically
shaped. Even the occasional use of the aside (as when the Clerk
compares Griselda to Job or condemns the "stormy peple" for

4. Charles Edward Mallet observes in his *History of the University
of Oxford,* Vol. I, that "whatever Oxford taught men in the Middle
Ages there is no doubt that she taught them to dispute" (New York:
Longmans, Green, 1924), p. 203. In fact, J. Mitchell Morse believes
that the Clerk is carrying on a private disputation — or at least an
interior debate — with himself, based on the vexatious intellectual problems that tormented Oxford at the time. See "The Philosophy of the
Clerk of Oxenford," *Modern Language Quarterly,* 19 (1958), 3–20.

5. Among the *Canterbury Tales,* only in the *Tale of Melibee* is the
noun *will* used more frequently than it is used by the Clerk — and that
tale is at least twice as long as the Clerk's.

their fickleness — 932ff. and 995ff.) is a judicious (because in-
gratiating) pedagogical tactic.

The Clerk's teaching, then, is skillful and appropriately
"sownynge in moral vertu." On the other hand, despite the pedagogical skills with which the Clerk carries out his narrative task,
he is plainly not triumphant over his professorial adversary. If
his severe logic is persuasive, her disarming illogic is entertaining; if his doctrine of the will is morally elevated, her assertion
of "maistrie" seems oddly more humane. The Clerk is an earnest
teacher, but he is a cold fish — and in the peripatetic school of
pilgrims to whom he addresses his lesson, merriment and
"solaas" are more welcome than clerical "sentence." The Clerk
himself may have some inkling of this — the heavily sarcastic
song with which he ends his lecture suggests as much; even so,
the response of his ad hoc students must have discomfited and
disappointed the teacher: neither Harry Bailly nor the Merchant
seems to have understood the lesson so patiently and earnestly
delivered. In any case, Chaucer's tribute to the learned profes-
sion of teachers is not without overtones of amusement.

CHRISTOPHER BROOKHOUSE

In Search of Chaucer: The Needed Narrative

Who was Geoffrey Chaucer? Boy, man; husband, father, widower; servant of kings, writer: these are the conditions of his life; facts giving us fuller knowledge of these conditions do not illuminate the ultimate condition of his being any more than his "portrait" illuminates the physical importance of his life. Some of the facts are fascinating. For example, Chaucer probably traveled more in his century than most of the Nobel Prize recipients for literature have traveled, under easier conditions, in their own century. Shakespeare never traveled very far, measured in physical miles, from London, but he journeyed through worlds within his mind. The final measure must be the works themselves; the last measure, the true identity.

As a writer myself, I want to go back to the fundamental existence of another writer, a man who lived some six hundred years before me. Can I find in his writings anything to tell me why he wrote, what he was trying to do? Can I illuminate in any way the one fact which itself becomes a condition — Geoffrey Chaucer was the first writer to give us a body of work in the English vernacular, written over most of a lifetime, and to put or ascribe his name and reputation, perhaps his soul, to that body of work.

I

Chaucer's own work began with the *Book of the Duchess,* a mannered and imitative poem, sometimes outright funny (" 'Awake!' quod he . . . And blew his horn ryght in here eere"), sometimes straining for humor ("He made of rym ten vers or twelve," followed by eleven lines of verse, 475–486),[1] but ultimately a moving, stately, handsome poem, a poem whose significance goes beyond Chaucer the narrator or persona, or Chaucer the writer at the beginning of his career showing off his reading, beyond even the form of dream vision and elegy. For me the poem's importance begins in these lines:

> Good sir, telle me al hooly
> In what wyse, how, why, and wherfore
> That ye have thus youre blysse lore.   (746–48)

Essentially the middle line translates the words of a priest at confession. John Mirk in his *Instructions,* though later than Chaucer's poem, suggests under the Latin heading *quis, quid, ubi* that the parish priest translate into English the requirement of confession as: "what man he was/wharfore, & why." [2] Regardless of verbal parallels (both men using the conventional phrase "wherfore & why," which is common enough in Middle English romances, for example), the main idea, which no doubt came close at hand from the Church itself rather than the techniques of classical rhetoric or elsewhere, is the need to speak and the need to listen. In one way or another "wherfore" and "why" occur over and over again in Chaucer's work.

At the start of the *Book of the Duchess,* the narrator is alone, "a mased thyng." How seriously we are to take the introduction is a problem, a problem of Chaucer's tone as he skips along telling us that to ease his "sicknesse" (eight years!) he asks for a book. His cure is practical though artificial, perhaps as artificial as the eight years; but all the artifice, or convention, is leading

1. In all citations I use F. N. Robinson, ed., *The Works of Geoffrey Chaucer,* 2nd ed. (Boston: Houghton Mifflin, 1957).
2. John Myrc, *Instructions for Parish Priests,* ed. Edward Peacock, Early English Text Society, Orig. Ser. 31 (London, 1902 [rev.]), 44.

parallel by parallel (narrator alone, Alcione alone, mourning Knight alone) to a reality — death, a woman's death whether or not she is Blanche, a reality which poetic convention may include, but nevertheless a fact from the real world, the most certain fact of all life. Whatever the poem owes to French literature, or any other, the poem deals with the fact of death, of loss, and Chaucer chooses to deal with loss as a listener to an example of its existence, a listener who willingly pretends not to know in order to know; a listener who depends on the teller, the mourning Knight, to complete the essence of the story, to admit death (" 'She ys ded!' 'Nay.' 'Yis, be my trouthe,' " 1309). Then, despite the clumsy abruptness of the narrator's last remark to the Knight (" 'hyt ys routhe!' "), the recall of the hunters hunting the hart/heart brings, except for a final stanza, a graceful conclusion in which the narrator, the listener, the dreamer, is silent. He has no comment to make, no explicit, meaningful summation. He simply describes and is done. The need of one man, the Knight, to talk is enough if there is someone to listen (the narrator and each reader). The quiet return of the hunter is a sufficient ending on the part of the narrator/listener. Chaucer seldom concludes his early work on his own behalf or in his own voice, with a sustained didactic comment. His faith is in the words of others, words he may have devised out of his own beliefs and then given to others to say, but words to which the narrator listens, thus making us listen.

Though the Knight's Queen perished, she lived; by words she continues to live, a memory, whether a fiction or not, of such force as to endure in the Knight and his listeners. Although clearly admitting death, the *Book of the Duchess* celebrates life and the potential beauty within life. Yet, I think, Chaucer begins more and more to question what is not in us beautiful, to question the state of our human world and the world beyond us; to examine our lives as a journey. I assume that Chaucer is also examining himself, who he is. For one thing, he is alone, and there is pain in solitude. There must be someone outside one's self to ease the pain. Chaucer, or the narrator/listener, was that someone in the *Book of the Duchess*. In the *Book of Fame* the narrator is alone and cannot function, it seems, without the aid of dreaming as well as the help of an eagle. Chaucer's tendency to display his knowledge continues, but usefully — the stories Chaucer mentions at the onset are sad ones: the fall of Troy, the loss of Creusa, the unblessedness of Dido, and so on. There is a darkness here despite the eagle's humor, and a sense of failure, of service unrewarded.

The eagle will guide the narrator on a journey to benefit him, but after witnessing the hazard of reputation, the narrator, who once believed in human words, encounters that place where all words gather, a place of whisperings and loud speeches about war and peace, marriage, voyages, death, life, love and hate, sickness and health, in short, all the essential conditions of human kind. The very length of the list, sixteen lines, enforces a sadness and seriousness despite the frequent humor of the poem. Also, I believe, the lines imply a questioning on Chaucer's part; the list ends at the threat of fire (what a terror to the medieval world!) and various other accidents (1976). The questioning is not an asking of what is just or unjust, but an observation of multiple misfortunes. To me the poem is about a man who writes poetry and wonders what his effort will produce. At the poem's end, what the narrator, now a pilgrim himself, a voyager, is to learn is not learned. At least not by us. Did Chaucer really know where he was going? Like many writers after him, did he begin to write and find something which would not let him finish? Did he find that the words he had so nicely given to us once could not be spoken again? It seems to me, the *Book of Fame* is a message to himself, a message about art, or skill, or reputation, or being a man in a body of flesh, a message often written humorously, with a light heart, but at the end, in essence, a sad, serious question — "can I hear or know more, even if I could be where all human voices gather, than a wrangle of voices speaking out our human condition, our mortality?" In human voices did Chaucer fear he might drown? Is the confusion of the poem's tone Chaucer's own confusion?

The man of "gret auctorite" does not speak. In the *Parliament* there is a sense of authority, too, in the person of the elder Africanus. The younger Scipio's questions, his needs to know, are Chaucer's, who again is a voyager, a dreamer, a listener to someone else, a man who is to be rewarded for his continual

efforts to learn through his reading, to understand through inherited authority.

The *Parliament* seeks affirmation, first through the authority
of the elder Africanus, and then through the poetry itself, which
enforces order, even the ordered disorder of the competing birds.
The *Parliament* is Chaucer's attempt to assert poetic order
against the human disorder implied in the *Book of Fame*. To
do so Chaucer depends on the rhetoric of the poetry itself, its
structure, to convey another structure, which is Nature's fullness. The poetry is not only a finished, rhetorical whole which
will be received as an occasional or public poem; the poetry
represents an attempt, perhaps successful for the moment, to
define an order for the writer himself within himself; the attempt to create art to order life. To use a word from our own
time, abiding as we do in the long shadow of Freud, Chaucer's
attempt is an effort at sanity, an effort to find rule and design
where so often there are only the words of human confusion,
the voices heard in Fame's house.

Chaucer's translation of Boethius probably derives from the
time when Chaucer completed the *Parliament,* that is 1380–
1386. At its core, the *Boece* is an intense speculation on order
and design, and Chaucer's effort to translate it further suggests
Chaucer's personal search. Next, in *Troilus and Criseyde,* Chaucer returns to the theme of loss, the lives of those involved in
loss, the narrowing cricuit of history and the inevitable defeat
of Troy. Chaucer returns as well to the theme of human love,
but above all else he returns to the theme of silence and talk;
the conflict between isolation or silence and the need to speak
or be spoken to is essential in *Troilus.* First there is Chaucer's,
or the narrator's, need to speak. Now, the narrator is not a pas-
sive man taken through dreams on various journeys. This narrator has a purpose, "the double sorwe of Troilus to tellen,"
and this narrator gives the impression of knowing what will
happen and how it will happen. This narrator is now our authority. We will hear his voice at various places in the poem.
We shall hear other voices too.

Troilus is a poem about silence, isolation, and knowledge. If
Chaucer has been called the poet of love, he should be called

the poet of knowledge, knowledge which is often gained in isolation. Calchas divines the fall of Troy. He leaves the city, isolating Criseyde and confusing her position in Troy both as a widow and the daughter of a traitor. Troilus is briefly seen in the company of others, "his yonge knyghtes." But when he sees Criseyde in the temple, his immediate attraction to her removes him from the company he keeps and isolates him also. Even his cynicism toward lovers cannot protect him. Knowledge held pridefully and abstractly does not withstand the test of the particular, as the narrator's voice makes clear: "How often falleth al the effect contraire/Of surquidrie and foul presumpcioun" (I.212–213). The narrator then suggests the power of love and makes this power concrete by the physical way Troilus comes under love's authority: "Love hadde his dwellynge/Withinne the subtile stremes of hir yen" (I.304–305). Troilus bears his pain, predestined ("Thow most loven thorugh thi destine," I.520), as is the fate of Troy itself, with sorrow and solitude until Pandarus, with his words, seduces Troilus into sharing the source of his grief. Pandarus, with his wordiness and proverbs, functions to make Troilus speak, as if Pandarus' role was a reshaping of Chaucer's role in the *Book of the Duchess*. In *Troilus,* of course, the listener's power is greater to the extent that Troilus and Pandarus are more or less equals, which is not true of Chaucer as narrator and the mourning Knight. However, Pandarus is a comic pragmatist and at the end of the poem a futile man of limited vision.

Pandarus would not succeed so well if Criseyde could endure uncertainty and isolation. Although she does not give in immediately, Pandarus' words prepare her to see Troilus riding by and to consider him as she has not before. If, when Pandarus has gone from her side, she continues to waver, there are other words — Antigone's song extolling love.

Pandarus visits Troilus (II.989ff.) with more words, in particular the art of words as he instructs Troilus in writing a letter to Criseyde. On one level there is a humorous conflict between Pandarus' advice and Troilus' practice. Pandarus says: "No jompre ek no discordant thyng yfeere,/As thus, to usen termes of phisik/In loves termes . . ." (II.1037–39). Troilus begins by calling Criseyde "his hertes lif, his lust, his sorwes leche"

(II.1066). Much of Pandarus' advice derives from Horace through John of Salisbury, and I wonder if Chaucer is not questioning the ends for which good advice and art may be used. I wonder if Chaucer is not using advice serious and worthwhile in one context to raise a question of motive in another context. I wonder if Chaucer questions his own motives, his own reasons for writing, through Pandarus. Is Chaucer warning himself that the power of art may be used for trivial or questionable ends, that the listener who listens to another's sorrow may use such sorrow for private and petty purposes? Pandarus, having brought Troilus to Criseyde, "took a light, and fond his contenaunce,/As for to looke upon an old romaunce" (III.979–980). Does Chaucer imply that the role of seer, of listener, can become the role of voyeur?

Books IV and V are the winter of the poem.[3] The comedy, which, despite deeper tones surrounding Pandarus, lies brightly on the surface, falls away. When Troilus laments the terms of exchanging prisoners, his words express a greater sorrow than any he has previously spoken (IV.260–336), and all Pandarus, who has never seen beyond the limits of the moment, says is: "This town is ful of ladys al aboute,/. . . fairer than swiche twelve/As evere she was" (IV.401–403).

Slowly we see Troilus more and more on his own, becoming free of Pandarus' influence, a freedom which ultimately will allow Troilus to travel through deeper despair but then upward toward a higher knowledge than ever he could have learned from Pandarus. In the meantime Troilus accepts Criseyde's promise that she will return after ten days, words calculated to protect Criseyde from any impulsive move that might thrust her beyond the security of either the Greeks or the Trojans: "We may wel stele awey . . ./But afterward, ful soore it wol us rewe" (IV.1529–31). Criseyde will not risk isolation. She wavers, she accepts Diomede with full knowledge that her once cherished reputation will be "rolled . . . on many a tongue." "She was allone and hadde nede/Of frendes help" (V.1026–27).

3. Specifically I refer to the similes which convey a time structure in themselves: March (II.764–770); May (III.351–357); Winter (IV. 225–231). These similes give an emotional zone of time to the poem which relates to the other chronologies in and around the story.

Pandarus has little to offer anymore, except to doubt Troilus'
dreams and to suggest the old standby, the letter. Troilus' letter
accomplishes one thing — Criseyde's answer reveals the truth.
Ironically, Pandarus' last words in the poem are, "I kan namore
seye" (V.1743). Troilus goes his own way to death, and his
final vision of worldly vanity is the truth he learns in the isolation of death and the vastness of space beyond "this wrecched
world."

II

I believe anyone who writes fiction himself must look upon
the *Canterbury Tales* with wonder and envy. Its structure combines a fundamental interest in the power of words and the importance of the listener as artist with the idea of a journey. Here
the journey is not one of dreams. The journey takes place in
Chaucer's contemporary reality, the road from London to Canterbury, which is both a real road and a spiritual one; for the
idea of a journey is the Christian notion that all human life is
a journey, one that will end, it is hoped, with a vision of the
heavenly city. Chaucer's people are taking a realistic pilgrimage
and a metaphorical one; they have always been pilgrims and
always will be.

Words: Chaucer opens himself to the words of many, to a
variety of men and women speaking, apparently, for themselves.
Chaucer has come upon a stunning truth: the words people use,
how they use them, and the stories they tell are not mere narrative; words are the deepest clues to a speaker's identity. Chaucer has found that speakers need to speak about themselves.
Even when they do not appear willingly to reveal their deepest
nature, their choice of words and stories will necessarily portray
what they would wish kept secret, or what consciously they may
not even understand about themselves. Thus Chaucer as artist
finds a way to reveal, and, without overt comment, to judge his
speakers as he unmasks them: this is the moral resolution of
Chaucer's art.

Of course the Canterbury journey is in Chaucer's mind. Ultimately all the words are Chaucer's words as he enters into the
lives of those he creates, the "positive" capability of any good
writer. In some tales, the need to speak is more Chaucer's own

than his surrogate's, the pilgrim's. In other stories, though, Chaucer enters the mind and body of the pilgrim and portrays that pilgrim's need to speak as if he stood by himself. However, in these instances, Chaucer's need to judge the pilgrim is always evident behind what otherwise might seem an objective creation.

Let me examine five examples of Chaucer's use of the "needed" narrative. Two examples, the *Knight's Tale* and *Melibee*, are instances of Chaucer's finding a surrogate voice (in *Melibee* Chaucer the pilgrim as a speaker for Chaucer the artist). The *Pardoner's Prologue* and *Tale,* the *Wife of Bath's Prologue* and *Tale,* and the tale of the Canon's Yeoman reveal the needs of separate pilgrims to speak.

The *Knight's Tale* is one of doubt. Chaucer introduces us to the teller, a man who has spent an exceptional part of his life in Christian combat and service; the Knight is an ideal. And yet, and yet . . . the tale Chaucer selects for the Knight is a serious questioning of survival, a painful examination of human limitations (the problem of knowing) and our relationship to gods or God. Although the setting is pre-Christian, in a dark time of our spirit do we as Christians doubt the power of Palamon's description of mankind as "sheep that rouketh in folde"? Chaucer has chosen the metaphor with care (pastoral care to make a bad but useful pun), for the shepherd/sheep metaphor is central to Christian writing and extends the context of the *Knight's Tale* beyond pre-Christian time. Both Palamon and Arcite, lover of the ideal and lover of the person, endure uncertainty and chance. As Egeus remarks, "this world nys but a thurghfare ful of wo,/ And we been pilgrymes, passynge to and fro" (2847–48). Egeus' statement is central as a comment on the structure of the *Canterbury Tales* and almost every teller whom Chaucer develops.

Although we may consider the *Knight's Tale* to end in a happy marriage, the tale is full of pain; the long catalogue of sufferings depicted in the temple of Mars, a bitter list for a soldier, Christian or not, to catalogue, and the sufferings Saturn claims for his control are so complete as to haunt the poem as a whole and bring all joy into question. Theseus' speech near the tale's conclusion (2787ff.) deals in mute tones with necessity and the fact of death. Theseus even suggests that while we cannot lengthen our life-days beyond our allotted term, we can shorten them, implying, among other possibilities, suicide (2998–99). Theseus does not question suicide as an alternative, or, rather, Chaucer does not. In conclusion, Theseus, though acknowledging a stable force above mankind, still refers to our life as "this foule prisoun" (thus the confinement of Palamon and Arcite behind walls and bars was as metaphorical as real). Granted that Christian feelings often despise this world, Chaucer's ideal Knight seems, by Chaucer's control, to speak of human pain without the clear relief of Christian reward. And though Theseus' own conduct confirms mercy and a hard-earned wisdom, the *Knight's Tale* is a dark beginning which does not hide the grief men endure on their pilgrimages. In the character of the Knight, Chaucer has presented someone who might reasonably need to question his life; however, the questions and the need are, finally, Chaucer's.

The Wife, the Pardoner, and the Canon's Yeoman disclose certain details about their lives; through Chaucer's use of language, they reveal more than they may intend. Their stories are emblems of their deepest needs and imply Chaucer's judgment upon each teller.

The Pardoner ("I trowe he were a geldyng or a mare") is an outsider, sexually alienated and professionally suspect. In his *Prologue* he insists he preaches for private, material gain ("I preche of no thyng but for coveityse"). However, such gain cannot heal him physically or spiritually. He fears something he will not define in his *Prologue,* but in the *Tale* he gives us the definition — loss of grace, a loss far more horrible than any other.

In the *Pardoner's Tale,* he continues to talk about himself while seeming to tell a story about three other men. But these men are extensions of the Pardoner, men seeking the physical pleasures the Pardoner admits he himself seeks. Throughout the tale, the teller's spiritual point of reference is Christ and grace. Four times the Pardoner alludes to Christ: "til Crist hadde boght us with his blood agayn" (501); "they been enemys of Cristes croys" (531); "by the blood of Crist that is in Hayles" (652); "for the love of Crist, that for us dyde" (658). The Pardoner cannot flee his knowledge of the Crucifixion, the saving of mankind, the redeeming of the old world by the new life. The Pardoner's sensuality and his new fashions ("newe jet," *General Prologue,* 682), and his self-proclaimed youth ("us yonge men," *Wife of Bath's Prologue,* 187) are no relief to his spirit. His narrative of the rioters is a story of dying and damnation. The rioters make a pact to "sleen deeth." They do not know, or acknowledge, as the Pardoner does, that victory over death is through Christ alone. Yet the Pardoner seems unable to act for his own salvation. He is afflicted by his knowledge, and his constant references to Christ come from this affliction.

In essence the Old Man of the *Pardoner's Tale* is also a comment on the Pardoner's spiritual failure. The Old Man is unbearably conscious of death and the flesh, but he is opposite to the sensualism of the rioters and to the Pardoner's own emphasis on money and pleasure. The "cheste" the Old Man keeps in his room is probably a *memento mori,* a coffin (Chaucer elsewhere uses "cheste" in this way, *Clerk's Prologue,* 29); the Old Man is always ready to send his body back to the earth from which it came. Although the Old Man is a sad and painful figure, there is no reason to doubt the possibility of his ultimate salvation. He does not doubt it himself; his last words are "God save yow, that boghte agayn mankynde" (766). The Old Man's denial of flesh and insistence on grace is the Pardoner's own self-condemnation.

The Pardoner needs to admit his failure, and he does so by implication in the narrative and language Chaucer gives him to speak. Furthermore, the fabric of the artistry is without flaw, because Chaucer has found that a speaker's tale can be made appropriate to the speaker's inner needs so well that the artist himself may disappear from the creation, thus allowing the illusion of an autonomous speaker to exist simultaneously with the artist's implicit judgment of the speaker.

In her *Prologue,* the Wife of Bath confesses a life dominated by sexual pleasure. She attacks all tradition and authority that might deny her right to "use my instrument/As frely as my Makere hath it sent." However, the Wife's point of reference is "engendrure" (28, 128, 134). Yet she has no children. She has confused sex and money (405–410), she has acquired physical goods in her youth, and she must endure the result — the process of growing old with material wealth and little else. Her need is to reverse the process, to be young again. The Hag of the Wife's tale is a physical projection of the Wife's inner self just as the Old Man was a projection of the Pardoner's self. In her fantasy, the Wife can become young through the story of an Old Woman who becomes young again in the fictions of the mind. Of course the fantasy will never be literally true. The Wife must live out the pattern of life she has made for herself. The Wife's tale is the story she must tell, the only relief possible.

The Canon's Yeoman confesses both his failure at alchemy and his master's, and yet he never specifically confesses the spiritual error of their materialism. The Yeoman speaks of his disfigurement (665–668) without understanding the analogy between the body and the spirit, the physical appearance representing the soul's state.

The failure stressed in the *Yeoman's Tale* is the physical, alchemical one. The Yeoman, always conscious of the failure, cannot interpret it and cannot tell of it in any terms but material ones. The elaborate listing of chemicals, instruments, and processes emphasizes the inability of the Yeoman to see beyond them. When each experiment ends in loss, the Yeoman reckons the loss in time and money only.

The Yeoman really tells a tale within a tale, and the second story, how the other Canon cheated a priest, is the symbolic epitome of spiritual corruption, the drawing of the spirit away from the Church to materialism. The second tale is not as difficult in content as it is in the manner of its telling. The Yeoman clearly distinguishes between the Canon his present master and the other Canon (1090). But the Yeoman is inordinately upset by the trickery of the other Canon:

> On his falshede fayn wolde I me wreke,
> If I wiste how, but he is here and there
> He is so variaunt, he abet nowhere.   (1171–74)

Is the Yeoman's anger against a general wrong or a specific one? Does the emphatic separation of one Canon and the other make the reader question the identities of the Yeoman and the priest? Is the revenge the Yeoman seeks directed at the other Canon because the Yeoman was that priest, and now, although he knows the other Canon was a cheat, he follows the present Canon who is as much a victim of materialism as the Yeoman is? The questions are hard to resolve, but it seems possible that the Yeoman is confessing more than the loss of his complexion, time, and money.

What of Chaucer himself, or the character he assumes on the pilgrimage? After World War II several critics, whose perceptions were influenced by the horror of Jewish persecution, suggested that Chaucer was a man of conscience, too, that the *Prioress's Tale* is the self-revelation of her anti-Semitism and therefore Chaucer's oblique acknowledgment of the problem. The problem with arguing for Chaucer's feelings against anti-Semitism has been that the argument places Chaucer in a moral position no one in England in the fourteenth century might have been expected to hold. There was plenty of Christian hostility against Jews because the Jews were responsible for Christ's death. Why should Chaucer's opinion be different?

Melibee suggests an answer, not to why Chaucer's view was different, but that it was different. The *Prioress's Tale* is a story of a crime and its punishment. A devoted Christian child is murdered by Jews. *Melibee,* the tale Chaucer took from a French version almost word for word as his own tale, deals with a crime also. Melibee's wife is beaten, and his daughter is wounded in five places. Melibee's daughter is not a Christ figure, but she is associated with Christ through the five wounds both receive.[4] Melibee's wife argues for mercy. Mercy, the virtue of Theseus and a few others in the *Canterbury Tales;* a Christian virtue which may extend even to the murders of Christ himself; at least, I think, Chaucer's tale hints at the possibility and as such opposes the Prioress' sense of justice. I believe *Melibee,* like the *Knight's Tale,* is an expression of Chaucer's need to speak, a need to seek beyond safe, superficial beliefs.

Geoffrey Chaucer was a moral man and a skeptical man. He saw great sorrow in the world; sorrow, chaos, and error. He

4. The association implied by the five wounds cannot be stressed too much; for a brief but excellent study of the metaphorical meanings of the wounds, see Douglas Gray, "The Five Wounds of Our Lord," *Notes and Queries,* 208 (1963), 50–51, 82–89, 127–134, 163–168.

senses our aloneness and isolation. In the beginning, he perfected his role of the writer as listener and insisted that there was comfort in our confessions of grief. Later he understood there was another need to speak, a need to confess, and that words themselves could reveal more than the speaker might want to reveal, a truth Chaucer found long before Freud. Through words, through the selection of narrative, Chaucer found a way to portray character and to judge it at the same time. Above all, Chaucer found a way to express his own need to speak. Chaucer, once the listener, became the speaker who assumed various identities. Speaking was the act of writing, and the act of writing became the perfection of a moral art.

For myself as a writer what I learn as I look for Chaucer's identity in his work is how the writer's self may, out of its pain and uncertainty, draw toward an art which uses that self without the abrasive and unrelenting exhibition of the self which we have come to expect from our contemporary writers; an art out of the self, of the self, in which the self of the creator dies into the new and separate life of the creation.

GEORGE F. REINECKE

Speculation, Intention,
and the Teaching of Chaucer

Shortly after William Wimsatt's *The Verbal Icon* appeared, Professor Whiting dryly took his Chaucer seminar to task for its heretical tendency to discuss auctorial intention in the *Canterbury Tales.* I was probably the chief sinner, and I still hold the consideration of intention as necessary to my work as a teacher of Chaucer. Generally, speculation and conjecture must play a major role in the work of English medievalists, because they are confronted with numerous uncertainties of text and with doubts as to the customs and ideas of their period. An even more telling reason for speculation and intentional conjecture is the imperfect or multiple textual state of such monuments as *Troilus, Piers,* the *Legend of Good Women,* and the *Canterbury Tales.* The old school taught that textual, historical, and lexical conclusions must be limited to the "scientifically" demonstrable. A second, aging generation of New Critics sought to limit admissible evidence to the ascertainable text. Neither has contributed much theory to the appropriateness of the guess when there is no proof in hand, no satisfactory text, and no clear line of inquiry to follow.

Of course, whatever the theory, major Chaucer critics and

scholars have in fact been given to conjecture. Passages from Kittredge's *Chaucer and his Poetry* and Robinson's introductions and notes, as well as Manly's *New Light,* immediately spring to mind.[1] Such conjecture goes on today. It is the purpose of this essay to examine several cruxes which are probably not to be resolved by scientific demonstration or by orthodox *explication de texte,* weighing what may be appropriately said about them in the college Chaucer course. The conclusions, whether given as my own or drawn from earlier and more distinguished work, are in no sense hard-and-fast. Taken all together, they may help set some norms for the lecturer. In passing, they might influence thought as to what is admissible in scholarly print.

1. *"Preestes thre" (CT* I.164). Let us consider this notorious passage of the *General Prologue.* When Manly and Robinson both committed themselves to rejecting Chaucer's authorship of the words "and preestes thre," they assuredly had no textual basis for their decision.[2] Why did they reject the phrase? Manly is quite explicit: two of the priests appear nowhere else, only one is needed, and the three fail to harmonize with the number of pilgrims as given some lines earlier in the *Prologue (CT* I.24). Robinson, not much impressed by Chaucerian arithmetic and bearing in mind the studies made since Manly's date of publication, suggests that the argument from the number of pilgrims is not overwhelming, but that the argument from historical data on Stratford-at-Bow, which was too small to provide such a retinue for its prioress, is telling indeed. Earlier, and quite perceptively, Skeat had pointed out that "wel nyne and twenty" must mean "at least twenty-nine," but then muddied the issue by saying that the real problem was to reconcile the crux itself with the twenty-nine pilgrims previously mentioned. Skeat obviously leaned to

1. George L. Kittredge, *Chaucer and his Poetry* (Cambridge, Mass.: Harvard University Press, 1915); F. N. Robinson, ed., *The Works of Geoffrey Chaucer* (Boston: Houghton Mifflin, 1933, 2nd ed. 1957); John M. Manly, *Some New Light on Chaucer* (New York: Henry Holt, 1926). Quotations and line references to Chaucer are from Robinson's second edition.

2. Robinson, p. 655, n.164; Manly, *New Light,* pp. 223–225. Robinson's note is useful bibliographically.

accepting the three priests, but conceded that they might have been inserted by a tampering hand. With an apparent contempt for the simplest way he suggested that the priests were inserted to complete the line after Chaucer had canceled a lost portrait of the Second Nun. He does not even advert to the possibility that such a portrait might not have been composed. More seriously, he fails to see that a rational man and competent writer would never for any reason cobble with nonsense any passage at all.[3] Edith Rickert's emendation (not textually founded) to "and the preest is thre"[4] at least absolves the cobbler of irrationality, leaving him charged only with a bad ear. E. T. Donaldson in his college text, *Chaucer's Poetry,* acknowledges, like other editors before and after, the probability of early tampering, but more recently has commended the editorial courage of Robert Pratt.[5] Here, perhaps, we find the difference between the charges of the editor and university lecturer. Robinson, Manly, and Baugh[6] all reject Chaucer's authorship, but all print the offending passage, indicating no lacuna.

Pratt, in his paperback selection from the *Canterbury Tales,* doubtless feeling less strictly bound because the book is directed to the less advanced student, moves from the Skeat-Robinson position, found in his earlier textbook; he both acknowledges the lacuna and, placing a period after "chapeleyne," omits "and preestes thre" from his text. The text itself, save for the short line, suggests no hiatus.[7] Except for this point I find myself in

3. W. W. Skeat, ed., *The Complete Works of Geoffrey Chaucer* (Oxford: Clarendon Press, 1894–1897), V, 19, n.164.

4. John M. Manly and Edith Rickert, eds., *The Text of the Canterbury Tales, Studied on the Basis of All Known Manuscripts* (Chicago: University of Chicago Press, 1940), III, 423.

5. E. T. Donaldson, *Chaucer's Poetry* (New York: Ronald Press, 1958), p. 895. See also pp. 193–194 of "The Ordering of *The Canterbury Tales,*" in *Medieval Literature and Folklore Studies: Essays in Honor of F. L. Utley,* ed. Jerome Mandel and Bruce Rosenberg (New Brunswick: Rutgers University Press, 1970).

6. Albert C. Baugh, ed., *Chaucer's Major Poetry* (New York: Appleton-Century-Croft, 1963), p. 314, n.164.

7. Robert A. Pratt, ed., *Selections from the Tales of Canterbury and Short Poems* (Boston: Houghton Mifflin, 1966), p. 7, n.164; see also R. A. Pratt, et al., *Masters of British Literature* (Boston: Houghton Mifflin, 1958), I, 26, n.164, where Pratt retains the entire line.

full agreement, and not only for more elementary students. This
is what ought to be offered students:

> Another NONNE with hire hadde she,
> That was hir chapeleyne . . .
>
> . . . .
>
> A MONK ther was, a fair for the maistrie,
>
> (*CT* I.163–165)

a text frankly imperfect and surely Chaucer's. Manly has
pointed out that only the Second Nun and the Nun's Priest
among the pilgrims lack a description in the *Prologue*.[8] This
seems a most telling argument that the text is not as Chaucer
intended it. If it cannot be as he intended it, then it had better
be published as he left it. Elsewhere, the *Canterbury Tales* give
evidence of imperfect revision and unreconciled details, for example in the famous case of the order of place-names along
Canterbury Way in the Ellesmere MS, and the matter of the
feminine speaker in the *Shipman's Tale*. Both of these, like the
crux of the three priests, are signs of work in progress. After all,
Chaucer could no more have fully developed all the pilgrims by
one act of his imagination than he could have written all the
tales simultaneously.

One or two undergraduates have sought to depart even further into speculation by writing characters (in limping S.E. Midland) to supply the *Prologue*'s deficiencies. There is a kind of
student for whom that sort of enterprise will bring to life a
course otherwise unstimulating. Presumably, then, such activity
is to a degree commendable, so long as it is kept to the paper
and the private conference; any attempt to induce reconstruction
and pastiche into the course proper would be to teach not Chaucer's work but someone else's, thus falling into the same error
that perpetuates "and preestes thre" in the editions and sometimes allows it to go by without a word in our lecture halls.

2. *"An Haberdasshere and a Carpenter . . ."* (*CT* I.361). Compared with the previous passage, this one, hardly a crux, has received little notice.

8. Manly, *New Light*, p. 224.

All but two of the pilgrims are indeed described in the *Prologue,* yet five of them, the Haberdasher and his companion guildsmen, are not individuated beyond the mention of their trades. All are dressed in the same livery, prosperous, married to wives who are socially ambitious, ripe for civic office. Beyond that, we do not know their names, ages, sizes, or complexions. They thus would do well for a pageant and figure prominently in several illustrations; they represent an important aspect of Chaucer's England; but they lack the individuation required for that later interaction of pilgrims in link and tale which is the hallmark of the *Canterbury Tales.* They are not imagined as part of the mature work. Did Chaucer determine fairly early to omit them when he perceived the difficulty of fitting five such similar people into his developed plan? Or did he intend to remake them individually at some later time? I find myself more in agreement with R. M. Lumiansky than with Carroll Camden, who suggested some years ago that the guildsmen were a late interpolation.[9] They never reappear. When the Miller announces his "legende" it is the Reeve and not the London carpenter who responds in anger: Alison of Bath has nothing to say to the *Webbe* and *Tapycer* of London.

It is a fact, then, that the guildsmen are not developed. Ought one to suggest that they be ignored or omitted like the two priests *de trop*? No, for unlike the priests they are certainly Chaucer's own creatures. He may deserve a degree of adverse criticism because they are relatively uninteresting, but beyond this, the teacher ought to go no further than to suggest that Chaucer quite possibly intended to drop them from his finished work and may have hesitated only because he would have had to find a new reason for the presence on pilgrimage of his highly characterized Cook.

3. *"Welcome the sixte . . ."* (*CT* III.45). B. J. Whiting used to suggest to his Chaucer students that much of the drama in the

9. R. M. Lumiansky, *Of Sondry Folk* (Austin: University of Texas Press, 1955), p. 59; Carroll Camden, "Query on Chaucer's Burgesses," *Philological Quarterly,* 7 (1928), 314–317. For the opinion that Chaucer postponed individualizing the guildsmen, see Lumiansky, "Chaucer's Retraction and the Degree of Completeness of the *Canterbury Tales,*" *Tulane Studies in English,* 6 (1956), 9.

early part of the marriage group turned on the Wife's marital interest in the Clerk of Oxford. This stimulating speculation differs from the two previous questions in being unrelated to the issue of revision and completeness; it is not affected by my argument for considering auctorial intention. Its success in the undergraduate course can be vouched for pragmatically by one who has adopted it in his own lectures. Yet there is no compelling textual reason to suppose that Alice of Bath pressed her marital quest in this particular quarter, though the words quoted above make it clear that she was still questing. But what is more likely than that her search for a husband would continue on pilgrimage, or that she would single out the Clerk as most like her favorite Jankyn? What more probable than that the devout professional celibate would recoil from these silent advances of leer and glance even more than from the Wife's heterodox opinions, and then be moved to counterattack with Griselda and the biting *Envoi*? To make a coherent unity of the Wife's and Clerk's links and tales, one does not wholly require Whiting's suggestion, but it strengthens the effect without running against the grain. If not Chaucer's it does not violate Chaucer. It is of his kind and worthy of his comic imagination. Here one has to risk the intentional fallacy and attribute to Chaucer that which is probable not from minute examination of the text but from the broad insight which comes with years of closeness to an author. The insight shared is worth the risk, so long as the student is not left to assume that this relationship of Wife to Clerk is stated rather than implied.

4. *"She is a shrewe at al"* (*CT* IV.1222). The pilgrim Merchant in his *Prologue* attributes his disenchantment with his new wife entirely to her "hye malice." Yet he proceeds to tell a tale about another wife whose chief fault is hypocritical infidelity. Is the Merchant's dissatisfaction with his marriage to be taken at face value? Certain cultural class attitudes may suggest otherwise. A bourgeois of Chaucer's time did not lose face if he admitted to a shrewish wife: consider Harry Bailly's remarks in the *Monk's Prologue* and perhaps the allusion to the shrews of Greenwich. Even more clearly, we know that to be a conscious cuckold was the most humiliating of conditions. We may then view the discontent expressed by the Merchant as a mask for his anger

at being cuckolded. Such an anger would give more meaning to his choice of January as chief character, the humiliation of January appearing as thinly veiled self-punishment.[10]

This conjecture, rather like the one concerning the Wife and the Clerk, is probably too tenuous for prolonged scholarly argument. It presents a possible extrapolation, turning on a perhaps excessively subtle irony. Since it adds a dimension to the student's perception of the *Merchant's Tale,* it seems to deserve mention in the Chaucer course, but not as a certainty or even a strong probability.

5. *"Squier, thow hast thee wel yquit . . ."* (*CT* V.673). Is the *Squire's Tale* intentionally incomplete or did Chaucer plan to bring it to an end? *The Monk's Tale* and *Sir Thopas* belong to the first category, the *Cook's Tale* to the second. Donaldson's textbook edition accepts the intentional interruption of the Squire by the Franklin as a possibility.[11] Chaucerian orthodoxy has regularly taught that the Squire was to end his story and that the Franklin's words to the Squire were written on that assumption. If this position be correct, this, like the first two *loci* discussed, is a case of incompleteness. If the Franklin interrupts the Squire, then, like the third and fourth instances, it becomes a matter of interpreting correctly an established and complete text.

Grant that it was clearly Chaucer's will to have the Knight cut off the Monk's tragedies and to have his own tale interrupted by Harry Bailly, then one must concede the possibility that the other tales were left incomplete for artistic reasons and not because time and invention failed. *The Squire's Tale* is more fitted to such a view than the Cook's because of the Franklin's subsequent remarks. These, coming after the last words of the Squire's unfinished narration, might be taken as an ironic means of cutting off this *oeuvre à longue haleine* by assuming that it has ended. One might thus be tempted to see a gradation in courtesy (supposing the Bradshaw order) among the three interruptions, with the Franklin's exceeding in subtlety and elegance the

10. See G. G. Sedgewick's interpretation, "The Structure of the Merchant's Tale," *University of Toronto Quarterly,* 17 (1947–48), 337–345; also *Of Sondry Folk,* p. 156.
11. Donaldson, p. 923.

Knight's directness and the Host's vulgarity. But such an interpretation differs from the two extrapolations just discussed in
running more against than with the characterization. Admittedly,
the Franklin is a clever old man, but his admiration for the
squire, reflected in his remarks on his own difficult son, penetrates his tale in the characterization of Aurelius, the noble
courtly lover. To see irony here is to destroy the tale in its obvious interpretation. Here, then, is an instance of speculation
which might well be entirely omitted unless the lecturer were
able to offer stronger reasons for it than can I.

6. *"I speke in prose . . ."* (*CT* II.96). A hard passage for teachers is the one where the Man of Law announces a tale in prose
just before telling one in rhyme royal. Skeat, in his notes, took
this to mean that the Sergeant usually spoke (like M. Jourdan,
one supposes) in prose. This explanation explains nothing. In his
chapter on sources, Skeat expands this notion: "We may even
suppose it to be feigned that the Man of Lawe did really, at the
time, relate the story in prose, on the understanding that Chaucer might versify it afterwards." [12] In his notes, Robinson declared that "it probably indicates that the *Introduction* was not
written to precede the Tale of Constance" but is "rather to be
understood like the similar remarks in the *Monk's Prologue,* the
Prologue to *Melibee,* and the *Parson's Prologue*" as introducing
a prose tale.[13] Robinson was probably right in diagnosing this
crux as another example of the incomplete state of the *Canterbury Tales,* and Furnivall was perhaps also correct in guessing
that *Melibee* was originally the Man of Law's. But Skeat's suggestion has a certain appeal, because Chaucer has elsewhere indulged in a playful switching among the several levels of existence in the *Tales* — narrator, pilgrims, characters in tales — so
that, like the interruption of Sir Thopas, this might seem a
comic mastery of the creation over its creator. The Man of Law
has in fact just passed judgment on Chaucer's poetic achievement. But then this earlier passage is a good argument against

12. Skeat, III, 406; V, 141, n.96.
13. Robinson, p. 690.

the Man of Law's being aware of the poet's presence on the pilgrimage. Such an awareness would change the focus from comedy and literary values to mere bad manners.

Yet another possibility which one may speculatively offer the student interests me, because it would add to the substantial number of passages in the *Canterbury Tales* dealing with literary values. Whiting has often insisted on the thematic aspect of literary criticism in the *Canterbury Tales,* and not long ago Alfred David applied the idea to the Man of Law's *Introduction,* though with a different emphasis from the present article's.[14] Perhaps Chaucer would have us believe that the lawyer who has just pontificated concerning the poet's corpus does not know the meaning of the word "prose." Just a few lines before, he has referred to Chaucer's verse as "sermons" (II.96); there seem to be no other instances in Chaucer of the word "sermon" meaning a poetic composition, but good evidence for the word in its modern meaning. Every one of us has had one student who referred to *Paradise Lost* as a play or *Tom Jones* as an essay. The Man of Law's difficulties with the critical vocabulary at its most elementary level would surely vitiate his earlier judgments of Chaucer. A special attraction of this explanation is that, like that of the Franklin's intentional interruption discussed above, it heals an otherwise defective passage. But such an attraction is no guarantee of correctness. Robinson burdens the text with the onus of imperfection; Furnivall complicates the history of its composition, the present suggestion at least removes us from the area of auctorial intention and reduces the number of entities instead of multiplying them. None of the interpretations above is strong enough to bring a sense of probability, so that the conscientious teacher must offer all the possibilities that occur to him as reasonable, then perhaps indicate which he prefers.

7. *"For I wol preche and begge . . ."* (*CT* VI.443). Though Jusserand thought of the Pardoner as a layman with no official status, and Marie P. Hamilton made him an Augustinian Canon,

14. "The Man of Law vs. Chaucer: A Case in Poetics," *PMLA,* 82 (1967), 217–225.

there are sound reasons for viewing him as a secular cleric not in priest's orders.[15] Yet the passage quoted above and much of the surrounding matter in the *Pardoner's Prologue* seem to contradict this generally held opinion and leave one with an uneasiness as to what Chaucer meant; for the Pardoner speaks in lines VI.412–453 unmistakably as though he were a mendicant friar. It was doubtless this passage which led H. B. Hinckley to say, without discussion, that the Pardoner was presumably a Dominican.[16] Hinckley's preference for the Blackfriars must be a recognition of the chief literary source for the Pardoner, Faus-Semblant in the *Roman de la Rose,* who is a satire on the Dominicans. A priori, the Pardoner might have belonged to any of the four categories. Though "pardoner of Rouncivale" (I.670–671) is probably quite literally what it says — a quaestor for the Hospital at Charing Cross — it might also be a metaphor for any dishonest, unscrupulous pardoner, who might be from any walk of life. The pardoners of Rouncivale themselves might have been either members of the religious institute (Augustinian Canons) or their substitutes.[17] These substitutes could have been almost anyone.

As to internal evidence, we conclude that he was a eunuch, and we know that eunuchs were commonly not considered candidates for the priesthood.[18] We see that he preaches and is termed "ecclesiaste" (I.708), both of which facts would suggest the diaconate, but there is external evidence that all pardoners, even laymen, preached. The chanting of the office ("lessons" and "stories") implies minor orders at least. We must dismiss

15. J. J. Jusserand, "Chaucer's Pardoner and the Pope's Pardoners," *Essays on Chaucer,* V, 423ff. (Chaucer Society, 2nd Ser., no. 19); Marie P. Hamilton, "The Credentials of Chaucer's Pardoner," *Journal of English and Germanic Philology,* 40 (1941), 48–72. Manly, *New Light,* p. 129, and Robinson, p. 667, are among those who see the Pardoner as most likely a secular cleric in minor orders, but Prof. Hamilton's case for major orders is more impressive than her argument for the Augustinians.

16. Henry Barrett Hinckley, *Notes on Chaucer,* 2nd ed. (New York: Haskell House, 1964), p. 45.

17. Samuel Moore, "Chaucer's Pardoner of Rouncival," *Modern Philology,* 25 (1927–28), 59–66.

18. But see A. Vacant and E. Mangenot, *Dictionnaire de Théologie Catholique* (Paris: 1903), s.v. "Eunuque" for information that involuntary eunuchs were at least technically admissible to the priesthood.

the Pardoner's remark to the Wife of Bath that he had been
about to marry, a statement which taken literally would rule out
any save the laity and minor clerics, because it is quite probably
comically intended. So, too, the phrase "I stonde lyk a clerk in
my pulpet" (VI.391) seems to imply that he is not a clerk, but
can in fact mean in the English of Chaucer and Lydgate, "I
stand like the clerk I am," or something of the kind. In the long
run, we must depend on negative and peripheral evidence. One
of the best pieces of the latter is the miniature of the Ellesmere
manuscript, which shows the Pardoner in a red tunic or cassock
of knee length, stockings, shoes, and a brimmed hat, whereas the
Friar is portrayed in black religious habit with scapular, white-
lined hood, and tonsure. So too, the miniaturist of the Cambridge MS, though his carelessness vitiates his evidence, certainly
did not conceive of the Pardoner as a friar.[19] Negatively, the
General Prologue and *Pardoner's Tale* nowhere suggest the friar.

But then, what of the passage in the *Pardoner's Prologue,*
where he refers to his "brethren," to preaching out of desire for
gain, to spitting out poison "under hewe of hoolynesse," to mendicancy and disinclination toward manual work, — in other
words, to the catalogue of faults which recur in the satirical literature against the friars, most notably in Jean de Meun as
noted above? [20] Robinson's note to VI.416 recognizes the mendicancy implicit in the passage we are discussing, pointing out
the inconsistency with III.166. The same scholars who concur
in seeing Faus-Semblant's influence on the *Pardoner's Prologue*
also find it present in the portraits of the pilgrim Friar and Summoner's Friar. But no one seems to have amplified beyond a
mere acknowledgment of its existence the contradiction between
this "Faus-Semblant" passage and the remainder of Chaucer's
treatment of the Pardoner, in which he appears as clerk and not
as "Third Friar."

19. Margaret Rickert, "Illuminations," in Manly and Rickert, *Text
of Canterbury Tales,* I, 590–593.
20. *Roman de la Rose,* ed. Ernest Langlois (Paris, 1914–1924), ll.
11181–11974. See also D. S. Fansler, *Chaucer and the Roman de la Rose*
(New York: Columbia University Press, 1914), pp. 162ff., and Germaine Dempster, "The Pardoner's Prologue," in *Sources and Analogues
of Chaucer's Canterbury Tales,* ed. W. F. Bryan and Germaine Dempster (Chicago: University of Chicago Press, 1941), pp. 409–411.

What should be said about all this in the Chaucer course? Obviously, we must refer to the inconsistency.[21] Chaucer has somehow failed to make a final adjustment of his parts. We are confronted with several strata of his imagination. My own more or less intuitive belief is that the *dramatis personae* originally contained no Pardoner as such, but only an "Ur-friar" based more heavily on the *Roman* than either the extant Friar or the Pardoner. It is quite likely that Chaucer made a false start by adding the quality of quaestor to this primitive Friar, only to decide after a good deal of writing that a process of imaginative gemination was taking place. Thus, the Pardoner would have lost his mendicancy and taken on the notes which still dominate his characterization, whereas the Friar emerged shorn of his pardons. One point which might lend credence to this hypothesis is the surviving close connection of both Friar and Pardoner with the Summoner, the one in angry enmity, the other in unhallowed intimacy.

But these are notions merely felt, not based on proof or logic. What is a teacher to do about such intuitive responses? It is doubtless better for the mature and dedicated student of Chaucer to indulge his bent for speculation and reconstruction of the poet's thought processes than to remain silent, hoping that the rank and file of undergraduates will themselves be prompted to produce similar answers.

Some may be tempted to protest that excessive attention is being drawn to the defects of the *Canterbury Tales* whereas the student ought to hear chiefly of its good qualities. I reply that we can learn from failures as well as triumphs. There are hundreds of things to praise in Chaucer. I think of a flawed canvas of Botticelli's in the Fogg Museum. It cannot be compared with the artist's greater works, but, displayed in an unrestored state, serves a teaching end in a way which the whole canvasses never could.

As to the matter of committing such speculation to print, the mere presence of this essay indicates something of its author's position. We need not always speak ex cathedra or write only when all must concede the invulnerability of our position. More

21. See Robinson, n. to VI.445.

and better voices ought to be heard in the field where speculation impinges on Middle English pedagogy.[22]

22. Though an attempt has been made throughout to attribute all opinions not the author's to their due source, it is most likely that some notions have been derived from teachers, fellow graduate students, and colleagues, Professor Whiting doubtless chief, and have been incorporated into my teaching without footnote. Professor Lumiansky, Professor Magoun, and the late Professor Robinson must also especially be cited.

EDMUND REISS

Chaucer's Courtly Love

Along with being the explicit subject of Chaucer's lyrics and early narratives, love provides a major structuring principle, perhaps even the basic theme, for the *Canterbury Tales*.[1] But merely to recognize the pervasiveness of love in Chaucer's writings is neither to distinguish him from a hundred other medieval writers nor to understand his view and use of love.

Love was, to be sure, "the great medieval theme," [2] the proper subject of both poets and philosophers. Although the terms varied, *amor, amicitia, caritas,* and their vernacular equivalents filled medieval writings, continuing the concern with passion, friendship, and charity that had derived from Ovid and Virgil, from Aristotle, Cicero, and Augustine, as well as from the Song

1. Such has been the view since early in this century. See especially George Lyman Kittredge, "Chaucer's Discussion of Marriage," *Modern Philology* 9 (1911–12), 435–467; repr. in *Chaucer and His Poetry* (Cambridge, Mass.: Harvard University Press, 1915), pp. 185–210; and Frederick Tupper, "Saint Venus and the Canterbury Pilgrims," *Nation,* 97 (1913), 354–356. See also the brief but cogent statement in Richard L. Hoffman, *Ovid and the Canterbury Tales* (Philadelphia: University of Pennsylvania Press, 1966), pp. 11–20.
2. See, e.g., D. S. Brewer, *Chaucer and His Time* (London: Thomas Nelson, 1963), p. 168.

of Songs and First Corinthians. Not only providing the common
denominator for writers as disparate as Guilhelm IX, Bernard
of Clairvaux, Alan of Lille, and Chrétien de Troyes, love is at
the heart of the most influential medieval writings, from the *Consolation of Philosophy* to the *Romance of the Rose* and the
Divine Comedy. It is hardly surprising to find in Chaucer's own
England, even at the court of Richard II, such major — though
still rather neglected — works on love as John Gower's *Confessio Amantis* and Thomas Usk's *Testament of Love*. Still,
merely to place Chaucer in this milieu, even to agree that love is
"his main concern in season and out of season," [3] is not to distinguish or define what his various writings do with love.

While we may be aware of the various shapes taken by love in
Chaucer's writings, from the most bawdy to the most courtly and
the most devout, we may still not be sure how Chaucer intended
all this love to be regarded. In particular, we cannot easily as-
certain whether he ever offers us a love or a lover to be taken
seriously. Notwithstanding assured assertions that "Chaucer is a
poet of courtly love," and protestations that critics too often
"read into Chaucer all manner of ironies, slynesses, and arch-
nesses," and "praise him for his humour where he is really writing with 'ful devout corage,'" [4] it would seem that Chaucer is
more surely than ever regarded as a master of wit, humor, irreverence, even of irony. And the subject that most provides a basis
for this humor and detached ironic view of life is love.

Readers have long been aware of an apparent dichotomy in
Chaucer's treatment of love. In some works, "notably his earlier,
shorter poems, the conception of the lover conforms apparently
in all particulars to the conventional pattern of the romantic
lover of chivalry. In other works he shows a definite deviation
from this concept." [5] The conclusion of such analysis has been

3. Howard R. Patch, "The Subjects of Chaucer's Poetry," *Franciplegius: Medieval and Linguistic Studies in Honor of Francis Peabody
Magoun, Jr.* (New York: New York University Press, 1965), p. 259.
4. C. S. Lewis, *The Allegory of Love: A Study in Medieval Tradition*
(London: Oxford University Press, 1936), pp. 161, 167. See also D. S.
Brewer's more recent assertion of Chaucer's "uniformly exalted conception of love" ("Love and Marriage in Chaucer's Poetry," *Modern Language Review*, 49 (1954), 464.
5. Agnes K. Getty, "Chaucer's Changing Conceptions of the Humble
Lover," *PMLA*, 44 (1929), 202.

that Chaucer was essentially opposed to the conventions of and that his "rebellion against the conventional concept of ... humble lover developed and increased in intensity." [6] Although the idea that Chaucer "progressed" in his detachment from the conventions of courtly love still has appeal, we may well wonder whether his earlier works are indeed the straightforward accounts of love they appear to be, whether, that is, in spite of surface appearances, Chaucer ever takes love seriously.[7] Recent scholarship questioning the essential nature of courtly love, even going so far as to doubt its very existence,[8] has pointed up the need for us to reassess both our general notions about medieval love and our particular understanding of its various literary expressions. We must, in effect, reexamine what we may have blithely accepted as straightforward accounts of love to be taken at face value. Such reassessment is especially necessary — and especially difficult — when we are faced with the writing of so obvious an ironist as Chaucer.

To examine Chaucer's presentation of love, we must first agree on what we mean by love and lover. It is not sufficient to limit discussion to the earthly Venus, or to specify heterosexual desire, or even to say that for Chaucer love is by and large something pre- or extramarital. Several of the particulars we encounter offer immediate obstacles to such vague definitions. What, for instance, do we make of Valerian in the *Second Nun's Tale*? Probably he should not even be thought of as a proper

6. *Ibid.*, p. 216.

7. Most recently an acceptance of this traditional view of "progress" appears in a foolish book by Ian Robinson, *Chaucer and the English Tradition* (Cambridge: Cambridge University Press, 1972), e.g., p. 69. A good recent discussion of the general subject of Chaucer's view of love may be found in the essays collected in *Chaucer the Love Poet,* ed. Jerome Mitchell and William Provost (Athens, Ga.: University of Georgia Press, 1973).

8. See especially John F. Benton, "The Court of Champagne as a Literary Center," *Speculum,* 36 (1961), 551–591; D. W. Robertson, Jr., "Some Medieval Doctrines of Love," *A Preface to Chaucer: Studies in Medieval Perspectives* (Princeton: Princeton University Press, 1962), pp. 391–503; E. Talbot Donaldson, "The Myth of Courtly Love," *Ventures,* 5, no. 2 (1965), 16–23; repr. in *Speaking of Chaucer* (New York: Norton, 1970), pp. 154–163; and *The Meaning of Courtly Love,* ed. F. X. Newman (Albany: State University of New York Press, 1968), esp. the essays by Robertson (pp. 1–18) and Benton (pp. 19–42).

lover, even though the tale clearly presents him as being in love with Cecelia. In the same work Cecelia's angel lover must be disqualified, not mainly because of his extrahuman identity but because of the explicitly nonsexual nature of his love. At the other extreme, how should we view Apius in the *Physician's Tale*? In his desire for Virginia he may qualify as lover, though here we might wish to distinguish lust from love. And what about Chauntecleer in the *Nun's Priest's Tale*? Although a bird, he is presented as a man; and in feathering Pertelote "twenty tyme," he may be regarded as a lover par excellence. Likewise, what of the Monk, Don John, in the *Shipman's Tale,* or Walter in the *Clerk's Tale*? Even though love is a significant detail, even an issue, in these tales, neither John nor Walter seems especially identifiable as a lover. It is thus necessary to define terms more precisely. Obviously, every scene of lovemaking does not a love or lover make.

Some scenes of love — even memorable scenes like John's and Aleyn's night with Simkin's wife and daughter in the *Reeve's Tale* — are not indicative of the main theme of the narrative containing them. On the other hand, some works that seem in retrospect to have little to do with love prove upon reexamination to be essentially concerned with the subject. Such is the case with the *House of Fame,* where not only does the dream begin with a detailed account of the love of Dido and Aeneas, but also the eagle tells the narrator that the whole point of his journey is to hear tidings of love. Although our attention in this poem is not much on matters of love, we cannot ignore the context love provides.

Even when we consciously limit our analysis to those characters who are noticeably lovers, we must make additional qualifications that have to do with taking them seriously. The courtly lovers, the "foules of ravyne," in the *Parliament of Fowls* are, for all their beautiful speeches, essentially ridiculous and more out of step with Nature and her work than even the boorish waterfowls. In the *Merchant's Tale* we can hardly accept January as a lover any more than we can John in the *Miller's Tale* or the Wife of Bath's first three old husbands. Similarly, we respond only with amusement at "hende" Nicholas's mixture of pragmatism and idealism in the *Miller's Tale,* as he grasps Alisoun by the "haunchebones" and begs her for "mercy." Nicholas, along with Absolon in the same tale, is an obvious parody of the courtly lover, as such resembling the eagles in the *Parliament of Fowls,* and his love is not to be taken seriously. If it were, we would wonder what happened to him and Alisoun after John recovered from his fall. Love in the *Miller's Tale* and in the other fabliaux is a trigger for the action and a means of allowing us to understand a character, not something designed to command our attention or to cause us concern.

A comparable love is that of Damian for May in the *Merchant's Tale* as well as that of Aurelius for Dorigen in the *Franklin's Tale.*[9] These squires may seem at first to be exceptions to what has been said about Chaucerian lovers, for, although serious in their love and their suffering, they are not noticeably ludicrous — certainly there is no comparison between January and Damian as lovers. But neither these squires nor their loves are intended to exist as objects of our attention; rather, they act largely as props to develop the narrative. Ultimately neither these characters nor their loves matter; otherwise, how could we accept the ending of the *Merchant's Tale* without wondering what is to become of Damian — who has apparently been left up the pear tree — and of his continuing love for May?

We respond with another kind of amusement to Sir Thopas' love-longing for his "elf-queene" and to the falcon's lament in the *Squire's Tale* about the perfidious tercelet who deserted her. Given the burlesque of romance clichés in *Sir Thopas* and the bombastic treatment of trivia in the *Squire's Tale,* it is doubtful that love or lover in either instance is meant to be taken seriously. And even though the narratives that make up the so-called Marriage Group of the *Canterbury Tales* might seem to be essentially concerned with love, these tales of the Wife of Bath, Clerk, Merchant, and Franklin in fact deal mainly with ques-

9. See Margaret Schlauch, "Chaucer's 'Merchant's Tale' and Courtly Love," *ELH,* 4 (1937), 201–212; and C. Hugh Holman, "Courtly Love in the Merchant's and the Franklin's Tales," *ELH,* 18 (1951), 241–252.

tions of sovereignty, patience, blindness, and gentilesse. Although the *Franklin's Tale* begins with the agreement between Dorigen and Arveragus about love and marriage, we never see Arveragus as lover. Indeed, his arrangement functions in the tale as a premise for the action to follow; and when trouble comes, we see the breakdown of his facile solution of equality in marriage as he asserts "maistrye" over his wife and forbids her ever to speak of her imminent rendezvous with Aurelius.

Whereas love, including its psychology and morality, fills Chaucer's writing, it is presented only rarely as something to be taken in earnest. After sorting out the various narratives and their lovers, we may conclude that Chaucer presents love in detail and with apparent seriousness only three times — in the *Book of the Duchess, Troilus and Criseyde,* and the *Knight's Tale.* And in these three instances he is concerned with courtly love. There is no need to fall back on the characteristics of such love that have become popular through C. S. Lewis's description: "Courtesy, Adultery, and the Religion of Love." [10] Even though this courtly love may differ in particulars from that which Chaucer refers to in the Prologue to the *Legend of Good Women* as "fyn lovynge" (F 544, G 534) — a love that involves "wyf-hood" and, as the G version of the Prologue makes clear, that excludes Criseyde — it still gives the impression of being noble and elevated.[11]

This is the same love that Chaucer parodies to such an extent that it would seem inconceivable for him ever to be able to present it credibly — the *Parliament of Fowls, Miller's Tale,* and *Wife of Bath's Tale* provide but three varieties of parody

10. Lewis, *Allegory of Love,* p. 2; cf. Donaldson, *Speaking of Chaucer,* p. 156.

11. Although the *Middle English Dictionary* lists under "fyn" the meanings "pure, true, genuine, perfect" (II, 565), the reference here is under the heading of "fyn" as "accomplished, expert, skilled" (II, 566). Scholars have long puzzled over the credibility of such "saints of love" in the *Legend of Good Women* as Cleopatra, Dido, and Medea; see, e.g., Harold C. Goddard, "Chaucer's Legend of Good Women," *Journal of English and Germanic Philology,* 7 (1908), 87–129; 8 (1909), 47–112; Robert M. Garrett, "Cleopatra the Martyr and Her Sisters," *JEGP,* 22 (1923), 64–74. All references to Chaucer are according to *The Works of Geoffrey Chaucer,* ed. F. N. Robinson, 2nd ed. (Boston: Houghton Mifflin, 1957), and are cited according to line number.

obvious to most readers.[12] Still, in the *Book of the Duchess,* the *Troilus,* and the *Knight's Tale* Chaucer seems to be asking his audience to take "fyn lovynge" in earnest. In each of these poems the narrative is very much concerned with love and its outcome, and the love-longing felt by the main characters — the Black Knight, Troilus, and Palamon and Arcite — cannot be immediately dismissed as foolish. At the same time, as will be seen, the love presented in these three works is ultimately of dubious value.

In the *Book of the Duchess,* Chaucer's only work to show the conventions of courtly love in a fully developed form,[13] love is initially and mainly seen as a debilitating sickness, something turning man into "a mased thyng" (12), even leading him to despair and to the verge of death (23ff.). These effects, as witnessed in the narrator at the outset of the work, reappear in the Black Knight when in his first words he asks for death. It would seem that for one like the Black Knight who has been from his earliest youth the "thral" of love, having put "body, hert, and al" in the "servage" of love (767–769), the main condition of life must necessarily be unhappiness. In making his lady what he terms "My suffisaunce, my lust, my lyf,/Myn hap, myn hele, and al my blesse,/My worldes welfare, and my goddesse" (1038–40), he only continues his thralldom to love. Apparently opposed to his grieving and feelings of unfulfillment is the happiness he experiences after his lady gives him "al hooly/The noble yifte of hir mercy" (1269–70). But although this new condition lasts "ful many a yere" (1296), it is actually only a hiatus in a general state of unhappiness; for after his lady dies, his sorrow returns more terribly than ever. Moreover, throughout the Black Knight's life what he experiences most are frustration and sorrow; these are, as it were, the beginning and end of his love. Whatever happiness there may be is but an interlude, a temporary respite, in the agony of loving. In the *Book of the Duchess* to love is to suffer, and the suffering contains nothing noble, notwithstanding the Black Knight's presentation of it.

12. See especially George R. Coffman, "Chaucer and Courtly Love Once More — 'The Wife of Bath's Tale,' " *Speculum,* 20 (1948), 43–50.
13. Robertson, *Preface to Chaucer,* p. 463.

Chaucer's view here would seem to be that love is a condition to be altered, not one to be celebrated or perpetuated.

In a sense, the Black Knight's complaint of his loss is less a *complaynt d'amours* than a *complaynt countre Fortune;* in fact, in this poem love seems necessarily bound up with Fortune — blamed by the Knight as "trayteresse fals and ful of gyle" (620). But his monologue is most of all an exordium of his lady and least of all an account of how he loved and gained and then lost, although the narrator keeps trying to direct him away from his praising and back to his story. The entire poem offers less a love story, and likewise less the study of a man in love, than the picture of love as a destructive force and the detailed account of a love not handled properly. The narrator is "a mased thyng"; so is the Black Knight. Neither figure is a trustworthy spokesman, and even the Knight's praise of his lady cannot be accepted at face value. His words are extreme and his love is unrealistic, as is made clear when, after the narrator tries to make him acknowledge his subjective view of his lady, the Black Knight refuses to make a basic distinction between his opinion and fact. His lady exists in his eyes as a creature of perfection, as the best of all women; and he presents her in terms more appropriate to the Virgin Mary than to a mortal woman. Unless we wish to say that "goode faire White" (948) is for Chaucer what Beatrice was for Dante and see her as a symbolic representation of the Virgin, we must realize that the praise given her by the Black Knight, extravagant and couched in language alluding to the Song of Songs, is in its excess necessarily ludicrous.

Even if we hesitate to make this evaluation of the Black Knight's effusions our final one, we may still see that the love presented in the *Book of the Duchess* is initially and finally pejorative, something to be excoriated rather than celebrated. The point of the "hert-huntyng" is precisely to exorcise the demon Love from the Knight and, concomitantly, from his alter ego, the narrator. And the exorcism is apparently successful, for, though aborted once, the hunt is finally concluded and the narrator freed from love; at least he is now interested in doing something constructive, albeit merely putting his curious dream into verse. He is at the end marked by a vitality lacking in him at the beginning of the work, and no further mention is made of the sickness and despair so dominant initially. No matter whether the narrator "really" understands his dream or whether the purging of the Black Knight's grief is successful — this figure is after all met only through the narrator's consciousness and, significantly, disappears after the explicit statement of the lady's death and the narrator's exclamation, "Be God, hyt ys routhe!" (1310)[14] — it is clear that "al was doon,/For that tyme, the hert-huntyng" (1312–13).

The accounts of love found in *Troilus and Criseyde* and the *Knight's Tale* are quite different in method and scope from that seen in the *Book of the Duchess*. It has long been realized that these two romances are closely related, both stemming from works by Boccaccio, both being romances of antiquity, and both showing notable similarities in tone and style. Strong arguments have been advanced that the two poems were written at more or less the same time, the story of "al the love of Palamon and Arcite/Of Thebes," as it is referred to in the *Legend of Good Women,* later being reworked as the *Knight's Tale.*[15] The two narratives may even be regarded as companion pieces in that the *Troilus* shows the final unhappiness of love whereas the *Knight's Tale,* after detailing unhappiness, concludes with a state of bliss. At the same time, the two works are quite different in the way love functions in their narratives. Whereas *Troilus and Criseyde* is in its entirety a story of love, the *Knight's Tale* seems only superficially concerned with love.

The tale begins as the account of "a duc that highte Theseus;/ Of Atthenes he was lord and governour,/And in his tyme swich a conquerour,/That gretter was ther noon under the sonne" (I, A, 860–863) — a subject reinforced by the title of Boccaccio's work, the *Teseida.* As the *Aeneid* celebrates Aeneas and the *Achilleid* Achilles, so the *Teseida* is apparently a celebration of Theseus (Teseo), especially in his roles of "lord and governour" and of "conquerour." And, in fact, the nature of right rule and

14. As I read this passage, it is the emperor Octovyen who at the end "Gan homwardes for to ryde" to the "long castel with walles white,/ Be seynt Johan! on a ryche hil" (1315–19), that is, to the heavenly Jerusalem. The Black Knight is not seen or heard from after his exclamation, "She ys ded!" (1309).

15. F 420–21, G 408–09. See the discussion in Robinson, *Works,* p. 669.

of justice seems to be a major subject in the tale that Chaucer takes from Boccaccio. Furthermore, Chaucer's additional use of Statius's *Thebaid,* along with the Old French *Roman de Thèbes,* would seem to indicate that the setting of Thebes — notorious in the Middle Ages as a representative of the corrupt City of Man — was essential, not incidental, to his purpose.

That Theseus is an ambiguous hero has recently been suggested by several critics of the *Knight's Tale.*[16] His arrogant words to the old women on his triumphant return from Scythia, his constant changes of mind, his extreme grief over the death of Arcite in contradiction to his earlier scorn of the Theban knights, his wanton ravaging of the forest to obtain wood for the funeral pyre, and, finally, his use of Boethian wisdom to justify political expedience, specifically to create an alliance with the Thebans that will place them in "servage" to Athens, are only some notable particulars. These instances not only make Theseus seem foolish and hypocritical, they also render him suspect as a representative of ideal rule and justice, and they make us wonder about Chaucer's purpose in having such a man as his initial if not his main protagonist. But the ambiguity provided by Theseus and the Theban origin of Palamon and Arcite, along with the incongruity of Emily's being an Amazon — hardly the most appropriate nationality for a heroine of courtly romance — may offer an ironic context for viewing the love in this tale.

This love has been seen as primarily offering a typical *demande d'amour:* "which of two young men, of equal worth and with almost equal claims, shall (or should) win the lady?"[17] If such were indeed the case, the relevance of the *demande* would be negated by the conclusion of the tale, where the knight who finally wins Emily does so through the manipulations of Saturn and Theseus, not at all because of his own merits or through his own efforts. At the same time, the love revealed by Palamon

16. See, e.g., Edward E. Foster, "Humor in the *Knight's Tale,*" *Chaucer Review,* 3 (1968), esp. 92–93; Joseph Westlund, "The *Knight's Tale* as an Impetus for Pilgrimage," *Philological Quarterly,* 43 (1964), 526–537; and Judith Scherer Herz, "Chaucer's Elegiac Knight," *Criticism,* 6 (1964), 212–224.

17. J. R. Hulbert, "What Was Chaucer's Aim in the Knight's Tale?," *Studies in Philology,* 26 (1929), 380; see also Robinson, *Works,* p. 670.

and Arcite when they first see Emily is actually the opposite of the medieval ideal of love as a creative and unifying force: it destroys their friendship, negates their blood brotherhood, and results in the death of one of the lovers. In fact, however, the only *demande* stated explicitly in the *Knight's Tale* is the narrator's question at the end of the first part after Arcite hears that he will be leaving prison, thereby losing the sight of Emily: "Who hath the worse, Arcite or Palamoun?" (1348), that is, not who is the more worthy, but who is in the worse condition, the one in prison but near his lady or the one who is free but apart from Emily? The question can hardly be thought of as a weighty one, and, given the blindness of these lovers and their topsy-turvy view of reality — seen especially in Arcite's lament that had he dwelled in prison "yfetered . . . everemo," then he would have been "in blisse, and nat in wo" (1229–30) — few in Chaucer's audience could take the lovers or their situation seriously. If anything, the debate between Palamon and Arcite serves to undercut their credibility and to render unacceptable their views, attitudes, and conclusions. To think that Chaucer's audience would gravely ponder the *demande* offered is to ignore Chaucerian irony and to presuppose a lack of sophistication and a level of childlike incredulity on the part of this courtly audience.[18]

In terms of the context created by the first book of the *Knight's Tale,* love can hardly be taken at face value. It has been rendered ridiculous by the lovers themselves, and the high seriousness with which it is viewed in the subsequent narrative is incongruous. Theseus' speech on love beginning "The god of love, a, *benedicite!*/How myghty and how greet a lord is he!" (1785ff.) provides something of a corrective to this seriousness in its unmistakable irony and in its explicit equation of love with folly: "Now looketh, is nat that an heigh folye?/Who may been a fool, but if he love?" (1798–99).[19] Such remarks continue the

18. It is equally difficult to take seriously the *demande* in the *Franklin's Tale,* where the audience is asked to decide which of the three men — knight, squire, or clerk — is the most "fre," when the gentilesse of all three is inadequate, even illusory.

19. See Robinson, *Works,* p. 676.

evaluation of love made earlier in the narrator's reference to "the loveris maladye/Of Hereos" (1373–74)[20] and lead to the picture of destructive love seen in the temple of Venus constructed by Theseus. In this temple are depicted "The broken slepes, and the sikes colde,/The sacred teeris, and the waymentynge,/The firy strokes of the desirynge/That loves servantz in this lyf enduren" (1920–23), as well as illustrations of those so caught in the snare ("las") of love that "they for wo ful ofte seyde 'allas!' " (1951–52).

Although the tournament called by Theseus is supposed to solve the problems caused by love, it, leading mainly to Arcite's death, functions ironically to rid the *Knight's Tale* of almost all further thoughts or words of love. Whereas love has seemed so urgent and all-encompassing, it is resurrected by Theseus only after a "lengthe of certeyn yeres" (2967), significantly after the Athenian parliament has decided to "have fully of Thebans obeisaunce" (2974). Calling in Palamon and Emily and striking a pensive pose — "His eyen sette he ther as was his lest./And with a sad visage he siked stille" (2984–85) — Theseus then presents his famous Boethian speech on "the faire cheyne of love" (2988). But after these first words paying lip service to love, nothing else in his speech is about this hitherto all-important subject, except for a puzzling reference to Arcite's love of Palamon and Emily (3063).[21]

The marriage of Palamon and Emily is, in Theseus's words, to make out of "sorwes two/O parfit joye, lastynge everemo" (3071–72). Although Theseus refers to Palamon's long service

20. See John Livingston Lowes, "The Loveres Maladye of Hereos," *MP*, 11 (1913–14), 491–546; and Robinson, *Works,* p. 673. For further discussion of the malady of love, see Robertson, *Preface to Chaucer,* pp. 108–110, 457–469; and John M. Steadman, " 'Courtly Love' as a Problem of Style," *Chaucer und seine Zeit: Symposion für Walter F. Schirmer,* Buchreihe der Anglia, 14 (Tübingen: Max Niemeyer, 1968), esp. pp. 20–26.

21. "Why grucchen heere his cosyn and his wyf/Of his welfare, that loved hem so weel?" (3062–63). As Robinson writes, "The better supported reading, *loveth,* might refer ... to Arcite's continued love of them after his death" (*Works,* p. 683). See also the variants in *The Text of the Canterbury Tales,* ed. John M. Manly and Edith Rickert (Chicago: University of Chicago Press, 1940), III, 124. The point may be to suggest the contrast between charity and self-serving love.

to Emily, as well as to his rank and to her "pitee," "grace," and "mercy," nothing is said explicitly about love until the very end, where the narrator prays that God might send Palamon "his love that hath it deere aboght" (3100). The terminology is such that the line might seem to be alluding to God's love of man, even to Christ's crucifixion; but it explicitly functions to describe Palamon's earthly condition.[22] Clearly emphasized is the woe that has come from loving and that has remained for years. In the light of such details it is difficult to take at face value the contrived happy ending of the tale or the Knight's assertion that in marriage Palamon is finally "in alle wele,/Lyvynge in blisse, in richesse, and in heele" (3101–02). That marriage is hardly "parfit joye, lastynge everemo" (3072) is amply demonstrated by half a dozen tales that follow the *Knight's Tale,* most immediately by the *Miller's Tale,* whose explicit purpose is to "quite the Knyghtes tale" (3127).

With love apparently not to be taken in earnest, in spite of first impressions, in either the *Book of the Duchess* or the *Knight's Tale,* we might wonder what we are to make of *Troilus and Criseyde,* a work that is clearly and unambiguously a story of love. As the title of the poem's main source, the *Filostrato,* suggests, the story as told by both Boccaccio and Chaucer may be thought of as the account of one laid low by love. But Chaucer also intimates at the outset how he intends for us to view this love. He writes that his story will be of Troilus' "double sorwe . . . In lovynge," that is, "how his aventures fellen/Fro wo to wele, and after out of joie" (I.1–4). Although it might be assumed that this "double sorwe" is Troilus' losing love and then dying — that which Chaucer refers to at the beginning of Book IV, when he states that he will show "the losse of lyf and love yfeere/Of Troilus" (IV.27–28) — this is not what is written in the Prologue to Book I, where the "double sorwe" is seen to be the rise and the fall of love. At the end of this Prologue, when Chaucer reiterates that his audience "may the double sorwes here/Of Troilus in lovynge of Criseyde,/And how that she forsook hym er she deyde" (I.54–56), the only death mentioned is

22. Again the variants of the line are many (Manly and Rickert, *Text,* III, 126), suggesting early difficulty in understanding the precise meaning and point of the passage.

Criseyde's, not Troilus'. The function of the "And" here (56) is not entirely clear, but as I read the passage, the "And" links what comprises the "double sorwes": Troilus' loving and Criseyde's leaving him. Twice in this Prologue the point is made that the very act of loving is the occasion of sorrow, that the gain of love, the movement "fro wo to wele," is involved in and a cause of unhappiness. Not only does Chaucer insist that love in the *Troilus* will necessarily end unhappily, he presents it *ab initio* as something bringing grief, something that is in effect a metonmy of sorrow.

This view is reinforced in the Prologue to Book I, where grief is shown to be the normal condition of lovers. Those lovers who "bathen in gladnesse" are exceptional and should, says the narrator, remember their "passed hevynesse" (I.22–24). He asks further that the prayers of lovers assist him in showing the "peyne and wo as Loves folk endure" and such is to be seen in Troilus' "unsely aventure" (34–35). Also in the invocation in Book III, though Chaucer ranges through the various kinds of love associated with the earthly and heavenly Venus, emphasizing the goodness of love, the conclusion rather incongruously alludes once again to the problems associated with love. The narrator asks Venus to aid him in speaking of the joy of love: "techeth me devyse/Som joye of that is felt in thi servyse" (III. 41–42). Whether or not the term "devyse" is ambiguous,[23] the implication may be more than that the narrator has never known joy and love; it may also be that such joy is something of a rarity. Moreover, in also calling on Calliope to assist him in his "destresse" of having to tell "the gladnesse/Of Troilus" (46–48), the narrator may be suggesting that talking of the "swetnesse" of love is not easy (44). It would seem to be more natural to "pleyne" of love and to relate the "peyne and wo" referred to at the outset.

The love between Troilus and Criseyde is itself set in a context of sorrow. On the morning when Pandarus is about to begin working to bring the lovers together, he awakens with a green sickness, a "teene/In love," that makes him return to bed "in

23. The *MED* apparently does not list this reference; see II, 1058ff.

wo" (II.60–62). The next morning is hardly more auspicious, for he awakens to the "waymentynge" of "the swalowe Proigne" (64–65). Although Pandarus is apparently unaware of the ill omen here, the "sorowful lay" of the swallow and her mythological associations with tragic love provide an ironic context for the imminent love between Troilus and Criseyde. The forecast of grief is reinforced by the song of the nightingale Criseyde hears when, later in Book II, she is lying in bed musing about whether or not to love. Although the nightingale's "lay/Of love" seems good to her — it "made hire herte fressh and gay" (II. 921–922) — it functions to call up the earlier song of the swallow and the sorrows associated with the mythological account of Procne, Tereus, and Philomela, who was transformed into a nightingale.[24] Along with the narrator's words, the details of the narrative itself seem to insist that love is necessarily unhappy.

Because of such insistence the "wele" between the two woes, detailed in Book III of the *Troilus,* should immediately be suspect. The "blisse" and "suffisaunce" that the lovers experience (III.1716) last only a short time. Hardly sufficient to minimize the final and total grief, this period of happiness is at best like the Black Knight's joy with his lady, an interlude in the sorrow. As Chaucer writes at the beginning of Book IV, "But al to litel, weylaway the whyle,/Lasteth swich joie, ythonked be Fortune" (IV.1–2). And the end of it all is death. Chaucer again insists on the connection between Fortune, death, and love, also writing at the conclusion of the entire narrative, "Swich fyn hath, lo, this Troilus for love" (V.1828), and again at the end of this bitter passage, "thus bigan his lovyng of Criseyde,/As I have told, and in this wise he deyde" (1833–34).

In relation to the final unhappiness of love seen in the *Troilus* and in the *Book of the Duchess,* it would appear that the ending of the *Knight's Tale,* where Palamon and Emily are said to be "in alle wele,/Lyvynge in blisse, in richesse, and in heele," is clearly an exception. That this ending also contradicts the medieval understanding of earthly happiness may be seen by com-

24. See, e.g., Ovid, *Metamorphoses* VI.412ff., though here Procne becomes the nightingale.

paring it with the ending of the *Man of Law's Tale,* where a comparable state of happiness is detailed.[25] Custance and her husband, after grief and separation, are finally united in great joy; but Chaucer insists on our viewing this joy in a larger context: "swich a blisse is ther bitwix hem two/That, save the joye that lasteth everemo,/Ther is noon lyk" (II, B, 1075–77). Although the couple live "in joye and in quiete," such cannot be their final state; for, as Chaucer writes, perhaps echoing the passage from Book IV of the *Troilus* cited above, "But litel while it lasteth, I yow heete,/Joye of this world, for tyme wol nat abyde" (1131–33). Mutability must necessarily have its way and give the final word.

Love is "joye of this world," and good as it may sometimes appear, it must obviously be bound inextricably to the world and to mutability. Although the lover may see himself and his condition to be tragic, from a broader perspective, *sub specie aeternitatis,* he must appear ludicrous and his situation comic. The lover who cannot see beyond his immediate condition cannot be taken seriously, and this is the courtly lover, the adherent of "fyn lovynge," that Chaucer consistently presents. The ideal love is doubtless that found in the oft-quoted passage at the end of *Troilus and Criseyde,* when the narrator addresses the "yonge, fresshe folkes" and advises them to leave their "feynede loves" and turn to God (V.1835–48). And in terms of this passage the ideal lover in all of Chaucer's writings would probably be St. Cecelia in the *Second Nun's Tale.* With such a love, however, we are out of the realm of both passion and courtly love. If we are to remain in this realm, we must expect to see love as the main ingredient in the human comedy. It may seem for a while to be something worthy and noble, but finally its inadequacies will be discernible and it will appear at best laughable and at worst destructive. Even when, as in the *Book of the Duchess,* the *Knight's Tale,* and the *Troilus,* Chaucer seems most sincerely to be presenting love and lover as noble and good, his final and real attitude seems to be one of ironic scorn. Like what may be seen

25. This comparison with the *Man of Law's Tale* may not be gratuitous. Not only do the two works show similarities in theme and purpose, they are paralleled in that each is the first tale told on a given day of pilgrimage.

in such significant writings as the *Art of Honest Loving* of Andreas Capellanus and the *Romance of the Rose* of Jean de Meun, Chaucer's method is to present earthly love as both good and bad. But, also as in these writings, his narratives bring out the ultimate destructiveness and folly of this love.

JOHN LEYERLE

The Heart and the Chain

Several of Chaucer's major poems have as a poetic nucleus either the heart or the chain. As such, the heart represents both love and its mutability; the chain represents order and its confinement. The word "nucleus" here is not italicized because the English word, first recorded in the *Oxford English Dictionary* in 1704, is meant, not the Latin. I use the word in two senses: the first is kernel, or seed, the latent beginning of growth or development; the second is the center around which other parts or things are grouped. As a critical term, nucleus means both seed, implying origin and growth, and center, implying a surrounding structure. The term is not difficult or new, but it provides a means to approach Chaucer's narrative poetry not often taken.[1] In this paper I propose to show how a number of

This paper was written for Jere Whiting, a man of gret auctorite.

1. The English word nucleus has been used as a critical term before. John Press, writing of Valéry, says that he "once admitted that sometimes God give him a line of poetry and that this single line was enough, for, having been granted a nucleus, he could then proceed to

Chaucer's poems are developed around such a nucleus lying at the core of the text that focuses the surrounding elements of the whole composition. In these poems the organizing effectiveness and centripetal force of each nucleus vary, but a strong nucleus controls the main narrative and thematic development of its work. Not all of Chaucer's poems have a nucleus, but those that do range from his early work to that of his poetic maturity.

His earliest long poem, *The Book of the Duchess,* ends as the man in black, usually taken to be John of Gaunt, and the dreamer emerge from the dark forest in which most of the poem is set.

> They gan to strake forth; al was doon,
> For that tyme, the hert-huntyng.   (1312–13) [2]

The nucleus of the poem is *hert-huntyng.* The deer, a hart, cannot be found by the hunters in their chase, nor can Gaunt recover his lady, usually taken to be his first wife Blaunch, who, he reports, had long possessed his heart; the two hunts proceed together and show how the nucleus has a literal and a metaphoric sense. The hunters pursue the deer, but lose their quarry.

> and so at the laste
> This hert rused, and staal away
> Fro alle the houndes a privy way.   (380–382)

The dreamer follows one of these hounds into a parklike forest and sees there "many an hert and many an hynde" (427). The dark wood, a refuge for harts and hinds that are beyond the hunt, is a medieval *topos* familiar from the opening of Dante's *Inferno*; the dress of the man in black, his manner, and his words all reinforce the associations of the ominous place with death.[3] The dreamer overhears Gaunt reciting a lament (lines

---

construct his flawless architectural patterns" *The Fire and the Fountain* (London: Methuen, 1966), p. 3. I am indebted to my colleague, R. A. Greene, for this reference.

2. All quotations are from *The Works of Geoffrey Chaucer,* ed. F. N. Robinson, 2nd ed. (Boston: Houghton Mifflin, 1957). Line references are to this edition.

3. The black and white imagery of the poem develops from the

475–486) about the death of Blaunch and then describes his state.

> Hys sorwful hert gan faste faynte,
> And his spirites wexen dede;
> The blood was fled for pure drede
> Doun to hys herte, to make hym warm—
> For wel hyt feled the herte had harm—
> To wite eke why hyt was adrad
> By kynde, and for to make hyt glad;
> For hit ys membre principal
> Of the body. (488–496)

Following the specific statement about the death of Blaunch in Gaunt's lament, this passage shows how the loss has affected his heart, the *membre principal of the body*. The relevance of the story of Seys and Alcyone which the dreamer read before he fell asleep becomes apparent here, for it indicates the risk that Gaunt, who has lost Blaunch to death, may die of grief as Alcyone had died of grief over the loss of Seys. The dreamer has just left the literal hunt in which the hart *staal away,* overhears the lament, and utters what must be a calculated ambiguity.

> "Sir," quod I, "this game is doon.
> I holde that this hert be goon;
> These huntes konne hym nowher see." (539–541)

Gaunt's reply, "Y do no fors therof," (542) elicits from the dreamer an explicit offer of help.

> For, by my trouthe, to make yow hool,
> I wol do al my power hool.
> And telleth me of your sorwes smerte;
> Paraunter hyt may ese youre herte,
> That semeth ful sek under your syde. (553–557)

---

death in September 1369 of Blaunch, or White, as she is called in the poem, as a result of black plague. This black and white contrast occurs several times in the poem, for example, in the dark forest and the white-walled castle at the end. The point is not to be pressed, however, because black death is a post-medieval term.

The balance of the poem is the working out of this offer to ease the heart sickness of Gaunt by getting him to articulate his sorrows; the cure is thus to have him talk about his loss. At this point the dreamer starts a metaphoric game of *hert-huntyng*.[4] Contrary to a critical commonplace about the poem, Gaunt is the one who does not comprehend what is afoot, not the dreamer who sets about to make him whole. The dreamer is concerned about the risk that Gaunt's heart, which he gave to Blaunch, *staal away* at her death to the dark forest, as the hart had done in the literal hunt, there to remain. In less metaphoric language, the dreamer fears that Gaunt, like Alcyone, will die of grief. Whatever may have been the truth about Gaunt's actual reactions to the death of his wife in 1369, Chaucer attributes to his patron a profound grief with lightness of touch by presenting his loss in metaphoric language so delicate and graceful that its point is easy to miss; Chaucer's narrator is not obtuse.

In telling the dreamer of his *sorwes smerte* Gaunt makes four long speeches that show an interesting progression. The first, lines 560 to 709, reveals a self-pity evident in the fifty-two repetitions of the first-person pronouns, *I, me* and *my,* in the first sixty lines. The main point of this speech is a wish for death, showing that the diagnosis made by the dreamer about Gaunt's grief sickness is accurate. He then elaborates the metaphor of the chess game with fortune in which he lost his queen and was mated. The next move would be the final checkmate[5] when the king, Gaunt himself, would, as had happened to his *fers* Blaunch,

---

4. A similar interpretation is made by Joseph E. Grennen, *"Hert-huntyng* in the *Book of the Duchess," Modern Language Quarterly,* 25 (1964), 131–139. The game of hunting is one of several connected games in the poem, such as the game of chess with fortune, ll. 617ff., and, less evidently, the game of love itself. Similar interlocking games of love and hunting occur in *Sir Gawain and the Green Knight* in which various games, complexly related to each other, form the nucleus of the poem. See John Leyerle, "The Game and Play of Hero," in *The Concept of the Hero in the Middle Ages and Early Renaissance,* ed. Christopher Reagan (Albany, N.Y.: State University of New York Press, forthcoming).

5. The English word checkmate is derived, by way of Old French, from the Arabic, *al-shah mat,* "the king is dead." In Middle English usage, the word appears in collocations with death; see the relevant citations in the *Middle English Dictionary* under *chek-mat,* 2(a).

be swept off the board by fortune. Gaunt concludes his first long speech with a question and his own answer to it:

> but yet, what to doone?
> Be oure Lord, hyt ys to deye soone.   (689–690)

The dreamer makes a skillful reply, saying that no man would "for a fers make this woo" (741). By taking Gaunt's metaphor of the chess game literally, he leads Gaunt to praise Blaunch in an effort to show how great a loss he had indeed suffered. The difference in tone in Gaunt's second long speech, lines 758 to 1041, is important, because he moves from the self-pitying grief of his first long speech to the eloquent praise of his dead lady. Gaunt's preoccupation has shifted from himself to the dead duchess, and the curative process of consolation, the heart-hunting, is well under way. In his third long speech, lines 1052 to 1111, Gaunt compares her to riches of all sorts and decides that she was superior to them all. In the fourth long speech, lines 1144 to 1297, Gaunt answers the dreamer's specific questions and reverts to his courtship, the time when Blaunch first possessed his heart.

> She was lady
> Of the body: she had the herte,
> And who hath that, may not asterte.   (1152–54) [6]

He then repeats the first love song to Blaunch, one that he made his "herte to glade" (1172). This song is a sharp contrast to the earlier, self-pitying lament and shows how his mood has shifted. Gaunt then recalls how Blaunch took pity on his sorrowful heart and gave him "The noble yifte of hir mercy" (1270), which caused his heart to be joyous (1275–76). In his mind Blaunch

---

6. The colon in l. 1153 here is my substitution for the semicolon printed by Robinson, because the second part of the expression explains the first as may be seen in the source for the passage: "Il est assez sires dou cors/Qui a le cuer en sa comande" (1996–97), Guillaume de Lorris, *Le Roman de la Rose,* ed. Ernest Langlois, Société des Anciens Textes Français (Paris: Firmin-Didot, 1914–1924), II, 103. Compare the *Romaunt* version: "For of the body he is full lord/That hath the herte in his tresor" (2084–85).

has now returned in death to her first inaccessibility and he has resumed his attitude of courtship; then he was happy to love her at a distance, but now the distance is the permanent one of death. At the same time she is shown to be fixed in his memory; in medieval times the memory was commonly thought to be a thesaurus where treasures of the past would be safe. While Gaunt lives, Blaunch is wholly his own and her heart has been found within his heart. To the dreamer's insistent questioning, he replies, with a hint of impatience, that Blaunch is dead. At once the dark forest is left and the heart-hunting is over.

> And with that word ryght anoon
> They gan to strake forth; al was doon,
> For that tyme, the hert-huntyng.   (1311–13)

The word *hert* is used nearly forty times in the poem, and this frequency is significant. The word occurs so often and so naturally that one hardly notices its full importance, but once that importance is recognized and the nucleus is identified, the supporting evidence is found throughout the text. This point has an obverse; if there is no repeated, specific statement, a poetic nucleus, as defined here, does not exist in a work.

Another of Chaucer's treatments of courtship and death — a combined theme that he liked — is *The Knight's Tale,* which also has a nucleus, but one less apparent than the *hert* of *The Book of the Duchess.* This nucleus is bonds in the literal sense of confinement, the poem's *prisoun,* and in the metaphoric sense of order in the created world, the *faire cheyne of love.* The idea that love is a bond was a medieval commonplace;[7] the lofty speech of Theseus at the end of *The Knight's Tale* draws on the last meter of Book II of the *Consolation of Philosophy,* one of Chaucer's favorite passages in that text. Use of an actual prison may derive from the fact that Boethius wrote while in prison, and he uses his confinement metaphorically to stand for the human condition. Chaucer's contemporary, Thomas Usk, uses the same device in *The Testament of Love,* a work dating from

7. See Arthur O. Lovejoy, *The Great Chain of Being* (Cambridge, Mass.: Harvard University Press, 1936).

1385–1386, about the time when Chaucer was writing *The Knight's Tale* and *Troilus and Criseyde*.

Near the beginning of the tale Arcite and Palamon are found half dead in a pile of slain warriors outside Thebes and are carried to the tent of Theseus. He arbitrarily sends them to Athens "to dwellen in prisoun/Perpetuelly" (1023–24). From a window in their tower of confinement the two glimpse Emelye and suffer love sickness. Their argument over priority of claim to her threatens the bond of sworn brotherhood between them (1131–51 and 1604), an indication that the breaking of social bonds easily leads to anarchy. Through the arbitrary intervention of a certain Perotheus, Arcite is released and then protests that his figurative prison of exile away from Athens is worse than the actual prison of the tower (1224 and 1244–48). Palamon remains in the prison and complains to the cruel gods who control the world with "byndyng of youre word eterne" (1304). In his view man is little better than an animal cowering "in prison and arreest" (1310). Palamon is a prisoner, not only because of walls, but also because of the bonds that love has laid upon him, a metaphorical way of describing man's condition in the deterministic world of the poem where the actions of the characters are controlled by the gods, or the numinous Theseus.

> In derknesse and horrible and strong prisoun
> Thise seven yeer hath seten Palamoun
> Forpyned, what for wo and for distresse.
> Who feeleth double soor and hevynesse
> But Palamon, that love destreyneth so
> That wood out of his wit he goth for wo?
> And eek therto he is a prisoner
> Perpetuelly, noght oonly for a yer.   (1451–58)

Venus has caught him in her snare (1951), and that is harder to escape than the tower.

Palamon manages to break free from the prison after the seventh year of confinement and flees to a grove near Athens where he meets Arcite. They attempt to resolve their quarrel over Emelye with a duel, but Theseus interrupts their unsupervised battle; he imposes the elaborate rules and order of a tournament

that is to end when either Arcite or Palamon is slain or driven
from the lists. Just before the tournament a year later Theseus
alters the rules so that the end will come when one or the other
is caught and brought to the stake, another example of the way
Theseus imposes order by placing those around him under
bondage of one sort or another. This bondage is, in fact, a form
of order and proceeds from the "Firste Moevere" (2987)
through the planets to man on earth. The planetary gods take
precedence according to their proximity to the *primum mobile*
(Saturn, Jupiter, Mars, Sun, Venus, Mercury, and Moon).
Saturn controls the outcome; Mars has his wish granted first and
Arcite wins the tournament. Venus has her wish granted next
and Palamon wins Emelye; this overrides the wish of Diana, the
moon, goddess of maidenhood. Without order, the condition of
the world and all the men in it would be anarchy; examples of
such chaos in the poem are the absence of funeral rites at
Thebes, the argument between Palamon and Arcite, the duel in
the forest, and the strife among Diana, Venus, and Mars. In the
poem this order takes the form of bonds — prison at the most
extreme — and the rationale given by Theseus in his long, eloquent speech at the end of the tale is that order on earth is natural and is linked by a great chain with divine order above.

> The Firste Moevere of the cause above,
> Whan he first made the faire cheyne of love,
> Greet was th'effect, and heigh was his entente.
> Wel wiste he why, and what thereof he mente;
> For with that faire cheyne of love he bond
> The fyr, the eyr, the water, and the lond
> In certeyn boundes, that they may nat flee.   (2987–93)

He goes on to say that Arcite has departed "Out of this foule
prisoun of this lyf" (3061) and ends by establishing the bond
of wedlock between Palamon and Emelye, "the bond/That
highte matrimoigne or mariage" (3094–95). The wedding at the
end of the tale recalls the beginning when Theseus returned
from the Scythian war in which he captured his enemy Ypolita,
queen of the Amazons, and married her, thereby ending the
chaos of war with the bond of marriage. As women were thought

to have less capacity for reason than men, the women in the poem are forced to submit to the order decreed by men, Ypolita and Emelye to Theseus, Venus and Diana to Saturn. This submission of women, especially in marriage, is another example in *The Knight's Tale* of imposition of rational order. Clearly the knight gives the opening statement in *The Canterbury Tales* of two major themes of the whole poem, love and order.

Saturn and Theseus are the controlling figures of *The Knight's Tale,* and they impose on others an order associated with divine causation. Theseus before the tournament is described as being "at a wyndow set,/Arrayed right as he were a god in trone" (2528–29), and he presides over the poem with numinous presence imposing order, bonds, and captivity on those subject to him. Saturn also imposes order on those subject to him and says that he is patron of prisons, "Myn is the prison in the derke cote" (2457). One result is that the human condition portrayed in the poem has a dark side to it, because the choice seems to be between freedom and anarchy on the one hand and bondage and order on the other. Chaucer gives the knight a tale with a highly developed sense of order, as is appropriate for a professional soldier, and his tale has a markedly deterministic attitude toward events. As such, it is notably lacking in humour, one of Chaucer's special talents, an absence that reinforces its somber mood. As often, Chaucer's silences are significant, and the absence of laughter in *The Knight's Tale* compared to its presence in *The Miller's Tale* following it makes clear the close connection in Chaucer of comedy and disruption of order.

The word *prisoun* and equivalents such as *cage, cheyn, dongeon, fettre, laas,* and *tour* occur over fifty times in the tale. The specific and repeated statement of the nucleus is as pronounced here as in *The Book of the Duchess.* Actual or figurative bonds form the nucleus of *The Knight's Tale* and establish the theme for what follows. *The Canterbury Tales* are, in effect, a "faire cheyne of love" on the themes of love and order, especially the bond of marriage. When the bonds of order are most evident, as in *The Knight's Tale* or *The Clerk's Tale,* the mood is serious, even somber. Chaucer's comic touch is most evident where these bonds rest lightly and slip, as in *The Wife of Bath's Prologue* or *The Miller's Tale.*

The Miller's Tale concerns *deerne love* (3200) set up by a wild story of chaos imminent in a second flood, and culminating in hilarious disorder. It has an appropriate nucleus: holes, both apertures and pits. The action of the tale involves two levels of *privitee; hende* Nicholas pretends to have knowledge of *Goddes privitee* in order to involve the superstitious carpenter in a far-fetched plot that will enable Nicholas to enjoy Alisoun's *privitee*. Some of the holes are in the carpenter's house, put there, no doubt, by his own gnarled hands. The carpenter's house-boy Robin uses a cat hole to spy on Nicholas whom he discovers gaping upward with open mouth. The carpenter is reminded of another clerk who fell into a *marle-pit* (3460) while star-gazing, yet sees no danger in listening to Nicholas who had, supposedly, been doing the same. He breaks open the door, another of the holes, with the help of Robin. Like the clerk who fell in the *marle-pit,* the old man has a tumble in the night, but his is more humiliating even than the clerk's, for he occupies a pit he has provided himself (cf. Psalm 7.16), the *tubbe* "hang-ynge in the balkes" (3626), and unintentionally provides a pit for Nicholas who has a somewhat different tumble in the night, finally satisfying his *queynte fantasye*. All this takes place on a Monday night inverting the rites due Diana, goddess of chastity, and mocking the careful astrological orderings of *The Knight's Tale*. Other holes in the tale are human: *yen, nether yen, towtes,* and *mouthes*. They all come together in yet another hole, the *shot-wyndow,* scene of the chaotic climax of the tale. Absolon, whose mouth "hath icched al this longe day" (3682), has his ardent passion quenched by its object, described in one of the many indecorous puns of the tale, "His hoote love was coold and al yqueynt" (3754). To gain revenge, Absolon offers Alisoun a ring, another of the holes in the tale, hoping that she will expose herself a second time so he can brand the offending part with the red-hot iron, but Nicholas incautiously decides that he will "amenden al the jape" (3799) and gets scalded by the glowing plowshare applied "amydde the ers" (3810). His wild cry for water causes the carpenter to axe the rope holding his *tubbe* thinking, "Allas, now comth Nowelis flood" (3818); the old man never gets a chance to use the axe on the gable end to make the one hole he planned for. In sum, *The Miller's Tale*

has an apparent nucleus, holes and the chaotic license that results from their very complex connections. This nucleus is, like
the tale itself, a parodying inversion of *The Knight's Tale;* bonds
and decorous order of love are turned into holes and wild chaos
of licence almost as if Chaucer noticed that every link in the
"faire cheyne of love" had a hole in it and wrote two poems as
a result, one on the links and the other on the holes. Wild laughter accompanies *The Miller's Tale* in contrast to the unsmiling
seriousness of *The Knight's Tale;* order is a grave business.

In Chaucer's poetry order is also a subtle business, because
his work resists simplification. *The Parliament of Fowls,* for example, presents a balance of attitudes to love and order without
reaching any firm conclusion about the conflicting attitudes. Like
much of what Chaucer wrote, this poem presents no single re-
solving doctrine, a situation too often ignored by the poem's
critics.[8] *The Parliament of Fowls* has an appropriate nucleus; it
is *place.* In the poem *place* has the senses of area and of degree,
both controlled by

> Nature, the vicaire of the almyghty Lord,
> That hot, cold, hevy, lyght, moyst, and dreye
> Hath knyt by evene noumbres of acord.   (379–381)

The *sterry place* (43) in the passage drawn from Macrobius and
the walled garden are *places,* "areas" where *place,* "degree,"
should prevail, although the mortal creatures in the poem do
not always follow this order of divine intelligence because of
the chaotic promptings of desire engendered by Venus, who
also has her *place* in the poem. The word and its variants are
repeated over twenty-five times in this short text. Nature can
no more enforce degree and order on the classes of birds than
the knight can do the same on the other pilgrims. The reverse
is true; serious high-mindedness draws out the cries of the worm
fowls just as it draws out the drunken Robin to "quite the
Knyghtes tale" (3127).

---

8. An important exception is the book by J. A. W. Bennett, *The
Parlement of Foules* (Oxford: Clarendon Press, 1957), which presents
the complex intellectual and literary traditions behind the poem, not
one particular reading of it.

This tendency in Chaucer's poetry to leave conflicting view-points unresolved must be kept in mind in discussing any of the texts that are organized about a nucleus so as to avoid reductive interpretations. Indeed, the nucleus itself is usually ambiguous in significance. Each nucleus has a contradiction within itself: the hunting of the *hert* is accomplished when its loss is finally recognized; the *prisoun* of order imposes a restrictive captivity; and the holes of license produce a love that famishes the craving. A nucleus does not, of course, explain everything in a poem where it is found, but it does reinforce from the core the ambiguities present in the whole. Each nucleus has a literal sense, but as the poem develops, each also tends to become invested with metaphoric sense representing the main abstract ideas present.

Here one sees Chaucer as the poet of ideas; he was not a philosopher, and his ideas in abstract statement are commonplace, because so many of them are taken from *The Consolation of Philosophy,* a work of wide influence throughout the Middle Ages. In his imagination, however, these ideas produced a creative reflex in which abstract conceptions took specific form in the nucleus. Perhaps this formation was a carefully worked-out process; more likely, it was the way his imaginative perception instinctively worked. Either way, a nucleus, once identified, provides a very powerful tool for discovering the center and seed of a narrative poem and the way the poet perceived ideas. The nucleus is, of course, very different from the passages of versified ideas inserted into a poem, such as the soliloquy of Troilus on free will and foreknowledge, set down like a lump in Book IV of *Troilus and Criseyde.*

Troilus has an extremely simple and pervasive nucleus, the heart. It is the cause of love and its variable fortune in the poem, thus subsuming both of the main themes. There is a significant difference between the two lovers' hearts, however. Troilus has a stable heart, and this steadfastness in love accounts, I think, for his ascent from the mutable love of the world to the stable love of the heavens. Criseyde, on the other hand, is "Tendre-herted, slydynge of corage" (V.825) and moves to the arms of another man, the "sodeyn Diomede" (V.1024). References to the heart abound in the poem and are prominent at every crucial development of the love affair. Owing to the length and complexity of this work, arguably the finest narrative poem in the language, there is need to trace the nucleus in some detail, for it is less obvious than the others discussed above.

In the temple of the Palladion Troilus scoffs at the men in his company whom he suspects of showing signs of love, conduct that betrays his ignorance of the strength of love and its application as a universal bond. He supposes that

> nothing hadde had swich myght
> Ayeyns his wille that shuld his herte stere,
> Yet with a look his herte wax a-fere.   (I.227–229)

In falling in love he becomes one more example of the power that love has as the binding force of the world (I.253–259). At the end of Book III Troilus acknowledges this bond in his song in praise of love and its binding force, a passage translated from meter 8 of Book II of *The Consolation of Philosophy* and already noted in connection with *The Knight's Tale.* Love in terms of a bond or knot is also present in *Troilus,* and the discussion of the nucleus of *The Knight's Tale* should be kept in mind here.[9] As Troilus looks about him, his glance penetrates the crowd and falls on Criseyde. "Therwith his herte gan to sprede and rise" (I.278); a deep and fixed impression of her sticks "in his hertes botme" (I.297). In Book II he uses the same expression of himself, saying

> so soore hath she me wounded,
> That stood in blak, with lokyng of hire eyen,
> That to myn hertes botme it is ysounded.   (II.533–535)

The process follows the traditional pattern of "loveris maladye": the "subtile stremes" (I.305) from Criseyde's eyes enter the eyes of Troilus, sink to the root of his heart, and cause love, which is regarded as a disease.[10]

9. In *The Parliament of Fowls* love is twice described in terms of a knot, ll. 435–438 and 624–628.

10. The standard study remains John Livingston Lowes, "The Loveres Maladye of Hereos," *Modern Philology,* 11 (1913–14), 491–546.

> hym thoughte he felte dyen,
> Right with hire look, the spirit in his herte. (I.306–307)

This is the first part of the "double sorwe" that Chaucer announces as his subject in the opening line of the poem. The connection between eye and heart is taken further when the narrator states that Troilus' "herte, which that is his brestes ye,/ Was ay on hire" (I.453–454).[11]

Criseyde, so far as the text indicates, is unaware in Book I of the effect she has produced and is not especially concerned with Troilus until Pandare informs her of his friend's love in Book II. The scene at the window follows this news, and Criseyde watches Troilus, who does not notice her, for his eyes are modestly cast down at the acclaim of the people, enthusiastic over his day's achievements against the Greeks in the field.

> Criseÿda gan al his chere aspien,
> And leet it so softe in hire herte synke,
> That to hireself she seyde, "Who yaf me drynke?"
>   (II.649–651)

Lowes is mainly concerned with the medical doctrine behind the lines of *The Knight's Tale,* which, like so much else in the poem, is directly relevant to *Troilus.* A late, but clear, statement of the process occurs in Book III of Castiglione's *Il Libro del Cortegiano.* See *The Book of the Courtier,* trans. Sir Thomas Hoby, intro. W. H. D. Rouse (London: Dent, 1928), pp. 246–247.

11. The idea that the heart was the eye of the breast, or that the heart itself had eyes, is interesting because of the explicit connection of vision with the seat of love. The heart is often reported in Middle English texts to have eyes; see the relevant citations in the *MED* under *ei.* The usage is traditional and is common in the fathers. It occurs, for example, in Jerome's commentary on Isaiah: "Istos cordis oculos et sponsa habebat in Cantico canticorum, cui sponsus dixit: *Vulnerasti cor meum, soror mea sponsa, uno ex oculis tuis,*" *S. Hieronymi Presbyteri Opera,* Pars 2, *Commentariorum in Esaiam Libri I–XI,* Corpus Christianorum, Series Latina, vol. 73 (Turnholt: Brepols, 1963), Book I.1, ll. 42–45, p. 6. The verse from the Song of Songs, 4:9, may be the most important single source for the idea of love as a wound in the heart inflicted by the eyes of the beloved. References to *oculi cordis* are common in Augustine; see, for example, *Sermo* 159 (Caput 3.3) *Patrologia Latina,* ed. J. P. Migne, 38, col. 869, *Sermo* 286 (Caput 8.6) *PL* 38, col. 1300, *Epistola* 147 (Caput 17.41), the famous *De Vivendo Deo, PL* 33, col. 615, and other references given in the index to Augustine in *PL* 46, cols. 469–470.

In her the process of love is slower (II.673–679) than ir
lus, and she is deliberate and cautious before committin
self, unlike him whose love is a headlong, final plunge from the
first. Her measured reaction may be due to the fact that his eyes
with their streams from his heart are not on hers, and she does
not at once suffer lover's sickness as a sudden onslaught. Her
love is also wavering, "Now was hire herte warm, now was it
cold" (II.698). Her mood shifts back and forth. In this unde-
cided state she leaves the window (II.809–812). The vacilla-
tion here is a hint of the variable nature of her heart which
leads her, eventually, to forego Troilus when the circumstances
turn against their love.

She goes to her garden and hears Antigone singing a lyric
vowing service to love.

> But I with al myn herte and al my myght,
> As I have seyd, wol love unto my laste,
> My deere herte, and al myn owen knyght,
> In which myn herte growen is so faste,
> And his in me, that it shal evere laste.   (II.869–873)

These lines make a strong impression on Criseyde; the suggestion of exchange of hearts is probably what prompts Criseyde's
subsequent dream, for she is acute in picking up hints and then
in acting on them. The development of her awakening love for
Troilus is summarized a few lines later by the narrator.

> But every word which that she of hire herde,
> She gan to prenten in hire herte faste,
> And ay gan love hire lasse for t'agaste
> Than it dide erst, and synken in hire herte,
> That she wex somewhat able to converte.   (II.899–903)

The dream of the eagle that changes hearts with her is a particularly vivid and specific manifestation of the nucleus, and it
further inclines her to love Troilus.

> And as she slep, anonright tho hire mette
> How that an egle, fethered whit as bon,
> Under hire brest his longe clawes sette,

And out hire herte he rente, and that anon,
And dide his herte into hire brest to gon,
Of which she nought agroos, ne nothyng smerte;
And forth he fleigh, with herte left for herte. (II.925–931)

Here the exchange of hearts happens in a dream in which the
white eagle stands for Troilus. In Book III the exchange is carried out symbolically, a token of the deep love that has by then
developed between the pair. A similar symbolic exchange accounts for the *hert-huntyng* of *The Book of the Duchess* and is
so important to Chaucer's poetic treatment of love that some
discussion of it is necessary here, but is best left to the end.

In Book II the development of Criseyde's love is described
in terms of her heart; and we see how it arises, less from Pandare's urgings than from a series of chance circumstances: the
glimpse of Troilus from her window, Antigone's song, and the
dream of the eagle. One characteristic of this development is her
wavering attitude, which is particularly clear as she debates with
herself over sixteen stanzas beginning at II.694. She balances a
growing emotional involvement with Troilus against her own
circumstances in Troy, the same process that afterward characterizes her waning love for Troilus and her growing involvement
with Diomede in the Greek camp.

Book III begins with the meeting of Troilus and Criseyde at
the house of Deiphebus. The first words that Troilus utters directly to Criseyde are "Ye, swete herte?" (III.69), and this is
the form of address he uses for her, with a few exceptions,
throughout the poem.[12] He calls her *swete herte, dere herte,* or
simply *herte* thirteen times and refers to her the same way, when
she is absent, ten more times. Eight of these references or apos-
trophes to his absent lady are in Book V. The last time he addresses her is at the end of his letter, "And far now wel, myn
owen swete herte" (V.1421); his final words of address to her
are thus the same as his first. Surprisingly enough, Criseyde uses
the word *herte* in addressing Troilus, or referring to him, even

12. The constant address of Troilus by Criseyde as *herte* is noted
by Sanford B. Meech, *Design in Chaucer's Troilus* (Syracuse, N.Y.:
Syracuse University Press, 1959), pp. 315–316.

more frequently. There are thirty-four instances, all of
Books III and IV. The only example in Book V is at line
where Troilus quotes Criseyde's promise to return, a promise
that includes her words to him, "O deere herte swete." The fact
that Criseyde in the Greek camp never refers to Troilus with
the word *herte* bears out the change taking place in her love for
him and reveals the deftness of Chaucer's control of dialogue;
here, as elsewhere, his silences are significant.

After the evening at the house of Deiphebus, the love sickness
of Troilus improves.

> His olde wo, that made his herte swelte,
> Gan tho for joie wasten and tomelte.   (III.347–348)

He is compared by the narrator to "thise holtes and thise hayis"
(III.351) that are dead and dry in winter only to reclothe themselves in green when May returns. In the same way "wax so-
deynliche his herte ful of joie" (III.356).

In the consummation scene during the "smoky reyn"
(III.628) the two lovers refer to their hearts repeatedly. Pandare tells Criseyde that Troilus, who is supposedly out of Troy,
has suddenly arrived because he has heard a report that Criseyde
has taken a lover named Horaste. This unworthy device is
ironic; what is here a complete fabrication becomes fact in the
Greek camp afterward. Her gentle rebuke of Troilus for mis-
trusting her strikes home since he knows she is guiltless and he
feels death's cramp creep "aboute his herte" (III.1069). The
lovers are soon accorded, and Criseyde opens "hire herte, and
tolde hym hire entente" (III.1239). Later she pins to his night-
shirt a brooch of gold and azure in which a ruby "set was lik an
herte" (III.1371), a symbolic gift of her heart to Troilus and
a gift he cherishes faithfully. The two lovers make their fare-
wells as the day approaches. Troilus protests that he feels his
heart break in two (III.1475) and wishes that he were certain that he is as firmly set in her heart as she is in his
(III.1486–89). Her reply is one of the few places where she
abandons her usual circumspection and says that natural order

will be disrupted "er Troilus out of Criseydes herte" (III.1498)
will move, because he is "so depe in-with myn herte grave"
(III.1499).

The book ends with the two in a state of temporary joy.
Criseyde is firmly knotted in the heart of Troilus (III.1730–36);
his subsequent song in praise of love as a universal bond has already been noted, but the last of the four stanzas of this song is
worth quoting here.

> So wolde God, that auctour is of kynde,
> That with his bond Love of his vertu liste
> To cerclen hertes alle, and faste bynde,
> That from his bond no wight the wey out wiste;
> And hertes colde, hem wolde I that he twiste
> To make hem love, and that hem liste ay rewe
> On hertes sore, and kepe hem that ben trewe!
>
> (III.1765–71)

The emphasis on *hertes* is Chaucer's addition to the original,
which mentions *animos* but once.

> O felix hominum genus,
> si uestros animos amor
> quo caelum regitur regat! [13]

In his *Boece* Chaucer is more literal with the passage and ren-
ders *uestros animos* as "yowr corages" (II, metrum 8, 26). The
added emphasis on *herte* in the song indicates that Troilus re-
gards his love as part of the ordering bond of universal love;
the song also bears out the invocation in the Prologue of Book
III to the planet Venus and her universal power in love. The
third book ends quietly with the lovers together.

> And Troilus in lust and in quiete
> Is with Criseyde, his owen herte swete. (III.1819–20)

---

13. *Philosophiae consolatio,* ed. Ludwig Bieler, Corpus Christianorum,
Series Latina, 94 (Turnholt: Brepols, 1957), II, metrum 8, ll. 28–30,
p. 36.

The ideas in the third book are related to those in *The Knight's Tale,* and comparison of the two is instructive, because the bond of love in *Troilus* also has a dark aspect; Troy is a besieged city, and the Trojans "alle and some/In prisoun ben," as Diomede in later days cruelly points out to Criseyde (V.883–884), a situation brought about in the first instance by the love of Paris for Helen and the harsh consequences for all concerned.

Bondage in Troilus is the subject of an admirable paper by Stephen A. Barney,[14] who shows that there are three types of bondage evident throughout the poem. The first type is the bondage of the world controlled by fortune, who binds all creation to her mutable wheel; this category includes the Boethian ideas of order coming from the stars, "the faire cheyne of love" discussed as the nucleus of *The Knight's Tale.* Second is the bond of earthly love, in literal language, the attractive net of sexuality. Third is the snare of sin and, ultimately, of the devil. The heart is involved in all three types of bondage, for the heart is what is caught, whether by the world that leads it to the devil or by the woman who may do the same, although the woman may also lead the heart to God, as happens to Troilus.

Including three variant readings — which might well be accepted on the basis of the present discussion — there are ninety-six uses of the words *herte* or *hertes* in Book III alone. The concentration and substantial use of the term at each crucial stage of the action are here, as in Books I and II, significant. Although only a fraction of the instances in the first three books has been discussed, the evidence indicates that the nucleus of the poem is the heart.

Book IV adds further evidence, but it can be presented briefly. Here the second sorrow of Troilus begins when the Trojan parliament agrees to exchange Criseyde for Antenor. Troilus is compared to a wild bull "idarted to the herte" (IV.240). His eyes stream like wells "for piete of herte" (IV.246), and his heart is twisted and vexed with torment. He beseeches his soul to "fle forth out of myn herte" (IV.306) to follow Criseyde,

14. "Troilus Bound," *Speculum,* 47 (1972), 445–458. Relevant studies are cited there; of particular interest is Pierre Courcelle, "Tradition platonicienne et traditions chrétiennes du corps-prison (Phédon 62b; Cratyle 400c)," *Revue des Études Latines,* 43 (1966 for 1965), 406–443.

and he prays that she will receive it when "myn herte dieth" (IV.319).

On hearing the news of the exchange, Criseyde is, as usual with her, afraid, but her heart remains firmly fixed on Troilus.

> As she that hadde hire herte and al hire mynde
> On Troilus iset so wonder faste,
> That al this world ne myghte hire love unbynde,
> Ne Troilus out of hire herte caste,
> She wol ben his, while that hire lif may laste.
>   (IV.673–677)

So long as she remains with Troilus she is steadfast. She ends her soliloquizing complaint by wondering how the "tendre herte" (IV.795) of Troilus will sustain her departure.

Pandare comes to visit her and suggests (IV.935) that she might be able to return immediately after she has gone; from this hint she formulates her plan to return in ten days. Pandare goes to Troilus and says that she

> Hath somwhat in hire hertes privete,
> Wherwith she kan, if I shal right arede,
> Destourbe al this of which thow art in drede.
>   (IV.1111–13)

Her "hertes privete" does indeed bring Troilus out of his distress, but in a way very different from what Pandare supposes as he speaks. Her heart changes and leads to the death of Troilus. The narrator says that her plan was made in good intent and that her heart was faithful (IV.1417) when she spoke. Troilus hears the plan "with herte and erys spradde" (IV.1422), but is loath to let her go.

> His herte mysforyaf hym evere mo.
> But fynaly, he gan his herte wreste
> To trusten hire, and took it for the beste.
>   (IV.1426–28)

He agrees to her plan, but continues to have misgivings in his heart (IV.1518–19), which prompts him to steal away with her.

The fourth book ends as they make their last private farewell, very different from the joyous end of the third book. The difference, as might by now be expected, is specifically stated in terms of his heart.

> For whan he saugh that she ne myghte dwelle,
> Which that his soule out of his herte rente,
> Withouten more, out of the chaumbre he wente.
> (IV.1699–1701)

In the fifth book Criseyde departs, escorted by Diomede, who woos her with practiced and cynical swiftness, the competitive urgency of an army-camp seduction. He does not suffer lover's malady; he merely sets about winning her with what seems like complete emotional detachment. His calculating smoothness is a complete contrast to the spontaneous blundering of Troilus in the first part of the poem. He speaks about his heart twice to Criseyde (V.138 and 156), but there is little evidence that his words reflect any true bond of love in his heart. The only metaphoric knots he ties are to a fish hook or in a net to catch Criseyde.

> This Diomede, of whom yow telle I gan,
> Goth now withinne hymself ay arguynge
> With al the sleghte, and al that evere he kan,
> How he may best, with shortest taryinge,
> Into his net Criseydes herte brynge.
> To this entent he koude nevere fyne;
> To fisshen hire, he leyde out hook and lyne. (V.771–777)

For Diomede the bond of love is not the great chain of being, but merely a snare for catching delicacies.

Troilus, meanwhile, suffers real affliction at heart; the contrast between the two men is reinforced by this difference. After Criseyde's exchange, he returns to his palace "with a swollen herte" (V.201) and turns on his bed like Ixion on the wheel. Although weeping assuages his heart a bit (V.214–215), he laments that he is dying.

> O herte myn, Criseyde, O swete fo!
> O lady myn, that I love and na mo!
> To whom for evermo myn herte I dowe,
> Se how I dey, ye nyl me nat rescowe!   (V.228–231)

He suffers a tremor "about his herte" (V.255) and is so full of despair that he gives Pandare instructions for his funeral pyre. He asks that the ashes of his heart be sent in a golden urn to Criseyde (V.309–315); this gesture, if carried out, would actualize the metaphoric gift of his heart often alluded to earlier in the poem. His thoughts and love are all on her.

> For evere in oon his herte pietous
> Ful bisyly Criseyde, his lady, soughte.
> On hire was evere al that his herte thoughte.
>   (V.451–453)

He suffers continuing affliction in his heart; for example, when he visits the barred palace of Criseyde, "Hym thoughte his sorwful herte braste a-two" (V.530) and "his herte gan to colde" (V.535).

Although Criseyde worries about Troilus, her heart is so filled with fear that she is paralyzed, caught between desire to return to Troy and fear of exposing herself in the attempt. Her situation in the Greek camp is the reverse of what it was in Troy, and circumstances turn her away from Troilus, not toward him. Within two months her heart has let her love for Troilus slide away: "bothe Troilus and Troie town/Shal knotteles thoroughout hire herte slide" (V.768–769). This reference is to the bond of love which should be knit and tied in her heart. A few lines later she is described as "Tendre-herted, slydynge of corage" (V.825); the sense is that her heart is too weak and soft to stand adverse circumstances and lets slip the bond of love. She is sliding of heart and does not keep the knot of love knit tight. The knot in the heart, without its sexual implications, was borrowed from *Troilus and Criseyde* by Thomas Usk and used in his *Testament of Love* as the central metaphor for stable, binding love.

Diomede keeps up his insistence that she let her circumstances rule her heart. She yields to his influence and begins to adapt her emotions to her new situation. At lines 953–954 she is said to have "hire herte on Troilus/So faste, that ther may it non arace." Yet in the speech that follows she denies to Diomede ever having loved anyone but her husband, already dead when the poem starts.

> "I hadde a lord, to whom I wedded was,
> The whos myn herte al was, til that he deyde;
> And other love, as help me now Pallas,
> Ther in myn herte nys, ne nevere was."   (V.975–978)

The narrator disclaims knowledge of whether or not she gave her heart to Diomede (V.1050), but she does vow to be true to him, "To Diomede algate I wol be trewe" (V.1071); this vow seems based on a more superficial love than she had for Troilus and is even less likely to be one she can keep. Certainly in the literary tradition subsequent to Chaucer she becomes regarded as a wavering woman, loose in the bonds of love, a view taken of her, for example, by Ulysses in Shakespeare's *Troilus and Cressida.*

> Fie, fie upon her!
> There's language in her eye, her cheek, her lip;
> Nay, her foot speaks. Her wanton spirits look out
> At every joint and motive of her body.[15]

On the last day of the period in which Criseyde promised to return to Troy she talks with Diomede and agrees to see him again the next day, the eleventh, thereby effectively abandoning any real plan to go back to Troy.

Throughout the period of waiting the faithful Troilus is torn between hope and dread. "Bitwixen hope and drede his herte lay" (V.1207; cf. V.1102 and 1118). His affliction grows worse when she does not keep her promise.

15. *The Complete Works of Shakespeare,* ed. George Lyman Kittredge (Boston: Ginn, [1936]), IV.v.54–57, p. 911.

> His hope al clene out of his herte fledde;
> He nath wheron now lenger for to honge;
> But for the peyne hym thoughte his herte bledde.
>
> (V.1198–1200)

As time goes on he realizes that she will not return as she had promised. His disability is obvious to all, for he is thin, pale, and so feeble that he walks with a crutch; *loveris maladye* has beset him again. Whenever asked about his sickness, he says that "his harm was al aboute his herte" (V.1225) and that "he felte a grevous maladie/Aboute his herte, and fayn he wolde dye" (V.1231–32). His dream of the boar which embraces Criseyde makes him so fear that she has turned her heart elsewhere that he writes her a letter filled with references to their hearts. He ends the letter "And far now wel, myn owen swete herte" (V.1421). As noted earlier, his last words of direct address to her are the same as his first in Book III. Cassandra interprets the dream correctly, adding a bit of information that the narrator claimed not to know, "This Diomede hire herte hath, and she his" (V.1517).

Troilus returns vindictively to war, but his heart is firmly fixed on Criseyde (V.1571). His remaining slight hope is finally dashed when he sees on a coat taken from Diomede in battle the same pin he had given Criseyde the morning she left Troy. This discovery convinces him at last of her "hertes variaunce" (V.1670), and yet he remains true to her, exclaiming to the absent Criseyde that he cannot "withinne myn herte fynde/To unloven yow a quarter of a day" (V.1697–98). He dies in battle, and his soul ascends into the heaven; he gets what he freely chose, enduring and stable love, but not where he looked for it with Criseyde. From on high his spirit laughs at those who weep at his death and, if I understand the difficult syntax correctly, urges that all ought "oure herte on heven caste" (V.1825). The presence of the nucleus in the epilogue reinforces the now general view that it is an integral part of the poem, not a loosely attached palinode. The point is that the heart, as seat of love, should be fixed on Christ "For he nyl falsen no wight, dar I seye,/That wol his herte al holly on hym leye" (V.1845–46).

The same point is made in more poetic language in the famous stanza just before.

> O yonge, fresshe folkes, he or she,
> In which that love up groweth with youre age,
> Repeyreth hom fro worldly vanyte,
> And of youre herte up casteth the visage
> To thilke God that after his ymage
> Yow made, and thynketh al nys but a faire
> This world, that passeth soone as floures faire.
>
> (V.1835–41)

The "visage" "of youre herte" recalls the reference in the first book to the heart as the "brestes ye."

There are repeated, specific textual references that show how the heart is the nucleus of *Troilus and Criseyde* and controls the main narrative development of the poem. The word is so ordinary that readers miss its pervasive force and frequency in the text; first reaction to the data, once they are presented and analyzed, tends to be surprise. The analysis here is incomplete, because less than half the more than 350 occurrences of the word are discussed. The significance of this nucleus is clear, nevertheless. The heart is source and seat of love and makes man subject to love's universal bond. Since earthly love is imperfect, love's bond may, for a time, be mocked, as Troilus mocks, or it may allow for some sliding, as Criseyde slides. The self-absorbed Troilus mocks what he does not understand, and for a time he suffers unrequited love for Criseyde; this is his first sorrow. She loves him for a time, but her sliding heart lets slip the bond. Again he suffers unrequited love for Criseyde; this is his second sorrow. He dies, and his soul ascends to the stable love of the heavens. In the process sorrow is revealed as a means to higher love, as the narrator observed, "sondry peynes bryngen folk to hevene" (III.1204), both worldly and divine. The poem shows the continuity as well as the progression from worldly to divine love, a progression not unlike the one presented in *The Divine Comedy,* if less explicit and systematic in the English poem than in the Italian.

Chaucer's use of the heart and the chain as nucleus metaphors for love and order belongs to long-existing literary traditions. Lovejoy's classic study, already cited, is a systematic history of the idea of the chain as a metaphor for order and degree. There is no equivalent single work on the heart as the seat of love, but enough studies have been written to make clear the long history of the idea.[16] One aspect of this tradition does need some attention here, the tradition of the movable heart exchanged in love.

The exchange of hearts is implicit in the *hert-huntyng* of *The Book of the Duchess* and explicit in *Troilus and Criseyde*. Not surprisingly, the idea of a movable heart occurs in religious writing long before the rise of aristocratic love poetry. An example is a passage in a homily by Gregory the Great on the Ascension.

Unde, fratres charissimi, oportet ut illuc sequamur corde, ubi eum corpore ascendisse credimus.[17]

16. Of particular help are two long papers by Xenja von Ertzdorff, "Das Herz in der lateinisch-theologischen und frühen volkssprachigen religiösen Literatur," *Beiträge zur Geschichte der deutsche Sprache und Literatur*, 84 (1962), 249–301, and "Die Dame im Herzen und das Herz bei der Dame. Zur Verwendung des Begriffs, Herz in der höfischen Liebeslyrik des 11. und 12. Jahrhunderts," *Zeitschrift für deutsche Philologie*, 84 (1965), 6–46. Von Ertzdorff traces the literary use of the heart from the Bible through the fathers up to the high Middle Ages. The apparatus provides useful bibliographical information. I am indebted to Prof. James Rochester Shaw of the University of Rochester for these references and helpful advice on medieval medical views on the heart.

17. Sermon 29, In Ascensione Domini, *PL* 76, col. 1219. This passage is the source for Cynewulf's *Christ II*, lines 751–755:

Is us þearf micel

þæt we mid heortan	hælo secen,
þær we mid gæste	georne gelyfað
þæt þæt hælobearn	heonan up stige
mid usse lichoman,	lifgende god.

The Exeter Book, ed. George Philip Krapp and Elliott van Kirk Dobbie (New York: Columbia University Press, 1936), p. 24. For a discussion of this connection, see Colin Chase, "God's Presence through Grace as the theme of Cynewulf's *Christ II* and the relationship of this theme to *Christ I* and *Christ III*," *Anglo-Saxon England*, 3 (1974), forthcoming.

The actual exchange of hearts with Christ can be found in saints' lives, notably in that of Catherine of Siena, whose experience of 1370 is recounted in considerable detail by her contemporary biographer, Raymond of Capua. Christ appeared to her while she prayed, and he removed her heart; she reported the event to her confessor, who merely laughed. She maintained her story, however, and several days later as she finished praying and was emerging from an abstracted meditation, Christ reappeared to her, holding a radiant heart in his hands; he opened her left side again and inserted the heart, telling her that he had given her his own heart which she had prayed to have. Christ then healed her side, but an elongated scar remained as a visible token, afterward seen by many, of the exchange.[18] Exchanges of hearts recounted in medieval literature either have such miraculous aspects of divine intervention or else they are metaphors; there seems to be no indication in medical literature of the period that the heart, like the womb, could move.[19]

As so often happened in the Middle Ages, the religious tra-

18. The material is discussed by Pierre Debongnie, "Commencement et recommencements de la dévotion du coeur de Jésus," in *Le Coeur,* Les Etudes carmélitaines, 29 (1950), 147–192. For the text of the story, see *Acta Sanctorum Aprilis,* ed. J. Carnandet (Paris: Victor Palmé, 1866), III, 907. The feast day of St. Catherine is April 30; the account of her exchange of hearts with Christ is in Part II of her *Vita,* chap. 6, secs. 178–180. See also Jean Leclercq, O.S.B., "Le Sacré-Cœur dans la tradition bénédictine au moyen âge," in *Cor Jesu,* ed. Augustinus Bea, S.J., Hugo Rahner, S.J., Henri Rondet, S.J., and Friedrich Schwendemann, S.J. (Rome: Casa Editrice Herder, [1959]), II, 3–28. Other papers in this collection are also of interest to the subject here.

19. Alfredus Anglicus, for example, in his tract *De Motu Cordis,* written about 1210, reflects medical opinions then current and ultimately derived from Galen; he has nothing whatever about a shift or transfer of the heart; *Des Alfred von Sareshel (Alfredus Anglicus) Schrift De Motu Cordis,* ed. Clemens Baeumker, Beiträge zur Geschichte der Philosophie des Mittelalters, 23 (Münster: Verlag der aschendorffschen Verlagsbuchhandlung, 1923). See also James Otte, "The Life and Writings of Alfredus Anglicus," *Viator,* 3 (1972). Nor does "the cursed monk, daun Constantyn" (*CT,* IV.1810) allude to any exchange of hearts; see Paul Delany, "Constantinus Africanus' *De Coitu*: A Translation," *The Chaucer Review,* 4 (1969), 55–65. For medieval medical opinion on the movable womb, see Vern L. Bullough, "Medieval Medical and Scientific Views of Women," in *Marriage in the Middle Ages,* ed. John Leyerle, *Viator,* 4 (1973).

dition of the exchange of hearts in divine love has parallels in profane love. Sometimes the religious aspects are explicit, such as those evident in *Troilus and Criseyde*. In the first book Troilus prays to the god of love and remarks that he does not know whether Criseyde is a goddess or a woman, a confusion also apparent in Palamon's reactions to Emelye in *The Knight's Tale*; the religious vows that Troilus makes in the consummation scene (III.1254ff.) and his apostrophe to Criseyde's empty palace as a "shryne, of which the seynt is oute" (V.553) are other examples, and the list could be extended. Sometimes the religious aspects are only implied, and the exchange itself indicates a religious devotion in love and the deep bond existing between the man and the woman, especially when they are forced by circumstances to conceal their love or must spend much of the time apart. A familiar example occurs in Chrétien's *Lancelot* when the knight must leave Guenievere after spending the night with her in Meleagant's castle.

> Au lever fu il droiz martirs,
> tant li fu griés li departirs,
> car il i suefre grant martire.
> Ses cuers adés cele part tire
> ou la reïne se remaint.
> N'a pooir que il l'an remaint,
> que la reïne tant li plest
> qu'il n'a talant que il la lest:
> li cors s'an vet, li cuers sejorne.[20]

It cost him such pain to leave her that he suffered a real martyr's agony. His heart now stays where the queen remains; he has not the power to lead it away, for it finds such pleasure in the queen

20. *Les Romans de Chrétien de Troyes,* vol. III: *Le Chevalier de la Charrete,* ed. Mario Roques, Les Classiques Français du Moyen Age, 86 (Paris: Honoré Champion, 1958), ll. 4689–97. The translation is from Chrétien de Troyes, *Arthurian Romances,* trans. W. W. Comfort (London: J. M. Dent, 1914). 329. The motif also occurs in Chrétien's *Yvain* (ll. 2635ff.) and, from there, in Hartmann von Aue's *Iwein.* For other examples of the exchange of hearts, see *La Mort le Roi Artu,* ed. Jean Frappier, 10th ed. (Geneva: Droz, 1956), p. 35, and Juan Ruiz, *Libro de Buen Amor,* ed. and trans. Raymond S. Willis (Princeton: Princeton Univ. Press, [1972]), stanzas 209ff.

that it has no desire to leave her: so his body goes and his heart remains.

An extended treatment of the motif of the exchange of hearts occurs in a work of the fifteenth century, *Le Livre du cueur d'amour espris,* written about 1457 by King René d'Anjou, an allegorical prose account of love interspersed with verse and written in the tradition of the first part of *Le Roman de la Rose.*[21] The exchange of hearts also occurs in more than one fabliau, an indication that the motif was well enough known to make its cynical employment an amusing parody.[22]

Chaucer's use of the heart as the nucleus of a poem about human love, its mutability, and its capacity to lead to divine love thus has historical probability. Both the narrative and the nucleus of *Troilus and Criseyde* are drawn from well-established literary traditions of great antiquity; Chaucer does not so much invent his material as reimagine it. With characteristic economy of means Chaucer put a traditional metaphor at the core of his poem and thereby transformed complex, abstract ideas about love and its relative stability into a nucleus that is so apt and simple that it has remained all but invisible to readers despite its appearance, often in repeated statement, at every crucial turn in the narrative.

In Chaucer's immediate source, *Il Filostrato,* the heart is mainly mentioned in casual references to inner thought or in connection with the affliction of love sickness. There are, however, three times where Troilo refers to Criseida as *cor del corpo mio,* "heart of my body," and two times where Criseida refers

21. For a miniature illustrating this text showing Amour entrusting the heart of the sleeping king to Vif-désir, see Germain Bazin, "En quête du sentiment courtois," in *Le Coeur,* Les Etudes carmélitaines, 29 (1950), 129–146, pl. 1 facing p. 138. Bazin also gives three other plates of late medieval/early renaissance illustrations of the exchange of hearts, or the offer to make such an exchange. In Jeanine Moulin, *Christine de Pisan* (Paris: Seghers, [1962]), the plate facing p. 113 shows Venus, in a circle of stars, collecting hearts in her skirt held up to form a lap; her votaries, both men and women, offer to her their hearts which they hold in the hand.

22. For example, see *Fabliaux: Ribald Tales from the Old French,* trans. Robert Hellman and Richard O'Gorman (New York: Thomas Y. Crowell, [1965]), pp. 137 and 148–149. One of these fabliaux is by Rutebeuf and the other by Gautier le Leu.

ιο him the same way.[23] This expression implies the exchange of hearts, a motif explicit only in Troilo's dream of Criseida and the boar.

> E poi appresso gli parve vedere
>   Sotto a' suoi piè Criseida, alla quale
>   Col grifo il cor traeva, ed al parere
>   Di lui, Criseida di così gran male
>   Non si curava, ma quasi piacere
>   Prendea di ciò che faces l'animale.   (VII.24)

> And then afterward it seemed to him that he saw
> beneath its feet Cressida, whose heart it tore
> forth with its snout. And as it seemed, little
> cared Cressida for so great a hurt, but almost
> did she take pleasure in what the beast was
> doing.

In Chaucer's poem Troilus dreams that Criseyde lies with a boar, but no mention is made of losing her heart. Chaucer uses the motif in Criseyde's dream of the eagle, an episode which is not in *Il Filostrato*. This shift seems to indicate that the episode in *Il Filostrato* provided Chaucer with a hint for his treatment of the heart. Certainly, the shift from animal to bird is indicative of the delicacy of Chaucer's poem in contrast to the vivid sensuality of his source, evident here.

If the hint came from *Il Filostrato,* sustained use of the heart as the nucleus of *Troilus and Criseyde* may be explained by Geoffrey of Vinsauf's advice near the beginning of his *Poetria Nova* on how to start a poem, a passage Chaucer repeated at the end of Book I of *Troilus.*

---

23. *The Filostrato of Giovanni Boccaccio: A Translation with Parallel Text,* Nathaniel Edward Griffin and Arthur Beckwith Myrick (Philadelphia: University of Pennsylvania Press, 1929); the expression occurs in the following stanzas: III.50, IV.90 and 145, V.25 and 59. The *cor/corpus* trope in love poetry is found widely in romance languages and may be no more than an ornament arising from the verbal closeness of the words.

For everi wight that hath an hous to founde
Ne renneth naught the werk for to bygynne
With rakel hond, but he wol bide a stounde,
And sende his hertes line out fro withinne
Aldirfirst his purpos for to wynne.   (I.1065–69) [24]

The Latin phrase translated in line 1068 is *intrinseca linea cordis,* which applies the heart and the bond to the initial act of writing poetry. The suggestion made earlier that *The Canterbury Tales* form a "faire cheyne of love" may have a basis in poetic theory known to Chaucer. If so, the links of *The Canterbury Tales* appear more aptly named than might be thought. The extent of this specific debt to the *Poetria Nova* must not be pressed, however. *The Consolation of Philosophy* has so many passages on order described in terms of bonds and *The Romance of the Rose* sufficient passages on love described in terms of the heart that one need look no further for Chaucer's source of the heart and the chain as organizing metaphors for love and order than in those two works which he translated, works that influenced him profoundly throughout his entire poetic career from first to last.

Chaucer's use of a poetic nucleus illustrates a medieval literary theory that is of more significance than the few lines from the *Poetria Nova.* The heart as nucleus of a poem about love and its variance and the chain as nucleus of a poem about order and its confinement are significant instances of a medieval attitude toward poetic language in which key metaphors such as these were apprehended as we would apprehend abstract statement; the metaphor of the chain would thus be thought to have the same literal truth about the organization of the cosmos that we would find in abstract statements about order and degree. This attitude toward poetic language is the subject of an important paper by Judson B. Allen. Using evidence from medieval

24. For the Latin text see Edmond Faral, *Les arts poétiques du XIIe et du XIIIe siècle* (Paris: É. Champion, 1924), 198: "Si quis habet fundare domum, non currit ad actum/Impetuosa manus: intrinseca linea cordis/Praemetitur opus . . . ." A useful English version is *Poetria Nova of Goeffrey of Vinsauf,* trans. Margaret F. Nims (Toronto: Pontifical Institute of Mediaeval Studies, 1967).

accessus, especially those on hymn collections dating from Hilarius in the twelfth century to Johannes Baptista Cantalycius in the fifteenth, Allen presents evidence that in late medieval poetic theory, the transfer of meaning inherent in metaphor was thought of as the literal truth, because the cosmos "was already, in modern terms, so poetic that there was no need to claim for the poet greater powers than those of an honest reporter." [25] The chain of order and the heart of love were as real to the medieval mind as, for example, were the crystalline spheres of the Ptolemaic universe, which are only metaphoric to us. The analysis here presents independent support and illustration for Allen's analysis by showing that what he suggests about poetic theory can be documented with extensive citation from several works of one of the major philosophical poets of the late medieval period. Chaucer has long been recognized as a philosophical poet, but the centrality of philosophical thought in his poetry has not been grasped, because the essence of his thought has been expressed in the highly creative form of a poetic nucleus. The modern separation of poetic language into concrete and abstract vocabulary is misleading in Chaucer's poetry because of the way that the poetic nucleus is given abstract significance even as it continues to be concrete.

Use of a nucleus in a long text may be a fairly rare occurrence and is difficult to detect in a poem of any considerable complexity.[26] Once found, however, a nucleus can provide a lu-

25. "Commentary as Criticism: Formal Cause, Discursive Form, and the Late Medieval Accessus," in *Acta Conventus Neo-Latini Lovaniensis: Proceedings of the First International Congress of Neo-Latin Studies Louvain 23–28 August 1971,* ed. J. IJsewijn and E. Kessler (Munich: Wilhelm Fink Verlag, 1973), p. 39. The present paper was in substantially finished form when Allen's work first came to my attention as a conference lecture.

26. *The Shipman's Tale* has *dette* as a nucleus, but the poem's relative lack of the usual Chaucerian complexity makes its existence very clear. in this tale *dette* operates at both a commercial and sexual level; the reckoning of the *dette* is another pun with *tailles* referring to tallies, tails, and, perhaps, tales. The point has been discussed before; see Albert H. Silverman, "Sex and Money in Chaucer's *Shipman's Tale," Philological Quarterly,* 32 (1953), 329–336. Janette Richardson, *Blameth Nat Me: A Study of Imagery in Chaucer's Fabliaux* (The Hague: Mouton, 1970), pp. 100–122, discusses image clusters in the tale including those pertaining to *dette.*

cid perception "of a work's centre, the source of its life in all its parts, and response to its total movement" which is Helen Gardner's lucid definition of the purpose of critical activity.[27] The molecular cohesion and focus of the work are, so to speak, apprehended from within, and the reader's basic experience of the text alters as a result. An apprehension of the functions of the heart and the chain in Chaucer's poetry provides a new perspective on familiar material as when the city dweller, long used to a night sky hazy with reflected artificial light, goes into the country and sees, as if with new eyes, the stars come out in the evening sky until the dark is full of light.

27. *The Business of Criticism* (Oxford: Clarendon Press, 1959), p. 23.

In a rather different form this paper was read at the annual meeting of the Mediaeval Academy of America in April 1967. Thanks are due three of my Toronto students, Ms. Linda Marshall, Ms. Anne Quick, and Mr. Gernot Wieland, who have provided me with assistance in the research on the heart in medieval medical and religious writing.

ALAIN RENOIR

The Terror of the Dark Waters: A Note on Virgilian and Beowulfian Techniques

In a brief essay published in 1966,[1] I argued that a somewhat exaggerated concern with imitation, influence, and originality has too often misled literary critics into making originality a criterion for quality, and literary historians — especially those of the comparative ilk — into allowing themselves to neglect the intrinsic values of literature in order to devote their efforts to ferreting out all kinds of influences and proudly exposing minor instances of imitation. I insisted, however, that the comparative analysis of similar elements in texts which need not be genetically related may prove a legitimate and useful critical method, and I suggested that such a comparative examination of the descriptions of Avernus in the *Aeneid* and Grendel's Pond in *Beowulf* would probably bear out my contention. The present note is an attempt at such an examination.

The fact that Hrothgar's account of Grendel's Pond in *Beowulf* (1357b–76a)[2] is somewhat reminiscent of the descrip-

1. Alain Renoir, "Originality, Influence, Imitation: Two Mediaeval Phases," *Proceedings of the IVth Congress of the International Comparative Literature Association* (The Hague: Mouton, 1966), II, 737ff.
2. This and all subsequent references and quotations from *Beowulf* are from the edition by Elliot Van Kirk Dobbie, *Beowulf and Judith,* in

tion of Avernus in the *Aeneid* (VI.237–242)[3] has naturally prompted scholars to surmise the influence of the latter epic upon the former.[4] But the concept of influence, and especially of imitation, in respect to *Beowulf* has become uncertain territory since 1953, when Francis P. Magoun, Jr., advanced the theory that Anglo-Saxon narrative poetry must have been composed according to an oral-formulaic method [5] which would make it almost impossible to determine whether obvious similarities between two poetic texts must be considered, on the one hand, illustrative of influence or actual imitation or, on the other hand, illustrative of the fact that both poets may have drawn their materials from a common fund of formulas and themes. Four years later, Adrien Bonjour referred to the theory as "revolutionary" and asserted that it "raises more questions than it tries to solve. Be this as it may, one thing is certain: there is bound to be some issue, within no distant future, between those critics who still consider *Beowulf* as the work of one author, and read this poem as a structural whole, and the supporters of an orally composed *Beowulf* . . . ." [6] Though Bonjour — who has usually been right — was dead wrong in his unwarranted assumption that the supporters of the oral-formulaic theory must automatically reject single authorship and structural unity, his prediction has come true; and the issue has since been fought over with enough enduring energy to warrant his remarking in 1967 that the controversy showed "no sign of abating." [7] Indeed, it has brought to the lists such formidable

---

Anglo-Saxon Poetic Records, IV (New York: Columbia University Press, 1953). References to other Anglo-Saxon poems are likewise to the texts in the *Poetic Records.*

3. This and all subsequent references and quotations from the *Aeneid* are from the edition by Henri Goelzer (Paris, 1961).

4. See Friedrich Klaeber, *Beowulf and the Fight at Finnsburg* (Boston: Heath, 1941), p. 183, note to lines 1357ff.

5. Francis P. Magoun, Jr., "The Oral-Formulaic Character of Anglo-Saxon Narrative Poetry," *Speculum,* 27 (1953), 446–467, and subsequent essays in *Speculum,* 30 (1955), 49–63, and *Neuphilologische Mitteilungen,* 56 (1955), 81–90.

6. Adrien Bonjour, *"Beowulf* and the Beasts of Battle," *PMLA,* 72 (1957), 563–573, especially 563–564.

7. Adrien Bonjour, "Jottings on *Beowulf* and the Aesthetic Approach," in *Old English Poetry*, ed. Robert P. Creed (Providence: Brown University Press, 1967), p. 179.

scholars as the late Arthur G. Brodeur, who referred to Magoun's theory as a "dubious assumption," [8] and Robert P. Creed, who set out to establish its validity by actually composing an oral-formulaic poem in Anglo-Saxon.[9] The publication of Albert B. Lord's epoch-making *The Singer of Tales*[10] has shown beyond doubt that an unlettered singer can indeed produce a long and carefully structured oral-formulaic poem; and Stanley Greenfield, Tauno Mustanoja, Robert Diamond, and Morton Bloomfield are among those who have entered the debate at one point or another.[11] The affair has appropriately had its own inconclusive oral stage, in the form of papers delivered by Larry Benson and Robert Creed at the 1964 convention of the Modern Language Association. Whereas Benson brilliantly and convincingly demonstrated statistically that certain religious poems which were presumably written reveal as high a formulaic count as *Beowulf* and went on to suggest that Anglo-Saxon poetry in general and the Cynewulfian corpus in particular must therefore be considered written rather than oral,[12] Creed equally brilliantly and convincingly rejected the suggestion that the pen had much to do with composing the bulk of Anglo-Saxon poetry. Status is as transitory a commodity today as it was in the

8. Arthur G. Brodeur, "A Study of Diction and Style in Three Anglo-Saxon Narrative Poems," in *Nordica et Anglica,* ed. Allan H. Orrick (The Hague: Mouton, 1968), p. 113. In *The Art of Beowulf* (Berkeley: University of California Press, 1959), p. 3, Brodeur accepts the theory with serious reservations.

9. Robert P. Creed, "The Making of an Anglo-Saxon Poem," *ELH,* 26 (1959), 445–454.

10. Albert B. Lord, *The Singer of Tales* (Cambridge, Mass.: Harvard University Press, 1960), e.g., pp. 13–29.

11. See, e.g., Stanley B. Greenfield, "The Formulaic Expression of the Theme of 'Exile' in Anglo-Saxon Poetry," *Speculum,* 30 (1955), 200–206. Greenfield's account of the principles of formulaic composition, in his *A Critical History of Old-English Literature* (New York, 1965), pp. 74–76, is especially useful. See also Tauno F. Mustanoja, "The Presentation of Ancient Germanic Poetry — Looking for Parallels: A Note on the Presentation of Finnish Runos," *Neuphilologische Mitteilungen,* 60 (1959), 1–11; Robert E. Diamond, "The Diction of the Signed Poems of Cynewulf," *Philological Quarterly,* 38 (1959), 228–241, and *The Diction of the Anglo-Saxon Metrical Psalms* (The Hague: Mouton, 1963); and Morton W. Bloomfield's review of Robert Creed's *Old English Poetry,* in *Comparative Literature,* 21 (1969), 285–286.

12. See Larry D. Benson, "The Literary Character of Anglo-Saxon Formulaic Poetry," *PMLA,* 81 (1966), 334–341, especially 340.

days of *Beowulf* (e.g., 1760bff.), however, and even statistics
seem to have lost some of their former claim to infallibility, so
that the validity of Benson's empirical argument was assessed
one way by Lionel Friedman in 1967 and another by Joseph
Duggan in 1973.[13]

In view of the blatant and apparently irreconcilable disagree-
ment between the experts, it would be foolish to base a critical
evaluation of the description of Grendel's Pond either on the
assumption that it is a conscious literary imitation of Virgil's
description of Avernus or on the contrary assumption that it is
the exploitation of an oral-formulaic theme by a poet who had
never heard of the *Aeneid*.[14] If the passage has significant qualities of its own, it will surely retain them in either case, and
comparison with its Latin counterpart will help us detect and
evaluate them.

Comparison between the Latin and Anglo-Saxon texts reveals
obvious similarities: both passages describe a body of black water surrounded by foreboding cliffs and darkling woods; either
vapors or waves rise to the skies; and the place is so weird that
no normal animal-life dares approach it. Beyond these admittedly striking resemblances, the two passages are vastly different, and I believe that the differences are much more significant
than the similarities.

Perhaps the most obvious quality of the picture which Virgil
draws for us is the sense of deathlike stillness which it conveys:

13. Lionel J. Friedman, in a review of Renate Hitze's *Studien zu
Sprache und Stil der Kampfschilderungen in dem "Chansons de Geste,"*
Romance Philology, 22 (1969), 334–336; and Joseph J. Duggan, *The
Song of Roland: Formulaic Style and Poetic Craft* (Berkeley: University
of California Press, 1973), pp. 30–33. For an up-to-date glance at the
arguments of both sides of the question, see also Duggan's "Oral Composition in the Old French Epic: A Computer-Aided Method of Formula Analysis," *Hasifrut,* 4 (1973), 488–496.
14. To this day, the clearest illustration of the use of a common formulaic theme by Anglo-Saxon poets is probably David K. Crowne's "The
Hero on the Beach," *Neuphilologische Mitteilungen,* 61 (1960), 367–372.
In my own footnote to Crowne's essay, "Oral-Formulaic Theme Survival," *Neuphilologische Mitteilungen,* 65 (1964), 70–75, I have tried
to show that a similar phenomenon may be found in the *Nibelungenlied.*
Attention is called to Donald K. Fry's brilliant essay, "Old English Formulas and Systems," *English Studies,* 48 (1967), 193–204.

> Spelunca alta fuit uastoque immanis hiatu,
> scrupea, tuta lacu nigro nemorumque tenebris,
> quam super haud ullae poterant impune uolantes
> tendere iter pennis: talis sese halitus atris
> faucibus effundens supera ad conuexa ferebat:
> unde locum Grai dixerunt nomine Aornon. (VI.237–243)

Here there is no life in sight, the point of view is totally inde-
terminate, and the only suggestion of motion comes through the
mention of the noxious vapors rising toward the sky. Along with
the darkness of the waters, the oppressive stillness and the chill
impersonality of the picture are clearly connotative of death and
thus set the tone for Aeneas' descent into the land of the dead.
Within context, the effectiveness of the passage lies not so much
in its intrinsic artistry as in its function as a tone-setting preface
to the subsequent action. Furthermore, we must note that this
is the only account which Virgil gives of Avernus and that we
are never allowed to go through the motion of approaching the
lake ourselves. If we ever get the faint sensation that we are
moving toward it, we do so only when we are told that the two
doves that guide Aeneas toward the golden bough fly off to their
goal as they reach the unhealthy caves by the lake:

> Inde ubi uenere ad fauces graue olentis Auerni,
> tollunt se celeres liquidumque per aera lapsae
> sedibus optatis geminae super arbore sidunt,
> discolor unde auri per ramos aura refulsit. (VI.201–204)

As a result of this technique, we sense no tangible location for
the otherworldly stillness that faces us. This surrealistic quality
of the scene reminds the modern reader of Jean Cocteau at his
best; and we should not be surprised at the coincidence, for it
is here that Aeneas will enter a world so far beyond mere physical reality that he will have to leave it through the Gate of
Ivory:

> His ibi tum natum Anchises unaque Sibyllam
> prosequitur dictis portaque emittit eburna.
>   (VI.897–898)

Thus, the initial impression created by Virgil's account of Avernus is one of awe-inspiring stillness. In contrast, the initial impression created by Hrothgar's account of Grendel's Pond is one of terrifying motion:

>   Hie dygel lond
> warigeað, wulfhleoþu,   windige næssas,
> frecne fengelad,   ðær fyrgenstream
> under næssa genipu   niþer gewiteð,
> flod under foldan.   Nis þæt feor heonon
> milgemearces   þæt se mere standeð;
> ofer þæm hongiað   hrinde bearwas,
> wudu wyrtum fæst   wæter oferhelmað.
> þær mæg nihta gehwæm   niðwundor seon,
> fyr on flode.   No þæs frod leofað
> gumena bearna,   þæt þone grund wite;
> ðeah þe hæðstapa   hundum geswenced,
> heorot hornum trum,   holtwudu sece,
> feorran geflymed,   ær he feorh seleð,
> aldor on ofre,   ær he in wille
> hafelan hydan.   Nis þæt heoru stow!
> Þonon yðgeblond   up astigeð
> won to wolcnum,   þonne wind styreþ,
> lað gewidru,   oðþæt lyft drysmaþ,
> roderas reotað.   (1357b–76a)

We have seen that in the Latin the only suggestion of motion is the faint rising of vapors from the lake (VI.240–241). In the Anglo-Saxon text, on the contrary, the second line hits the audience with all the wild force of the wind sweeping across a headland (1358b), and the remainder of the passage presents us with a bewildering succession of physically and emotionally striking motions leading to the grand conclusion that the very heavens weep (1376a). Of the total twenty lines, twelve specifically describe some sort of motion: in addition to the blowing wind at the opening and the weeping heavens in the conclusion, we see a torrent plunging under the earth (1360b), fire burning on the water (1366a), a stag pursued by hounds (1368a–70a) and panting by the side of the Pond (1370b–72a), dark waters rising to the sky as the wind blows (1373a–74b), and the air itself turning into darkness (1375b). We must further note that the density of motion increases as the passage progresses: whereas only three half-lines (1358b, 1360b, 1366a) suggest motion in the first eleven lines (1357b–67b), twelve half-lines (1368b, 1369b–72a, 1374b, 1375b–76a) do so in the last nine lines.

In contrast to the surrealistic imprecision through which we perceive the stillness of Avernus, the sense of overwhelming motion which characterizes the account of Grendel's Pond is brought to us through a series of sharply delineated visual and auditory images. We can hear the howling wind and see the terrified stag, and we can clearly contrast the tumbling mountain stream to the motionless forest overhanging the Pond (1363a–64b). Only three statements in the passage fail to evoke a sharply delineated image: the mention of the proximity of the Pond (1361b–62b), the assertion that no man has explored the bottom of the Pond (1366b–67b), and the conclusion that the Pond is not a safe place (1372b). Two of these, however, are mere statements of empirical facts, and the last is an effective and appropriate formulaic summation of the description which precedes it.[15] In addition to its sharpness, the entire image pattern seems designed to evoke a weird but entirely realistic total picture, for the things which we are forced to visualize are without exception taken from the realm of human experience. After all, a stag at bay was by no means an uncommon sight until the nineteenth century; and one need not range far afield to meet the man who has heard the weeping of a storm and seen waves stirred upwards by the wind, the air grow dark at the approach of a thunderstorm, windswept headlands, mountain streams, or even the multicolored fires that burst out of ponds at night and are still taken as signs of the fairy world by some villagers today.

Just as we have noted the impersonality of the Latin account, so we must note the opposite quality in the Anglo-Saxon. With the statement that no human being, however wise, has ever explored the bottom of the Pond (1366b–67b), the poet makes man himself the scale against which the weirdness of the scene must be measured and beyond which it goes, with the result that the audience becomes irresistibly involved by association. This

15. E.g., *Beowulf*, 11b, *Dream of the Rood*, 56b, *Genesis B*, 318b, etc., etc.

personal involvement gains immediacy with the next six lines
(1368a–72a), as we are made to share the despair of the lone
stag who chooses to be torn to pieces by the dogs rather than
face the horror of the Pond. In addition, the series of terrifying
motions whose realism we have noted above somehow takes on
the air of conscious human action, as when the heavens weep.
The result is that, whereas the atmosphere of the Latin passage
is awesome and remote, that of the Anglo-Saxon is terrifying
and immediate. This observation brings to the fore a paradox:
whereas the Latin account remains within the realm of reasonable possibility despite its surrealism, the Anglo-Saxon is clearly
outside the realm of reasonable possibility despite its realism.

Virgil, I have argued above, never allows his reader to go
through the actual motion of approaching Avernus; he merely
lets him know that the lake is within proximity and then presents him with the still picture which has already been discussed.
The Anglo-Saxon poet, on the contrary, takes us through the
motions of a progressive approach to the Pond. To draw an
analogy from the visual arts, we might say that Virgil presents us
with a simple photograph and the Anglo-Saxon poet with a
motion picture. If we imagine a motion-picture screen before us,
we begin with a general view of the entire area (1347b–61a),
and we then proceed in the direction of the Pond (1361b–62b)
until we come within sight of its waters (1363a–67b). The view
then narrows to a close-up of the stag on the shore (1368a–
72b) before moving on to the waves (1373a–75a), whose rising crest we follow up to the sky and away from the Pond
(1375b–76a). It is as if a camera mounted on an airplane had
swept down on the territory, centered upon its target, and swept
up again — and all this in a single, uninterrupted motion. If we
recall my previous remarks about the distribution of images, we
must now note that the image density increases as the view
narrows upon the center of action. I submit that this masterful
technique is largely responsible for the tremendous impact of
the Anglo-Saxon passage: instead of being presented with a still
picture as in the *Aeneid,* the audience of *Beowulf* is irresistibly
swept toward the mounting terror of the scene. This technique,
incidentally, is the same which Sergei Eisenstein admiringly
noted in *Paradise Lost* and which led Joseph Frank to entitle his

famous essay on *Madame Bovary* and other recent works, "Spatial Forms in Modern Literature." [16] Since both Eisenstein and Frank were clearly indebted to Lessing, to whom the analogy of the motion-picture screen was regrettably not available, it is relevant to the present discussion that the technique in question corresponds precisely to this mobility of point of view which is offered in *Laocoön* as the very essence of poetry in contrast to the rigidity of painting. [17]

The foregoing observations call forth another and a last consideration of the stag passage. When Virgil writes that the birds do not fly over Avernus because of the noxious vapors that emanate from the lake, he accomplishes two things. In the first place, he suggests that the lake is death to normal living organisms, so that "pius Aeneas" (VI.232) will approach it only through heavenly decree and his own great courage, as the words of the Sibyl will make clear a few lines later:

> "Procul o, procul este, profani,"
> conclamat uates, "totoque absistite loco;
> tuque inuade uiam uaginaque eripe ferrum:
> nunc animis opus, Aenea, nunc pectore firmo."
>
> (VI258–261)

In the second place, he takes our attention *away* from the lake and toward the sky. In contrast, the Anglo-Saxon poet uses two different positive images to accomplish what Virgil accomplishes with the single negative image of the absent birds: the lone stag's willingness to die on the shore rather than to take the plunge impresses us with the terrifying quality of the Pond, and the rising waves take our attention away from the Pond and toward the sky. The device presents at least two obvious advantages. The first is that we are permitted to dwell momentarily upon the stag before the waves themselves force our attention toward the sky. The result is that, in contradistinction to the

16. Sergei M. Eisenstein, *The Film Sense,* trans. and ed. Jay Leyda (New York: Harcourt, 1947), pp. 57–62; Joseph Frank, "Spatial Forms in Modern Literature," *Sewanee Review,* Spring, Summer, and Autumn, 1945.

17. Gotthold Ephraim Lessing, *Laocoön,* trans. Ellen Frothingham (New York: Noonday, 1957), e.g., pp. 21 and 67.

Virgilian technique, the Beowulfian technique allows us to visualize almost concurrently both the result of terror (the stag)
and the cause of it (the waters). The second is that, whereas the
absent birds of the *Aeneid* can obviously convey no emotion of
their own, the stag of *Beowulf* delivers a formidable emotional
impact.

Though the Anglo-Saxon audience had neither *Sir Gawain
and the Green Knight* to show them the deer that "brayen &
bleden" pitifully as "ay rachches in a res radly hem folȝes" nor
Alfred de Vigny to sing for them "les pleurs de la biche aux
abois," [18] they had surely seen, or at least heard of, the heart-
rending and humanlike tears which a deer sheds when his last
stand against men and dogs has proved futile. They must accordingly have been aware of the fact that the animal at bay
usually makes no effort to ward off death but rather submits
without further fight to his inevitable fate. Within the context of
a poem where fate is specifically mentioned eleven times and
where the hero who is now about to grant a request to pursue a
man-eating monster to the bottom of the Pond has already expressed his conviction that "Gæð a wyrd swa hio scel" (455b),
the image with which we are presented acquires immediate and
powerful significance.

Although the principal aspects of the entire passage under discussion have already been mentioned, a closer analysis of the
concluding four and one-half lines (1372a–76b) is in order here
because much of their effectiveness depends on some of the
elements of the stag image which have merely been pointed out
in the preceding paragraph. As already noted, the account of the
stag concludes with the statement that he will rather let himself
be torn to pieces by the dogs than "in . . ./hafelan hydan"
(1371b–72a). We should further note that it is so organized that
the mention of the beautiful animal's head occurs as the first
word of an initial half-line, receives the accent on the initial syllable, and carries the alliteration on that same initial syllable: in
other words the very nature of the organization and the versifica-

18. *Sir Gawain and the Green Knight,* ed. Israel Gollancz, Early English Text Society (London, 1957), lines 1163 and 1164; Alfred de Vigny,
Le Cor, in *Oeuvres complètes: Les Poèmes,* ed. Jean Chuzeville (Paris,
1929), p. 102, line 2.

tion forces us to center our attention on the very source of the tears which experience tells us must be there. The next half-line wrenches us away from this close-up picture of the stag and uses what has by now become a truism — "Nis þæt heoru stow!" (1372b) — to return us to the entire Pond for a momentary pause. With the next statement, introduced by the kinetic adverb "þonon" (1373a) at the beginning of the initial half-line, our attention is again swept away from the Pond and forced upwards with the irresistible swirl of dark waters which rises to the sky (1373a–74a) as the winds blow (1374a–75a) until the air itself grows dark and the heavens weep (1375b–76a). Schematically, the visual progression to which we are thus exposed goes from a close-up to a medium-sized picture and finally to a picture as immense as the skies themselves. Just as the magnitude of the image increases with each subsequent statement, so does the emotional impact, for the silent tears of the stag at bay find a powerful and terrifying voice in the weeping of the heavens, to which they are irremediably linked by the rhetorical progression of the concluding four and one-half lines of the passage.

I have suggested throughout this essay that, in contrast to the Avernus passage, Hrothgar's description of Grendel's Pond owes something of its impact upon the audience to a descriptive technique which forces us to participate in the approach to the source of terror in a quasi-physical manner. The full effectiveness of this technique, however, becomes fully apparent only if we consider the passage within the context of the narrative to this point, and realize that the poet has been preparing us for Hrothgar's account ever since the beginning of the poem, where he has described Grendel as an "ellengæst" (86a) who "earfoðlice . . ./in þystrum bad" (86b–87b) and "moras heold,/fen ond fæsten" (103b–104a), thus impressing upon the audience the mysterious quality of the invader's habitat as well as the weirdness of its location in the undefined moors. The impression has been graphically strengthened with Grendel's attack upon Heorot:

> Da com of more   under misthleoþum
> Grendel gongan. . . .   (710a–711a)

It has further been confirmed with the account of his desperate flight from Heorot, and we have learned that his retreat lies in the highlands:

> scolde Grendel þonan
> feorhseoc fleon   under fenhleoðu,
> secean wynleas wic. . . .
>   (819b–821a)

We have even been allowed a brief glance at the pond itself after its waters had been momentarily tainted with the monster's blood:

> Ðær wæs on blode   brim weallende,
> atol yða geswing   eal gemenged
> haton heolfre,   heorodreore weol.
> Deaðfæge deog,   siððan dreama leas
> in fenfreoðo   feorh alegde,
> hæþene sawle;   þær him hel onfeng. (847a–852b)

Two observations are worth making here in respect to the passages cited. The first is that, although they never afford us a complete view of Grendel's retreat, each new account tells us a little more about it than we knew before. We learn, in this order, that the monster dwells in *darkness* somewhere about the *moors and fens,* that he moves into human ken from unspecified *misty slopes,* that he must seek his retreat in *fen-slopes* after receiving his death wound, and finally that the *fen-retreat* in question is a body of water whose gory waves bear witness to the death he has found therein. In effect, the poet avails himself of the most appropriate spots over nearly 1,300 lines to create in his audience the proper anticipatory mood for Hrothgar's description. One might almost say that, between the first mention of Grendel's activities and the opening of the stag passage, we know and yet do not know, and fear to know where the fearful retreat lies.

The second observation is that the stag passage precisely reproduces and elaborates upon the collective organization of the four passages I have cited. Just as the first passage cited lets us know that Grendel lives in some vague and mysterious place, so the opening statement of the stag passage tells us that he and his kin dwell in a "dygel lond" (1357b); just as the second and third passages cited somewhat narrow the location to the highlands, so the stag passage goes on to locate the retreat near "wulfhleoþu,   windige næssas" (1358a–b); and just as the fourth passage cited takes us to the actual pond and affords us a glance at the bloody waves, so the stag passage takes us to the place where "se mere standeð" (1362b) and makes us see "fyr on flode" (1366a) before focusing on the stag himself. Thus, we may say that the quasi-cinematographic motion through which the poet has inexorably forced us to approach the pond acts with all the psychological force of a faster rerun of the equally inexorable motion which has slowly taken us toward the same pond during the previous narrative. I believe that this complex and emotionally exhausting technique belongs to what Brodeur has most aptly termed "Design for Terror" in *Beowulf*:[19] against the terror of the unknown which the poet has thus conveyed to his audience — to use Beowulf's own expression ("eafoð uncuþes" [960a]) to describe his previous fight with Grendel — Beowulf's exploit in diving in the dark waters a few lines later (1494aff.) must necessarily be received with the admiring awe it deserves.

Although our fortuitous ignorance of the authorship and precise date of composition of *Beowulf* has done much to shield the poem from the depredations of biographical and sociological criticism, one may be tempted to wonder whether the technique which I have tried to isolate in the foregoing discussion is merely a lucky accident or the product of a conscious undertaking directed at an audience of literary critics. It is at this point that more certitude about the oral or written composition of the poem would be helpful, for Albert Lord has shown that the audience before which the oral poet composes does indeed act as a critical panel whose reactions strongly influence the shape of the completed product.[20] Be this as it may, two things are certain. In the first place, the technique under discussion is by no means an isolated phenomenon: simpler instances of it, for example, have

19. Brodeur, *Art of Beowulf,* p. 91.
20. Lord, *Singer of Tales,* e.g., pp. 14–17 and 26–29.

been studied in *Judith* and in other parts of *Beowulf*.[21] We may thus contemplate the possibility that it was neither utterly unconscious on the part of the poet nor necessarily unnoticed by the audience. In the second place, whether or not *Beowulf* was composed in front of its original audience, I think most of us would agree that it was performed orally, and experience shows that oral recitation of *Beowulf* at a speed corresponding to that of the South-Slavic poems in the Milman-Parry Collection requires a little under four hours, including occasional breathing spells. The events discussed above would accordingly have been narrated within about one and one-half hours of possibly uninterrupted performance, and there is no reason to believe that Anglo-Saxon singers resisted the temptation to emphasize relevant passages in a manner similar to that attested by the South-Slavic singers and discussed by Mustanoja[22] in respect to Finnish oral poets: in other words, by the time the *Beowulf*-Poet got to Hrothgar's account of Grendel's Pond, he could reasonably expect his audience to recall all the relevant details which had preceded it, and he had had both the opportunities and the means of emphasizing these details in the course of the performance. In this light, we must accept the possibility that, whether or not poet and audience were consciously aware of the technique discussed above, the former fully intended to create for the benefit of the latter the impression of progressively mounting terror which has been the subject of our discussion.

In conclusion, if one is willing to grant the facts of the foregoing analysis, one must also accept the contention that comparison between the Virgilian and Beowulfian texts helps us understand an important aspect of the Anglo-Saxon poet's superb mastery of his craft.

21. Alain Renoir, "Point of View and Design for Terror in *Beowulf*," *Neuphilologische Mitteilungen,* 63 (1962), 154–167, and *"Judith* and the Limits of Poetry," *English Studies,* 43 (1962), 1–11.
22. Mustanoja, "Presentation of Ancient Germanic Poetry."

ANTHONY E. FARNHAM

The Art of High Prosaic Seriousness:
John Gower as Didactic Raconteur

An anecdote, especially one about B. J. Whiting, is not out of place in the opening paragraph of an essay on narrative comedy. One chilly fall morning after I had been a graduate student at Harvard for some three years, I sought from Mr. Whiting a direct answer to a plain but problematical question: "What should I read in order to pass the medieval portion of my oral examination next spring?" It was with distinct relief that I saw my inquiry received — was I mistaken that it seemed even to be welcomed? — with judicious consideration, and heard it answered in the manner of one who takes pride in his reputation for sound advice, and pleasure that another should ask it of him. Adequate beginning preparation for the examination could be made, I learned — with the understanding, of course, that the suggested reading, though offering fair certainty of success, was minimally impressive and probably less than most conscientious students would want to do anyway — if one first read carefully all the items described in J. E. Wells's *Manual of the Writings in Middle English*!

My memory has persisted in associating this advice with John Gower's *Confessio Amantis,* despite my pained and irritated attempts at the time to suppress even the slightest gesture of appreciation for the performance. The eccentric Maine irony, the infuriating down-east delight in contrived verbal ambush, in labored under-preparation for outrageous overstatement, has always struck me as an amusing and vivid parallel to Gower's narrative style in his last major work. The parallel might even point towards a partial explanation of the predominantly hostile tone which has characterized critical estimates of Gower's work over the last three centuries:[1] the record of those estimates is not unlike that collection of horrors I remember in Child Library, a file of misinformation about previous oral examination requirements put together by generations of earnest graduate students like myself. I was fortunately not quite earnest enough to enter there a solemn statement, "B. J. Whiting requires candidates to read ALL items listed in Wells"; but neither was I wise enough to understand that I might have borrowed wit from Chaucer and exclaimed, as Chaucer did of Gower, "O moral Whiting!" Typical eighteenth and nineteenth-century critical pronouncements on Gower's life and works appear to me to be similarly lacking in both sympathy for and understanding of the moral and didactic intention which is his central concern.

An obvious turning point in critical judgment of Gower came nearly forty years ago when C. S. Lewis published *The Allegory of Love,* and though it took some time for Lewis' views to make themselves felt, they prepared the way for the increasingly favorable estimates of Gower's achievement which have appeared since Maria Wickert published her *Studien zu John Gower* in 1953. Current appreciation of Gower's extraordinary skill as a narrative artist should support and give perspective to an attempt to understand the brilliance of his moral concern and the manner of its expression, and it is my hope in this essay to build upon the important observations about Gower made by J. A. Burrow in his recent study, *Ricardian Poetry.*[2]

1. For the history of Gower's critical reputation, see John H. Fisher, *John Gower: Moral Philosopher and Friend of Chaucer* (New York: New York University Press, 1964), chap. 1; parts iii and iv (pp. 20ff.) are concerned with the period in question, from the late seventeenth century to the present.
2. C. S. Lewis' remarks about Gower in *The Allegory of Love* (London: Oxford University Press, 1936) are concerned only with the *Confessio Amantis*; see pp. 198–222. The final chapter of Maria Wickert,

Burrow is the first critic of Gower to observe that Matthew Arnold's famous censure of Chaucer — that his poetry lacked "high and excellent seriousness" — ought to be taken as equally true of all the great English poets who were his contemporaries: "In Arnold's context, as one can see from his choice of 'touchstone' examples ('In la sua voluntade è nostra pace' is one of them), 'seriousness' implies speaking straight, not obliquely, to some great matter. Neither Chaucer nor his great contemporaries are often in this sense 'serious'. Their characteristic manner lies, to adopt a favourite phrase of the period, 'betwixt earnest and game'." [3] In a later chapter, Burrow argues that this characteristic manner requires us to judge warily in assessing the intent and effect of stories told by Ricardian poets. Ricardian narrative, he believes, is notably different from "the illustrative stories, or *exempla,* to be found in medieval sermons and books of religious instruction. Ideally, these stories just illustrate the writer's or the preacher's point. Any obliquity in their bearing on that point, any unexpected implication, any irony or wit, will strike us as merely unintentional and unfortunate." Obliquity,

---

Studien zu John Gower (Köln: Universitäts-Verlag, 1953), is an essay on Gower's narrative technique; the book has been reviewed by J. A. W. Bennett, *Review of English Studies,* n.s. 8 (1957), 54–56. Besides the study of Gower by Fisher (n.1 above), other recent contributions of importance include Peter Fison, "The Poet in John Gower," *Essays in Criticism,* 8 (1958), 16–26; Eric W. Stockton, trans., *The Major Latin Works of John Gower* (Seattle: University of Washington Press, 1962); Derek Pearsall, "Gower's Narrative Art," *PMLA,* 81 (1966), 475–484, some of which appears in revised form in Pearsall's later study, *Gower and Lydgate,* Writers and Their Work, No. 211 (Harlow, Essex: Longmans Green, 1969); Arno Esch, "John Gowers Erzählkunst," in *Chaucer und seine Zeit: Symposion für Walter F. Schirmer,* ed. Arno Esch (Tübingen: Max Niemeyer Verlag, 1968), pp. 207–239; and, most recently, the study by Burrow, *Ricardian Poetry: Chaucer, Gower, Langland and the* Gawain *Poet* (London: Routledge & Kegan Paul, 1971). This list is by no means exhaustive, but if considered in chronological order it will, I think, support the assertion that a change in critical estimate is in progress.

3. *Ricardian Poetry,* p. 45. As Burrow indicates in a note, Arnold's discussion of Chaucer is found in "The Study of Poetry," in *Essays in Criticism, Second Series.* The title of Burrow's book refers to English poetry written during the reign of Richard II; see pp. 1–2 for his choice of adjective. I wish here to discuss only Gower's characteristic narrative manner, without considering Burrow's interesting and original hypothesis that this manner may characterize an entire period.

however, is exactly what we encounter in a writer like Gower;
the exempla in the *Confessio Amantis* "cannot be taken for
granted as flat illustrations. The relationship between the story
and its prescribed signification within the schema of the seven
deadly sins is something for the reader to think about. It chal-
lenges him to an intellectual response, almost like the relationship between tenor and vehicle in a metaphysical conceit." [4]

Why so many readers of Gower have found this challenge
offensive, and have chosen to view it as a dull failure, is not easy
to explain. The view has become so orthodox and habitual that
even recent critics of the *Confessio* have felt it necessary to
temper their praise by acknowledging its dullness in some way.
Burrow, for example, in an earlier chapter on Ricardian style,
judges that "Gower's plain style is often not so much plain as
threadbare. The 'metrical smoothness' of which Macaulay speaks
is sustained with astonishing consistency, and there are many
moments of great beauty; but the staple style is always danger-
ously close to sheer hebetude and dullness." [5] Hebetude in the
style of a work which deserves praise for irony, surprise, wit, and
intellectual challenge? Either the style is unsuited to its content,
or else the relation between the two has been mistaken. This latter
possibility is the more likely explanation for the astonishing pattern of continued censure in Gower criticism. The style, like the
exempla it conveys, may be oblique in its effect; where it appears
plain, simple, and staple, it may in fact be operating at a less obvious and more witty level, somewhere between earnest and
game. Such a style is certainly part of Chaucer's repertory,
though he never chooses to sustain it during an entire narrative
with the bland unwinking earnestness which is Gower's characteristic pose. Chaucer, one is tempted to say, seems unable to
keep from laughing out loud at what he is doing, and these moments relieve the tension between earnest and game and make us

4. *Ricardian Poetry*, pp. 83–84. The discussion which there follows, of
the stories about "lachesse" (procrastination) in Book IV of the *Confessio*, illustrates Burrow's point.

5. *Ricardian Poetry*, p. 31. G. C. Macaulay was the editor of *The
Complete Works of John Gower*, 4 vols. (Oxford: Clarendon Press,
1899–1902), which I shall use for all quotations from Gower's writings.
The comment alluded to will be found in II, cxx.

see him as more human than Gower. Nearly all the many com-
parisons of Gower with Chaucer leave behind them an uneasy
feeling of dissatisfaction: their assertion of Chaucer's superiority
is too facile, and their tone betrays an inability to respond to and
enjoy the work of one assumed to be so very obviously the lesser
man. We quite rightly refuse to look down on Chaucer because
he does not possess the range of Shakespeare or the power of
Dante; it is time to accord Gower a similar courtesy and recognize that his achievement invites both appreciation and enjoy-
ment. The excellence of his narrative art is inseparable from its
peculiar style, from that almost perverse comic sense, that keen
awareness of the didactic value of misdirected seriousness, which
suffuses the entire *Confessio Amantis*.

The scheme of the *Confessio* calls for illustration of supposed
sins by means of stories, told to the lover by Genius, his Confessor. In the very first of these (the tale of Acteon and Diana,
told to illustrate sins of sight and hence of the five senses), the
reader's awareness of underlying comedy — an awareness which
may have lurked uncertainly in the recesses of his thought during his reading of the Prologue, but which has been more and
more insistently demanding attention during the first 332 lines
of Book I — is brought to the forefront of consciousness with a
suddenness that would be painful were it not so laughable. It is
only fair to Gower to assume a reader of mildly earnest medieval tastes, one who would have relished (as we in general do
not) the Latin marginalia and elegiac meters as an elegance
well suited to moral wisdom. Such a reader, able to consult Ovid
for himself and the more likely to read Gower's Latin for delight
as well as for instruction, would have found in the marginal summary preceding the tale that the Confessor is to narrate an exemplum "de visu ab illicitis preseruando." [6] Acteon, of the royal

6. Printed in Macaulay, II, 45 margin, next to I.335–336 of the *Confessio*. References to Macaulay will hereafter be indicated parenthetically
in the text. The page layout of the best MSS of the *Confessio* (many of
which Fisher believes were produced in Gower's own scriptorium) gives
the impression that the Latin marginalia are an integral part of the
work — more so than Macaulay's typographical arrangement suggests. A
reader who assumes the marginal notes are mere summaries of the English verses will miss some of Gower's humor. On MSS of Gower's

blood of Thebes, taking his privileged ease in hunting through the nearby woods, unexpectedly came upon Diana bathing. Sensitive to the beauties neither of her attendant nymphs nor of the natural setting, he glued his unchivalrous eyes on the figure of the goddess, "quam diligencius intuens, oculos suos a muliebri nuditate nullatenus auertere volebat." Understandably indignant, Diana transformed him on the spot to a stag, "quem canes proprii apprehendentes mortiferis dentibus penitus dilaniarunt." His own dogs, seizing him with death-dealing teeth, tore him thoroughly to pieces. More just and satisfying punishment was never meted out to so shameless a girl-watcher.

The earnest medieval reader would have been aware that the thrust of this marginal summary, toward making Acteon a responsible moral agent, is a striking reversal of Ovid's explicit statement,

> At bene si quaeras, Fortunae crimen in illo,
> Non scelus invenies; quod enim scelus error habebat? [7]

On the whole, however, he would have both accepted and approved of the change, for it was the fashion of his time to moralize all "auctoritee." He may nevertheless have experienced some misgivings over the quality of moral sensibility which has replaced Ovid's sportive and careless sadism, and these could hardly have been alleviated by the opening lines of the Confessor's English version:

> Ovide telleth in his bok
> Ensample touchende of mislok.   (I.333–334)

"Mislok" indeed! Either the Confessor is capable of a flippancy worthy of Ovid himself, or his sense of moral proportion is

---

works, see Fisher, Appendix A, pp. 303–309; the present location of item 49 has been traced by J. A. W. Bennett, *Selections from John Gower* (Oxford: Clarendon Press, 1968), p. xxi, n.1. On Gower's scriptorium, see Fisher, pp. 116–117, 124, 352, n.8.

7. *Metamorphoses* III.141–142; text from Frank Justus Miller's 2nd ed. for the Loeb Classical Library (New York: G. P. Putnam's Sons, 1921).

somewhat askew. He proceeds to sketch Acteon as a lord of haughty pride, one who because of his royal blood "above alle othre caste his chiere" (I.341), whose position allowed him leisure to pursue the pleasures of the chase as a habitual amusement. His natural vices were only too susceptible to the influence of natural beauty:

> So him befell upon a tide
> On his hunting as he cam ride,
> In a Forest al one he was:
> He syh upon the grene gras
> The faire freisshe floures springe,
> He herde among the leves singe
> The Throstle with the nyhtingale:
> Thus er he wiste into a Dale
> He cam, wher was a litel plein,
> All round aboute wel besein
> With buisshes grene and Cedres hyhe.   (I.349–359)

Did Acteon respond to this setting as an upright man of virtue should? Did he enjoy its beauty passively, without grasping after more? Did he allow that lovely thicket to remain inviolate? It is with a shudder of moral repugnance that the Confessor continues,

> And ther withinne he caste his yhe.   (I.360)

As to be expected, once he had cast it and it had landed on Diana in her bath, he was not the sort of decent chap to avert his gaze out of consideration for a girl's feelings.

> Bot he his yhe awey ne swerveth
> Fro hire, which was naked al.   (I.366–367)

For such a deliberate sinner, the worst of fates is too good, and the Confessor adopts the forthright moral approach of quick and retributive justice:

> And ate laste unhappely
> This Hert his oghne houndes slowhe
> And him for vengance al todrowhe.   (I.376–378)

There follows the inevitable *moralitas* which the lover is apparently expected to deduce from the exemplum:

> Lo now, my Sone, what it is
> A man to caste his yhe amis,
> Which Acteon hath dere aboght;
> Be war forthi and do it noght.
> For ofte, who that hiede toke,
> Betre is to winke than to loke.   (I.379–384)

The earnest medieval reader will be forgiven if he is seen shaking his head in both despair and laughter at a morality more obtuse and more earnest than his own, which has attracted his sympathy but repelled his common sense, and so won a comic victory over his sensibility and taught him some of its shortcomings.

This didactic success has been brought about not by flippancy, but by Gower's ability to create in the person of the Confessor a character whose moral imagination is almost as prosaically deficient as the literary imagination of Chaucer's narrator of the tale of *Sir Thopas*. It is no piece of carelessness on Gower's part that the moral to the tale of Acteon is morally ridiculous, nor need one appeal to the end of the *Nun's Priest's Tale* ("For he that wynketh, whan he sholde see,/Al wilfully, God lat him nevere thee!")[8] to argue that a medieval audience would recognize it as awry. The Latin marginal summary makes no mention of any moral; I discussed that summary first because, as part of Gower's "game," it is a come-on for the earnest reader, who is led to believe that here is respectable and profitable material obviously worth his time. Once caught in the trap, he must cope with a seriousness which is continually sinking beneath the level of his intelligence and a morality which pretends to the sublime and achieves the ridiculous. The game, of course, does not depend on the Latin summaries; they are functional but not essential decoration. What is essential is the comedy of high prosaic serious-

---

8. *The Canterbury Tales* VII.3431–32; text from F. N. Robinson's 2nd ed. of *The Works of Geoffrey Chaucer* (Boston: Houghton Mifflin, 1957).

ness, of the ironically obtuse earnestness by means of which Gower compels us to laugh at our own capacity for moral perception and judgment, to consider seriously and with genuine earnestness Ovid's flippant assertion that those who ask rightly, know whom to blame. To turn Ovid against himself in this way, and moralize him by means of his own jest, is an achievement of moral and literary genius.

From first to last, each of the tales in the *Confessio* is a comparable achievement, some of them so successful that it is easy to forget their relation to the single frame story of which they are all subordinate parts. Gower created not only the Confessor, but the creator of the Confessor, the author-narrator in whose image the Confessor is made, whom we meet in the very first line of the Prologue, dusting off his library preparatory to explaining to us the grave motives which have compelled him to bend our ear to the tune of at least 33,000 lines:

> Of hem that writen ous tofore
> The bokes duelle, and we therfore
> Ben tawht of that was write tho:
> Forthi good is that we also
> In oure tyme among ous hiere
> Do wryte of newe som matiere,
> Essampled of these olde wyse
> So that it myhte in such a wyse,
> Whan we ben dede and elleswhere,
> Beleve to the worldes eere
> In tyme comende after this.   (Prol. 1–11)

With commendable broad-mindedness, the narrator admits his sympathy for those who find wisdom boring if indulged in excessively, and he promises a work which will touch on fun as well and will hence please everybody, since at no point will it not please somebody. God knows, he says, what the world is coming to; in the good old days when men were virtuous, princes were worthy, and everyone loved books, men of letters performed an agreeable and pleasant task:

> For hier in erthe amonges ous,
> If noman write hou that it stode,
> The pris of hem that weren goode
> Scholde, as who seith, a gret partie
> Be lost: so for to magnifie
> The worthi princes that tho were,
> The bokes schewen hiere and there,
> Wherof the world ensampled is.   (Prol. 40–47)

Authors in those days wielded honest pens:

> And tho that deden thanne amis
> Thurgh tirannie and crualte,
> Right as thei stoden in degre,
> So was the wrytinge of here werk.   (Prol. 48–51)

(The golden age, if one stops to reflect, seems on occasion to have had problems not unlike those the narrator so clearly perceives in his own time.) The narrator does not permit such parenthetic reflections to intrude on his train of thought, however, and after apologizing for both illness and ignorance, he assures us he will do all he can to compose a prologue "so assised/That it to wisdom al belongeth" (Prol. 66–67). His readers can look forward, once this chore is out of the way, to a bit of relaxation and even titillation:

> Whan the prologe is so despended,
> This bok schal afterward ben ended
> Of love, which doth many a wonder
> And many a wys man hath put under. (Prol. 73–76)

For the present, however, he will keep sternly to his task of composing unadulterated wisdom, and he launches section ii of the Prologue with some grim Latin verses on the degeneracy of times present,[9] adding a marginal note which proclaims the sub-

---

9. Like the Latin marginalia, the elegiac meters which occur throughout the poem are a trap for earnest readers. Their high and elegant moral sentiments are impeccably phrased, but the solid edifice of meaning they appear to buttress totters precariously if examined and collapses if leaned on with serious intellectual intent. The imagination behind the joke is

ject at hand to be "De statu regnorum" (next to Prol. 94 in Macaulay). Macaulay, apparently influenced by the narrator's suggestion, heads the entire section, "Temporal Rulers" (II, 7ff., top margin); Peck follows the marginal Latin still more in his heading, "The State" (Peck, p. 4). Even a cursory reading of this section of the Prologue, however, will lead to the conclusion that its true subject is not kings or governments, but the disordering of worldly love. Again and again the note is sounded, "That love is fro the world departed" (Prol. 169). The narrator has hit on a point of central moral concern — but does not realize he has done so. Incredible as it may sound, the remainder of the Prologue, and the eight long books which comprise the body of the poem, are in a sense only an elaboration of this one simple joke. Too stupidly prosaic to understand the truth he has stumbled over, too academic to think consciously of "love" as anything other than a social pastime, the narrator is unable to see the foolishness of his "wisdom." A modern reader of the final section of the Prologue, especially one accustomed to superserious exegesis of medieval texts, may well have difficulty accepting Nebuchadnezzar's dream as a joke. Nevertheless, from another point of view, it is hard to resist the temptation to call the great statue, as it appears in the *Confessio,* a colossal jest: its feet of earth and steel prove at great length, much to the narrator's satisfaction, a fact nobody can deny — that the reason we stand divided is because we are apart.

With the opening of Book I, the narrator confides to his read-

---

like that which designed the medieval choir stall, the seat of which offers a weary chorister the appearance and promise of physical comfort but collapses ignominiously the instant he ceases to keep his spine erect and rigid. Any reader still unconvinced should turn to the Latin verses which introduce the tale of Acteon already discussed (Book I, between lines 288 and 289). If he does not end in laughter, the fault surely does not lie with Gower. Unfortunately, the only edition of the *Confessio* in which there is an attempt at translation of the Latin meters into modern English, Russell A. Peck's useful and extensive paperback selection (*Confessio Amantis,* New York: Holt, Rinehart and Winston, 1968), cannot be relied on for this purpose; the translations there given are all too often inaccurate. Nor does Stockton include any passages from the *Confessio* in his *Major Latin Works* (n.2 above). Possibly this lack is not to be regretted: a sense of humor does not always survive translation easily.

ers that the role of sage has been too much for him; from now
on he will change his style, and, by writing of love, become an
entertainer. The promise to change his style (I.8–9), like the
implied assent of Chaucer's Clerk to the Host's request that he
eschew rhetoric, never has any discernible effect. Bent on conveying the sensational power of the irresistible sickness and in-
curable passion which is "love," the narrator casts about for
some happy means whereby his asseverations may be rendered
more convincing. What more tangible proof of his veracity than
the solid facts of personal experience? With labored humor, he
buttonholes us in a confessional tone:

> I am miselven on of tho,
> Which to this Scole am underfonge.   (I.62–63)

He too, he tells us, is one of the devotees of this terrible malady.
Lest we mistake the skills of rhetoric for an embarrassing truth,
however, he is careful to point a marginal finger of caution:

> Hic quasi in persona aliorum, quos amor alligat, fingens se auc-
> tor esse Amantem, varias eorum passiones variis huius libri
> distinccionibus per singula scribere proponit.
>   (next to I.60–64 in Macaulay)

From this pretentious pose of the narrator to be one of those
others whom love fetters — of course, he wants us to understand
that in actual fact a person of his serious concerns would not be
caught dead in such a situation — there unfolds with growing
brilliance the great joke of the entire *Confessio,* the comic frame
story of Amans, the would-be dirty old man, frustrated and be-
wildered by an emotional commitment of embarrassing purity,
and Genius, the affable Confessor forever in a muddle over
which god he serves, too garrulous to listen with understanding,
too obtuse to grasp any of the realities which lie behind the
moral platitudes with which his prosaic mind is plentifully furnished. Both figures are creatures of the narrator's deficient imagination, the one a projection of his fantasies (not always impure)
about "love" and "lust," the other of his beliefs (not always
foolish) about "wisdom" and "lore." The joke is however with-

out malice, for it is in didactic earnest: only by laughter can we come to recognize our moral beliefs and intellectual assumptions for what they are. Life yields no easy harvest of either morality or truth, and the wisdom of age may be the knowledge that what we once believed could be thrashed out only with a flail, must in the end be winnowed by hearty and plentiful laughter.

Such I take to be the lesson of the *Confessio Amantis,* addressed not solely to Richard II or to Henry IV, but to every person, of royal station or not, who must eventually learn to rule the kingdom which is himself and must therefore be brought to understand the true meaning of Love. The poem is indeed the confession of a lover, of a poet who loved men and language and life, of a great wielder of words and a passionate believer in moral truth, who tried in his earliest work to hold up a mirror in which men might see the outrageous sinfulness of their daily existence, who cried out publicly in his middle years at the moral wilderness he saw around him, yet who had hope in his neighbor and faith in his God enough to end his life's work in jest at himself and his own best efforts. It would be entirely characteristic of John Gower that we should last see him with a twinkle in his eye and a solemn set to his lips; I think he would have been delighted to have it said that by way of introduction to his greatest work, he provided it with an epitaph — not an epigraph, but an epitaph:

> Ossibus ergo carens que conterit ossa loquelis
> Absit, et interpres stet procul oro malus.[10]

10. These lines are the last of the three elegiac distichs which introduce the Prologue; a clumsy translation might run as follows: "Then I implore that he who, missing the bones, destroys them with words,/Be absent; and that the clumsy translator keep far away."

FLORENCE H. RIDLEY

A Plea for the Middle Scots

For over four hundred years the greatest poets of medieval Scotland have stood in the shadow of Chaucer, their work judged in the light of his, they themselves categorized as "Scots Chaucerians," a term which puts them in the wrong time and the wrong place, assigns them characteristics they do not have, and denies them talents they do.[1] This intellectual Chaucerian straitjacket,

1. The linking of Chaucer and the Scots began quite early when William Thynne printed the *Testament of Cresseid* as Book VI of *Troilus and Criseyde* in *The workes of Geffray Chaucer* (London, 1532). Then in 1667 Franciscus Junius praised Douglas' translation of the *Aeneid* as a gloss for Chaucer, *The Life, Diary, and Correspondence of Sir William Dugdale,* ed. W. Hamper (London, 1827), p. 383. Allan Ramsay, who printed the first sizable selection of the Scots' works, took but slight notice of Chaucer's influence, *The Ever Green* (1724; rpt. Glasgow, 1874), I, 132; II, 36. However, subsequent eighteenth-century anthologists and historians considered their work in the light of Chaucer's. Cf. D. Dalrymple, Lord Hailes, *Ancient Scottish Poems* (Edinburgh, 1770), pp. 224, 279; J. Pinkerton, *Select Scotish Ballads* (London, 1783), pp. xxxiv–xxxvi; *Ancient Scotish Poems* (London, 1786), pp. ix, xciv; T. Warton, *History of English Poetry,* ed. R. Wellek (1774; facsimile rpt. New York, 1968), II, 257, 264, 279. The sobriquet "Scottish Chaucer" appears to have been popularized early in the nineteenth century by Walter Scott and his circle; cf. D. Laing's citing the use of the term by Scott and Lockhart in his edition of Dunbar, *The Poems of William Dunbar* (Edinburgh, 1834), I, 49; II, 451–452. It has now as "Scottish Chaucerian" become the ac-

presupposing the nature of their work and forestalling its objective appraisal, has resulted in persistent neglect of the Scots' poetry. Admittedly the dialect of these writers, Robert Henryson, Gawin Douglas, and William Dunbar, is difficult for us today; but so is the dialect of *Sir Gawain and the Green Knight,* and that poem is neglected by neither students nor critics.[2] In the present space the effect and extent of the Chaucerian blight can perhaps be best suggested by representative quotes from a great body of commentary and a detailed analysis of the actual as opposed to the traditionally accepted relationship between one Scots poem widely touted as "Chaucerian" and the relevant English poem.

Chaucer is a giant among poets, surpassed in English literature only by Shakespeare and perhaps Milton, though the point is arguable. Comparison between him and the Scots would inevitably make them appear in some way inferior — F. P. Magoun once suggested that making such a comparison was to put a New York skyscraper in a California patio. Both accommodations have their uses, and the Scots have excellences of their own; yet even when they do not aim at those of the master, time and again in appraising them critics drag in Chaucer whether his presence is relevant or not. Dunbar is criticized because he lacks Chaucer's chivalry and figures ."admirable in the ways of the parson, Constance, or Griseld." [3] Why not criticize Chaucer for lacking Dunbar's vitriolic bite and figures admirable in the ways of the Lady Solistaris who dance their minuet of vice

---

cepted terminology of literary historians and some of the most influential commentators upon the Scots. *The Kingis Quair* is omitted from the present discussion since its "Chaucerianism" in meter, diction, imagery, outline, and philosophy is obvious, even to the most stalwart defender of the independence of Scottish poetry, A. M. Mackenzie, *An Historical Survey of Scottish Literature to 1714* (London: A. Maclehose, 1933), p. 62.

2. For example, the *MLA Bibliographies* for 1967–1971 list for some 120 poems of the Scots 3 critical books and 33 articles, for *Sir Gawain and the Green Knight* alone, 5 books and 67 articles.

3. J. Nichol, "A Sketch of Scottish Poetry up to the Time of Sir David Lyndesay," in *The Monarche and Other Poems of Sir David Lyndesay,* ed. J. Small, Early English Text Society, Orig. Ser. 11 (London, 1883), xxx; cf. also W. Godwin, *Life of Geoffrey Chaucer,* 2nd. ed. (1803; rpt. London, 1804), I, 494–495, and H. H. Wood, *Two Scots Chaucerians,* Writers and Their Work, No. 201 (London: Longmans, Green & Co., 1967), p. 31, who are quoted subsequently.

at court? Henryson "was incapable of rising to the refinements, or conceiving the delicacies" of Chaucer. But Henryson gives no indication of ever attempting such refinements and delicacies. In "The Thrissil and the Rois" and "The Goldyn Targe" "there is nothing . . . to recall the discursive dialogues between 'Geoffrey' and the eagle in upper space." Why on earth should there be? Relevant or not, Chaucer's presence seems inescapable in criticism of Middle Scots poetry and has resulted in misinterpretation of the poets' work and persistent underestimation of their achievement both as individuals and as a school. Chaucer, sole begetter of the movement, is the master influence who brought fresh literary life to Scotland, "quickened the fallow ground" making it "sessonabill, sappie, and to resave all seidis abill," and only thus able to produce the likes of Henryson, Douglas, and Dunbar.[4] The critics' name is legion, but perhaps G. G. Smith speaks best for those who give Chaucer full credit for the flowering of Scotland's poetry. In discussing "the Chaucerian revival," Smith says: ". . . the North deliberately put itself to school and by a rhetorical, and somewhat bookish, discipline, rather than by a natural facility, reproduced, and at times improved upon, the models."[5]

The nature of the conventionally conceived relationship is illuminated by the terms in which it is described. Chaucer is the master and lantern, moulder, model, and king; the Scots are his pupils, disciples, followers, successors, and liegemen. To his genius first, their ability second, is due their high achievement; they are dependent upon him as inspiration, stimulus, source. Their great works are modeled upon, borrowed from, suggested and inspired by those of Chaucer. They are good when they imitate most, bad when they imitate least. Frequently it is suggested that without Chaucer the Scots would never have been poets at all, much less good poets! Even when critics praise them, they

4. Kurt Wittig, *The Scottish Tradition in Literature* (Edinburgh and London: Oliver and Boyd, 1958), p. 57. Cf. also W. J. Courthope, *History of English Poetry* (London, 1895), I, 368; T. Wright, "On the Scottish Poet Chaucer," in *Essays* (London, 1846), II, 291; and W. Minto, *Characteristics of English Poets from Chaucer to Shirley* (Boston, 1889), p. 98.
5. "The Transition Period," *Periods of European Literature* (Edinburgh, 1900), IV, 42.

often do so in terms of Chaucer, making him the standard of excellence, "Chaucerian" a synonym for "good," and assigning Dunbar and the rest certain ill-defined, but inevitably Chaucer-related, traits.[6] Henryson has humor finer, slyer, more Chaucerian than Dunbar's, and is "the only one of the major Makars who is really Chaucerian in his breadth of mind and largeness." Douglas "attains a robuster versification than you are like to find in Chaucer." [7] Why must the praise always be by comparison, and why must the comparison always be with Chaucer?

Why should commonplaces of content, meter, and language be taken as evidence of dependency? Henryson is "prone, like Chaucer, to draw a comic parallel between the bestial and the human." The assemblage of creatures in "The Thrissil and the Rois" is "in imitation of Chaucer's 'Parliament of Fowls'"; Douglas' pentameter couplets are "Chaucer's rhyming couplets of ten-syllabled lines"; the southern forms of his dialect, the result of Chaucer's influence.[8] But other such parallels were commonly drawn in the great body of beast epic and fable; other assemblages were described, other pentameter couplets composed by poets other than Chaucer; and the southern forms of Douglas' dialect were frequently enough found from Edinburgh to the channel during the late fourteenth, fifteenth, and early sixteenth centuries.

Comprehensive citation of all the relevant commentary is not possible here; perhaps the sampling in the footnotes will suggest

6. For the use of such terms and such an approach cf. D. F. C. Coldwell, *Selections from Gavin Douglas* (Oxford: Clarendon Press, 1964), p. xiv; M. W. Stearns, "Henryson and Chaucer," *Modern Language Quarterly,* 6 (1945), 284; J. G. R. McElroy, "The Thrissill and the Rois," *The Penn Monthly,* 12 (1880), 541; G. Eyre-Todd, *Mediaeval Scottish Poetry* (Glasgow, 1892), p. 51; H. H. Wood, "Robert Henryson," in *Edinburgh Essays on Scots Literature,* ed. H. J. C. Grierson and others (Edinburgh: Oliver and Boyd, 1933), p. 29.

7. H. J. C. Grierson, "Robert Henryson," in *Essays and Addresses* (London: Chatto and Windus, 1940), p. 42; Tom Scott, *Dunbar: A Critical Exposition of the Poems* (Edinburgh: Oliver and Boyd, 1966), p. 88; Ezra Pound, *A B C of Reading* (Norfolk, Conn.: New Directions, 1951), p. 115.

8. James Kinsley, "The Mediaeval Makars," in *Scottish Poetry* (London: Cassell, 1955), p. 18; W. A. Neilson and K. G. T. Webster, *Chief British Poets of the Fourteenth and Fifteenth Centuries* (Boston: Houghton Mifflin, 1916), p. 434; H. Morley, *English Writers* (London, 1890), VII, 164.

its abundance. Consistently Henryson, Douglas, and Dunbar are held up to Chaucer and found wanting. Of course not all critics interpret the Scots solely in this manner; recently a number have been at pains to reject both the term "Scots Chaucerian" and the concept. Yet they have remained curiously persistent, and even these critics seem unable to escape entirely the Chaucerian set. Fox says, "The 'Chaucerian' part of 'Scottish Chaucerian' . . . [is] so equivocal as to be almost meaningless" but entitles his essay "The Scottish Chaucerians," calls the *Testament of Cresseid* a continuation and companion piece, an analysis of and parallel to *Troilus* which uses Chaucer's characters and situation "to explore the same problems that Chaucer deals with." MacQueen asserts that Henryson is not the disciple of but rather a fellow innovator with Chaucer, yet describes the *Testament* as the "most Chaucerian" of Henryson's works, "The Cok and the Fox," as an "adaptation" of "The Nun's Priest's Tale," "The Taill of the Lyon and the Mous" as "directly modelled on the 'Prologue' to Chaucer's 'Legend of Good Women,' " and finds Henryson's burgess mouse reminiscent of the Wife of Bath. Even the redoubtable Agnes Mure Mackenzie, after firmly stating "the Scottish Chaucerians are a myth," feels compelled to point out that Henryson is "superficially, most like Chaucer in temper and out-look and in the peculiar quality of his humour," and she approaches the Scots poet by comparing him to Chaucer.[9]

9. As early as 1931, P. H. Nichols, "William Dunbar as a Scottish Lydgatian," *PMLA,* 46 (1931), 214–224, demonstrated that Dunbar borrowed more from Lydgate than from Chaucer, but cf. as quoted Denton Fox, "The Scottish Chaucerians," in *Chaucer and Chaucerians,* ed. D. S. Brewer (University, Ala.: University of Alabama Press, 1966), pp. 165, 167, 171, and *Testament of Cresseid,* ed. Denton Fox (London: Nelson, 1968), pp. 20ff.; John MacQueen, *Robert Henryson: A Study of the Major Narrative Poems* (Oxford: Clarendon Press, 1967), pp. 55, 221, 65, 125; A. M. Mackenzie, *An Historical Survey,* pp. 62–63. For others who reject yet in varying degrees reflect the Chaucerian bias see David Murison, ed., *Selections from the Poems of Robert Henryson* (Edinburgh: Oliver and Boyd, 1952), pp. 2–4; James Kinsley, ed., *William Dunbar Poems* (Oxford: Clarendon Press, 1958), pp. xiii–xvii; A. C. Spearing, "Conciseness and 'The Testament of Cresseid,' " *Criticism and Medieval Poetry* (London: Arnold, 1964), p. 118; A. M. Kinghorn, "The Mediaeval Makars," *Texas Studies in Language and Literature,* 1 (1959–60), 73–75, 77–78; Del Chessel, "In the Dark Time: Henryson's 'Testament of Cresseid,' " *The Critical Review,* 12 (Melbourne, 1969), 61–72.

Yet, evidence of the Scots' indebtedness is surprisingly slim.
Douglas and Dunbar call Chaucer "master." Henryson refers to
him, occasionally uses rime royal as he does, and bases two
poems on narratives which derive either from Chaucer or sources
common to both. Douglas' "Palice of Honour," like Chaucer's
"House of Fame," is a dream vision involving the journey of a
comic persona to the palace of a personified abstraction. Dunbar's "Goldyn Targe," like Chaucer's "Legend of Good
Women," is a dream vision involving a company of ladies and a
dreamer attacked by a god of love; the ladies in his "Twa Marriet Wemen and the Wedo" appear to be descended, as was the
Wife of Bath, from La Vieille in *Romance of the Rose,* and his
satire on the court fool, Thomas Norny, employs a mock-heroic
technique and meter comparable to those in Chaucer's "Rime of
Sir Thopas." [10] But the purpose of Henryson's "Cok and the
Fox" and the *Testament of Cresseid* is quite different from that
of Chaucer's comparable poems; Douglas' "Palice of Honour"
is minor work, perhaps one tenth as long as his *Eneados* and
one hundredth as significant; and there are indicative resemblances to Chaucer in no more than four, at most five, of over
one hundred poems attributed to Dunbar. On the whole, the
main reason for calling the Scots "Chaucerian" seems to be that
they were the first to write good verse in the British Isles after
Chaucer.

Nearly anyone who wrote English poetry for two hundred
years after Chaucer would have been hard put not to show his
influence somehow. Spenser's Acrasia bears a family likeness to
Chaucer's Venus — though it is possible that both enchantresses

10. Details cited are possibly significant evidence. The image cited by
Priscilla Bawcutt, "Dunbar's 'Tretis of the Tua Mariit Wemen and the
Wedo' 185–187 and Chaucer's 'Parson's Tale,' " *Notes and Queries,* 11
(1964), 332–333, seems inadmissible; it too easily could have been suggested to Dunbar by a common sight in daily life rather than by its one
appearance in Chaucer. E. R. Eddy, "Sir Thopas and Sir Thomas Norny:
Romance Parody in Chaucer and Dunbar," *Review of English Studies,*
n.s. 22 (1970), 401–409, has most recently studied the relation, formerly
noted by F. N. Snyder, " 'Sir Thomas Norny' and 'Sir Thopas,' " *Modern
Language Notes,* 25 (1910), 80, between the two. As Eddy concludes,
the similarity in technique and diction indicates Dunbar's familiarity
with Chaucer's poem, but the effect and purpose of his own are quite
different.

hark back to Prudentius' glowing Luxuria. Should we then call Spenser "Chaucerian," or both Chaucer and Spenser "Prudentian"? Shakespeare tells of Troilus and Criseyde; and it is doubtful that he would have described Troilus on the Trojan walls gazing toward the Grecian tents had Chaucer not done so before him. Donne's aubade to the sun reflects that of Chaucer, and Dryden, like Henryson, retold the tale of Chauntecleer and Pertelote.[11] But neither Shakespeare nor Donne nor Dryden is called "Chaucerian." Why the Scots? Because, says H. H. Wood, "it is quite impossible to overestimate their debt in inspiration, in form, and in doctrine, to their master and original, Chaucer . . . without [whose] inspiring and fructifying influence . . . the movement would never have been." Without *Troilus* there would have been no *Testament*; without the Wife of Bath, no "Twa Marriet Wemen and the Wedo." Sprutok's song, "Was never wedow sa gay," reminds Wood of Chauntecleer's "My leif is faren on lande"; Makyne reminds him of Criseyde. We may well agree with Golding, "happier had the fate of the Scottish Chaucerians been had they . . . been born in China," set as they are "dubiously upon a border-line of appreciation," their virtues "blurred in the glory thrown about them by the sun of Chaucer," deriving "their immortality, alas! more from his name than from their own high merits." [12]

Despite its Scottish idiom, Henryson's *Testament of Cresseid* was long attributed to Chaucer, and in 1803 William Godwin established the standard mode of its criticism in writing that the poem had "a degree of merit calculated to make us regret that it is not a performance standing by itself, instead of serving merely as an appendage to the work of another." Subsequently Bennett

11. Cf. *The Faerie Queene* II.xii.77–78; *The House of Fame* I.130–137, *The Parliament of Fowls* 260–274, *Troilus and Criseyde* V.666–672, III.1464–70 (*The Works of Geoffrey Chaucer*, ed. F. N. Robinson, 2nd. ed. [Boston: Houghton Mifflin, 1957]; all quotations from Chaucer are from this edition). Cf. also Prudentius, *Psychomachia* 310–330; *The Merchant of Venice* V.i.1–7; "The Sunne Rising," *The Poems of John Donne*, ed. H. J. C. Grierson (London: Oxford University Press, 1933), pp. 10–11; "The Cock and the Fox," *The Poems of John Dryden*, ed. James Kinsley (Oxford: Clarendon Press, 1958), IV.1605–26.
12. Wood, "Robert Henryson," pp. 1–2, 13, 16, 29; *Two Scots Chaucerians*, p. 8. Louis Golding, "The Scottish Chaucerians," *The Saturday Review of Politics, Literature, Science, and Art*, 134 (1922), 782.

designated it "a not unworthy pendant," Huxley, "merely a short
sequel" to Chaucer's *Troilus and Criseyde,* McDermott, "the
most successful of Chaucerian imitations." [13] The *Testament*
begins its story where Chaucer left off, is in the same stanzaic
form as *Troilus,* and was first printed as Book VI of that poem.
Beyond that what is Henryson's actual debt? If the two poems
are compared in detail, it becomes apparent that the *Testament*
is neither a slender appendage to nor an imitation of *Troilus.*
Henryson perceived in Chaucer embryonic concepts which he
developed and carried through to their logical end. In a sense,
his poem takes its departure from Chaucer's, but achieves great
dramatic force by means of contrast with rather than resemblance to it. Chaucer tells of the birth, blossoming, and betrayal
of a love which is an earthly shadow of the cosmic force that
creates, vitalizes, and binds together the universe. Henryson tells
of the corruption and death that follow the betrayal of such love
and its debasement into lust.

He must have meant to set his poem against Chaucer's, for he
tells initially of reading Chaucer's account of the sorrow of
Troilus; then throughout he inserts echoes from *Troilus* which
call it persistently to mind and help to make clear that his poem
is at once consistent with it and yet quite different. Despite his
title, Chaucer is concerned primarily with Troilus, whose growth
he traces from ignorance of any sort of love through the puppy
love of a young Romeo, to adult passion and a mature but finite
questioning of God's ordinance, to final, reconciled comprehension of the nature of all human happiness — including love. But
Chaucer presents a static Criseyde who never learns and never
changes, who simply disappears from the story with her fate left

13. The *Testament* was printed as Chaucer's by Thynne in his 1532
edition and in editions based upon his until well into the eighteenth cen-
tury, and it was attributed to Chaucer by J. Leland, *Commentarii de
Scriptoribus Britannicis* (1540), ed. A. Hall (Oxford, 1709), II, 424;
J. Bale, *Illustrium Maioris Britanniae scriptorum* (1548), fol. 198; and
T. Tanner, *Bibliotheca Britannico-Hibernica* (London, 1748), p. 168.
Godwin, *Life of Geoffrey Chaucer,* p. 489; Bennett, *Chaucer and the
Fifteenth Century,* p. 176; Aldous Huxley, "Chaucer," in *Essays New
and Old* (London: Chatto and Windus, 1926; rpt. New York, 1932), p.
271; J. J. McDermott, "Henryson's 'Testament of Cresseid' and Hey-
wood's 'A Woman Killed with Kindness,'" *Renaissance Quarterly,* 20
(1967), 20.

obscure. Henryson traces the progress of Criseyde become Cresseid, a figure whose corrupt end grows logically and inevitably from seeds in Chaucer's poem. However, by continually pointing up the contrast between that poem and his own, between what love and Criseyde had been and what they become, he enhances the grimness of his heroine's lot, underscores the lesson it illustrates, and explores an irony left undeveloped by Chaucer: we make our own fate, but are blind to that fact until it is too late.[14]

Chaucer commences his tragedy of Troilus with a plea to Tesephone for aid in writing, for the manner of its telling should suit a tale; and Henryson in the first lines of his tragedy of Cresseid strikes the same note, "Ane doolie sessoun to ane cairfull dyte/Suld correspond and be equiualent." [15] Both poets then set their narratives in spring, the appropriate season for each, but with a notable difference.[16] For Chaucer spring is an

14. My interpretation of the relation between the two poems differs somewhat from that of Fox, *Testament*, pp. 20–58. For instance, I believe that the development of Henryson's heroine is continued along the same lines hinted at in the *Troilus* rather than in an opposite direction, is consistent with, indeed inevitable in the light of, Chaucer's poem; that the *Testament*'s irony evolves from a contrast between what Criseyde had been and what Cresseid becomes rather than from its being "an imitation of 'worthie Chaucer glorious' "; that Cresseid does not change from "a weak woman" into a "much-abused beauty," but far from being abused causes her own misfortune; that Henryson writes not "to reveal the vanity of sexual love" but to reveal the wrongness, of which sexual promiscuity is a part, of violating the natural laws which rule the world and constitute the order of God, who is love. Moreover, to call, as Fox does, the natural order symbolized by the planets "inexorable," Cresseid "pitiful and helpless," the gods "terrible," and the poem "bleak and cruel" seems to contradict the basic truth, which Fox himself finds therein: "there is justice in the world, but not a justice always comprehensible to man." Tatyana Moran, " 'The Testament of Cresseid' and 'The Book of Troylus,' " *Litera: Studies in Language and Literature,* 6 (1959), 18–24, finds Henryson expressing a puritanical "personal revenge on love," at cross purposes with Chaucer on all points, the *Testament* an "anti *Troylus*." My interpretation perhaps indicates our differences. Ronald Marken, too, has compared the two poems, reaching the unfortunate conclusion that Henryson's "If anything . . . has served as a foil to accentuate the immortal greatness of its predecessor," "Chaucer and Henryson: a Comparison," *Discourse,* 7 (1964), 381–387.

15. *Testament*, ed. Fox, ll. 1–2. Quotations from the poem are from this edition.

16. Fox, *Testament*, p. 50, finds that Henryson makes an unorthodox combination of weather, beginning with hot, i.e. "feruent," spring, then switching to cold. But "Aries, in middis of Lent," means the end of

English April, filled with new green and the sweet scent of
flowers, a suitable setting for the birth of Troilus' idealistic love.
For Henryson spring is the very opposite, a northern mid-Lent of
hail, frost, and bitter wind, at once an effective setting for his
story and a means of emphasizing the difference between it and
Chaucer's: the warm, fresh, young love of which Chaucer wrote
has now passed, to be succeeded by age, cold lust, disease, and
death.

Henryson disposes quickly and, in the light of Chaucer's account, logically of the affair between Criseyde and Diomede.
Chaucer had presented Diomede's speedy wooing, begun in the
short space of a ride from Troy to the Greek camp, as a parody
of Troilus' long, formal courtship, and suggested Criseyde's in-
cipient falsity in her early responses to the Greek warrior:

> "But as to speke of love, ywis," she seyde,
> "I hadde a lord, to whom I wedded was,
> The whos myn herte al was, til that he deyde."
>
> (V.974–976)

After her husband, as we know, came Troilus; but Criseyde continues, "And other love, as help me now Pallas,/Ther in myn
herte nys, ne never was" (V.977–978). Thus we see that she
can lie, and having denied a previous betrayal, she concludes:

> I say nat therfore that I wol yow love,
> N'y say nat nay; but in conclusioun,
> I mene wel, by God that sit above!   (V.1002–04)

It is the utterance of a woman tragically weak; and surely any
love between such a one and Chaucer's Diomede would from the
start have been doomed to end as Henryson perceived and, in
resuming her story, depicts in a few devastating lines:

March or beginning of April, springtime yet quite chilly in Scotland; and
"feruent" weather could be "turbulent, violent, raging," as well as hot.
Cf. *Middle English Dictionary, fervant,* 2, where *Beryn,* 1583, is cited:
"The wedir was so fervant of wynd & eke of thundir."

> Quhen Diomeid had all his appetyte,
> And mair, fulfillit of this fair ladie,
> Vpon ane vther he set his haill delyte,
> And send to hir ane lybell of repudie
> And hir excludit fra his companie.   (71–75)

The most consistent motivation of Chaucer's Criseyde is a proud concern for honor which she equates with her reputation, as Pandarus says, initially that of a saint. Having accepted Troilus, her greatest fear is that "Men myghten demen that he loveth me" (II.730), although she reasonably concludes:

> May ich hym lette of that? Why, nay, parde!
> I knowe also, and alday heere and se,
> Men loven wommen al biside hire leve;
> And whan hem leste namore, lat hem byleve!
>
> (II.732–735)

Her refusal of his plea that they flee Troy together is based on this concern:

> And also thynketh on myn honeste,
> That floureth yet, how foule I sholde it shende
> And with what filthe it spotted sholde be,
> If in this forme I sholde with yow wende.
> Ne though I lyved unto the werldes ende,
> My name sholde I nevere ayeynward wynne.
>
> (IV.1576–81)

Near the end of the story she does give over care for the Mrs. Grundys of the world and resolves to return to Troilus; but Diomede's persuasion suffices to change her resolve, and Criseyde herself predicts the loss of the name she has so jealously guarded, "O, rolled shal I ben on many a tonge!" (V. 1061). In the *Testament* Henryson shows the heroine's regard for her hallowed reputation debased to fear lest men know, not that a great prince loves her, but that the surfeited Diomede has indeed "when hem liste namore" thrown her out. Chaucer's Criseyde once stood proudly among the other worshippers in the

temple of the Palladion. Henryson's Cresseid will not enter a
temple to sacrifice as she should, but hides outside, afraid the
people may suspect her disgrace. And she will endure the fate
Criseyde predicted: her name foully ruined, spotted with filth,
will be rolled on every tongue.

Chaucer's Criseyde is almost never alone. She lives surrounded by ladies, is visited by Pandarus, sought out by Troilus
and Diomede. But Henryson emphasizes the isolation of Cresseid, who journeys to her father's house without fellowship and
alone in a secret oratory angrily cries out against the gods for her
lack of lovers:

> Vpon Venus and Cupide angerly
> Scho cryit out, and said on this same wyse,
> "Allace, that euer I maid ȝow sacrifice!
>
> "ȝe gaue me anis ane deuine responsaill
> That I suld be the flour of luif in Troy;
> Now am I maid ane vnworthie outwaill,
> And all in cair translatit is my ioy.
> Quha sall me gyde? Quha sall me now conuoy,
> Sen I fra Diomeid and nobill Troylus
> Am clene excludit, as abiect odious? . . .
> And fra luifferis left, and all forlane."   (124–33, 140)

The Scots poet, recognizing that a woman with the character
Chaucer assigned Criseyde would inevitably lose her company of
ladies and lovers and be isolated, assigns just such a fate to
Cresseid.

Following her outburst, Henryson tells how in a vision Cresseid sees a convocation of gods to whom Cupid appeals for
justice:

> "Lo," quod Cupide, "quha will blaspheme the name
> Of his awin god, outher in word [or] deid,
> To all goddis he dois baith lak and schame,
> And suld haue bitter panis to his meid.
> I say this by ȝone wretchit Cresseid,
> The quhilk throw me was sum tyme flour of lufe,
> Me and my mother starklie can reprufe, . . .

> This greit iniure done to our hie estait
> Me think with pane we suld mak recompence; . . .
> Thairfoir ga help to reuenge, I ȝow pray!"
>
> (274–280, 290–291, 294)

One of the more troubling aspects of Henryson's poem is the cause assigned here for the punishment of his heroine.[17] Since Criseyde's sin was infidelity, Cupid's charge of blasphemy seems somewhat inconsistent. But again, I believe, Henryson is developing a rudimentary concept of Chaucer's and, by so doing, suggesting that it is not mere angry words against two pagan gods which bring down punishment upon Cresseid's head. The crux of the matter would seem to be against whom or what she blasphemes, and how.

Chaucer identifies love with an omnipotent life force, "Thorugh which that thynges lyven alle and be." Book III of *Troilus* opens with an invocation which moves from praise of Venus to that of the power whose emanations vitalize the universe, to that of God's redemptive love, and closes with further praise of love which, as Troilus says, governs earth and sea, holds peoples joined, knits the law of company, diversifies the seasons, and binds together the discordant elements, bringing forth day and night and keeping the sea in check (III.1–16, 1744–64). Clearly it is no subjective passion to which the young prince responds, but a cosmic creative force of which his own emotion, at once physical yet spiritualizing, is at least a shadow if not a part. Henryson does not identify love in these explicit terms; rather, he assigns something of the same role Chaucer had assigned love to the seven planet gods who judge and punish Cresseid,

> Quhilk hes power of all thing generabill,
> To reull and steir be thair greit influence
> Wedder and wind, and coursis variabill . . .
> . . . seuin deificait,
> Participant of deuyne sapience.   (147–150, 288–289)

---

17. For a brief summary of various interpretations of Cresseid's crime and its punishment cf. E. D. Aswell, "The Role of Fortune in 'The Testament of Cresseid,'" *Philological Quarterly,* 46 (1967), 471.

In crying out against the gods of love, Cresseid has, as Cupid says, done shame to all these gods, violence "Asweill for ʒow as for my self," and thus has blasphemed against the power that generates and rules the world.[18] Her blasphemy, however, consists not just of words, but of a series of actions which began with Criseyde's lies, betrayal of Troilus's ennobling love and response to Diomede's debased wooing, and has now progressed to Cresseid's prostitution and sacrilegious outcry.[19] The wrongness of these actions is underscored by the rightness of those of Troilus.

Troilus speaks and acts perfectly in accordance with the laws of love, is ennobled by and faithful to it. For aid he prays devoutly to the same gods who punish Cresseid; for his happiness, he thanks Venus, Cupid, and "Benigne Love, thow holy bond of thynges," with a reverent acknowledgment of its power, "Whoso wol grace, and list the nought honouren,/Lo, his desir wol fle withouten wynges" (III.1261–63), which ironically suggests the nature of Cresseid's later offense. On the other hand, Criseyde breaks the laws of love and feels but little of its ennoblement. Henryson then makes clear the full significance of these contrasting actions, showing to what end the course upon which Criseyde embarks would lead, if indeed love be as Chaucer describes it. Having dishonored the divine power Troilus honors, she will inevitably suffer.

In her vision Saturn and Cynthia, representatives of the gods, decree that Cresseid is to be afflicted "with seiknes incurabill,/ And to all louers be abhominabill" (307–308). What she seems to see here is a metaphorical statement of her crime and its pun-

18. Cf. MacQueen, *Robert Henryson,* p. 70, and Aswell, "The Role of Fortune," pp. 471ff., who also identify the planet gods with physical laws or natural forces. To maintain further, as Aswell does, that Henryson depicts a purely naturalistic world without divine providence or an omniscient dispenser of justice and mercy, where all man can do is try to control himself, seems to contradict the characteristically religious bent of Henryson's other poems, "The Bludy Serk," "The Abbay Walk," "Ane Prayer for the Pest," and "The Annunciation," and destroy the concept of Cresseid's wrongdoing as blasphemy.

19. Although a *TLS* reviewer also sees Cresseid's offense as blasphemy in "deed," he finds it a mere "failure to live according to the code on which her happiness had been based," Henryson concerned only with "the courtly theme of the betrayal of a lover," *TLS,* April 9, 1964, p. 290.

ishment, for just as the gods represent the creating, ruling force of the universe, which Chaucer interpreted as love and against which she has blasphemed in action and word, so the punishment they mete out represents the logical consequences of such blasphemy. With or without the intervention of pagan gods, Cresseid would experience loss of beauty, disease, abandonment, and death because those are the natural results of her behavior, of her violation of the laws which govern "all thing generabill." Her dream represents dawning comprehension of what she has done and the beginning of a new self-awareness.

Blindness to herself and to the nature of true love is the hallmark of Chaucer's heroine, blindness which for Cresseid is gradually mitigated. Initially Criseyde, a widow, has greater maturity and common sense — shrewdness might be a better term — than Troilus. Yet despite her experience, her comprehension of love never equals that he achieves, but remains instead comparable to that of Pandarus. For the uncle love is but "casuel plesaunce" (IV.419), for the niece it begins in nothing and ends in nothing, "That erst was nothing, into nought it torneth" (II.798). When Antigone praises love, the right life, which leads one to flee all vice and live in virtue, Criseyde can only wonder, "Lord, is ther swych blisse among/Thise loveres" (II.885–886). Moreover, despite her shrewdness, Criseyde's understanding of human nature, including her own, remains limited. She is certain she can trick her father and return to Troy — were she not she would die on the spot. But of course Criseyde cannot trick Calkas, and she neither returns nor dies. She swears to mourn forever should Troilus die:

> And, Troilus, my clothes everychon
> Shul blake ben in tokenyng, herte swete,
> That I am as out of this world agon.   (IV.778–780)

But she has worn black before for another man, and as Troilus had displaced that dead husband in her heart, Diomede displaces him. When Criseyde promises, "To Diomede algate I wol be trewe" (V.1071), inevitably we wonder who will be next.

Perceiving in Criseyde's words and actions the implications for subsequent development, Henryson tells us most graphically what, if not precisely who, will be next in her downward progress. While Chaucer's heroine ends as she began, "slydinge of corage" and totally unaware of it, Henryson's learns and changes, her mind's eye ironically becoming ever clearer as her physical eyes become blurred with disease. After sentence is passed upon her, Saturn blasts Cresseid's beauty with a touch of his frosty wand and Cynthia inflicts disease upon her:

> Thy cristall ene mingit with blude I mak,
> Thy voice sa cleir vnplesand hoir and hace,
> Thy lustie lyre ouirspred with spottis blak,
> And lumpis haw appeirand in thy face:
> Quhair thow cummis, ilk man sall fle the place.
>
> (337–341)

This is the concrete expression of the ultimate degradation which would befall Chaucer's lovely heroine, for the ravaging of beauty symbolizes corruption which began with Criseyde's falsity and grew with Cresseid's lust and irreverence.[20] With the vision and the disease, Cresseid's understanding of the significance of her actions begins, and again it is a development partially anticipated but left unrealized by Chaucer. Pandarus had once urged Criseyde to love, warning that beauty would pass:

> 'And sende yow than a myrour in to prye,
> In which that ye may se youre face a morwe!'
> Nece, I bidde wisshe yow namore sorwe.   (II.404–406)

20. Beryl Rowland, "The 'Seiknes Incurabill' in Henryson's 'Testament of Cresseid,'" *English Language Notes,* 1 (1964), 175–177, takes Cresseid's disease to be syphilis. But Henryson might not have known the symptoms of that disease if, as Rowland says, it were first identified at Naples in 1495, while he could well have been aware of those of leprosy, cf. J. Y. Simpson, "On Leprosy and Leper Hospitals in Scotland and England," in *Archaeological Essays* (Edinburgh, 1872), II, 139. S. V. Larkey, "Leprosy in Medieval Romance," *Bulletin of the History of Medicine,* 35 (1961), 77–80, and Fox, *Testament,* pp. 26ff., have pointed out that leprosy was sometimes considered a venereal disease. In view of Cresseid's sexual misdeeds such an affliction would be logically and thematically appropriate; but of greater significance than its actual nature is its role as an outward sign of corruption.

Now Cresseid wakes from her dream:

> ... than rais scho vp and tuik
> Ane poleist glas, and hir schaddow culd luik;
> And quhen scho saw hir face sa deformait,
> Gif scho in hart was wa aneuch, God wait!   (347–350)

Pandarus' idle prayer has been fulfilled, and indeed he could have wished his niece no more sorrow.

Still pathetically concerned to protect her reputation, Cresseid asks Calkas:

> ... Father, I wald not be kend;
> Thairfoir in secreit wyse ȝe let me gang
> To ȝone hospitall at the tounis end,   (380–382)

and retires to the spital house. There as she remembers her fairness, lovers, riches, honor, fame, all irrevocably lost, Cresseid feels the force of another of Pandarus' earlier warnings:

> The worste kynde of infortune is this,
> A man to han ben in prosperitee,
> And it remembren, whan it passed is,   (III.1626–28)

and offers herself as a mirror wherein other women may see the truth of such an admonition:

> ... in ȝour mynd ane mirrour mak of me:
> As I am now, peraduenture that ȝe
> For all ȝour micht may cum to that same end.
>
>   (457–459)

Of course to be aware that such loss may come is not necessarily to know how to avoid it; and Cresseid still, accepting no responsibility for her plight, blames the "craibit Goddis" and, like Criseyde, fortune and fate. But Cresseid keeps on learning. As she continues to weep and chide her destiny, she is counseled by a leper lady to make virtue of necessity, "[G]o leir to clap thy clapper to and fro,/And lei[f] efter the law of lipper leid"

(479–480); and having broken the law of lovers, Cresseid
learns to follow that of lepers.

Her moment of final illumination comes with recognition of
Troilus, which brings full awareness of what he represents and
is, and of the contrast, so damning to herself, between them.
The passage describing these reactions (498–546) has caused
some difficulty, but I believe the key to its meaning may be
found in Henryson's adroit development of another suggestion
in Troilus, where the psychological ground for this recognition
is laid. Chaucer describes the manner in which Troilus was affected by his first sight of Criseyde in all her beauty and pride:

> And of hire look in him ther gan to quyken
> So gret desir and such affeccioun,
> That in his hertes botme gan to stiken
> Of hir his fixe and depe impressioun. . .
> [He] Was ful unwar that Love hadde his dwellynge
> Withinne the subtile stremes of hir yen;
> That sodeynly hym thoughte he felte dyen,
> Right with hire look, the spirit in his herte.
>   (I.295–298, 304–307)

Then upon this concept of the onset of love Henryson builds,
telling how when Troilus rides past a leper huddled by the road-
side, although he does not recognize her, those bleared eyes
where love once dwelt bring to mind, "The sweit visage and
amorous blenking/Of fair Cresseid, sumtyme his awin darling"
(503–504). And as once before his lady's look had seemed to
slay his spirit, so now:

> Ane spark of lufe than till his hart culd spring
> And kendlit all his bodie in ane fyre;
> With hait fewir, ane sweit and trimbling
> Him tuik, quhill he was reddie to expyre.   (512–515)

Henryson explains:

> Na wonder was, suppois in mynd that he
> Tuik hir figure sa sone, and lo, now quhy:

> The idole of ane thing in cace may be
> Sa deip imprentit in the fantasy
> That it deludis the wittis outwardly,
> And sa appeiris in forme and lyke estait
> Within the mynd as it was figurait.   (505–511)

It is the sense impression of Criseyde fixed in his heart long ago as Chaucer had told which moves Troilus, and he tosses the beggar alms.

Criseyde had once felt the aspect of Troilus sink into her heart, seeing him ride from the battlefield among the cheering Trojans. But Chaucer had not said that the image became fixed in its depths; and now the figure of Troilus, which could be but dimly perceived by leprous eyes, rouses no impression in Cresseid's imagination as she asks, "Quhat Lord is ȝone .../Hes done to vs so greit humanitie?" (533–534). Only with the revelation, "Schir Troylus it is, gentill and fre" (536), does she feel a bitter pang of memory, understanding, and self-knowledge and see at last what Criseyde never saw: the difference between love like that of Diomede and that of Troilus and the significance of her actions. Seeing that she has shaped her own destiny, she no longer blames fortune or the gods but only herself, and for the first time laments the wrong done Troilus rather than her own misery:

> All faith and lufe I promissit to the
> Was in the self fickill and friuolous:
> O fals Cresseid and trew knicht Troilus!   (551–553)

This marks a considerable advance over Criseyde's blindness, but even Cresseid's understanding never approaches the cosmic wisdom of Troilus who, as Chaucer tells, not only comprehends true love but ultimately sees all earthly felicity, of which love is a part, in proper perspective. Only at the moment of death does Cresseid comprehend anything of the nature of real love; and she ends as Henryson knew, given the character Chaucer originally assigned his heroine, she would, not like Troilus laughing in the heavens but comparatively unenlightened, dead beneath a stone.[21] Thus the *Testament,* primarily through the relationship between the two heroines, develops consistently yet in an unexpected way action and character anticipated in *Troilus,* and by so doing evokes pathos and powerful dramatic irony.

The narrator of Chaucer's *Troilus* displays no attitude of significance for any major theme of that poem; but the attitudes of Henryson's narrator serve to emphasize further the lesson of the *Testament,* particularly by their contrast with those of Cresseid. This narrator first appears trying humbly to invoke Venus, whom he has promised to obey and now trusts will renew his success in love. But he is repelled by frost and bitter wind for the fire of passion is no longer for him — he is old, and "Thocht lufe be hait, ȝit in ane man of age/It kendillis nocht sa sone as in ȝoutheid" (29–30). Lovelessness on the part of Chaucer's narrators is a standard joke, the result of ineptness; here it is the natural result of age which the narrator, blaming no one, accepts philosophically. Cresseid too had once worshipped Venus, trusting that the goddess would always prosper her suit. Now she too is loveless, but in sharp contrast to the narrator she blames the gods for infelicity she has brought upon herself and is neither obedient, humble, nor reverent.[22] Initially the narrator shares Cresseid's blindness as to the cause of her fate, attributing to cruel fortune the distress which, he says, has come

21. Cresseid does not seem "healed" by her experience, for there is no sense of peaceful reconciliation in the poem's last lines. Fox, *Testament,* p. 58, says that repentance which "brought no healing" would imply a questioning of the divine order — precisely what Douglas Duncan maintains the poet engages in, "Henryson's 'Testament of Cresseid,' " *Essays in Criticism,* 2 (1961), 129. Yet Henryson depicts blasphemy, of which such questioning is a part, as wrong and punishable. Perhaps it should be remembered that Cresseid was not subject to the Christian scheme of salvation, but a pagan for whom repentance did not necessarily bring healing. On the question, see Spearing, "Conciseness and 'The Testament of Cresseid,' " pp. 144ff.

22. Henryson emphasizes the parallel and contrast between the two and their condition by figures of vegetation and cold. Cf. ll. 22–24 with 136–139, and the narrator's cold, result of the natural banking of passion's fire by age and an old man's susceptibility to chill, with the cold Cresseid suffers figuratively from untimely loss of beauty — the seed of love in her face "with froist is slane" — and physically from disease — deprived of heat of body her moisture and heat are changed into cold and dry (139, 334, 318). For the narrator there is remedy; but for Cresseid, "to thy seiknes sall be na recure" (335).

about "nathing throw the gilt/Of the," and anticipating her protest against the crabbed gods by himself upbraiding Saturn, "O cruell Saturne, fraward and angrie,/Hard is thy dome and to malitious!" (323–324). In his concluding admonition to women, however, the narrator again like Cresseid reproves no one and nothing save her own false deception.

Obviously Henryson considered the deception of Troilus important, for his final words relate Cresseid's punishment specifically to that offense. Yet, it had been committed only in Chaucer's poem and is not included among those sins of blasphemy, slander, defamation, injury, and violence done the gods which Cupid cites as reasons for punishing Cresseid. I believe the apparent contradiction is resolved by the fact that Henryson considered this specific sin against love to be only one aspect, though perhaps the most important, of a whole complex of wrongdoings, of blasphemy in word and deed which began in *Troilus* and continued in the *Testament*. This woman's end about which Chaucer remained silent is the just, inevitable result of a progress spanning both poems. "Troilus moot wepe in cares colde," says Chaucer's narrator:

> Swich is this world, whoso it kan byholde:
> In ech estat is litel hertes reste.
> God leve us for to take it for the beste!   (V.1747–50)

When youthful passion ends as it must, Henryson's narrator takes it for the best. He does not rail against fortune, fate, or the gods, but turning to comforts appropriate to old age — a fire, a drink, warm wraps, and a book — wisely adapts himself to natural law. Cresseid in violating all the laws of love violates the natural law of gods and men; by infidelity she brings down lovelessness, by lecherous living disease upon herself; she attacks the gods and dies a disgraced outcast. Perhaps the lesson is best stated in "The Knight's Tale," where Theseus says:

> Thanne is it wysdom, as it thynketh me,
> To maken vertu of necessitee,
> And take it weel that we may nat eschue,
> And namely that to us alle is due.

And whoso gruccheth ought, he dooth folye,
And rebel is to hym that al may gye.
                    (*The Canterbury Tales*, I (A) 3041–46)

The leper lady who counseled Cresseid would have agreed. Such
is the testament illustrated by the downward course of a heroine
whose character is consistently developed from the beginning of
Chaucer's poem to the end of Henryson's, a testament for anyone who "gruccheth," rebels or blasphemes in word or deed
against the gods — or, as the masque of seven planets suggests,
the laws which rule and steer all things generable in the world.

Now if in light of this comparison of the two poems we again
ask what was Henryson's debt to Chaucer, perhaps it will be apparent how misleading "Scots Chaucerian," with its connotations
of dependency, really is. For in the *Testament* Henryson did
not imitate Chaucer, did not adopt his material or manner or
themes. He found in Chaucer's poem a latent idea and the outline of a static character which he proceeded to develop fully in
such a way as to illustrate that idea and make it a lesson univer-
sally applicable. The greatest teachers point the way for others;
and that, I believe, is what Chaucer did for Henryson, though
it is a way he himself did not, perhaps even could not, go. To
see the *Testament of Cresseid* as weaker because it begins where
Troilus and Criseyde leaves off and gains irony from its contrast
with that poem — much less because it is not a perfect imitation
— is to miss the point and artistry of Henryson's achievement
and do far less than credit to a poet who was a genius completely
in his own right.

JAMES REPPERT

F. J. Child and the Ballad

Among the Child MSS preserved in Harvard College Library there is a piece of yellow notepaper with a single paragraph at the top and several abbreviated notes, mostly references to books, at the bottom. This little scrap Child scribbled out in August 1896 in an effort to begin at last his long-awaited essay on ballad literature. He died almost in the very act of writing it.

Child's essay on ballads remains one of the great unwritten works of American scholarship. Yet only one systematic attempt to reconstruct Child's ballad theory has so far been printed. Walter Morris Hart tried to meet this need by publishing in *PLMA,* 21 (December 1906), 755–807, an article, "Professor Child and the Ballad," which collects Child's *obiter dicta* from *English and Scottish Popular Ballads* and from Child's article on ballads in Johnson's *New Universal Cyclopedia.* These opinions Hart has admirably summarized at the end of his article.

We are now in position to attempt a summary of Professor Child's conception of the popular ballad. He regarded it as a distinct species of poetry, which precedes the poetry of art, as the product of a homogeneous people, the expression of our common nature, of the mind and heart of the people, never of the person-

ality of an individual man, devoid, therefore, of all subjectivity
and self-consciousness. Hence the author counts for nothing;
hence, too, the ballad is difficult to imitate and most attempts in
this way are ridiculous failures. In transmission the ballad regularly departs from the original form, least in the mouths of un-
learned people, more in the hands of professional singers and
editors. (P. 805)

Child's remarks on the subject matter of the ballad Hart con-
denses as follows:

Of the Subject-Matter of the ballad, the sources may be, and in
the best instances are, purely popular, consisting of material which
appears only in popular literature. Professor Child mentions no
instance of where a prose tale is the source of a ballad, but the
ballad, he says, may sometimes be resolved into a prose tale.
Popular origin is attested by foreign parallels in folk-literature.
(P. 806)

Hart's summary concludes by touching upon two other important aspects of the ballad, technique and style:

So far as Technique is concerned, the ballad must have plot. The
story may not be completely told; conclusions, transitions, and
preliminaries may be omitted; but the result is not nonsense, the
ballad is not incoherent. At its best it is, however, brief. (Pp. 806–
807)

In Style the ballad is artless and homely, and in it the conceit,
and literary or learned words and phrases are out of place. Yet it
has certain conventions of its own . . . . It is essentially lyrical,
and its lyrical quality is not less essential than the plot. (P. 807)

To these general statements, which are a literal presentation
of Child's sayings, I shall add a further list of Child's critical remarks designed to amplify the themes of ballad content, style,
and transmission.

One of the most immediately striking features of Child's critical comments is his constant appeal to the original form of a
ballad as a referent from which to judge its merit. A ballad becomes better and better as it gets closer and closer to the earliest

form of the story which it relates. The manifest gaps and corruptions in many ballads lend an obvious force to this argument, as Child was tireless in pointing out.

"The Elfin Knight" (No. 2): J, K, and L have completely lost sight of the original story.   (I, 14)[1]

"The Twa Sisters" (No. 10): this is a wide departure from the original story, and plainly a modern perversion.   (I, 123–124)

"Leesome Brand" (No. 15): though injured by the commixture of foreign elements, A has still much of the original story. (I, 177)

"Thomas Rymer" (No. 37): The ballad is no worse and the romance would have been much better, for the omission of another passage, impressive in itself, but incompatible with the proper and original story.   (II, 320)

"Sweet William's Ghost" (No. 77): A alone, the first published, has perhaps retained the original form.   (III, 227)

"Fair Annie" (No. 62): There are other variations in the story, and some additional particulars in one or another version: none of these, however, seems to belong to the original ballad. (III, 64)

"Lady Maisry" (No. 65): The genuineness of H. Buchan's version may be doubted both on general and particular grounds, and both because of its departures from the common story and because of its repeating some peculiarities of the Jamieson-Brown copy, A.
(III, 112n.)

"Robin Hood's Chase" (No. 146): This is a well-conceived ballad, and only needs to be older.   (V, 206)

"A Gest of Robyn Hode" (No. 117): The earliest of these ballads, on the other hand, are among the best of all ballads, and perhaps none in English please so many and please so long.
(V, 42)

1. The Roman numerals refer to the ten paperbound parts of *ESPB*, not the volumes.

"The Braes O Yarrow" (No. 214): L 19 is also found only in that copy. It seems to me, but only because L does not strike me as being of an original cast — rather a ballad improved by reciters — to be an adaptation of No. 215, A2.   (VII, 163)

"Bonny Lizie Baillie (No. 227): The story is told in a somewhat disorderly way even in a, and we may believe that we have not attained the original yet, though this copy is much older than any that has appeared in previous collections.   (VIII, 267)

To judge from the choicest examples, the Child-type ballad is a ballad with a past. Itself an antique, it tells a story older still. It preserves ancient traits or features — facts and fictions from verifiable folklore. Given two modern ballads of approximately the same quality and date, one with analogs in tradition, one without, Child would give precedence to the former. In the case of a single ballad with a long transmission history, the earlier text would be the A version. Of two ballads of approximately equal antiquity and quality, the preference is for the one closest to the original form of its story. If both were close to their originals, then the story which preserves the more antique features is accorded the more important position. As a further reduction, where there are equal amounts of folklore, the preference seems to be for the Nordic or Scandinavian tradition.

It was characteristic of Child to postulate an Ur-ballad, made up of the "best" elements from each of its versions, as a measuring stick for evaluating the relative position each version was to occupy in a graded hierarchy of beauty. Child's conception of the first form of a ballad story is the keystone for all of his ballad criticism.

Child judged himself to be near the original form of a story when he encountered a simple, direct plot which was in every way economical, reasonable, and logical. Wherever a ballad was irrational, fulsome, or inconsistent, it was to that extent corrupted. Each element in the story line had to succeed the last in a logical fashion. Child accepted the ballad on its own terms, but he was extremely vigorous in his attack upon inconsistency within the world of ballad story. He hammered away endlessly at the idea that a ballad is only as good as its story.

"Earl Brand" (No. 7): has preserved most of the incidents of a very ancient story with a faithfulness unequalled by any ballad that has been recovered from English oral tradition.   (I, 88)

"Twa Sisters" (No. 10): the restoration of the younger sister, like all good endings foisted on tragedies, emasculates the story.
                                                                              (I, 123)

"Leesome Brand" (No. 15): but the great majority has a single nightingale, and, as Grundtvig points out, the single bird is right, for the bird is really a vehicle for the soul of the dead Redselille.
                                                                              (I, 180)

"Hind Horn" (No. 17): it must be admitted that it was better for the ring to change, to the temporary clouding of the Lady's character, than for the forced marriage to go on.   (I, 193)

"Willie's Lyke-Wake" (No. 25): This version gives us some rather unnecessary previous history.   (I, 248)

"Tam Lin" (No. 39): What is of more account, the style of the piece, as we have it, is not quite popular. Nevertheless, the story is entirely of the popular stamp, and so is the feature in it, which alone concerns us materially.   (II, 336)

"The Cherry Tree Carol" (No. 54): Some of these [versions] are very imperfect, or have even lost chief points in the story. (III, 2) The proper story of this highly popular carol is derived from the Pseudo-Matthew's gospel, chapter xx.   (III, 1)

"Fair Janet" (No. 64): He would not survive Janet in any pure and full form of the story.   (III, 101)

"The Gay Goshawk" (No. 96): In this ballad the goshawk is endowed with a nightingale's voice. The substitution of a parrot in G, a bird that we all know can talk, testifies to the advances made by reason among the humblest in later generations. A parrot, says Buchan, 'is by far a more likely messenger to carry a love-letter or deliver a verbal message'.   (IV, 357)

"Brown Robin" (No. 97): It does not seem to have been tampered with so much as other ballads in the same manuscript. The story undoubtedly stops at the right point in A, with the escape of the two lovers to the wood. The sequel in C is not at all beyond the inventive ability of Buchan's blind beggar, and some other blind beggar may have contrived the cane and the whale, the shooting and the hanging, in B.   (IV, 368)

"The Famous Flower of Serving-Men" (No. 107): A great deal of nonsense passes in ballads, but I am impelled to ask just how a lover would go about to clothe a bower with lily-flower. Is the ballad lily a climbing plant?   (IV, 429)

"Hughie Grame" (No. 191): The high jump which Hugh makes in A 18, C 12, D 4 (fourteen, or even eighteen feet, with his hands tied on his back), is presumably an effort to escape, though, for all that is said, it might be a leap in the air.   (VII, 10)

"Bewick and Graham" (No. 211): I am persuaded that there was an older and better copy of this ballad than those which are extant. The story is so well composed, proportion is so well kept, on the whole, that it is reasonable to suppose that certain passages (as stanzas 3, 4, 50) may have suffered some injury. There are also phrases which are not up to the mark of the general style, as the hack-rhymster lines at 7^3, 19^2. But it is a fine-spirited ballad as it stands, and very infectious.   (VII, 145)

"Geordie" (No. 209): The English ballads, however, are mere 'goodnights.' The Scottish ballads have a proper story, with a beginning, middle, and end, and (save one late copy), a good end, and they are most certainly original and substantially independent of the English.   (VII, 126)

"The Rose of England" (No. 166): It is a remarkably lively narrative, with many curious details, and in its original form (which we cannot suppose we have) must have been nearly contemporary.
(VI, 332)

"Jamie Douglas" (No. 204): D 10–15, N are palpable and vulgar tags to a complete story.   (VII, 92)

Child was deeply concerned with the technique of determining excrescence in a ballad by taking the measure of a given circumstance's probability or credibility. Elements which in Child's opinion retarded the progress of the ballad story were, we have just seen, regarded as suspicious. They were now subjected to the scrutiny of reason, and Child was meticulous in his application. The criterion of probability proved a singularly handy tool. It provided the necessary legitimization of taste without which Child would have been forced to admit, finally, that he was editing by *Sprachgefühl.* Where the burden of ballad correctness might have proved troublesome, Child was enabled to pronounce upon the structural disfigurements or architectonic beauties of his ballads with careful authority. Moreover, Child thoroughly enjoyed making literal interpretations of his ballads, and some of his most amusing comments are in this vein.

"The Laily Worm and the Machrel of the Sea" (No. 36): It would be a mere cavil to raise a difficulty about combing a laily worm's head. The fiery beast in 'Kemp Owyne', A, has long hair, and the laily worm may have had enough to be better for combing.
(II, 315)

"Lady Isabel and the Elf-Knight" (No. 4): Had she put him to sleep with a charm, and killed him with *his own knife,* as Lady Isabel does, there would have been nothing to shock credibility in the story. . . . It must be admitted that the transaction in the water is not a happy conception in the latter, since it shocks probability that the woman should be able to swim, and the man not.
(I, 23n.)

Comments of this nature abound in almost every other ballad throughout the whole collection.[2] Frequently they are buttressed by subsidiary criteria which are too contextual to resolve into general statements. On occasion one finds Child examining the motive for an action in a ballad story.

"Erlinton" (No. 8): No sufficient motive is furnished for introducing him (Gunther).   (I, 107)

2. See especially II, 314, 320, 391; III, 1, 13, 18, 65, 66, 84, 100, 102, 126, 127, 173, 243; V, 90, 96, 102, 103, 120; VII, 192, 217; VIII, 383, 437.

"Young Johnstone" (No. 88): Motherwell remarks of his version, what is true of all the others, but E, that the ballad throws no light on Young Johnstone's motive for stabbing his lady.

(IV, 288)

"Sir James the Rose" (No. 213): No motive is furnished in a-f for the woman's betraying her leman.   (VII, 156)

Another approach to the problem of how to recognize the oldest forms of a story was Child's reference to the occurrence (or nonoccurrence) of ancient traits, as he called them. He meant, apparently, story elements drawn from the kind of material found only in popular literature and whose popular origin is attested by foreign parallels in folk literature. Child is here at his best. He brought to the ballad a knowledge of popular literature unparalleled by any ballad editor before or since. His remarks in this connection are among the most cogent and interesting he ever printed.

"Lady Isabel and the Elf-Knight" (No. 4): It is quite beyond question that the third class of German ballad is a derivation from the second. Of the versions T-Z, Z alone has preserved clear traits of the marvellous. A king's daughter is enticed from home by Ulrich's singing, and is warned of her impending fate by the dove, as in Class II. The other ballads have the usual marks of degeneracy, a dropping or obscuring of the marvellous and romantic incidents, and a declension in the rank and style of the characters.

(I, 48)

"Twa Sisters" (No. 10): Perhaps the original conception was the simple and beautiful one which we find in England B and both the Icelandic ballads, that the king's harper, or the girl's lover, takes three locks of her yellow hair to string his harp with.

(I, 121)

"Glasgerion" (No. 67): The oath by oak, ash, and thorn, A 18, is a relic or trait of high antiquity.   (III, 137)

"Sir Hugh, or, The Jew's Daughter" (No. 155): The fine trait of the ringing of the bells without men's hands, and the reading of the books without man's tongue, occurs only in A.   (V, 235)

"Jellon Grame" (No. 90): It is interesting to find an ancient and original trait preserved even in so extremely corrupted a version as C of the present ballad, a circumstance far from unexampled.

(IV, 303)

"Tom Potts" (No. 109): Unequal matches are common enough in ballads and romances, and very naturally, since they are an easy expedient for exciting interest, at least with those who belong to the humbler party.   (IV, 441)

"Crow and Pie" (No. 111): This is not a purely popular ballad, but rather of that kind which, for convenience, may be called the minstrel-ballad. It has, however, popular features, and markedly in stanzas 13, 14; for which see pp. 444, 446 of the first volume, and the ballad preceding this, A 5, 6, B 3, 4, etc.; also Buchan's *Ballads of the North of Scotland, II,* 144, 'The Baron oLeys.'

(IV, 478)

"Rose the Red and White Lily" (No. 103): The only part of the ballad which has the stamp of indubitably ancient tradition is the child-birth in the wood, and this scene is the rightful, and perhaps exclusive, property of 'Leesome Brand', No. 15.   (IV, 416)

That "declension in the rank and style of the characters" which Child speaks of in "Lady Isabel" deserves further comment as illuminating a rather confusing point in his attitude toward the traditional ballad. When Child tells us that the comic portrayal of a ballad hero is a sure mark of degeneracy in the story, we can only agree. The difficulty comes in reconciling his remarks about certain aristocratic aspects of ballads with his remarks about their transmission (of which more in a moment). He seems to have taken to heart the admonition in "Little Musgrave,"

> But lay my lady on the upper hand,
> For she came of the better kin.

Is the quality of a ballad affected by the rank or social condition of the personages it portrays? Child seems at times to come close to maintaining something very like that proposition.

"Twa Sisters" (No. 10): The sisters are king's daughters in English A, B, C, H, O, P, Q, Ra, and in Swedish B and two others of Afzelius's versions. They are an earl's daughters in Swedish F, and sink to farmer's daughters in English Rb, c, Swedish A, G, Norwegian C.   (I, 120)

"The Lass of Roch Royal" (No. 76): In the other versions Love Gregory is somewhere over sea, and in B, F his lass is indebted for his direction, not to a company who are raking over the lea, but to a sea-rover, who shows a consideration not to be looked for from his class.   (III, 214)

"A Gest of Robyn Hode" (No. 117): Yeoman as he is, he has a kind of royal dignity, a princely grace, and a gentleman-like refinement of humor. (V, 43) In the oldest ballads Robin Hood is simply a stout yeoman, one of the best that ever bare bow; in the later ballads, he is repeatedly foiled in contests with shepherds and beggars.   (V, 47)

"Young Allan" (No. 245): At this point, especially in A, Allan's seamanship appears to very little advantage; he is more of a fair weather yachtsman than of a skeely skipper .... The ballad indeed suffers almost as grieviously as the comedy cog. (VIII, 376)

These remarks are close to some of Louise Pound's observations, an engaging circumstance in view of Miss Pound's assault on the most distinguished of Child's pupils, Kittredge and Gummere. In the following paragraph particularly it seems to me that Louise Pound states plainly everything that Child implied.

The social atmosphere of the ballads is the atmosphere of the upper classes. Certainly no peasant audience or authorship is mirrored in them. The picture we get from them is a picture of the life of chivalry, not of the doings of the common people; such as we have, for example, from genuinely "communal" ranch or lumbermen or cowboy or fisherman or negro songs today .... The English and Scottish ballads seem to have affiliations with classical narratives, mediaeval romances, scriptural matter, lives of saints.[3]

3. Louise Pound, *Poetic Origins and the Ballad* (New York: Macmillan, 1921), pp. 99–100.

If it is reasonable to perceive an analogy between Child and Pound in the matter of the aristocratic aspects of ballads, it is difficult to interpret Child's remarks about the popular ballad in process of transmission. Not only do Child's comments establish a dichotomy between ballad content and ballad transmission, but his criticisms are in themselves contradictory. In "The Twa Brothers" (No. 49) we are told that "It is interesting to find the ballad in the mouths of children in American cities, . . . in the mouths of the poorest, whose heritage these old things are" (II, 435). Yet we have only just been told in "Hind Etin" (No. 41) that "It is scarcely necessary to remark that this ballad, like too many others, has suffered severely by the accidents of tradition. A has been not simply damaged by passing through low mouths, but has been worked over by low hands. Something considerable has been lost from the story, and fine romantic features, preserved in Norse and German ballads, have been quite effaced" (II, 360). Of version B of "Glasgerion" (No. 67) it is stated that "Scottish B is mainly of good derivation (a poor old woman in Aberdeenshire)" (III, 136). But version B of "Thomas Rymer" (No. 37), "never published as yet, has been corrupted here and there, but only by tradition" (II, 317). Child's statements about transmission of ballads seem to me to be vague and unsatisfactory, although he occasionally wrote out his ideas on this subject at some length.

"The Boy and the Mantle" (No. 29): This ballad and the two which follow it are clearly not of the same rise, and not meant for the same ears, as those which go before. They would come down by professional rather than by domestic tradition, through minstrels rather than knitters and weavers. They suit the hall better than the bower, the tavern or public square better than the cottage, and would not go to the spinning wheel at all. An exceedingly good piece of minstrelsy 'The Boy and the Mantle' is, too; much livelier than most of the numerous variations on the somewhat overhandled theme.   (II, 257)

"The Laily Worm and the Machrel of the Sea" (No. 36): Somewhat mutilated, and also defaced, though it be, this ballad has certainly never been retouched by a pen, but is pure tradition.
                                    (II, 315)

"The King's Dochter Lady Jean" (No. 52): This copy has been extremely injured by tradition; so much so as not to be intelligible in places except by comparison with A.   (II, 450)

"The Clerk's Twa Sons O Owsenford" (No. 72): We have here a strong contrast with both the blind-beggar and the housemaid style of corruption.   (III, 173)

"Johnie Cock" (No. 114): This manuscript, which Fry bought in Glasgow in 1810, contained several other ballads, 'but written so corruptly as to be of little or no authority'. It did not occur to Fry that the illiteracy of the drummer gave his ballads the best of authority.   (V, 1)

"The Bent Sae Brown" (No. 71): The silliness and fulsome vulgarity of Buchan's versions often enough make one wince or sicken, and many of them came through bad mouths or hands: we have even positive proof in one instance of imposture . . . . But such correspondences with foreign ballads as we witness in the present case are evidence of a genuine traditional foundation.
                                                    (III, 170)

"Child Maurice" (No. 83): Aytoun considers that E is the only copy printed in the middle of the last century purged, in the process of oral transmission, of what was not to the popular taste, and 'altered more.' There is no doubt that a copy learned from print may be transformed in this way, but it is certain that old tradition does not come to a stop when a ballad gets into print.   (IV, 264)

"Robin Hood and the Monk" (No. 119): It is very perfection in its kind; and yet we have others equally good, and beyond doubt should have had more, if they had been written down early, as this was, and had not been left to the chances of tradition. Even writing would not have saved all, but writing has saved this (in large part), and in excellent form.   (V, 95)

In using the phrase *Child-type ballad,* there is a danger that we may infer a greater homogeneity in the collection than in fact exists. Child labored for years over the problem of how best to classify and group his ballads. Sigurd Hustvedt has discussed the influence of Svend Grundtvig upon Child in this matter and has shown that Child took from his Danish friend the idea of starting the collection with the two-line ballads.[4] But he was unable to follow the scheme Grundtvig had used in editing the Danish ballads, for the English and Scottish ballads differed too much both in content and form from their Scandinavian counterparts. Child never really settled the problem of classification to his own satisfaction. He wrote to Macmath in 1886 an appraisal of the grouping of ballads in *ESPB:*

> Arrangement is now a vexatious question. Decidedly it is not a strong point in my collection. I started perversely: I should in making a new edition be tempted to arrange in three classes: 'Romantic'; 'Historical'; 'Anecdotes' or Stories, meaning such things as no one imagines, or which don't profess to be real (Boy & Mantle, Gawain: Heir of Linne, etc. etc.). But there would be trouble anyway. After Part IV, there will still be still [*sic*] a few ballads which I shall not know where to stow . . . . I reserve for the end a quantity of Buchanish and the like stuff in which the genuine is about 10% of the whole matter.   (IV, 398)[5]

Child's letters to Macmath frequently comment on the problem of which ballads to include and where in the collection to place them:

> The hunting ballad would scarcely be of our sort — I mean a traditional story of the *lyrical* description — so I should think from the verses you cite.   (II, 153)

> 'May Colvin' affords almost enough matter for a volume. I shall put first the *two* line ballads, that is, those of which I have *any* two line text. Luckily I have *one* of the Douglas tragedy and one of May Colvin, so that these very ancient ballads may come in early.   (II, 185)

> Next I thought I would put in all the *four* line ballads which, as to subject, belong with the two-liners already printed.   (III, 354)

4. Sigurd B. Hustvedt, *Ballad Books and Ballad Men* (Cambridge, Mass.: Harvard University Press, 1930), pp. 241–335.
5. Macmath MSS. The Roman numerals refer to the volume number, the Arabic to the article. Originals in possession of E. A. Hornel estate, Castle Douglas, Kirkcudbrightshire, Scotland; microfilm copy on deposit, HCL.

I have not quite enough of the better sort [of ballads] to fill Part
IV so I fear. There are rather more than 30 ballads as against 27
or 28 of the other parts, but some of the thirty are short. I mean
to end with Robyn and Gandelyn, & Johnie Cock, which are
nearest to Robin Hood in character, so as to begin Part V with R.
Hood . . . . The Historical & Border ballads will follow R. Hood,
and then all the later things, including much rubbish, will come at
the tail. I purpose such an Index as never was made for Ballads
before . . . .   (IV, 404)

Robin Hood will not fill Part V, and I think I shall go on with
'Historical Ballads'. When I said I should use that term liberally
['loosely' is here deleted] I meant that since some of the 'historical' ballads are 9/10 fiction I should not hesitate to put with them
ballads not commonly called historical which are of the same
general description . . . I shall begin 'Historical' ballads (not
applying any name to them) with the Jew's Daughter. (IV, 420)

I am sorry to think that after Part VI the ballads will begin to
decline in merit till they sink very low.   (V, 546)

It is a poor lot that is left — the Andrew Lammie, Ritchie Story,
Duke of Gordon's Daughter Lady Stopat lot: there are some 80 to
choose from. I cannot in the case of these give all the texts, for
the texts are very numerous often and the ballads next to worthless. After them come a set in which there are good ballads (I
will finish the Domestic ones first).   (VII, 701)

'The Lass of the Logan Lea', though, generally referred to as a
Ballad, is really only a Song — having no story.   (VII, 763)

I have been spending quite too much time on a very worthless
ballad . . . . The difficulty now is in selection. I really do not
think it would matter much if I stopped nearly where I am [Part
VIII], for pretty much all that remains has a very slight claim to
come in. But I will be liberal.   (VIII, 847)

Writing to his Glasgow correspondent, James Barclay Murdoch, Child remarked briefly on his intentions:

I shall begin to Print Part IV in March [1889]. It will contain the historical ballads, so called, and a few others which it is convenient to put with them.[6]

Part III has many beautiful ballads of the Romantic sort, and even Part IV will have some.[7]

With these comments in mind, it is possible to make a reconstruction of the outline around which *ESPB* was organised.

Part I, Nos. 1–28, "Two line ballads."
Part II, Nos. 29–53, "Four line ballads on subjects similar to the ballads in Part I."
Part III, Nos. 54–82, "Romantic ballads."
Part IV, Nos. 83–113, "Historical ballads."
Part V, Nos. 114–155, "Robin Hood ballads."
Part VI, Nos. 156–188, "Historical and Border ballads."
Part VII, Nos. 189–225, "Buchanish stuff."
Part VIII, Nos. 226–265, "Buchanish stuff."
Part IX, Nos. 266-305, "Domestic ballads" and "Anecdotes."
Part X, Glossary and Indexes.

This list is merely an informal gathering of descriptive phrases used by Child in letters never intended for publication, and there is no need to exaggerate its importance. Child did not print any kind of descriptive headings to the various parts of *ESPB*, nor do his notes to the individual ballads make any application of the above divisions. Yet the phrases are his, and they may help us to understand what was in Child's mind as he progressed from part to part.

The grouping of Part II is made clearer by a comment Child wrote to Grundtvig in 1872: "My *Trylleviser* will make a natural class, and I have no doubt that this class should come first." [8] Child had in mind here ballads of magic and marvels, a division used by Grundtvig and a division which in fact operates to a considerable extent in Part II of *ESPB*. It may be recalled from

6. Murdoch MSS, Article 41. Originals in possession of J. B. B. Murdoch, Glasgow; microfilm copy on deposit, HCL.
7. Article 36.
8. Hustvedt, *Ballad Books,* p. 254.

the discussion given earlier that Child regarded traits of the marvelous as a sure mark of antiquity in a ballad.

Parts VII and VIII are really a miscellany of ballads which did not find very much favor in Child's eyes but were included simply because he thought they contained remnants of traditional features or had been at one time, at least, popular ballads.

Taking the collection as a whole, Part V seems to be the pivotal volume; the four volumes before it contain the best ballads, those after it contain inferior ballads, with some exceptions in Part IX. The completed work as we have it did not represent Child's final judgment upon the canon of English and Scottish ballads. He was already planning a new edition before he had printed a quarter of *ESPB*. At that time (1875) he still lacked most of the important ballad manuscripts for which he had been searching and remarked to Macmath that perhaps people would be more willing to contribute their manuscript material to a second edition. Moreover, it was inevitable that versions, good versions, of ballads already printed should be found too late to be included except in an appendix. Child was sure he had not exhausted the possibilities of versions of ballads from Ireland, Shetland, Aberdeenshire, and from old magazines, to name instances he cited himself. Perhaps not enough account has been taken of the dynamic aspect of *ESPB;* the collection was constantly being expanded, Child was constantly changing his mind, new material and fresh problems were constantly arising.

Although he did not make general statements about popular balladry at large, Child did succeed in developing criteria for a good ballad. He gave a highly individualized treatment to most of his ballads, emphasizing their particular features, content, and stylistic nuances against a background of world literature. In the end, the Child-type ballad is primarily a study in comparative literature; it is a good story, ancient, coherently told, with features that can be verified by analogs in folklore and oral tradition.

ALBERT B. FRIEDMAN

"When Adam Delved . . .":
Contexts of an Historic Proverb

> Whan Adam dalf and Eve span,
> Who was þanne a gentil man?

This first extant record in English of this momentous couplet occurs in a recension of Thomas Walsingham's *Chronica Maiora* made sometime in the 1390s.[1] The circumstances are well known. John Ball, a Kentish priest freed by a mob a few days before from prison in Maidstone, used the lines as the text for an inflammatory sermon delivered June 13, 1381, to the rebellious peasants on Blackheath menacing London. Ball preached that the claim of prelates and nobles to the services of the peo-

1. British Museum Royal MS E ix, fol. 287a. Ptd. from later and worse MSS in *Historia Anglicana,* ed. H. T. Riley, Rolls Ser., II (London, 1864), 32, and in *Chronicon Angliae,* ed. E. M. Thompson, Rolls Ser. (London, 1874), p. 321. The dates and authority of the various recensions and MSS are established by V. H. Galbraith, "Thomas Walsingham and the Saint Albans Chronicle 1272–1422," *English Historical Review,* 47 (1932), 12–29. B. J. Whiting, *Proverbs, Sentences, and Proverbial Phrases from English Writings Mainly before 1500* (Cambridge, Mass.: Harvard University Press, 1968), p. 4, following the Brown-Robbins *Index* (No. 3922), gives Balliol MS 354 for the entry under 1381, but this MS is c. 1520. I am grateful to Dr. Peter French for checking my MS references.

ple because of their superior birth contradicts the biblical fact
of all men's common descent from the original sinful pair, "for
if it had pleased God to create serfs, surely in the inception of
the world He would have appointed who should be a serf and
who should be a lord."

The history of these lines before 1381 can only be conjectured. Walsingham calls the text on which Ball preached a proverb (*verba proverbii*), implying that it was an old popular saying current orally. The proverb in a Latin form is found in
sermons preached in 1374 and 1377 by Thomas Brinton, bishop
of Rochester, a diocese which furnished a large number of the
Kentish agitators. Brinton simply gives the opening clause of the
proverb ("Cum vanga quadam tellurem foderat Adam"), cutting it short with an "et cetera." [2] He apparently expected his
audiences to complete the saying for themselves, and his abbre-
viation is further evidence that the lines were common knowledge. The same deduction may be made from another early record. "A Song of Mortality" written by a lyricist of the school of
Richard Rolle begins,

> When adam delf & eve span, spir, if þou wil spede,
> Whare was þan þe pride of man þat now merres his mede.[3]

Though the song appears only in fifteenth-century MSS, Carleton Brown ascribes the poem to the 1370s,[4] about the time Ball
was actively agitating in Kent, and Hope E. Allen is led to conjecture that Ball "may have caught up and adapted a folk-saying
long current . . . or he may even have met this Northern poem
and taken a hint from it for his rhyme." [5] In one document Ball
is cited as having been early in his career "Seynte Marie prest

2. *Sermons,* ed. Sister Mary A. Devlin, Camden Soc., 3rd Ser., 85
(1954), 154, 195–196. In the second instance, *quandam* for *quadam;* in
later references, *foderat* is more correctly given as *foderit.*

3. *Religious Lyrics of the XIVth Century,* ed. Carleton Brown (Oxford: Oxford University Press, 1957), pp. 96–97.

4. *Ibid.,* p. xix. Cf. Alois Brandl's dating (end of the fourteenth century) in Hermann Paul, *Grundriss der germanischen Philologie* (Stras-
bourg, 1900–1909), II, i, 667.

5. *Writings Ascribed to Richard Rolle* (New York: D. C. Heath,
1927), p. 296.

of York," [6] a bit of information that could connect him however slimly with the Northern poem, but the first part of Miss Allen's conjecture, namely that Ball adapted a folk saying for his text, is more apt. Indeed the Northern poet, I would suggest, is doing precisely the same thing in the opening lines of his poem. In the six-stanza version of the poem, he has twelve opportunities for internal rhyming, but only once aside from the "span/man" of the opening lines does he use internal rhyme. Clearly the second halves of both these lines are more or less vapid expansions; the second half of the first is particularly obvious filler. The alliteration, not carried through consistently in the poem as a whole, is used here to bind on the additions.

W. C. Hazlitt assumed that the proverb derived from a Latin "parent-phrase." [7] Bishop Brinton uses the Latin form, but then he is preaching in Latin. Walsingham, on the other hand, though writing in Latin, quotes the proverb in English, one of the rare times he resorts to the vernacular, and this condescension, of course, implies the priority of the English. It is true, however, that in three of the eight or so pre-1550 records of the English saying it appears as a gloss on the Latin lines Brinton was alluding to: "Cum vanga quadam tellurem foderit Adam,/Et Eva nens fuerat, quis generosus erat?" [8] This Latin version is unvaried in England, but in Germany and the Low Countries, where the proverb was well known in the fifteenth and sixteenth centuries, the Latin versions vary widely. The seminal Dutch *Proverbia Communia* (c. 1475) offers the succinct "Adam fodiente, quis nobilior, Eva nente?" [9] Heinrich Bebel's *Proverbia Germanica* (1508) is better prose: "Dum Adam agrum coleret et Eva ne-

6. Walsingham, *Historia Anglicana,* ed. Riley, II, 33–34; *Fourteenth Century Verse and Prose,* ed. Kenneth Sisam (Oxford: Clarendon Press, 1921), pp. 160–161.

7. *English Proverbs and Proverbial Phrases* (London: Reeves and Turner, 1907), p. 523.

8. Harley MS 3362, fol. 5a (c. 1470); Rawlinson MS D 328, fol. 142b (c. 1475) — Samuel Meech, "A Collection of Proverbs in Rawlinson MS D 328," *Modern Philology,* 38 (1940–41), 121; Balliol MS 354, fol. 200b (c. 1520) — *Songs and Carols . . . from Balliol MS 354,* ed. Roman Dyboski, Early English Text Society, Extra Ser. 101 (1907), 131.

9. Ed. Richard Jente, Indiana University Publ., Folklore Ser. No. 4 (Bloomington: Indiana University Press, 1947), pp. 106, 297–298 (No. 778).

ret, quis tunc nobilis?" [10] Dedekind in his timidly Rabelaisan
Grobianus (1552) elaborates the sentiment into a quatrain,

> Primus Adam duro cum verteret arva ligone,
> Pensaque de vili duceret Eva colo:
> Ecquis in hoc poterat vir nobilis orbe videri?
> Et modo quisquam ante alios locandus erit? [11]

From these facts we must conclude that the Latin version in
England descended in a MS tradition parallel to the oral, vernacular tradition; the Continental Latin versions are ad hoc
translations of the vernacular proverb; and the proverb was diffused popularly from England to Germany in the vernacular
form. If the proverb were originally Latin, we would expect the
Continental and English versions of the Latin to be much more
similar.

In contrast, the North European vernacular versions of the
proverb could hardly be closer translations of the English. One
of the earliest (c. 1450) runs, "Wo was ein graff, ritter und
edelman,/Do Adam hackt und Eva span?" [12] A poem published
at Bamberg in 1493, "Wer der erst Edelmann gewest ist," contains the lines: "Da Adam reütet und Eva span,/Wer was die
zeit da ein Edelman?" [13] Agricola (1529) has, "Do Adam
reutte und Eva span/Wer was do eyn Edelman?" [14] His master
Melancthon's version (c. 1550): "Da Adam hackte undt Eva

10. Ed. W. H. Suringar (Leyden, 1879), p. 354, No. 247; cp. Sylvia
Resnikow, "The Cultural History of a Democratic Proverb," *Journal of
English and Germanic Philology*, 36 (1937), 398, and Jente, p. 298.
Resnikow and Jente offer virtually a full spread of the German, Dutch,
and Scandinavian appearances of the proverb.

11. Friedrich Dedekind, *Grobianus* (Frankfort, 1552), I chap. 4; cf.
Resnikow, p. 400. A completely different Latin quatrain, beginning "Si
pater est Adam cunctis, si mater est Eva," appears in André Tiraqueau,
De Nobilitate (Lyons, 1559), p. 44.

12. *Die Wolfenbüttler Handschrift,* ed. Karl Euling (Berlin: Weid-
mann, 1908), p. 60, No. 418.

13. Ed. Emil Weller, *Serapeum,* 24 (1863), 231. Wilhelm Stammler,
Die deutsche Literatur des Mittelalters: Verfasserlexikon I (Berlin: De
Gruyter, 1933), col. 178, erroneously gives this as the source of the prov-
erb; cf. Jente, p. 298, and Resnikow, pp. 394–395.

14. *Die Sprichwörtersammlungen,* ed. S. L. Gilman (Berlin: De Gruyter, 1971), No. 264, pp. 207–212.

span,/Wer war da ein Edelman?" [15] A Swedish poem on chess
Schack-tafvels Lek (c. 1485) quotes the proverb: "Ho war tha
een ädela man/Tha Adam groff ok Eva span?" [16] — lines which
probably derive from the Dutch "Wie was doe die edel man,/
Doe Adam groef ende Eva span?" in the *Proverbia Communia*.[17]

In modern proverb collections one comes across Italian, Polish, and even Czech renderings of "When Adam delved . . . ,"
but these are learned concoctions transparently imitating the
German or English. There is, however, a closely related proverb,
though without the distinctive rhetorical form of "When Adam
delved . . . ," which was widely used throughout Europe in important contexts. This is Whiting A 37 (pp. 3–4), "We are all
come from Adam and Eve." Mannyng of Brunne inserts the
proverb into *Handlyng Synne* (1303) without warrant from his
French source:

> ȝyf þou for prydë art outrage
> Þat þou art come of hygh lynage
> Beþenke þe weyl fro when þou cam;
> Allë we were of Adam:
> ȝyf þou be comë of hygh blode
> And þou dost more evyl þan gode,
> Unwrþyly art þou made gentyl
> ȝyf þou yn wurdys and dedys be yl.[18]

Whiting's earliest citation is from Hilton's *Scale of Perfection*
(c. 1396), his next from Wyclif's *Sermons* (c. 1400); a passage
from Banester's *Guiscardo* (c. 1485) shows the proverb — Eve

15. *Analecta Lutherana et Melanthoniana,* ed. Georg Loesche (Gotha,
1892), No. 227; cf. Resnikow, p. 396.
16. Cited by Jente, p. 298; cf. Resnikow, p. 396. Archer Taylor, *The
Proverb* (Cambridge, Mass.: Harvard University Press, 1931), p. 24,
gives a modern Swedish version in which Adam weaves to accompany
Eve's spinning.
17. Ed. Jente, p. 106, No. 778.
18. Ed. F. J. Furnivall, EETS, 119, 123 (1901–1903), ll. 3031–38.
The proverb is also used to argue the equality of men and women; see
Alexander Scott, *Poems,* ed. James Cranstoun, Scottish Text Society
(Edinburgh, 1896), pp. 26–27, cited in B. J. Whiting, *Mediaeval Studies,* 11 (1949), 130, and Carleton Brown, *Religious Lyrics of the XIVth
Century,* p. 177.

substituted for Adam — making the same point as "When Adam delved . . .":

> Furst when oure modyr Eve brought forth Abell and Caym, Who cowde prefer hymself of byrth or of lynage, And of theym tweyne infauntes, who could a tytell claym In gentyll blood, in nobleness, or in hygh parage? But every man was fayne to put him in devoir Hys lyvyng for to gete with swetyng and gret labour.

The functional equivalence of the two proverbs is shown by the fact that Froissart in his description of John Ball's agitation supplants "When Adam delved . . ." with the blander proverb:

> A ye good people, the maters gothe nat well to passe in Englande, nor shall nat do tyll every thyng be common; and that there be no villayns nor gentylmen. . . . What have we deserved, or why should we be kept thus in servage? We be all come fro one father and one mother, Adam and Eve: wherby can they say or shewe that they be gretter lordes than we be? Savynge by that they cause us to wyn and labour for that they dispende.[19]

The earliest Continental analogue of Whiting A 37 occurs in Freidank's *Bescheidenheit* (1229): "Swie die liute geschaffen sint,/Wir sin doch alle Adames kint." [20] In a poem of Jean de Condé (c. 1285) we find:

> Quanqu'il est de fames et d'omes,
> D'un pere et d'une mere sommes:
> D'Adan, que Diex fist, et d'Evain;
> Tout sommes presti d'un levain
> Et tout ouni selon la char
> Gentil, vilain, large et eschar,
> Haut et bas, roi et duc et conte
> Si com poure gent, qui voir conte.[21]

19. *Chronicle,* trans. Sir John Bourchier, Lord Berners, 1523–1525, Tudor Translations, III (London: D. Nutt, 1901), 224.

20. Ed. Wilhelm Grimm (Göttingen, 1860), p. 86, ll. 10–11.

21. *Dits et contes,* ed. August Scheler (Brussels, 1866–1867), III, 97, ll. 41–48; cited by G. M. Vogt, "Gleanings for the History of a Sentiment: *Generositas Virtus, Non Sanguis," JEGP,* 24 (1925), 106.

The antifeminist *Lamentations* (c. 1290) of Matheolus, a Norman cleric, furnishes this expressive if not very elegant set of verses on the theme:

> Nobilitas sola est animum que moribus ornat,
> Non ea quam sanguis turgens ad vana sobornat.
> Heu! cur confidit vir in alto sanguine? funus
> Mox genus elidit. En cunctis est pater unus
> Adam. Dico phy! de carnis nobilitate;
> Exaltanda tamen est, quando sapit probitate.[22]

Nearer to what was later to be the standard wording is a passage from Gervais du Bus' *Roman de Fauvel* (1310):

> Tous summes neiz d'une semence,
> Si qu'il n'a point de difference
> Entre vilain et gentil homme;
> Tous summes d'Eve et d'Adan neis,
> Et tous fusmes a mort dampneis
> Pour ce qu'il mordrent de la pomme.[23]

The proverb was current in southern Europe as well. "Tutti siem nati di Adam e di Eva" is urged as a reason for the sharing of wealth in a sonnet of Folgore da San Gimignano (c. 1325),[24] and in Fernando de Rojas' *La Celestina* (1499) Areusa advises,

> Las obras hazen linaje, que al fin todos somos hijos de Adán y Eva. Procure de ser cada uno bueno por sí, y no vaya a buscar en la nobleza de sus passados la virtud.[25]

Since, then, all men have a common origin, to boast of one's lineage is arrogant and foolish. Actually, commencing the gen-

22. Ed. A. G. van Hamel, I (Paris, 1892), 267, ll. 4121–26; unnoticed by Vogt.

23. Arthur Langfors, *Société des Anciens Textes Français* (Paris, 1919), p. 44, ll. 1107–12; unnoticed by Vogt.

24. *Sonetti Burleschi,* ed. A. F. Massèra (Bari: G. Laterza e figli, 1940), p. 173.

25. Ed. Julio Cejador y Frauca (Madrid: Ediciones de 'La Lectura,' 1931), II, 34–35, Act IX.

erations with Adam was a species of flattery; mankind's begin-
nings were even earthier. Centuries before, Juvenal had cited
the heterodox myth of Prometheus' fabrication of the first generation of men from clay to mock those who gloried in their
pedigrees,[26] and there were many medieval preachers, Wyclif
among others, who liked to humble nobles and church digni-
taries and further degrade the already humble by reminding
them that man's origin may be traced even beyond Adam to
the soil he tilled. "Alle we byeþ children of one moder," says
the *Ayenbite of Inwit* (1340), "þet is, of erþe and of wose,"
referring to Genesis 2:7.[27] But if men are base, as sons of dust,
they are also exalted, as sons of God, a paradox the Church
fathers exploited tirelessly; and in both baseness and exaltation,
all men are naturally equal. Boethius furnished the seminal text
for such egalitarian notions. In the *Consolation* "nobilitatis nomen" is called a vain and futile thing to desire "quae si ad clari-
tudinem refertur, aliena est," and Dame Philosophy goes on to
proclaim that

> Omne hominum genus in terris simili surgit ab ortu.
> Unus enim rerum pater est,

a Father who created all men from "nobile germen." "Why
then," asks Philosophy, "do you brag about your ancestors?" [28]
Curiously enough, when King Alfred or his committee of epis-
copal scholars translated these lines of Boethius, the Father of
all things is transmuted into the father and mother of the race:

> Hwæt ealle men hæfdon gelicne fruman, forþan hi ealle coman
> of anum fæder and of anre meder, and ealle hi beoð git gelice
> acennede.[29]

Seemingly Alfred preferred the concept of a concrete biblical
blood cousinry to the abstract mystical brotherhood of men, sons

---

26. *Satires,* IV.133, VIII.133; cf. Ovid, *Metamorphoses,* I.80ff.
27. Ed. Richard Morris, EETS, 23 (1866), 87.
28. Book III, prose 6 and metrum 6.
29. *King Alfred's Boethius,* ed. W. J. Sedgefield (Oxford, 1899), p. 69.

of a spiritual Father, which his text, influenced by late Stoicism, intended. The Boethian passage resonated through the Middle Ages. Over six centuries after Alfred, Dame Scotia in *The Complaynt of Scotlande* (1549) quotes this very speech of Dame Philosophy in the course of arguing that "it is grit arrogance, and na les folie, quhen ony person gloris in his genoligie, considerand that evyre person is discendit of ane origyne," whether Adam and Eve or "eird and puldir." [30]

As the contexts adhering to many of my abstracts anticipate, the medieval moralists were doing something more than warning their audiences against the sin of pride when they reminded them of their common and lowly origins. Their ulterior purpose was to prepare the ground for asserting that the qualities of nobility and gentility were not matters of blood, position, or possessions, but stemmed from an inherent impulse, inspired by God's grace, to conduct oneself virtuously. All the great medieval poets, Jean de Meun, Dante, Petrarch, Chaucer, were obsessed with this theme and rang endless changes on it. The loathly lady's coverlet lecture in the Wife of Bath's Tale is a cento of commonplaces on the subject. Yet, although the assumption of hereditary virtue was regarded by the poets as morally monstrous, they lived more or less comfortably in a social order in which power and status were inherited, and riches, new or old (Aristotle found it important to distinguish between new and ancient wealth), counted for virtually everything. Precept and practice confronted each other uneasily, and matters were not much helped by those who, like Chaucer's Parson, urged a distinction between the gentry of the body and the gentry of the soul.[31] The whole gentilesse discussion was further bedeviled by a massive semantic confusion: villany, gentility (*gentilezza, gentilesse*), and nobility denoted ambiguously birth, class, and membership in an estate on one hand, and personal viciousness or virtue on the other, an ambiguity which promoted a bias inherent in medieval society. Neutral terms like probity, goodness, virtue, and their opposites were available to the poets and oc-

30. Ed. J. A. H. Murray, EETS, ES 17, 18 (1872–73), 152.
31. *Works,* ed. F. N. Robinson, 2nd ed. (Boston: Houghton Mifflin, 1957), pp. 241–242 (*De Superbia,* ll. 460ff.).

casionally employed by them, but they seem to have felt a heuristic value in the ambiguous ones. If it was morally mistaken
to think that the merits of illustrious ancestors automatically de-
volved upon the bearers of the name along with titles and lands,
being called a nobleman or a gentleman and accorded the privi-
leges of rank might stimulate *noblesse oblige* and make the noble who committed a villany (so Jean de Meun reasoned)[32]
aware that he had betrayed his degree and shamed his forebears.
But no one was threatened in a practical way by the poets' high-
minded pronouncements on gentilesse. Seldom if ever was a noble degraded in rank for acting in a way unbecoming a noble,
nor was the baseborn man who acted nobly automatically, or
even exceptionally, exalted to the rank his personal merit de-
served. Virtue, as always, had to be its own reward. Of course
the vicissitudes of Fortune were not to be denied, and always
in the backgrounds was the warning of the Magnificat that "He
hath put down the mighty from their seats, and hath exalted
those of low degree," but since such capricious social reversals
could neither be guarded against nor invited, they were irrelevant as moral sanctions. In these circumstances, the chastening
sermons of the preachers and the graceful ethical formulations
of the poets could be tolerated, indeed complacently approved
by the privileged and propertied because prepotent social institutions rendered them just so many innocuous pieties.

For over a hundred years at least, "When Adam delved . . ."
has been labeled a "democratic proverb," [33] and thanks to the
history manuals, Ball's proverb has become the tag under which
the Peasants Revolt of 1381 is filed in our minds. Consequently,
when we hear any medieval saying that sounds at all like this
leveling sentiment, we smell a Lollard in the wind. But before
Holinshed and later chroniclers had fixed the association, this
and related sayings had no such threatening subversive connotations. As late as 1450, the couplet could be used as the refrain
of a light-hearted carol ("Now bething the gentlemen/How
Adam delved and Eve span"), lines employed simply for their

32. *Le Roman de la Rose,* ed. Ernest Langlois, SATF (Paris, 1914–
1924), IV, 246–247, ll. 18864ff.
33. *Notes and Queries,* 4th ser., 9 (1872), 415; cf. the title of Resnikow's article.

cadence since they have little connection with what the carol goes on to sing.[34] Gower, a Kentish landowner who suffered through the sack of London in 1381 and left a circumstantial account of it in *Vox Clamantis,* is not inhibited, either by this experience or by his anger at the demands of laborers even before the Revolt, from invoking the aboriginal parity of human blood. Riches are no basis for gentilesse, the priest of Love tells the Lover in the *Confessio Amantis,* nor is gentilesse a matter of birth:

> Adam, which alle was tofore
> With Eve his wife, as of hem tuo,
> Al was aliche gentil tho;
> So that of generacion
> To make declaracion,
> Ther mai no gentilesce be.[35]

And in the earlier (1378) *Mirour de l'Omme,* addressing a representative of the lords and knights, Gower reminds him

> Tous suismes d'un Adam issuz.

All come into the world nude; none emerge wearing fancy shoes. If you are rich but without virtue and given to mischief, God will change your six to an ace. And again, a few lines later,

> Tous suismes fils de dame Evian.
> Seigneur, tu qui me dis vilain,
> Comment voes dire q'es gentil? [36]

G. C. Macaulay, Gower's editor, comments that such passages show that Gower

... though a thorough believer in the principle of gradation in human society, emphasizes constantly the equality of all men

34. Sloane MS 2593, fol. 2b; *The Early English Carols,* ed. R. L. Greene (Oxford: Clarendon Press, 1935), No. 336, p. 230.
35. Book IV, 2220ff.; *Works,* ed. G. C. Macaulay (Oxford: Clarendon Press, 1901), II, 361.
36. L1. 23389ff.; *Works,* ed. Macaulay, I,258.

before God and refuses absolutely to admit the accident of birth
as constituting any claim whatever to 'gentilesce.' The common
descent of all from Adam is as conclusive on this point for him
as it was for John Ball, and he is not less clear on the subject of
wealth.[37]

The facile implicating of John Ball in this interpretation is unfortunate. John Ball was not the least interested in courtly dis-
quisitions on gentilesse. What he refuses absolutely to admit is
that the accident of birth should entitle any man to hold others
in servitude. He would obliterate the distinction between serf
and lord entirely, a distinction he regarded as unnatural because
it was not original and not established by God. Clearly Gower,
"a thorough believer in the principle of gradation in human society" and a man who had written thousands of lines on the
distinct duties of the estates in promoting the common good,
would regard Ball's radical deductions as a diabolic perversion
of natural law and Christian order.

    And so, too, would the preachers who inadvertently laid the
groundwork for Ball's ministry. The first record of "When Adam
delved . . . ," we recall, is as an allusion in two of Bishop Brinton's sermons, and G. R. Owst has demonstrated how some of
the popular preachers, especially the friars with their exaltation
of evangelical poverty, prepared the way for Ball.[38] But like the
poets on gentilesse, the preachers in their homiletic invectives
on wealth and privilege were innocent of any revolutionary intent. Owst quotes a sermon of the Dominican Bromyard:

All are descended from the same first parents, and all come of
the same mud. For, if God had fashioned nobles from gold, and
the ignoble from mud, then the former would have cause for
pride . . . . True glory does not depend upon the origin or beginning from which anything proceeds, but upon its own condition.

Bromyard goes on to predict that the luxuries of the rich on
earth will be repaid with gruesome miseries in hell. The poor

    37. *Works,* I, lxiv.
    38. *Literature and Pulpit in Medieval England* (Cambridge: Cam-
bridge University Press, 1933), pp. 287ff.

who have suffered unjust exactions may console themselves with
the thought that their torments are temporary while their op-
pressors will suffer eternally. God may now seem to connive in
the injustice of the world, but in the end the powerful who in-
flict wrongs will perish.[39] The idea of the poor seeking earthly
and immediate redress for their grievances is unthinkable to the
preachers. The poor must endure patiently their God-appointed
lot and not begrudge other men their high estate if they want to
preserve their heavenly reward. The court prelate Brinton's
"Cum vanga . . . foderit Adam . . ." is similarly swathed in ex-
hortations to submit to the divine purpose which effectively de-
fuse it of any incendiary force.

The preachers could risk criticizing the pompous pride of the
rich because the stratification of feudal society was so secure.
Like the conservative writers who censured the failures and ex-
cesses of the three estates, censured laborers no less than clerics
and nobles — Gower, for example, or Alain Chartier in the
Quadrilogue invectif — the preachers had no intention of bringing down the system. A stable social order, they knew, was
necessary to provide the material arena in which Christians
struggled to save their souls. From Aristotle's *Politics* to Caxton's *Chessbook,* the learned agreed that differences in rank
among men no less than division of labor was necessary for the
public good and the survival of the body politic. Plebeians and
peasants were instructed in organicism by Menenius Agrippa's
apologue, familiar to us from Livy (II, 32) and *Coriolanus,* of
the strike against the belly mounted by the limbs, nerves, and the
other organs. The strikers soon came to realize that their strength
came from the pampered organ whose demands they destruc-
tively resented. Plato, Cicero, and St. Paul had dignified the
fable by alluding to it; John of Salisbury applied the corporate
image it dramatized to the medieval state.[40]

There were, to be sure, cynical versions of how class differences arose. Jean de Meun conjectured that the differentiation
began when the original, natural society of equals chose one of
their number to settle disputes among them, gave him bullies for

39. *Ibid.,* pp. 292–294.
40. *Policraticus,* trans. John Dickinson (New York: Alfred A. Knopf,
1927), p. 65.

guards, and so corrupted the golden age of equality.[41] Others in-
timated that the ruling class had not waited to be elected:

> For when Adam dolf and Eve span,
> Who was then a gentylman?
> But then cam the churl and gederyd good,
> And ther began furst the gentyll blood.[42]

Both religious teachers and most political theorists, of course,
held that the social order was Providential: "God in his divine
wisdom ordained degrees in society just as in all the rest of the
universe, and God desires we keep our due degree." [43] In heaven
as on earth: were there not grades of angels? Rank, like salvation, was predestined by divine grace. According to a German
legend, when the Emperor Maximilian I read "Da Adam reutet
and Eva spann,/Wer was da ein Edelmann?" on an oven, he
answered the question by writing "Ich bin ein Mann wie ander
Mann,/Allein dass mir Gott die Ehr vergan." [44]

For fundamentalists there was a quasi-biblical explanation for
the origin of social distinctions, namely the fable best known
through the Grimms' *Kinder- und Hausmärchen* as *Die un-
gleichen Kinder Evas*.[45] After their expulsion from Paradise,
Adam delved and Eve spun wool, but they still had the energy
to produce a numerous brood. Preparing for a visit from God,
Eve washed the handsome ones among her children and dressed
them in their best clothes; the ugly children she hid in the hay,
in the stoves, under vats, or in the attic or cellar. God blessed
the eight children presented to him, all boys, promising one he

41. *Roman,* ed. Langlois, III, 127ff., ll. 9587ff.
42. John Heywood or John Rastell in *Gentylnes* (c. 1525); quoted by
Whiting under A 38.
43. Edmund Dudley, *Tree of Common Wealth* (c. 1500), quoted in
Ruth Mohl, *The Three Estates in Medieval and Renaissance Literature*
(New York: Columbia University Press, 1933), p. 154. On the divine
origin of estates, see pp. 277ff.
44. *Analecta Lutherana,* ed. Loesche, No. 227; see Johannes Bolte and
Georg Polívka, *Anmerkungen zu den Kinder- und Hausmärchen der Brü-
der Grimm* (Hildesheim: Georg Olms, 1963), III, 311.
45. No. 180; quotations from *The Grimms' German Folk Tales,* trans.
F. P. Magoun, Jr., and A. H. Krappe (Carbondale: Southern Illinois
University Press, 1960), pp. 583–585.

would become a king, another a count, another a merchant, another a scholar, and so on. When Eve saw how kind the Lord was, she fetched her twelve misshapen children, "the whole coarse, dirty, scabby, sooty troop." These God blessed too, telling one child "You shall become a farmer," another, "You a fisherman"; the others were destined to be smiths, tanners, potters, servants, and other menial occupations. When Eve complained of the unequal distribution, God replied:

> "Eve, you don't understand. It is proper and necessary for me through your children to provide for the whole earth. Were they all princes and lords, who would cultivate grain, thresh, grind, and bake? Who would forge, weave, hew, build, dig, cut, and sew? Everybody must have his place, so that one may support the other and all, like the parts of a body, be nourished."

The Grimm version is a *Schwanke* of Hans Sachs (1558), latest of four forms the mastersinger put the tale through. Another form, in which Sachs follows Melancthon, has the Lord catechize the children. Abel heads the good performers, Cain the bad boys. Sachs' source for the *Schwanke* was a Latin eclogue of Mantuan written in the 1470s but not published until 1498. (Alexander Barclay translated the eclogue into English in 1514.) The French printer Ascensius, commenting on Mantuan's eclogue in 1502, reports that the story was a well-known old folktale, and its wide distribution in later centuries, both in Europe and among the Arabs, makes his report highly probable.[46]

Perhaps the reason the fable of Eve's children circulated only among the medieval folk, if indeed it did, is that the learned would have found it irrelevant. God's arrangement of ranks in the post-Edenic world was washed out by the Flood. Obviously the estates of mankind derive not from the sons of Adam but the sons of Noah — Shem, Japheth, and Ham. "In Noah's time," writes Honorarius of Autun about 1125, "divisum est genus humanum in tria: in liberos, milites, servos. Liberi de Sem, milites de Japhet, servi de Cham." [47] The biblical license

46. Bolte and Polívka, III, 308–311.
47. *De Imagine Mundi,* III, 2; Migne, *Patrologia Latina,* CLXXII, 166.

for this dispensation is the passage in Genesis (9:18–25) where the descendants of Ham were cursed by Noah and condemned to be "the lowliest of slaves" because Ham had ridiculed the nakedness of his drunken father. The story is used prominently in Hugo von Trimberg's *Renner* (1296–1313) to justify the divisions of society and — by a peculiar twist of reasoning — to illustrate that nobility does not depend on ancestry or wealth but on virtue. If Ham had been virtuous, his descendants would not have been condemned to servitude.[48] In Heinrich Wittenweiler's *Ring* (c. 1400) a farmer who cannot see where the princes get their right to rule — "Sein seu nicht als wol sam wir/Adams Kinder?" — is answered feebly by an old councilor that the good are elected to be noblemen, the wicked bondsmen, as happened to the sons of Noah.[49]

These uses of the story are sufficiently clumsy, but they are at least skillful in sidestepping its greatest difficulty. From the sons of Noah came the three social classes; as the *Cursor Mundi* (c. 1300) puts it:

> O sem freman, o Iaphet knytht,
> Thrall of cham the maledight.[50]

The territorial world had also been divided among the sons:

> Asie to sem, to cham affrik,
> To Iaphet europ, þat wil-ful wike.[51]

How then, asks Eike von Repgau in the *Sachsenspiegel* (1200), could the serfs of Europe descend from Ham, whose descendants

48. Ed. Gustav Ehrismann (Tübingen: Bibliothek der litterarischen Verein in Stuttgart, 1909), ll. 1315ff.

49. Ed. Edmund Wiessner (Leipzig: P. Reclam, 1931), pp. 252–253, ll. 7218ff.

50. Ed. Richard Morris, EETS, 57, 59, 62, 66, 68, 99, 101 (1874–1893), ll. 2135–36.

51. *Ibid.*, ll. 2089–90. This division appears as late as the earliest printed map of the world, the famous "T-map" in Guenther Zainer's printing of Isidore of Seville's *Etymologiae* (Augsburg, 1472), Bk. XIV, chap. 1. In the more accessible Venetian edition of 1483 the map is reproduced on p. 68b. Donne alludes to the legend in *Hymn to God, my God, in my sickness*, 1. 20.

peopled Africa? And were these descendants not black? — a punishment visited on them, if the rabbis are to be believed, because Ham had copulated with a raven on the ark.[52] *The Boke of St. Albans* (1486) propounds a solution of sorts, though it garbles Genesis and geography and overlooks the negritude of Ham's issue to do so. According to Dame Juliana Berners or whoever the author was, after cursing Ham, Noah assigns him the northern part of the world, where he is doomed to live in "sorrow and care, colde and myschef" in a region "wich shall be calde Europe, that is to say the contre of churlys." Japheth is given the West, Asia, "the contre of gentilmen," and Shem the East, Africa, "the contre of tempurnes." Presumably the nobles and gentlemen of Europe are Asian or African immigrants.[53]

With More and Elyot, the theory of the original equality of mankind entered the realm of philosophical controversy, and neither in England nor on the Continent was there much tolerance for the testimony of naive biblical lore.[54] The courtesy books on the making of gentlemen are silent on natural equality, as we should expect. In any case, they would scorn the vulgar wisdom of proverbs, though Chesterfield, who has harsh things to say about proverbs, reverts to the Adam and Eve motif when warning his son that, before God, he was no better than the servant who wiped his shoes.[55] Actually our proverbs had very little popular currency after 1600, and allusions to the concept they expressed crop up infrequently in literature. When they do, it is usually in a somewhat facetious manner, as in Prior's *The Old Gentry* or his *Epitaph*:

> Nobles and Heralds by Your leave,
> Here lyes what Once was Matthew Prior,
> The Son of Adam and of Eve,
> Can Stuart, or Nassaw go higher? [56]

52. Ed. C. G. Homeyer (Berlin, 1861), III, 333–335; cf. Oskar Dähnhardt, *Natursagen*, I (Leipzig: B. G. Teubner, 1907), 291.

53. Sigs. A1a–A2a.

54. Mohl, p. 300.

55. John E. Mason, *Gentlefolk in the Making* (Philadelphia: University of Pennsylvania Press, 1935), pp. 108, 334.

56. *Literary Works,* ed. H. B. Wright and M. K. Spears (Oxford: Clarendon Press, 1959), I, 195.

The most notable English allusion occurs in a stanza from
Tennyson's "Lady Clara Vere de Vere" (1842) which Dickens
for obvious reasons liked to recite during his speeches to work-
ing-class audiences:

> Trust me, Clare Vere de Vere,
>   From yon blue heavens above us bent
> The gardener Adam and his wife
>   Smile at the claims of long descent.
> Howe'er it be, it seems to me,
>   'Tis only noble to be good.
> Kind hearts are more than coronets,
>   And simple faith than Norman blood.[57]

And with William Morris's *A Dream of John Ball* (1886), we
come full circle, for here we are back with the Kentish rebels
marching under a banner decorated with Adam and Eve, plow
and distaff, and the "democratic" proverb, now socialistic, in-
scribed underneath.

57. *Speeches of Charles Dickens,* ed. K. J. Fielding (Oxford: Clarendon Press, 1960), pp. 56, 133, 146.

PAUL THEINER

The Medieval Terence

Although known to us primarily as a dramatist, Terence could scarcely have presented himself to the Middle Ages in that light. E. K. Chambers, in sketching "the forces of humanism as they affected the history of the interlude during the first half of the sixteenth century," [1] gives us a succinct account of the postclassical lives of ancient comedy and tragedy:

> These, as vital forms of literature, did not long survive the fall of the theatres, with which, indeed, their connexion had long been of the slightest. In the East, a certain tradition of Christian book dramas begins with the anti-Gnostic dialogues of St. Methodius in the fourth century and ends with the much disputed Χριστὸς Πάσχων in the eleventh or twelfth. It is the merest conjecture that some of these may have been given some kind of representation in the churches. In the West the *Aulularia* of Plautus was rehandled under the title of *Querolus* at the end of the fourth century, and possibly also the *Amphitruo* under that of *Geta*. In the fifth, Magnus, the father of Consentius, is said by Sidonius, as Shakespeare is said by Ben Jonson, to have 'outdone insolent

1. E. K. Chambers, *The Mediaeval Stage* (Oxford: Clarendon Press, 1903), II, 206.

231

Greece, or haughty Rome.' Further the production of plays cannot be traced. Soon afterwards most of the classical dramatists
pass into oblivion. A knowledge of Seneca or of Plautus, not to
speak of the Greeks, is the rarest of things from the tenth century
to the fourteenth.   (II, 206–207)

But he goes on immediately to point out that Terence was a
"marked exception" to this rule, and he lends approval to
Ward's sentiment that Terence led "a charmed life in the darkest
ages of learning," attributing the charm to the readiness with
which Terence can be mined for sententious remarks (*ibid.*).
The rest of Chambers' argument deals, as one might expect from
his subject matter, with the occasional and tenuous connections
between Terence and the notion of drama in the Middle Ages:
with the request to Notker Labeo that he translate the *Andria*
into German, with the Terentian pieces of Hrotsvitha of Gander-
sheim, with the confused notions of Terence's dramatic practices
that abounded in the Middle Ages (II, 207–208). I would like
to leave all of these matters aside, taking instead as my point of
departure the following remark, which Chambers makes before
getting back to his dramatic theme: "[Terence's] vogue as a
school author was early and enduring, and the whole of mediae-
valism, a few of the stricter moralists alone dissenting, hailed him
as the master of the wisdom of life" (II, 207). For it is in fact
this solid vogue, and not what is connoted by the idea of leading
a charmed life, that characterizes the whole history of Terence's
writings and reputation from the close of antiquity to the end of
the Middle Ages. Charmed lives were led in the medieval period
by writers like Catullus, or Lucretius, or Tacitus, whose works
survived the millennium in rare and seldom noted manuscripts,[2]
and not by Terence, whose strength rendered elfin ministrations
quite unnecessary.

First of all, it should be noted that there is nothing eccentric
or exotic in the notion of the medieval Terence; there is in fact
a decided continuity and congruity from the ancient Terence
through the medieval Terence to the Renaissance Terence. That
is to say, there is no medieval Terence the Necromancer, no oc-

2. J. E. Sandys, *A History of Classical Scholarship,* 3rd ed. (Cambridge: Cambridge University Press, 1921), II, 413.

cult resorting to *sortes Terentianae,* to be triumphed over by the clear-eyed humanists of the Renaissance. Quite the contrary; while Erasmus may have had a characteristically Renaissance end in view when he urged the study of "models of pure Latinity" and put Terence on a par with Cicero in this respect (Sandys, II, 131), his medieval predecessors had already praised Terence for the elegance of his language, and Erasmus' proposed syllabus of school readings, which (Greek authors aside) included Terence, Vergil, Horace, Cicero, and Sallust, would scarcely have caused much of a stir had it been put forward five hundred years sooner.[3] Similarly, whether the rhymed prose of Hrotsvitha's Terentian adaptations is to be attributed to her inability to cope with the intricacies of Terence's verse forms, as Manitius would have it,[4] or with the prior inability of medieval scribes working on Terence's plays to recognize the writing as verse at all (Sandys, I, 506), we might simply observe that the *editio princeps* of Terence, which came out in 1470, also prints the text as prose.[5] There is no sudden break in attitude toward either the form or the substance of the Terentian comedies that can be conveniently used to separate the sensibilities of the Middle Ages from those of its descendants.

Unlike Plautus, only eight of whose twenty extant plays were known during the Middle Ages,[6] Terence had the benefit of a solid manuscript tradition that assured the acquaintance of a wide circle of medieval readers with the entire corpus of his work. Nor was there any period within the Middle Ages when copies of the writings of Terence ceased to be common, although the thirteenth- and fourteenth-century catalogues record the pos-

3. R. R. Bolgar, *The Classical Heritage and Its Beneficiaries* (Cambridge: Cambridge University Press, 1963), p. 340. Plautus and Caesar, who are also included, would have been less common in the Middle Ages; see Sandys, I, 658.

4. Max Manitius, *Geschichte der lateinischen Literatur des Mittelalters* (1911; rpt. Munich: C. H. Beck, 1969), I, 628.

5. John Sargeaunt, ed. and trans., *Terence,* Loeb Classical Library (Cambridge, Mass.: Harvard University Press), I, xiii. In fact when Bentley made his great edition of Terence in 1726, he corrected the text "in about a thousand passages, mainly on grounds of metre" (Sandys, II, 407), indicating that the true meter was not well understood for a considerable period.

6. Sandys, I, 630; also Manitius, III, 17.

session of fewer texts than those of the immediately preceding periods.[7] Therefore, although Bolgar professes surprise at the number of times Terence is quoted in monastic sources (p. 125), there would appear to be little reason for such surprise, unless we were still to be haunted by that specter of our humanistic educations that used to remind us constantly, and of course wrongly, that the Renaissance rediscovered all of the previously "lost" authors of antiquity. We will find instead that Terence is quoted, paraphrased, and alluded to by writers from one end of the Middle Ages to the other, for a wide variety of purposes, and in nearly as many genres as can be included in the Latin literature of the period. The problem is not one of finding traces of Terence, but of sorting out the pile. First, however, we ought to account for its existence.

Terence is, of course, a school author for the Middle Ages. No matter where we look in our period, it is difficult to find a respectable author espousing a program of readings that does not include him in its course.[8] Thus Curtius informs us that at the end of the tenth century, "students in the cathedral school at Speyer were reading 'Homer' [i.e., the Latinized paraphrase which was current at the time], Martianus Capella, Horace, Persius, Juvenal, Statius, Terence, Lucan; and of the Christian writers only Boethius" (p. 260), and that such a list is to be considered "normative" (p. 49). Not quite a century later, we find in the catalog of Winrich, teacher in the cathedral school of Treves, the following: "Cato, Camillus, Tully, Boethius, Lucan, Vergil, Statius, Sallust, and Terence" (Curtius, p. 260). Meanwhile Aimeric the grammarian, in his work *Ars lectoria,* which dates from about 1086, classes our author with the very best, as Manitius informs us:

Wie weit die Lektüre der alten Dichtung in der Schule ging, dafür haben wir in unsrer Periode mehrfach genauer Berichte. So

7. Bolgar, p. 413, notes that Terence is mentioned one, ten, and twenty-five times, respectively in catalogues of the ninth, tenth, and eleventh centuries; six and nine times for the thirteenth and fourteenth.

8. It is not impossible, of course; E. R. Curtius, *European Literature and the Latin Middle Ages,* trans. Willard R. Trask (New York: Harper and Row, 1963), p. 260, notes that the twelfth-century writer, Conrad of Hirsau, dropped Terence from his list in favor of Ovid.

teilt Aimericus in dem Werke *De arte lectoria* die zu lesenden Schriftsteller in drei Teile und führt an unter den aurei auctores Terenz, Vergil, Horaz, Ovid, Lucan, Statius, Juvenal, Persius, unter den argentei auctores Plautus und Ennius, unter den communes auctores Cato, Homer, Maximian, Avian, Asop. (III, 12)

Similarly, ancient poetry quoted in Isidore of Seville includes heavy doses of Terence, Virgil, Ovid, Lucan, Persius, and Juvenal, a bit less of Horace, and quite rare and scattered glimpses of Catullus, Statius, Martial, and Terentian (Manitius, I, 65).

We know, at the same time, that from Tertullian and Jerome forward there was a suspicion of pagan authors among Christian clerks, a suspicion that touched such diverse minds as Gregory, Alcuin, Odo of Cluny, Honorius of Autun, and Abelard, not to mention lesser figures.[9] And yet these men are apt, in the end, to urge caution rather than abstinence; Jerome, as we shall see, is not above a Terence allusion or two himself. And if the objections of an Abelard are grounded in a Platonic distrust of poets as fabricators of lies and deceptions, it is not the "fabulous" side of Terence that ordinarily attracts the attention of the medieval reader. As early as Quintilian, the rhetoricians found a distinction between the lyric poets and the writers of comedy that sheds light on the uses of Terence in the Middle Ages. In summarizing the *Institutio oratoria,* Curtius says, "The lyric poets too must be read, though with exceptions. Even Horace has passages which Quintilian would be loath to interpret in class. The erotic elegy is altogether rejected. Comedy, on the other hand, is recommended. It is important for students of oratory because it presents the various characters and passions, which Aristotle too had treated in his *Rhetoric*" (p. 437). The connection of the comic writers, then, is with the observation of human nature and the mores of men, and with the philosophical interpretation of that nature and those actions. In this sense, Terence, for all the admiration that his verbal art has always commanded, is for the medieval audience a thinker, specifically an authority on the human species and its behavior. It is the preeminent moral re-

9. See Sandys, I, 617–618.

spectability of this role that justifies his continued study in the
Middle Ages, just as it is his formal felicity that ensures his constant citation by the clerks who have been brought to the study
of his work.[10] When a medieval writer decides to make a com-
pendium of moral sayings, he is quite likely to include Terence
among his contributors. Thus Wernher of Elmendorf, stringing
together a book of moral precepts in the twelfth century, uses
quotations from Sallust, Boethius, Seneca, Juvenal, Horace,
Ovid, Lucan, and Terence (Curtius, p. 520), while a similar
compilation, the *Moralium dogma philosophorum,* has citations
of *auctores* as follows: "165 . . . from Cicero's *De Officiis,* 16
from other works of Cicero, 92 from Seneca, 12 from Sallust, 5
from Boethius, 104 from Horace, 40 from Juvenal, 18 from
Terence, 23 from Lucan," and this particular anthology proved
to be so popular that it was translated into Old French and a
number of other medieval vernaculars, much of it eventually
ending up in the *Trésor* of Brunetto Latini (Curtius, p. 529).
Having thus stocked their libraries, and their minds as well, with
the pith of Terentian wit, medieval writers were quite prepared
to make use of that stock in their own compositions; and they
did not hesitate for a moment.

It would be possible, but I think both confusing and misleading, to treat the medieval world of Terentian allusion in the
chronological order of authors citing the plays. This would lead
to a structure highly suggestive of historical development, and
although some generalizations along historical lines can be
drawn — e.g., that earlier writers are more likely than later ones
to reveal a consciousness of Terence's own literary genre by
referring to him as "comicus"; or that some later writers who use
words from Terence are not really quoting an author, but citing
a well-known "proverb" — it seems to me that even these observations can best be made in an atmosphere that avoids the
appearance of historical causality, that suggests that there is a
narrative history of allusions to Terence in the Middle Ages. For
that reason I propose rather to order the exposition around the

10. This is not of course to discount the possibility that many medieval writers who quote Terence came upon his words in *florilegia* or an-
thologies.

chronological order of the plays themselves. This procedure will also have the advantage of showing quite clearly which plays, and which parts of those plays, had the greatest appeal for medieval writers.

Of all the plays of Terence, the one most frequently cited — and that by a wide margin — is the first that he presented, the *Andria*.[11] We need not even get into the play proper. In the beginning of the Prologue to *Andria,* Terence complains that instead of being allowed to attend to the business of being a playwright, he is forced to answer the "maledictis" of a "malevoli veteris poetae," one Luscious Lavinius, by writing explanatory and apologetic prologues. And in the Preface to his *Liber Hebraicarum Quaestionum in Genesim,* Jerome — in spite of his wariness of the classics — sets himself up as a contemporary Terence: "Qui in principiis librorum debebam secuturi operis argumenta proponere, cogor prius respondere maledictis, Terentii quippiam sustinens. . . ."[12] The same Prologue to *Andria* also served Angelomus of Luxeuil as a model for a prologue to a proposed commentary on *Kings* (Manitius, I, 418) and was used by Bovo II of Corbie in a preface to a commentary on Boethius (Manitius, I, 528) and by Bern of Reichenau in the prologue of his *De consona tonorum diversitate* (Manitius, II, 71), both of whom play on the wording of Terence's opening line, "Poeta quom primum animum ad scribendum adpulit . . . ."

In the first scene of *Andria* there occur two *sententiae* that were cited an enormous number of times by medieval writers, both ending up more or less in the category of anonymous proverbs. The first occurs at lines 60–61, where the steward Sosia says, "nam id arbitror/adprime in vita esse utile, ut nequid nimis." This expression of the Mean so caught the eye of later writers that it is employed by Augustine in *De Doctrina Christiana,* II.xxxix: " . . . in quibus omnibus tenendum est, 'ne quid

---

11. All line citations from the plays are taken from Robert Kauer and Wallace M. Lindsay, eds., *P. Terenti Afri Comoediae* (Oxford: Clarendon Press, 1961).

12. J. P. Migne, ed., *Patrologiae Cursus Completus, Series Latina* (Paris: Garnier Fratres, 1844–1903), XXIII, 983. This work is hereafter cited as *PL,* followed by the volume and column numbers.

nimis' " (*PL,* XXXIV, 62), by Alpert of Metz (Manitius, II, 281), by Thangmar of Hildesheim (Manitius, II, 271), in the *Vita Abbonis* of Aimoin of Fleury (Manitius, II, 241), and in many other places. One writer, "der sogenannte Astronomus," simply refers to the "vetustissimum proverbium . . . ne quid nimis" (Manitius, I, 657). The other, if anything even more widely echoed, is *Andria,* 67–68, "namque hoc tempore/obsequium amicos, veritas odium parit." This is cited by Lactantius, *De Justicia,* V.9 (*PL,* VI, 576), with the tag ,"ut ait poeta, quasi divino spiritu instinctus." It is used as a paradigm case in *Etymologiarum,* II.ix.11 (*PL,* LXXXII, 129), where Isidore says, "Sententiale [membrum enthymematis] est quod sentencia generalis addicit, ut apud Terentium: 'Obsequium amicos, veritas odium parit.' " It is compared by Ratherius in *Praeloquiorum Libri sex,* III.126 (*PL,* CXXXVI, 219), to Luke 9:26. It appears in the same *Vita Abbonis* of Aimoin of Fleury as the "nequid nimis" tag above (*PL,* CXXXIX, 397). It is used by John of Salisbury in a letter to a church officer (*PL,* CXCIX, 211), and it appears over and over again in other places too numerous to list.

By now, the shrewd reader may have surmised that the outpouring of citations and allusions dealing with the passages discussed so far, all of which naturally occur within the first page or two of any text of Terence, owes its profusion to just that fact — that they are very near the beginning of the text — and that therefore a familiarity with them no more argues for a familiarity with the rest of the play — let alone the corpus — than an ability to recognize "Whan that Aprille . . ." argues a thorough knowledge of the *Canterbury Tales,* or even the rest of the *General Prologue.* And there is much to be said for this view. It is certainly true that the two *sententiae* dealt with so far account for more Terence allusions than anything else in *Andria*; and it is also true that there are more citations of *Andria* than of any other Terence play. Nevertheless, if we count the Terentian loci cited, rather than the total number of citations, the picture changes a bit; there are medieval uses of Terence spread pretty much throughout the corpus, even if there are only isolated cases of each particular citation. I am quite prepared to say that either the medieval writers themselves, or the anthologists and compilers of *florilegia* who may have provided many of them with their tags, covered the Terentian corpus fairly thoroughly.[13]

Thus we find Augustine, in the letter to his friend, Martianus,[14] saying, "Memento quid mihi duxeris profecturo, comicum quidem de Terentio, si recolis, versum, sed tamen aptissimum et utilissimum: 'Nunc hic dies vitam aliam affert, alios mores postulat,'" a close quotation of *Andria,* 189, and one that shows a certain sensitivity to the genre of the source as well. On the other hand, the word play of 218, "nam inceptiost amentium, haud amantium," catches the eye (or perhaps ear) of Isidore, who turns it into a lesson: " . . . Nomen est a nomine; Terentius: 'Inceptio est amentium, haud amantium.'"[15] For Hildebertus, in *Moralis Philosophia,* Quaestio I, 40, "de modestia," there is of course a moral to be seen: "Juvenis enim, ut ait Terentius [*Andria,* 266]: 'Dum in dubio est animus paullo momento huc [vel] illuc impellitur'" (*PL, CLXXI,* 1036). One span of half a dozen lines at the beginning of what is now usually called Act II of *Andria* provided Augustine and John of Salisbury with a total of four citations. In *De Civitate Dei,* XIV, 25, Augustine backs up an opinion of his own by citing a similar one in Terence: "Quoniam non potest id fieri quod vis, id velis quod possit" (*Andria,* 305–306) (*PL, XLI,* 433), after having a few chapters earlier (*PL, XLI,* 412) quoted the succeeding exchange, with approval of the servant's retort:

Charinus: Nihil volo aliud nisi Philumenam.
Byrria: Quanto satius est, te id dare operam, quo istum ex animo
                 amorem amoveas tuo,
             Quam id loqui quo magis libido frustra accendatur tua.
                                                        (306–308)

John of Salisbury here picks up the scene, quoting the next two lines in *Polycraticus,* VII, prol. (*PL, CXCIX,* 635):

13. In fact this spread may well argue against the widespread quotation from *florilegia,* where it would seem that the tendency to stay near the beginning of the text would be even more pronounced.

14. *Epistola* CCLVIII; *PL,* XXXIII, 1073.

15. *Etymologiarum* II.xxx.5; *PL,* LXXXII, 151.

Omnes cum valemus, recta consilia aegrotis damus.
Tu autem si hic sis aliter sentias.   (309–310)

He then proves his fondness for the general idea by quoting
"recta consilia aegrotis damus" again in a letter to his brother.[16]
The rest of *Andria* is also occasionally used, for example, in
more citations from Isidore, for the same general illustrative purposes that we have seen already.

The next play, *Heauton Timorumenos,* is less often cited than
Andria, but the chronological spread of the writers is comparable, and there is at least one astonishing occurrence to suggest
the play's popularity. That came when Petrus Liberius made use
of *Heaut.* 373, "gemitus screatus tussis risus abstine," in an exhortation to the sister of St. Ambrose on the occasion of her
reception as a nun.[17] Generally speaking, allusions to *Heaut.* are
not concentrated on the first part of the piece, although Manitius
reports an allusion in the foreword of Johann of St. Arnulf's
Translatio Sanctae Glodesindis to *Heaut.* 26, "qua re omnes vos
oratos volo . . . ," and reference by Alpert of Metz to *Heaut.*
222, in the phrase, "Set quid surdo narro fabulam" (Manitius,
II, 195, 281). Hildebertus cites *Heaut.* twice in his *Moralis
Philosophia*; once in Quaestio I.10, "de docilitate," with slight
grammatical accommodation to his context (*PL,* CLXXI, 1013):

Ita comparata est hominum natura omnium
Aliena ut melius videant, ut dijudicent,
Quam sua. Quod ideo fit quia in re nostra aut gaudio
Sumus praepediti nimio aut aegritudine.   (505–507)

and later in the same work, in Quaestio II.62, "de praelationibus" (*PL,* CLXXI, 1050), the sententious "deteriores omnes
sumus licentia" (483). Augustine, in *Contra Litteras Petiliani,*
III.21 (*PL,* XLIII, 359), uses "quid si nunc redeo ad illos qui
aiunt, 'quid si nunc coelum ruat?' " (*Heaut.* 719), where he improves the rhetorical balance (nunc . . . nunc) by disregarding
the meter. In Lactantius, *Divinarum Institutionum,* III.xviii, "de

16. *Epistola* CLXXIX, "ad ricardum fratrem suum"; *PL,* CXCIX, 175.
17. *PL,* XVI, 225; see also Sandys, I, 630.

falsa sapientia philosophorum," (*PL,* VI, 409), we find the following adaptation of *Heaut.* 971–972:

> Prius disce, quid sit vivere;
> Si displicebit vita, tum isthoc utitur [i.e., dying].

In making reference to a quotation from *Eunuchus,* Jerome gives early expression to the medieval notion of Terence as commentator on human nature:[18]

> ...etiam Comicus, cujus finis est humanos mores nosse atque describere, dixerit: 'Sine Cerere et Libero friget Venus.'
> (*Eun.* 732)

Augustine uses the following not only at *Confessiones* I.26, but also in *De Civitate Dei,* II.7 (*PL,* XXXII, 672; XLI, 53):

> At quem deum. Qui templa coeli summa sonitu concutit.
> Ego homuncio id non facerem? Ego vero feci illud ita ac libens.
> (*Eun.* 590–591)

And in the second case he also quotes other lines from the same scene. Both Isidore and also the Venerable Bede make use of *Eunuchus* for linguistic illustrations,[19] but Hildebertus, *Moralis Philosophia,* Quaestio I.33, "de magnificencia" (*PL,* CLXXI, 1032), is more interesting. He not only combines two separate Terentian lines in reverse order, but alters the text in the direction of pointing his own meaning, when he adds the word "verbis" to the first of them:

> Hic autem praeparatus in quattuor cernitur rebus:
> in clientelis, municipiis, sumptibus et verbis.
>   Terentius:
> 'Omnia prius experiri verbis, quam armis sapientem
>   decet.
> Malo ego nos prospicere, quam hunc ulcisci accepta
>   injuria.'   (*Eun.* 789, 762)

18. *Epistola* LIV, 288; *PL,* XXII, 554.
19. *Differentiarum,* I.507; *PL,* LXXXIII, 61; De Orthographia, "sero"; *PL,* XC, 148.

In another place[20] he cautions against telling secrets to talkative types, who, he warns, will respond with Terence: "Plenus rimarum sum, hoc atque illac perfluo" (*Eun.* 105).

John of Salisbury, of course, provides the most extensive and telling sample of exemplary use of Terence when he devotes the whole of Book VIII, chapter iii, of the *Policraticus*[21] to a discussion of the elusive values of worldly things; his text here is the plot of *Eunuchus,* which he introduces in the chapter's subtitle:

> Quod omnis professio suos Trasones habet; et de personis quae ad similitudinem Eunuchi Terentiani sint apud insaniter gloriantes; et quod vana gloria meretricis more loculos sequiter.

Since his quotations from *Eunuchus* range widely in the play, and especially because he is making specific use of the whole plot structure, it is quite clear not only that John of Salisbury himself knows the piece from a text and not from florilegial snippets, but more importantly that he fully expects his audience to be able to appreciate the allusions without any difficulty. His reference to the whole is smooth, almost offhand:

> In summa totius argumenti eo ad praesens universa haec arbitror posse referri, ut constet pro certo quia amicitiae prostitutae fides haberi non debet.

This apparent easy familiarity is also evident in at least two other citations of *Eunuchus* in the *Policraticus.*[22]

The next two plays, *Phormio* and *Hecyra,* are the least quoted by medieval authors; still they are not entirely unrepresented. The virtually proverbial "Quot homines, tot sententiae . . ." (*Phormio,* 454) is quoted by Hildebertus,[23] who also rearranges two other passages to give

20. *Moralis Philosophia,* Quaestio I.43, "de verecundia"; *PL,* CLXXI, 1040.

21. Clemens, C. I. Webb, ed., *Policraticus* (1909; rpt. Frankfurt: Minerva, 1965), II, 236–240.

22. III, iv (*Eun.* 252); VII, ix (*Eun.* 57ff.).

23. *Moralis Philosophia,* Quaestio I.38, "de modestia"; *PL,* CLXXI, 1035.

Quod fors feret, feremus aequo animo . . . .
                                    Inscitia est,
Adversum stimulum calces.

(Phormio, 138; 77–78)[24]

Paulus Albanus in a letter plays on "auribus teneo lupum"
(Phormio, 506), showing a willingness to indulge in casual or-
namentation by way of the odd classical allusion *(PL,* CXXI,
513).

Hecyra allusions are relatively uncommon, although we do
find Jerome, in the *Commentariorum in Michaeam,* Book II,
Chap. VII, citing a premise of much vaudeville humor: "omnes
socrus oderunt nurus," *(Hec.* 201), a line that also appears in
the Theophrastus section of the *Adversus Jovinianum (PL,*
XXV, 1221; XXIII, 292). And the reliable Hildebertus is also
in on the play. In the *Moralis Philosophia,* Quaestio II.62, "de
praelationibus" *(PL,* CLXXI, 1049), he takes a moral position:
"Praelationum contemperandus est appetitus; gravior enim est
casus altitudinis" and then backs it up with a string of *auctores,*
including Juvenal, Lucan, Seneca, and Horace, and ending with
Terence's "O fortuna ut numquam perpetuo es bona" *(Hec.*
406).

From *Adelphoe,* there is a somewhat greater harvest, beginning with Lactantius, who says, "Da mihi virum, qui sit ira-
cundus, maledicus, effraenatus: paucissimis Dei verbis:

'Tam placidum, quam ovem, reddam.' "

(Adelphoe, 534)[25]

Augustine, in one of his letters, cites the "sententiam cujusdam
saecularis auctoris: 'Pudore et liberalitate liberos/Retinere,
satius esse credo, quam metu' " *(Adelphoe,* 57–58), presumably
hedging the authority with anonymity because he does not want
to give his full endorsement to the view: "Hoc quidem verum
est; sed sicut meliores sunt quos dirigit amor, ita plures sunt

24. *Moralis Philosophia,* Quaestio I.35, "de patientia"; *PL,* CLXXI,
1034.
25. *Divinarum Institutionum,* Bk. III, chap. xxvi; *PL,* VI, 432.

quos corrigit timor." [26] In a letter to Licentius, he jests urbanely:
"Hic tu fortasse Terentiani servi mihi responsum dederis:

> 'Ohe, tu verba fundis hic sapientia!' "
>
> (*Adelphoe*, 769) [27]

More seriously, in *De Civitate Dei* (XIX.5; *PL, XLI,* 632):
"Audiant apud comicos suos hominem cum sensu atque con-
sensu omnium hominum dicere: 'Duxi uxorem, quam ibi miser-
iam vidi! Nati filii/Alia cura' " (*Adelphoe,* 867–868). Hildebertus, not to be outdone, also cites *Adelphoe* three times in his
Moralis Philosophia, once, in Quaestio I.40, "de modestia," saying, " . . . idcirco juvenis sit officium: 'Suspicere, tanquam in
speculum in vitas omnium . . . atque ex aliis sumere exemplum
sibi,' " (*Adelphoe,* 415–416), a fine example of what medieval
authors thought Terence was all about himself.[28]

This account, obviously just a sampling of the wares available,
has shown us a medieval Terence who is essentially two things,
neither of which has any direct connection with his role as dramatist per se. The first and most important is that he is an authority to be cited on the subject of human nature and the mores
of men, an authority who does not suffer even in juxtaposition
to biblical commentary and, in some cases, to the Scriptures
themselves. This role is indeed indirectly connected to the drama,
since there is a lingering tradition, which tries to ground itself in
Aristotle, that it is precisely the dramatists who fill this function
in ancient life. But there is certainly no awareness among the
medieval citers of Terentian texts of any kind of dramatic context, of any real feel for the dramatic situation; a quotation taken
from a passage in which Terence is trying to hold up a stuffy
father or treacherous slave to the light of irony is as good as the
word of the wisest character in the corpus, provided that it is
sentientious in itself, when detached from the rest of the play.

26. *Epistola* CLXXXV, to Boniface, "de correctione Donatistarum";
PL, XXXIII, 802.
    27. *Epistola* XXVI (a); *PL,* XXXIII, 104.
    28. *PL,* CLXXI, 1036–37; see also *Moralis Philosophia,* Quaestio I.41,
"de modestia," *PL,* CLXXI, 1037; and *Moralis Philosophia,* Quaestio
I.10, "de docilitate," *PL,* CLXXI, 1013.

Terence's second great function for these writers is to serve as a rhetorical and personal ornament. Letters, in particular, are fitted out with Terentian asides in order to add to their own verbal comeliness and also to call attention to the cultivation and urbanity of the writer who can so freely allude to the smallest tag of the ancient sage. What makes Terence work in this second function is of course his verbal surface, but what caused the surface to be so carefully scrutinized was the supposed sententious and moral underpinning.

Since we have leaned so heavily on relatively early medieval writers, it may prove useful to end with a fourteenth-century "life" of Terence. Walter Burley (d.1349), in his *De vita et moribus philosophorum,*[29] includes our playwright among the subjects treated, as indeed he includes all of the "standard authors" of antiquity he can think of. That such writers fit in the category "philosophers" is so natural to Burley, and presumably to his readers, that he never explains or apologizes for it. Burley does not do any original research into his subject; in fact it appears that he learned just about everything he knows about Terence from Vincent of Beauvais, but this is precisely why he is so interesting to us now. He is the bearer of the late medieval stock of Terence lore, and he delivers it with what we can only assume is a typical, not entirely uneducated, view of the Roman poet.

Actually the details of Terence's "life" are disposed of by Burley with a single sentence; then he proceeds to the value of the man. In Burley, as in the medieval authors we have already seen, this value is both esthetic and moral: "Scripsit autem comediarum librum elegantem in quo mores multorum ad precavenda pericula annotavit," a slightly gloomy view of the playwright's role as social scientist, but one which fits within the general confines of the overall medieval opinion of Terence. After a citation, apparently derived from Vincent of Beauvais,[30] of the supposed epitaph of Terence, in which Vincent takes essentially the same view of the philosophic value of his work as

29. Hermann Knust, ed., *Gualteri Burlaei Liber de Vita et Moribus Philosophorum* (Tubingen: 1886). The section on Terence runs on pp. 342–347.

30. Knust, p. 343, note (d).

Burley has already displayed for us, Burley goes on to list some
of Terence's better-known *sententiae,* which were also taken,
without exception, from among those already cited by Vincent,
although they are not all from one place. These *sententiae*
include:

> Ita fere corrupta est hominum natura ut aliena melius
> judicet quam sua.   (cf. *Heaut.* 503–505)

and

> Inspicere tanquam in speculum vitas hominum quemque
> iubeo atque ex aliis sumere exemplum sibi.
> (cf. *Adelphoe,* 415–416)

Both of these we have already come across in the *Moralis Philosophia* of Hildebertus; Burley, like the typical medieval scribe,
shows no awareness that the Terentian lines are anything other
than prose, and he also never indicates where in the corpus they
appear (the locations in Terence are all mine).

There are altogether in the *De vita* five quotations — not always exact, by any means — from *Heauton Timorumenos,* four
from *Adelphoe,* and three from *Phormio,* including one which
is made from two passages a few lines apart.[31] It is curious that
the five from *Heauton Timorumenos* are listed first, then the
ones from *Adelphoe,* and finally those from *Phormio,* without
any mixing, even though they do not come in that order in Vincent of Beauvais, nor does this follow the usual order of the
plays themselves. One might be tempted to conclude that Burley
worked from full texts of at least the three plays that he makes
use of, but this possibility, which suggests a pretty thorough
knowledge of Terence as a whole — even though the most
widely quoted play, *Andria,* and two others are never cited —
cannot stand with what follows these *sententiae* in Burley's text,
which reads, after the list of Terence's sayings is completed, as
follows:

31. They are, in order: *Heaut.* 503–505; 796; 805–806; 922–923;
1058–59. *Adelphoe* 98–99; 65–67; 386–388; 415–416. *Phormio* 41–42;
241–242; 245–246; 696–697.

Agellius vero libro nono has Publii refert sentencias: 'Malum est consilium quod mutari non potest.' 'Beneficium accipit dando qui digno dedit.' 'Feras, non culpes quod mutari non potest . . . '

and so forth through a total of eleven sayings that are not taken from the plays of Terence at all, and which can scarcely have been thought Terentian by a writer thoroughly familiar with the corpus, limited in size as it is. "Agellius" is of course Aulus Gellius, and the *sententiae Publii* are in fact sayings of Publilius Syrus, whose name was often incorrectly given as Publius,[32] and who has been taken, by Burley himself, or by some intermediary, to be identical with Publius Terentius Afer. There is for Burley no possibility of excluding the passages on metrical grounds, since they and Terence are alike prose to him, nor does there seem to be any knowledge of the whole of Terence such that it would suggest to our writer that the second set of *sententiae* looked rather unfamiliar. In the world of encyclopedic knowledge, fourteenth-century English style, Terence has become little more than a source of proverbial wisdom, and one that can scarcely be distinguished from any other such source.

32. Otto Friedrich, ed., *Publilii Syri Mimi Sententiae* (Hildesheim: Georg Olms Verlag, 1964), p. 3.

JOSEPH HARRIS

Christian Form and Christian Meaning in *Halldórs þáttr I*

Old Icelandic sources preserve two independent short stories or þættir about Halldórr Snorrason in addition to the numerous passages concerning him in *Haralds saga harðráða* and other texts. The better known of the þættir, *Halldórs þáttr II*, telling of a series of quarrels between Halldórr and King Haraldr and of Halldórr's old age, sketches an early and amusing portrait of this salty Icelander; the less well-known *Halldórs þáttr I* is almost certainly much younger, apparently exhibits a knowledge of Halldórr's character and times based partly on the earlier þáttr, and is of no historical value, being simply a fiction, a novella with historical setting.[1] From the purely literary point

For Bartlett Jere Whiting on his seventieth birthday: "opt er gott, þat er gamlir kveða" (*Hávamál*).

1. See Einar Ólafur Sveinsson, ed., *Íslensk fornrit* 5 (Reykjavík, 1934), where *Halldórs þáttr II* is also found; sources for Halldórr's biography are given, pp. lxxxv–xc. Sveinsson's introduction (pp. lxxxii–lxxxv) gives reasons for the dating and literary relations alluded to here and anticipates *in nuce* many of my remarks in this essay, but I believe he underestimates the literary value of the þáttr (p. lxxxii) and perhaps overestimates its historicity (pp. lxxxiv–lxxxv).

of view, however, *Halldórs þáttr I* is one of the most interesting and instructive of the þættir, despite its probable late date, and an analysis of the artistry with which theme here harmonizes with structure and invests it with significance — more exactly, the way *Christian meaning creates Christian form* — may be suggestive for criticism of the saga literature more generally. But we begin with structure.

The story opens when an Icelander named Eilífr arrives in Norway and offends King Haraldr; Halldórr attempts to intercede for him and, failing to win the king over, leaves the royal court in anger. Halldórr and Eilífr remove to the estate of the powerful Norwegian nobleman Einarr þambarskelfir; there Halldórr incurs the jealousy of a disagreeable young kinsman of Einarr's named Kali, who defames and lampoons the older man. When Halldórr then kills Kali, he comes in mortal danger from Einarr, but on the advice of Einarr's wife Bergljót Halldórr surrenders to Einarr's judgment. Einarr calls an assembly but before announcing his verdict recounts an anecdote from his youth that explains his decision in the case (a separate narrative about King Óláfr Tryggvason, summarized below). Einarr's judgment is that he himself shall pay compensation for Kali's death and that he will hold the peace with Halldórr. Then Halldórr succeeds in making peace for Eilífr and himself with King Haraldr, sends Eilífr home to Iceland, and remains long afterward with the king.

A first glance suffices to show that the þáttr comprises at least two complete narratives, one within the other like Chinese boxes: Halldórr's adventures and Einarr's narration at the assembly. But when examined in the context of the six-part narrative pattern which is characteristic of a large group of þættir, *Halldórs þáttr I* appears to be composed of four narrative structures, three with the Alienation/Reconciliation pattern common to the group and the fourth the tale told by Einarr.[2] The outermost structure concerns Eilífr and King Haraldr, the second

2. I have discussed the pattern, in which "alienation" and "reconciliation" form the central structural segments, in "Genre and Narrative Structure in Some *Íslendinga þættir*," *Scandinavian Studies*, 44 (1972), 1–27, and "The King and the Icelander: A Study in the Short Narrative Forms of Old Icelandic Prose," Ph.D. diss., Harvard University, 1969.

Halldórr and Haraldr, the third Halldórr and Einarr, and the inmost Einarr's recollections of King Óláfr Tryggvason, and these strands are related in a manner similar to that of syntactic "nesting structures." The relationship between Halldórr and Einarr replicates closely that between Eilífr and Haraldr, both having not only the common Alienation/Reconciliation structure but, in addition to the two essential role positions or "slots," also a third that is often found in þættir of this type, the intercessor (Halldórr as intercessor for Eilífr, and Bergljót for Halldórr). The relationship between Halldórr and Haraldr is quite similar, but no third person functions as intercessor.[3]

This analysis seems confirmed by the elegant and economical ending of the þáttr where the last three sentences knit up the three outer narrative strands. The opening of the þáttr had presented the Alienations in the order Eilífr/Haraldr, Halldórr/Haraldr, and Halldórr/Einarr (1, 2, 3); in the closing passage the inmost of these feuds is settled first (3); in the second sentence both the Halldórr/Haraldr and Eilífr/Haraldr feuds are composed, not in the expected order 2, 1, the mirror image of their introduction, but in the order 1, 2. Then the third and last sentence, which concerns only Eilífr and Haraldr, arrives to establish the pattern 1, 2, 3:3, (1), 2, 1, an instance of the aesthetic formula of establishing a strong presumption of a pattern, first violating it, and finally fulfilling it. The þáttr's last sentence, so untypical of saga conclusions,[4] is also remarkable for giving essential information that was withheld at the beginning of the story: we learn only in the last sentence that Eilífr's offense had been killing a courtier of King Haraldr's. This belated information, dropping into place like the keystone of an arch, has the effect of drastically underlining the parallelism between Eilífr's story and Halldórr's. Authorial control of the reader and sus-

3. Typical *dramatis personae* of these stories are discussed in "King and Icelander," pp. 151–167. In *Flateyjarbók* (Reykjavík, 1944) I, 562, the story is headed "Einarr hjálpaði Halldóri," as if the copyist were completing the analogies among the three pairs of antagonists.
4. Usual endings of such þættir are discussed in "King and Icelander," pp. 76–80 and p. 260, n.13. The three principal texts of the þáttr (F, S, and B) are, I think, similar enough to warrant this detailed commentary, though, of course, the punctuation of the last three sentences is editorial; on F_2 see Sveinsson, pp. lxxxii–lxxxiii, n.1.

pense of a sort extend literally to the last sentence, and by dramatically emphasizing the equivalence of two of the story's personal ratios (Eilífr : Haraldr :: Halldórr : Einarr), it "lays bare the device" (in the famous Russian Formalist phrase) and stimulates the reader's mind to seek the thematic relevance of the story's form.

Framed within the Alienation/Reconciliation structures, a story within the stories, we find Einarr's retrospective narrative: Bjǫrn, an old man, Kolbeinn, who was in middle life, and Einarr, aged eighteen, shipmates aboard the famous Long Serpent, were captured by Danes in the general defeat at the Battle of Svǫldr after King Óláfr Tryggvason had "disappeared in the light that shined over him"; they were kept bound in a wood to be sold as slaves. At the slave market a man in a blue cloak like a monk's and masked bargained with the slave master for the three and finally purchased them. As he led them away on a forest path, Einarr asked his name, but the stranger refused to tell. Then he predicted their lives: Bjǫrn had not long to live and should make disposition of his property for his soul's sake; Kolbeinn would be highly esteemed at home; but Einarr would be the greatest. And from Einarr the hooded man required repayment for buying and freeing them: Einarr was laid under obligation to free a man who had offended against him, even though his enemy should stand fully in his power. The stranger lifted his mask as he distracted the three by pointing, and when they looked back, he had disappeared. But they recognized him as Óláfr Tryggvason.

This reminiscence is introduced into the þáttr as an "entertainment" offered at the assembly:

Ok þenna sama dag stefnir Einarr fjǫlmennt þing. Hann stóð upp á þinginu ok talaði svá: "Ek vil nú skemmta yðr ok segja frá því . . ." (P. 255)

That same day Einarr called an assembly that was heavily attended. He stood up in the meeting and spoke as follows: "I mean to entertain you now by telling about . . ."

But its real integrative principle is explained in Einarr's closing words:

"Nú em ek skyldr til," segir Einarr, "at gera þat, er Óláfr konungr bað mik. Sýnisk mér nú eigi annat líkara, Halldórr, en hann hafi fyrir þér beðit, því at þú ert nú á mínu valdi." (P. 260)

"Now I am obligated," said Einarr, "to do what King Óláfr asked of me. Nothing seems more likely to me now, Halldórr, than that he was asking it for your sake since you are now in my power."

Mere entertainment is unmasked as the motivating principle of the remainder of the þáttr.[5]

It should be clear by now that our author's aesthetic sense is strongly symmetrical. The triple Alienation/Reconciliation structures and the retrospective speech are neatly "self-embedded"; the causal principle operates from outer to inner structures and out again from inner to outer: Eilífr's offense causes Halldórr's separation from the king, which leads to his presence at Einarr's and the resulting feud, the assembly, and the "entertainment"; that tale motivates Einarr's reconciliation with Halldórr, which (I shall argue below) leads to Halldórr's reunion with the king, in turn a necessary condition for Eilífr's reconciliation to Haraldr. The triple arrangement of the Alienation/Reconciliation structures suggests that the same action is being replicated at different social levels. Thus the sequence — king vs. otherwise unknown Icelander (Eilífr), king vs. famous Icelander from a great family (Halldórr),[6] great nobleman vs. famous Icelander from a great family — seems to be arranged in descending order of social distance between the antagonists. More obvious is the triple arrangement and gradation of the comrades in Einarr's tale: Bjǫrn is old, Kolbeinn evidently middle-aged, Einarr young; their prices as slaves are graded from Bjǫrn through Kolbeinn to Einarr (respectively one, two, and three marks); and in the prophecy Bjǫrn is told to make his peace with God in

5. Cf. the ostensible and real motivation for the tale-within-a-tale in *Morkinskinna*'s story about Úlfr inn auðgi (ed. C. R. Unger [Christiania, 1867], pp. 66–69): at a feast King Haraldr proposed to enliven the occasion with a story (*rœða*) and at the end made the application to his own immediate situation, motivating his ensuing actions.
6. Cf. *Halldórs þáttr II* on Halldórr's pride of family (*ÍF* 5, 269 and 273).

preparation for imminent death, while Einarr is to live to a ripe and powerful old age (Kolbeinn being somewhere between).

The most important structural feature (also manifesting a kind of symmetry) of the central "entertainment" leads from discussion of form to theme. Einarr's reminiscence has a symbolic dimension and is, more specifically, a figural or typological narrative. There should be nothing surprising in this since Óláfr Tryggvason was in popular conception very nearly a saint, and every saint's life is to some extent a typological recapitulation of Christ's, an *imitatio Christi;* what is remarkable is to find typology so well integrated into typical themes and structures of the saga literature. But first the details of the typology must be examined.

Svǫldr is Óláfr's last, great *agon,* and like Christ his "death" here is ambiguous; like Enoch and Elijah, Óláfr is taken mysteriously while yet alive, and those prophets were interpreted as types of Christ in the manner of their passing.[7] After three days Christ rose from the dead and came to his disciples, just as Óláfr comes to Einarr and his companions (members of Óláfr's crew, his "disciples") after some time; the interval between the battle and Óláfr's "epiphany" cannot be calculated exactly, but there can be no doubt that the author wished to make the parallel clear since he contrives to mention the number three in connection with this time period:

"ok Danir, menn Sveins konungs, tóku oss ok fœrðu konungi, en hann flutti oss til Jótlands, ok váru vér þar upp leiddir ok settir á eina lág ok þar fjǫtraðir . . . *ok í þeim skógi sátu vér þrjár nætr.*"

(P. 256)

"And the Danes, the men of King Sveinn, captured us and led us to their king, and he brought us to Jutland, and there we were

7. Gen. 5:24; 2 Kings 2:1–12 (cf. also Romulus, Ovid, *Met.* IV.816ff.). The translations of Enoch and Elijah were usually viewed as figuring Christ's Ascension (e.g., J. P. Migne, ed., *Patrologia Latina* CIX, col. 222–223), which does not fit the action schema of Óláfr's story perfectly, but the eclecticism of my typological interpretation has precedent in medieval methods of composition and interpretation.

led ashore, seated on a log, and fettered . . . And we sat three nights in that forest."[8]

The effect of Christ's victory over death was the *redemption* or "buying back" of mankind, and imagery of commerce, of slavery, and of bondage is commonplace in this connection; thus Óláfr returned from "death" to purchase his men literally out of thralldom and to release them literally from bondage.[9] Christ was not recognized by his disciples when he appeared to them after the resurrection; so the disguised Óláfr is not recognized at first by his men.

These parallels will be sufficient for the moment to establish a figural relation between aspects of the death and resurrection of Christ and Óláfr's role in our þáttr, though a few qualifications are in order. Óláfr's disappearance into a cloud of light and some other features of Einarr's tale are traditional, not invented by our author, and other stories do attribute supernatural powers to Óláfr Tryggvason; [10] nevertheless, most of the ele-

8. See W. Baetke, "Das Svoldr-Problem," *Berichte über die Verhandlungen der sächsischen Akademie der Wissenschaften zu Leipzig.* Philological-historical class, vol. 98 (1951), pt. 6, pp. 59–135; if our author thought the battle site near Jutland, he may have meant the interval to be exactly three days, but general Icelandic tradition favored the coast of Pomerania, while the other major tradition, locating it in the Öresund, was Danish. A third location at the Schlei in Schleswig-Holstein would place it near Jutland, but it seems quite impossible that our author belongs to this questionable tradition (Baetke, pp. 59–60) in spite of the fact that he does not name the place "Svǫldr" in the Icelandic manner; Jutland is probably chosen simply as a forbidding place deep in enemy country. With the image of captives fettered and sitting along a log; cf. the Jómsvíkings (*ÍF* 26, 284). The word *lág* seems to be old; it is used here by Snorri, glossed twice in his *Edda,* and used once in *Egils saga;* cf. n.10 below.

9. The Harrowing of Hell, a mythic elaboration of the idea of redemption, has only general relevance here; but cf. Jesus' words (from Isaiah): "He has sent me to proclaim release to the captives . . . to set at liberty those who are oppressed . . ." (Luke 4:18).

10. Sveinsson places the þáttr in the general tradition of the Óláfr sagas of Oddr and Gunnlaugr (p. lxxxiii). In Oddr (ed. Finnur Jónsson [Copenhagen, 1932]) the author could have found the light, the names of Einarr, Kolbeinn, and Bjǫrn in close proximity as three of the first four named as survivors (identities of Kolbeinn or Kolbjǫrn and Bjǫrn discussed by Sveinsson, pp. 255–256, n.3), the fact that the survivors

ments of the story and their constellation as a narrative whole
must be credited to him, and in view of the Christian parallels
offered so far, both the general and the specific, I think it would
"outrage probability" to consider this pattern accidental (R. E.
Kaske's criterion). The þáttr's style is "saga realism," and in accord with that peculiar brand of realism the author clothes his
figural narrative in the possible if unlikely theory that Óláfr
Tryggvason escaped from the battle and lived on as a monk in
a distant land; and the stage business at the slave market, the
mask and hood, and the sheer weight of mundane detail in
these scenes lend further plausibility. But Óláfr's role in the
story is supernatural — Sveinsson commented that if the king
had survived the battle he would have had better things to do
than hang about in his enemy's country — and scarcely to be
understood from a purely realistic point of view, without its figural schema and function in the semantic configurations of the
þáttr. In short, the author of *Halldórs þáttr I* was not interested
in presenting a version of either of the realistic theories of Óláfr's
end for its own sake but instead in the king as instrument and
spokesman for God and as *deus ex machina* in the realistic human drama of enmity and reconciliation that he laid in Norway.[11]

On this basis we may look for some more questionable parallels of detail. In the gospels Christ appears unrecognized three
times, in Luke 24, John 20:14–16, and John 21:4; of these the
epiphany on the road to Emmaus is most similar, and the parallels are extensive: the epiphany occurs out of doors, on a path,
to only a small number (two) of disciples; Christ instructs them

---

jumped overboard and were captured, that Óláfr lived on, became a
monk, and was seen by certain witnesses. But he may have had recourse
to Snorri's version for the information that Einarr was eighteen (*IF* 26,
346) and about the legal ages of the crew (p. 344; Sveinsson, p. 256,
n.2); cf. n.8 above.

11. Tradition, represented by Oddr, actually reports *three* versions
of Óláfr's end: disappearance in light, normal death of wounds or
drowning but in unspecified circumstances, escape by swimming to a
Wendish ship; the latter two are not only realistic but related, while
the first is quite separate. See Lars Lönnroth, "Studier i Olaf Tryggva-
sons saga," *Samlaren*, 84 (1963), 54–94, for discussion of the sources
of the realistic escape legend.

before he disappears; they recognize him just as he vanishes from their sight; after Christ has disappeared the men talk about the epiphany ("Did not our hearts burn within us while he talked to us on the road . . ."); then they return to Jerusalem. Similarly Óláfr leads his three men, a small portion of his crew,[12] down a forest path, instructs them about their future life, and is recognized fully by all only in the moment of his vanishing; afterward the men discuss the event and return to Norway.

One curious feature of the þáttr is possibly to be explained as a confused or, better, imaginatively altered imitation of the passage from Luke: The hooded man and the companions reach a clearing, and they catch a glimpse under his hood: "kippði upp lítt at hettinum" (p. 258) ("he pulled up a little on the hood"). After his prophecy they get a closer look: "Ok at svá tǫluðu lypti kuflmaðrinn grímu frá andliti sér" (p. 259) ("And this said, the cowled man raised the mask from his face"). At the same time he distracted them, and:

> "er vér litum aptr, var grímumaðr horfinn, ok síðan sám vér hann aldri. En þenna man kenndu vér allir fullgǫrla, at þetta var Óláfr konungr Tryggvason, því at þegar fyrra sinn, at hann lypti kuflshettinum, kennda ek hann fyrir víst; en síðan hann lypti upp grímunni ok sýndi oss sína ásjónu, kenndu vér hann allir." (P. 259)

> "When we looked back, the masked man had disappeared, and we never saw him again. But we all recognized the man quite clearly: it was King Óláfr Tryggvason. For as soon as he pushed back his hood the first time, I was certain I recognized him; but after he raised up his mask and showed us his face, we all recognized him."

It is strange that, having recognized Óláfr "for sure" the first time he gave a glimpse of himself, Einarr did not call him by name, give the Good News to his comrades, and "lay hands on him" as the three afterward agreed they should have done (pp. 259–260); instead Einarr waited for the final revelation with

---

12. The þáttr says nine survived from the Long Serpent; Oddr says eight but gives only seven names; conceivably Oddr's "eight" derives from the seven named crewmen plus Óláfr and the þáttr's "nine" in the same way from Oddr's "eight."

his two companions and only tells us after it is all over that he had known from that first glimpse. This is perhaps to be related to the fact that, while Luke states clearly that Jesus appeared to two disciples on the way to Emmaus, he also mentions an earlier epiphany to a single disciple: "And they [the two from Emmaus] rose that same hour and returned to Jerusalem; and they found the eleven gathered together and those who were with them, who said, 'The Lord has risen indeed, and has appeared to Simon!' Then they [the two from Emmaus] told what had happened on the road . . ." (24:33–35). Thus the Emmaus passage as a whole mentions three individual disciples (Cleophas, one unnamed, and Simon) as witnesses of Christ's return and seems to make the epiphany to Simon prior to that to the two on the road to Emmaus; in *Halldórs þáttr I* we have Óláfr's appearance to three followers but to one a little before the other two.

Perhaps this explanation is not necessary, but in addition to the questions posed above about the logicality of Einarr's actions judged from purely a realistic perspective, we must explain why, after the first glimpse when he knew with certainty that the stranger was Óláfr Tryggvason, Einarr nevertheless claimed not to know him: "Ek svaraða, at óhœgra væri at launa, ef ek vissa eigi, hverjum at gjalda var" (p. 259) ("I answered that it was very difficult to repay a man if I didn't know who was to be repaid"). It is possible, of course, that Einarr was boasting untruthfully when he said he had recognized the king before the other two or that the author imagined Einarr as having some unexpressed reasons for not making known his discovery immediately and for saying he did not know whom to reward — possible, but as it seems certain that the author had the Luke text in mind, it is at least a likely hypothesis that the illogicality or at least lack of realistic motivation in Einarr's actions here is caused by the imitation or, with Frye, "displacement."

This argument is not damaged by a series of striking if unsystematic agreements with John 21 where the risen Christ, at first not recognized, reveals himself to eight disciples beside the Sea of Tiberias and breakfasts with them (21:1–14). He then makes a speech (15–19) with strongly marked tripartite form ("Simon, son of John . . . Simon, son of John . . . Simon, son of John"; cf. "En þú, Bjǫrn . . . En þú Kolbeinn . . . En þú, Einarr . . ."); the climactic third part is longest and most developed (as with Óláfr's speech). The speech is given before the group but addresses an individual (as Óláfr addresses each of his men individually, and especially Einarr) and treats a commandment (thrice repeated) as an obligation ("do you love me? . . . Feed my sheep"; cf. Óláfr's injunction of forgiveness as the obligatory requital for freedom given). Besides the commandment the speech includes prophecy of Peter's old age and death (Óláfr prophesies Bjǫrn's death and Einarr's prosperous old age), and Jesus' words about Peter's life oppose youth and old age, suggesting the contrast between Einarr and Bjǫrn. Finally, an arresting detail: Peter is evidently singled out for the commandment and prophecy here *because* he stands out above the other disciples ("Simon, son of John, do you love me *more than these*? . . . Feed my lambs"; cf. Peter's individual actions in 21:7–8 and 11), while Óláfr sets Einarr apart in prophecy and selects him alone for his commandment because Einarr excels the others.[13] If, then, it seems reasonable to say that Einarr's role reflects to some extent Simon Peter's position in John 21, the probability of the same influence from the epiphany to "Simon" in Luke 24:34 seems to gain support.

13. Pp. 257–258, esp. 259: " 'En þú, Einarr . . . munt verða yðvar mestr maðr . . . af þér einum mun ek laun hafa . . . því at þér einum hygg ek at mest þykki vert, ef þú ert eigi þræll' " (" 'But you, Einarr . . . will become the greatest man of the three . . . from you alone I must have repayment . . . because I think you place the most value on not being a slave' "). An ambiguity in the Vulgate's "diligis me *plus his?*" is reflected in the English translation; the interpretation here is the most natural in context. The John 21 passage includes also "Follow me" (19 and 22; cf. the þáttr, p. 258 and below). Other texts that may have contributed: John 21:12: "Jesus said to them, 'Come and have breakfast.' Now none of the disciples dared ask him, 'Who are you?' They knew it was the Lord" (cf. p. 258: "gekk þá brott . . . ok bað fylgja sér . . . spurða ek hann at nafni. Hann svarar: 'Ekki varðar þik at vita nafn mitt . . .' "); John 20:17: "Jesus said to her, 'Do not hold me, for I have not yet ascended to the Father,' " and other passages about touching the risen Christ, John 20:27 and Luke 24:39 (cf. pp. 259–260: "tǫluðum vár í milli, at oss hefði mjǫk óvitrliga til tekizk er vér hǫfðum eigi hendr á honum . . ."); with Óláfr's directives to his "disciples," esp. Einarr, cf. Matthew 28:18–20 (the risen Christ's charge to the apostles); Luke 4:29–30 may perhaps be compared with the final disappearance.

Figural narrative can be considered a structural device in that a pattern of events is made or seen to conform to that of a part of sacred history,[14] but an examination of the *effects* of typology takes us out of formal analysis and into the realm of theme, the semantics of a narrative; in *Halldórs þáttr I* the typology associates Ólafr with Christ, lending his words a deeper resonance which perhaps only grows on the reader as he gradually realizes that Ólafr here is a type of Christ. Most obviously, of course, the dialogue dealing with purchase and sale takes on symbolic force, but perhaps also the harsh slave master (*meistari*) suggests the death to which mankind had been subject before Christ's redeeming victory. (Note that, like the hooded stranger in this scene, the meistari is identified only by his words and actions, an anonymity which increases his symbolic potential.) The universal ring of some of Ólafr's words and an irony (beyond that occasioned by the motif of the king in disguise) in his bargaining become explicable against the figural pattern (are men worthy of redemption?), and the syntactic and lexical balance between the expressions of the meistari's relation to the prisoners and Ólafr's, which cannot be accidental, takes on significance:

"En sá, er oss varðveitti, *vildi selja* oss í þrældóm; hann hét oss afarkostum ok limaláti, *ef* vér *vildim eigi þjásk.*" (P. 256)
" 'eru menn takmiklir, *ef* þeir *vilja mennask; sýnisk mér því ráð* at *kaupa* þá alla.' " (P. 258)

"The one who was guarding us meant to sell us into slavery; he threatened us with rough treatment and mutilation if we would not submit to being slaves."
" 'they will be strong if they are willing to act like men [or even: men will be strong...]; so it seems to me a good idea to buy them all.' "

14. This is not intended as a definition of typology, and no general treatment will be attempted here; see Erich Auerbach, "Figura," in *Scenes from the Drama of European Literature* (New York: Meridian Books, 1959), Jean Danielou, *From Shadows to Reality: Studies in the Biblical Typology of the Fathers,* trans. W. Hibberd (London: Burns' Dates, 1960), and Charles Donahue, "Patristic Exegesis: Summation," in *Critical Approaches to Medieval Literature,* ed. Dorothy Bethurum (New York: Columbia University Press, 1960), pp. 62–66 and passim.

The conventional symbolism of "forest" and "night" in Christian thought may go some way toward creating the reverberations of "í þeim skógi sátu vér þjár nætr" and to explaining why in a *merely* realistic fiction (in fiction an author has control of what he says and does not say) an assembly or market is called in an unnamed forest vaguely located in Jutland. Christian-symbolic ideas associated with "path" may also lend overtones that go beyond geography when Óláfr leads his men away from the slave market and, showing them the "path" to safety, immediately adds directives for the future lives of his freedmen.

Finally, of course, comes Óláfr's injunction to Einarr:

" 'því skaltu launa: ef nokkurr maðr gerir svá mjǫk í móti þér, at fyrir hvatvetna vilir þú hafa hans líf, ok hafir þú vald yfir honum, þá skaltu eigi minna frelsi gefa honum en ek gef nú þér.' " (P. 259)

" 'Here is the way you must repay me: if some man offends you so much that you want to take his life and you have him in your power, you must give him no less freedom than I have now given you.' "

In this way Einarr (and mankind) must repay the "gift of life and freedom" ("laun . . . fyrir lífgjǫfina ok frelsit," p. 259); Óláfr is not only enjoining upon Einarr the practice of forgiving an enemy but imagining a situation similar to Einarr's own predicament as a slave, thus an exemplification of the golden rule in a saga-specific form: if Einarr should one day find himself with power over an enemy, he shall act in imitation of the redeemer Óláfr/Christ and not identify himself with the forces of the meistari/death. More precisely, the imagined situation explicitly predicts the relationship between Halldórr and Einarr and by extension that between the other feuding pairs, giving the "correct solution" to any Alienation/Reconciliation story.

With this injunction we have arrived at the structural and moral heart of *Halldórs þáttr I*. This teaching of Óláfr's is now applied to Einarr's grievance against Halldórr and in turn to the feuds between the Icelanders and King Haraldr. The text, of course, simply juxtaposes Einarr's final words, quoted above, and his exemplary action with the reconciliation to King Haraldr and leaves the reader to imagine how it came about. As so often the saga literature presents us with the "half-sung song," but how *did* Halldórr reconcile himself and Eilífr with the king? Must we not imagine that he recounted Einarr's story, which applies to the situation of Eilífr almost as well as that of Halldórr, or at least that in some unspecified way Óláfr's teaching is extended to King Haraldr? (If Einarr can forbear revenge for his relative, cannot Haraldr do the same for his unnamed courtier?) This not very bold assumption allows further details to be integrated as thematically functional: Halldórr's first attempt to intercede in Eilífr's behalf is impetuous and demanding and results in an extension of the royal disfavor to himself and indirectly in his feud with Einarr; however, after hearing Óláfr's precept and profiting by Einarr's example, Halldórr succeeds in making peace with Haraldr; Bergljót's initial advice that Halldórr throw himself on Einarr's mercy led ultimately to the settlement, but she appears at the assembly with an armed force ready to fight against her own husband for her protégé Halldórr — just as Einarr is rendering his generous and peaceful decision. The story as a whole, of course, recommends conciliatory attitudes, but with the details of these attempts at intercession the author seems to be making a further statement: human mediation is not necessarily effective; if attempted in the wrong spirit it may cause further trouble (Halldórr's first attempt) or appear absurd in the face of Christian charity (Bergljót with her armed men); to have any effect at all peacemakers must proceed in humility and moderation (Bergljót's advice),[15] but to be finally blessed with success they must also be imbued with Christian intent, a reflex of divine directive (Einarr's exemplum and its effects).

The texture of the narrative in *Halldórs þáttr I* is denser in the center, in Einarr's tale, and thinner, less circumstantial, as we move outward: much is told about Halldórr's conflict with

---

15. Bergljót's advice is here simplified for the legitimate purpose of bringing out the chiastic pattern; the point to be emphasized is that her advice is sensible (in contrast to Halldórr's worse-than-useless attempt to mediate for Eilífr) but not religiously motivated and so incomplete without Einarr's story of Óláfr.

Einarr but very little about that of King Haraldr and the Ice-landers. This stylistic gradation seems associated with the fact that the theme of the þáttr is expressed most explicitly in Ei-narr's tale, and triplication of the Alienation/Reconciliation structure could be seen simply as a kind of "redundancy" that insures communication.[16] But the meaning of even didactic lit-erature is not the same as "information," and a better view is that the teaching of forgiveness and reconciliation takes effect in concentric circles, widening out from Óláfr's precept and passing through the story's three degrees of social relations; thus the thematic function of triplication may not be mere redundancy but a way of saying that reconciliation is a value that should be carried through these three, hence all social relations. Simi-larly the three comrades, Bjǫrn the old man, Kolbeinn the mid-dle-aged man, and Einarr the youth, suggest three ages of man in general and make Óláfr's words apply to everyman, including the medieval audience.

Other aspects of the art of this þáttr might be mentioned. Item: the didactic note struck when Einarr stifles his first in-stincts for revenge, foreshadowing the peaceful outcome and crystalizing the ethical-religious dilemma of reconciliation or revenge, and, like the final settlement, supported by a near saintly royal precept (p. 254). Item: the three examples of *sagnaskemtan* or "saga-telling for amusement" that grade off from good to evil: Einarr's implicitly religious "entertainment"; Halldórr's worldly heroic tales; and Kali's malicious satire "in prose and verse," especially his parody of Halldórr's Byzantine adventures. (Is it oversubtle to add as a fourth Óláfr's divinely sanctioned "sermon" and to compare the narrative structures of

16. Richard F. Allen, *Fire and Iron: Critical Approaches to Njáls saga* (Pittsburgh: University of Pittsburgh Press, 1971), pp. 47–48, also connects stylistic density with didactic intent, though I disagree about what is taught. (Didactic aims are likely to be ethical, religious, and social, but hardly tactical or strategic.) For two interesting comments on struc-tural replication in myth see Claude Lévi-Strauss, "The Structural Study of Myth," in *Structural Anthropology* trans. Claire Jacobson and Brooke G. Schoepf (New York: Basic Books, 1963), p. 229 (Formalist view), and Edmund R. Leach, *Genesis as Myth and Other Essays* (London: Cape, 1969), pp. 7–9 (information theory).

the þáttr as a whole?) Item: the choice of setting and persons, Haraldr, Einarr, and Halldórr, for the tale (compare their historical relationships and characters); conceivably even the numbers in the story and the naming of the presumably invented character Eilífr. But perhaps enough has already been said to make my point about Christian form and Christian meaning: *Halldórs þáttr I* embodies the theme of reconciliation in rather simple but skillfully articulated narrative structures that function intimately in the meaning of the story.

No ringing declarations will be risked here on the basis of one possibly isolated short story; however, few works of art are entirely *sui generis*. *Halldórs þáttr I* shows how intricately a "standard" generic form may be varied and related to theme and suggests semantic functions for structural replications and for the familiar saga aesthetic of symmetry. Formal typology is not to be expected as a widespread saga convention, of course, and I know of no exactly comparable case; however, this þáttr does suggest that some aspects of the allegorical sensibility in general and some of its techniques as found elsewhere in medieval literature may not be totally alien to the authors of ostensibly secular sagas. Like this story, most þættir and family sagas are built on conflicts manifested in violent actions and proud passions, but most end in reconciliation and restoration of social balance. However, the question posed for the family sagas by such a story as *Halldórs þáttr I* is rather how far the conciliatory values of the sagas are to be seen in specifically religious light and how a putative religious ethic is there artistically integrated with material partly transmitted by a secular tradition. Finally, the clarity of the didactic intention in the art of *Halldórs þáttr I* may partly be due to the *projective force* immanent in Christian typology, which views history as unfinished but divinely patterned, but it poses the question whether more sagnaskemtan than only that of Einarr þambarskelfir may not reveal itself in the fullness of time as directly relevant to Christian conduct. The Christian interpretation of the saga literature, despite brave hopes of a decade ago, seems now bogged down, and I suggest that if we are to realize the full consequences of the literary nature of our subject — to reap where Nordal sowed — the pot will have to be set boiling again.

DONALD B. SANDS

Reynard the Fox and the
Manipulation of the Popular Proverb

The anonymous Middle Dutch poem *Reinaerts Historie* (usually referred to as *R II*) was written sometime around 1375.[1] Its first half (3,480 lines) amounts to a close retelling of a poem written perhaps one hundred years before called *Van den vos Reinaerde*.[2] Its second half (4,314 lines) is a continuation and conclusion of the earlier poem. *Van den vos Reinaerde* (usually referred to as *R I*) is a surprisingly unified piece of narration, but it can also be said that a sense of unity — this, however, arising chiefly from tone and style — informs *R II*. A modern reader feels he has before him in the later poem the product of one man's creative skill; and *R II*, although it is lit-

1. Still the handiest annotated text of *R II* is Ernst Martin, ed., *Reinaert/Willems Gedicht Van den Vos Reinaerde und die Umarbeitung und Fortsetzung Reinaerts Historie* (Paderborn: Ferdinand Schöningh, 1874). Line references to *R II* in the present context are to the Martin edition, and quotations from *R II* are also from the Martin edition.
2. The most heavily annotated edition of the older poem is J. W. Muller, ed., *Van den vos Reinaerde*, 2 vols., Leidsche Drukken en Herdrukken (Leiden: E. J. Brill, 1939 and 1942). Diplomatic printings of both the early poem and its continuation are in W. Gs. Hellinga, ed., *Von den vos Reynaerde/I Teksten* (Zwolle: W. E. J. Tjeenk Willink, 1952), where line numeration differs slightly from Martin's edition (see n.1 above).

265

tle read outside Dutch- and Flemish-speaking areas, is the seminal work of much English and German Reynard material. Via
Caxton's translation of a prose version, it sired numerous English adaptations. Via its eventual translation into Low German
verse, and Gottsched's translation of this into prose, it is the
source of Goethe's *Reineke Fuchs*.

There are 73 proverbs in *R II*. For a medieval work of just
under 8,000 lines, the number is neither large nor small. It
means that there is 1 proverb, on the average, for every 100
lines. The statistic, however, does not give a true picture. *R I*
contains in its 3,500-odd lines only 13 proverbs — hence, approximately, 1 proverb for every 260 lines — and the *R II* poet
neither adds to nor subtracts from that number in his adaptation of it; but in the 4,300-odd lines he adds to *R I,* there are
60 proverbs — hence, about 1 proverb for every 70 lines. This,
indeed, is a high number, even for a medieval work; and it leads
to speculation as to whether the *R II* poet used proverbs with
an intention the *R I* poet either did not need to utilize or, more
probably, was really unaware of. Predominant in *R I* is a succession of narrative motifs; in *R II,* these give way to numerous,
chiefly hypocritical, confessional speeches. The *R II* poet, being, in all probability, a learned cleric, could have padded out
his speeches with learned "sentense," as Chaucer padded out
Pertelote's presentation of her "doctrine," and he could have
drawn heavily on the *topoi* of late medieval Latinity. In fact, one
is forced to conclude that the *R II* poet, however well he dupli-
cates the idiom of the earlier poem, is a very different fellow
from the man who put *R I* in final form. Not only is his narrative technique different from the *R I* poet's, his Reynard is an
altogether different fox from the Reynard of *R I,* where he is
primarily a prankish folk figure; the *R II* Reynard is psycho-
logically top-heavy, an angry brooder over the discrepancies between social appearance and inner intention.[3]

Criteria for proverb selection vary, but in culling the 73 prov-

3. Coverage of the literary history of Reynard the Fox in the Low
German areas is in my edition, *The History of Reynard the Fox Translated and Printed by William Caxton in 1481* (Cambridge, Mass.: Harvard University Press, 1960), pp. 14–30, and in N. F. Blake, ed., *The
History of Reynard the Fox Translated from the Dutch Original by William Caxton,* Early English Text Society, 263 (London, 1970), xi–xxi.

erbs from *R II* I followed those laid down by J. Allen Pfeffer in his *The Proverb in Goethe.*[4] A proverb, he says, is "human experience and reflection distilled in the form of a lucidly phrased, variable saying" of "known or unknown origin and of limited or wide prevalence" whose "currency must be attestable." Hence, I exclude, as some paroemiologists do not, metaphorical turns of phrase, any expression of incomplete predication, and numerous nonattestable proverb-like utterances.

What gives a proverb its aura of truth is not truth itself but the sheer currency of the proverb. The fact that a multitude of unreflecting minds accept a proverb as true makes it appear true. An illustration is that almost any proverb when negated contains just about as much "truth" as does the original. "Clothes do not make the man" is just as true, given proper context, as its more usual positive expression.

But the medieval *Spielmann* — why did he often interlard his fictions so heavily with proverbial lore? The answer, it seems to me, lies in the fact that as a purveyor of fictions, he, like the *pícaro,* views the world aesthetically, not morally. He uses the proverb, over and above the stylistic heightening it lends his tale, not for its "truth," but for the impact of credence it carries with it. If the *Spielmann's* game is primarily deception — making his audience believe for a period what is manifestly untrue — what better device than the proverb could he use to promote an audience's belief in his fictions?

But does the Middle Dutch *Reinaerts Historie* itself differ from the usual medieval narrative — whether romance, *Märchen*, lay, or fabliau? Its date of composition places it in the later stages of the medieval period, although by no means at its very shag end. Literary histories label it a "comic beast epic," and one can wonder how accurate the label is. If it is "comic," it is so in a "black humor" sense quite foreign to the slapstick of the fabliau and the *Fastnachtspiel,* the late medieval German Shrovetide play. If it is a "beast epic," it is also one of the few

4. New York: King's Crown Press, 1948, pp. 1–2. On the skepticism that must inevitably arise concerning anyone's clear-cut definition of the proverb, see B. J. Whiting, *Proverbs, Sentences, and Proverbial Phrases from English Writings Mainly before 1500* (Cambridge, Mass.: Harvard University Press, 1968), pp. x–xvii.

medieval narratives that produces characters, albeit in the personas of animals, that duplicate the treacherous contradictions in human makeup. And if it is indeed an "epic," it is so, I feel, because it is, unlike many long medieval narratives, whether by design or by accident, well plotted and well constructed. Nor do I feel, as is sometimes assumed, that it is someone's satire of something socially out of phase. It pillories humanity rather than human institutions — it is only incidentally anticlerical and antiestablishment. Finally, I question the occasional allegation that it is allegory or allegorical. Its orientation is foreign to the system of concepts on which medieval writers based their allegories — the moral philosophy, the theocratically sanctioned hierarchies, the mandarin conventions of an aristocratic society. It transcends the intermediary of allegory — it is more a direct appraisal of *zoon politikon* himself.

There is, furthermore, in the latter half of *R II,* an implied social ethic. Society splits into those covetous of power and those attempting to evade its machinations. The former, once in power, suffer from the myopic stupidity power engenders. The latter are constrained by the sheer effort of evading those in power to acknowledge the virtue of mutual loyalty. They develop Socratic adroitness. They become intuitive manipulators to whom proverbial "truth" is useful as a psychological ploy. They find the chink in the armor of moral pretense to be the public's unreasonable veneration of its own version of "truth" — and it may be that the implied social ethic of *R II* prompted Goethe to refer to it as an unholy universal Bible.

But turning to the proverbs themselves: How do they operate? They can be arranged according to the degree the import of "truth" disappears from their contextual use and the impact of ironic virulence takes its place. On one level, they are to be taken "straight." The narrator, for example, reassures his audience with comfortable words in proverb form. Grimbart the badger, within context, supplies a sort of choric wisdom — voices proverbially the reactions and conclusions any honest burgher might have. Reynard himself, in confession to his friend Grimbart, voices bitter wisdom in proverb form that could only come from a member of society with the tragic perspective of an outcast. In all three instances, the proverbs establish audience-narrator rapport, even though those of the narrator are platitudinous, those of Grimbart conventional, and those of Reynard in confession to Grimbart anguished and bitter. A few examples will help highlight the "ironic proverbs" to be noted later.

The narrator of *R II* does obtrude on occasion, as most medieval narrators do. He says of Reynard, who fails to appear at court, "Wie quaet doet, die scuwet dat licht" — "Whoever does evil shuns the light" (63). He remarks, as Reynard leads the credulous Bruin to a meal of honey in Lantfreit's farmyard (and to a physical disaster), "Mer het is dicke also ghesciet/dat hem die menich verblijt om niet" — "But it often happens thus/that many look forward to something in vain" (697–698). He observes, as the various animals gather to make accusations against an all-but-forsaken Reynard, "Die crancste heeft die minste crode" — "The weakest have the least retinue" (1911). At the very end of the poem, where Reynard emerges victorious from his trial by combat with Isegrim the wolf and wins thereby the support of king and queen, he directs a proverbial observation toward the audience which embodies a truism applicable to the whole narrative: "Diet wel gaet, gheeft man eer ende lof:/mer diet misgaet, daer vliet men of" — "To those with whom things go well people give honor and praise:/but those who fail, people flee from them" (7393–94). As if to drive home the point, he repeats it a few lines later in terser form: "Diet wel gaet, die crijcht veel maghen" — "Those who succeed get many relatives" (7409).

Grimbart, as noted earlier, is a choric figure. He reacts laconically and usually in proverb form. One can imagine that the narrator lets the audience via Grimbart into context and lets it speak the wisdom an honest audience might. In defending Reynard against the deluge of accusations leveled at him during his absence from court, Grimbart says, "Dat viants mont sprect selden wel" — "An enemy's mouth speaks seldom well" (189). When Courtois the hound accuses Reynard of stealing a pudding he himself had stolen, the badger excuses the act with "Met recht so wart mens qualic quijt/dat men qualic heeft ghewonnen" — "With justice is one dishonestly freed/of that which he has unjustly acquired" (269–270). At the end of Reynard's second

private confession of his sins, when the badger is less aghast at
Reynard's transgressions than overwhelmed by his wisdom, he
exclaims, "Die beste clerke ... dicke die wijste liede niet en-
sijn:/die leken vervroedense bi wilen" — "The best scholars ...
aren't often the wisest people:/the laity outwit them on occasion" (4102–03). He says, by way of giving Reynard absolu-
tion, "Die doet is, moet bliven doot" — "What's dead ought to
remain dead" (4116). As the pair make their way into a crowd
of hostile courtiers, he reassures his uncle, the fox, with three
proverbs on the wisdom of being bold in the face of danger:

> Die blode endooch tot gheenre ure:
> Den coenen helpt die aventure.
> Een dach is beter dan sulc een jaer.

> The cowardly aren't worthy of any honor.
> The courageous are helped by hazard.
> One day for many is better than for others a year.
>   (4285–87)

Reynard himself delivers four long confessions in *R II*. Two
are given before the court of Noble the lion, and these presumably are comic because the narrator's audience knows, though
the court is not quite sure, they are bare-faced fabrications. The
two other confessions are private. They are given on the way to
face various charges before a royal tribunal and are made to
Grimbart, Reynard's brother's son. The first consists chiefly of
Reynard's enumeration of his misdeeds against Bruin the bear,
Tibert the cat, and Isegrim the wolf. There are two encapsulated
Schwänke — Isegrim, as monk, caught and beaten when he becomes entangled in the bell-ropes of a monastery and Isegrim
duped into falling into a peasant's hen-house. There is only one
proverb and this an item of deceiving rhetoric. As Isegrim inches
his way into the blackness along the hen-roost in the peasant's
barn, Reynard urges him on with the words "Men moet wel pi-
nen om ghewin" — "One must take pain for profit" (1642). In
contrast, the second confession to Grimbart, even though it does,
like the first, contain encapsulated *Schwänke,* evolves into a
lengthy and angry denunciation of greed. One imagines the poet

in the persona of Reynard assessing the moral composition of the audience itself, and the lines might well create a narrator-audience nexus which in its potential impact might far surpass that produced by the few proverbial asides that the narrator as narrator addresses to his audience. Reynard admits transgressions, but observes, "Wie honich handelt, vingher lect" —"Whoever touches honey licks his fingers" (4129). Deception is a fault, he concedes, but a necessary art of survival: "Dus moet men hier ende daer/nu liegen ende dan segghen waer" — "Thus must one here and there/first lie and then tell the truth" (4189–90). Telling the truth consistently is fatal: "Want die altoos die waerheit sprake,/enconde die strate nerghent bouwen" — "For those who ever spoke the truth/couldn't travel anywhere" (4252–53). At the point when fox and badger draw near the court, Reynard, prepared to lie his way out of the charge of murdering Cuwart the hare, speaks three proverbs in a row:

> Man moet wel lieghen alst doet noot,
> Ende daer na beteren bi rade.
> Tot allen misdoen staet ghenade:
> Ten is niemen, hi endwaelt bi tiden.

> One has to lie as necessity dictates
> and afterward make amends according to experience.
> For all transgressions there's pardon.
> There's no one who doesn't at times transgress.
>
> (4260–63)

When the confession ends, there is little for the loyal Grimbart to say except concede the wisdom of his uncle's words and admit, "Ghi sout selve sijn die paep" — "You ought yourself to be the priest" (4269).

Elsewhere the narrator may also express his views, but more indirectly and precariously — namely, in those speeches given Martin the ape, speeches punctuated by proverbial summations of things as they are. Here the proverbs are probably to be taken "straight," just as "straight" as those the narrator addresses to his audience directly or as those spoken by Grimbart or as those spoken by Reynard privately during the second confession. But

Martin's proverbs possess an insulting quality. They express un-popular "truths," ones that might be expected from a *déclassé* opportunist like Martin himself, but ones that also unmask the righteous and godly pretentions which camouflage human motiv-ation. An audience, on hearing these particular "truths," prob-ably undergoes several reactions — first, a shock on hearing utterances they suspect are true, but are forbidden by convention to voice; second, a suspicion that repugnant imputations are ricocheting in their direction; third, an apprehension that one "truth" may exist for those respectably ensconced behind legality and another for those entangled in it. Such proverbial wisdom could probably produce a subtle and unsettling *Verfremdungs-effekt.*

Martin the ape is a repellent character. The poet seems to in-tend in him a caricature of a papal emissary whose one faith lies in the power of money. His long sermon on the ways of venality is addressed to Reynard and Grimbart just before the opening of the second trial. Justice, he begins, is a delicate matter: "Trecht is elken swaer ghenoech" — "Justice is for everyone hard enough" (4609). Faced with the possibility of becoming involved in it, one needs, above all, an extralegal prop: "Een trou vrient is een hulpe groot" — "A true friend is an enormous help" (4422). But one needs a particular kind of friend, one to whom personal loyalty transcends all else: "Een trouwe vrient sel lijf ende goet/voor sinen vrient setten, alst noot doet" — "A faithful friend ought to hazard life and property/for his own friend as necessity dictates" (4555–56). He adds that justice must be cajoled: "Want trecht heeft dicwijl hulpe noot" — "For justice often has need of help" (4576) — such "help" coming via petitions cushioned with money: "Die bede is mitter ghiften coen" — "A petition becomes bold with gifts" (4552). Hence, learning the value of the one means that can influence justice is the root of all wisdom: "Men sel den pennic houden leren/ter noot dat onrecht mede to keren" — "One must learn to cherish money/in order to avert injustice with it" (4553–54). And whoever does not use friend and money to buy himself off as occasion demands is lost: "Wel is die vrient ende tghelt verdoemt/daer niemen troost of baet of coomt" — "Indeed money and friend are damned/where no one derives comfort and advantage from them" (4557–58). When Martin hastens away, Reynard and the little badger look after him in wonder, and one senses that the poet has let him echo the judicial *Realpolitik* of his time.

With the figure of Martin's consort, Rukenaw the she-ape, the *R II* poet reduces proverbial wisdom to sophistical blather. Her great moment comes when she champions Reynard at the beginning of his second trial. She immediately thrusts at her royal audience with a weapon of highest potency — proverbial lore of Biblical origin. She quotes Luke 3:36, initially the Latin "Estote misericordes" (4776) and then the vernacular "Weest ontfermich" — "Be merciful" (4777). This she reinforces with Matthew 7:1, initially again the Latin "Nolite judicare,/et non judicabimini" (4778–79) and then the vernacular "Oordeelt niemen, so enseldi/selve oordeel liden gheen" — "Judge no one, thus you shall/yourself suffer no judgment" (4780–81). After relating the parable of the woman taken in adultery, she adduces her third Biblical proverb (Matthew 7:3): "Sulc siet in eens anders oghe een stro,/die selve in sijn oghe een balc heeft" — "Many a one sees a straw in another's eye/who himself has a beam in his own" (4792–93), which, just to be sure king and queen fathom its import, she paraphrases in plain words: "Tis menich, die over een ander gheeft/een oordeel, ende hi is selve die quaetste" — "There's many a one who makes judgment on others who himself is most evil" (4794–95). Biblical allusion persists. She notes that the lowly shall be exalted and that God shall receive those who desire him (4796–97 and 4798). She caps her exordium, her portentous call to justice, with a third and freer paraphrase of Matthew 7:3:

> Niemen ense den anderen condempneren,
> Al wist hi wat von sinen ghebreke,
> Hi endede eerst of sijns selfs bleke.

> No one ought to condemn another
> even though he knows something of his transgression
> unless he first be rid of his own blemish.   (4800–02)

Noble at first rejects her plea that Reynard be heard by remarking curtly, "Hi strijct altoos sinen steert" — "He's always

stroking his tail" (that is, always deceiving) — and her rejoinder
is a concatenation of six proverbs, all of which are, like the proverbs of Sancho Panza, overwhelming in their aura of wisdom
and none of which are particularly pertinent:

> Dat swaerste moet noch meeste weghen.
> Een sel sijn lief minnen to maten
> Ende sijn leet to seer niet haten.
> Ghestadicheit voecht wel den heren.
> Tis misselic, hoe die saken verkeren.
> Men sel den dach te seer niet
> Loven noch laken, eer men siet
> Dat hi ten avont is ghecomen.
> Goet raet can dic den ghenen vromen
> Die hem met vlijt daer keret an.

> The heaviest must indeed weigh the most.
> One ought to love his pleasure in moderation
> and not hate his anguish too much.
> Constancy well beseems a lord.
> It is unforeseeable how things will turn out.
> One ought not to praise too much
> or blame the day before one sees
> that it has reached evening.
> Good counsel can often help
> those who diligently apply themselves to it.   (4848–58)

The inundation of wisdom silences the royal couple. The she-ape
keeps the floor and eventually affords Reynard opportunity to
contrive his own defense. Here the sweet reason of the proverb
prevails: it subverts justice, and the rational king and queen
succumb to it where, by rights, they should have executed the
fox on the spot.

It is a curious fact that the *R II* poet gives no proverbs to the
three power figures — Bruin the bear, Isegrim the wolf, and
Tibert the cat — although there is one exception. Once and only
once the poet allows Bruin to proverbialize, and his wisdom
encourages his own downfall. As he is obviously on the verge of
being trapped within the tree-trunk in which Reynard has convinced him there is a cache of honey, he smugly reassures the

fox of his continent habits: "Waendi dat ic bem onvroet?/Maet
es tot alle spele goet" — "Do you think I'm foolish?/Measure is
good in everything" (723–24).

One assumes that the poet implies by not larding the speeches
of his power figures with proverbial truisms that they are so
obsessed with greed that they have lost all mental agility. But
king and queen, though power figures also, are of a different sort.
Their position is secure, and hence they have opportunity to
lapse into attempts at wisdom. When Noble tries to persuade
Tibert to bring Reynard to court, the cat is apprehensive. Bruin
has been mauled, and Tibert feels he might fare no better. The
king urges him on with "Het is menich die mit listen can/meer
dan sulc mit crachten doet" — "There's many a one who can do
more with cunning/than others can do with force" (1062–63).
When Noble wishes to execute Reynard without legal formality,
the queen, both Francophile and stickler for protocol, rebukes
her spouse with "Sir, pour dieu, ne croies mie/toutes chose que
on vous die (3665–66) and caps her demand with "Alteram
partem audite!/Sulc claect, die selve meest misdoet" — "Hear
the other side!/Many accuse who themselves misdo most"
(3678–79). When Reynard seems hopelessly within the clutches
of Isegrim and his henchmen, the king evokes Aesopic wisdom:
"So langhe gaet te water die cruuc,/Dat si breect ende valt aen
sticken" — "The pot goes only so long to water/before it breaks
and falls to pieces" (4356–57). When Reynard, victorious in
combat with Isegrim, desires to address those loyal to him, both
king and queen consent, saying:

> Tis reden, dat men den vrienden seit
> Grote saken, daer macht aen leit,
> Ende men des volghet haren rade.

> There's reason that one tell friends
> important matters that concern power
> and that he follow their counsel.   (7381–83)

Here, with the royal pair, the proverb is the cipher of unwisdom.
As in the speeches of Polonius, its function is to underscore
vacuousness of character.

The proverbs allotted Reynard are, with the exception of those addressed to Grimbart during the fox's second confession of his sins, ironic sallies that are both hypocritical and candid at once, that have both a surface pertinence and a subterranean barb. They are the *R II* poet's masterpieces of ambiguous truisms. Only a few may be cited here. One exhorts to religious renewal. Reynard quotes Matthew 24:44 — "et vos estote parati" (4458) — as he, in the guise of an eremite, is about to take the life of Lampreel the cony. Another enjoins legal impartiality. He cries, "Dat recht endoet niemen onghelijc" — "Justice treats no one unequally" (4627) — as he is about to demand special dispensations from the royal tribunal. Another warns against incompetents in authority. He says to king and queen that Isegrim, Bruin, and Tibert have dangerous ambitions and points up his argument with "Waer esels crighen heerscappien/daer siet ment selden wel ghedien" — "Where jackasses get power/one seldom sees things turn out well" (5749–50) — and here the listeners, both the animal courtiers of the poem and the human audience of the narrator, are fully aware that the dig is as appropriate to the royal pair as to the trio of political scoundrels. Several — hypocritically — warn against the prevalence of hypocrisy:

> Want daer veel op eerden leeft,
> Die van buten draghen schijn
> Anders, dan si van binnen sijn.
>
> For many live on earth
> who outwardly show appearances
> different from what they are within.   (4310–12)

On occasion, Reynard's proverbs are instruments of cruel sarcasm, of the *Schadenfreude* which characterizes much of the humor in the late medieval *Schwankbücher*. When Bruin is firmly caught in Lantfreit's tree-trunk and is about to suffer a horrible beating at the hands of the local farmers, Reynard announces their approach and tells Bruin they will give him something to drink since he has enjoyed Lantfreit's honey so thoroughly (which he certainly has not), adding as justification, "Het is goet dat men die spise wel net" — "It is proper that one moisten food (with drink)" (764). The cruelty of the remark is rounded off a few lines later when Reynard finds Bruin on a river bank where he has collapsed from exhaustion and, presumably, loss of blood. Seeing that the scalp has been torn from his head, the fox addresses him as "Sir priester, dieux vous saut" (957) and then asks, "In wat oorden wildi u doen/dat ghi draecht dat rode caproen" — "What order do you wish to enter/ by wearing that red cowl?" (969–70).

The ultimate purpose of any paper such as this is to enhance the aesthetic potential of its subject. Too much esteem, I feel, is allotted the progeny of the Middle Dutch poem and too little the progenitor. Few medievalists I know have ever bothered to read *R II*. Elsewhere, in an earlier paper, I attempted to give paternity its due.[5] I pointed out that if Lazarillo de Tormes and Guzmán de Alfarache are *pícaros,* then Reynard is also, just as much as Simplicius and Felix Krull are *pícaros,* even though they are outside the seminal picaresque tradition of the Spanish sixteenth and seventeenth centuries. I urged that *R II* be accorded the dignity of being read as picaresque fiction, despite the fact that it is written in iambic tetrameter couplets; despite the fact that its narrative technique is not linear, but complex and heavy with encapsulated flashbacks; despite the fact that its picaresque earthiness and vulgarity are informed by an ever ironic and worldly eloquence. Here I must concede that much of the humor in *Reinaerts Historie* is gross and heavy-handed. The two major crises of the poem utilize the motif of the "lying confession": in both we see Reynard condemned to death and allowed, grudgingly, to make public confession of his sins. We, the external audience, know he is lying and know also the internal audience, the assemblage of beasts at King Noble's court, eventually feel he is telling the truth. This sort of thing is pretty obvious, and its humor may strike us today as stale. I concede also that the numerous fabliau-like *Streiche* in *Reinaert* — like the two in the first half where Reynard does in both Bruin and Tibert — belong in *Schwankbücher:* their level of humor is that of the prat-

5. "Reynard the Fox as *Pícaro* and *Reinaerts Historie* as Picaresque Fiction," *The Journal of Narrative Technique,* 1 (1971), 137–145.

fall and custard pie. But the ironic humor that plays on conventional conceptions of "truth" is pervasive and subtle. It does not merely reverse the positions of apparent truth and apparent falsehood, but indirectly casts doubt on whether there is any basis for conventionally received "truth" outside of that produced by public consensus abetted by repressive power. The signal for this sort of epistemological irony is the persistent use of the popular proverb in ever-varied contextual situations. Indeed, the proverbs are, in a large sense, heuristic: they tend to disestablish any unreflected acceptance of "truth" and to keep Pilate's question open.

JAMES I. MILLER, JR.

Lydgate the Hagiographer as Literary Artist

John Lydgate is notorious as a poet in want of design and control, but the allegation, however time-honored and well established as a "fact" of literary history, is by no means unassailable.
Indeed, it may not stand up at all under more searching examination of his poems than has usually been accorded them. In discussing the epic legend *St. Edmund and St. Fremund*,[1] W. F.
Schirmer says of the miracles which occupy the second half of
the third book (848ff.), but "really constitute a separate" one:
"They have been selected from the great compilation of St.
Edmund without regard for chronological order, for the sake of
their paraenetic and edifying purpose." He then speaks of "the
irrational way in which they have been added." [2] While these

1. It was at Professor B. J. Whiting's suggestion that I became interested in this poem, and my first efforts to produce an edition were sustained by his advice and encouragement. A result was "John Lydgate's
Saint Edmund and Saint Fremund: an Annotated Edition," Ph.D. diss.,
Harvard University, 1967, now under revision for the Early English
Text Society. Citations in the present essay are by line only (as all are
to be found in Book Three), with punctuation deleted, from the edition
by Carl Horstmann in his *Altenglische Legenden,* n.s. (1881; rpt.
Hildesheim: Georg Olms, 1969).
2. W. F. Schirmer, *John Lydgate: A Study in the Culture of the XVth*

statements do have apparent validity and fairly represent much
that has been said about Lydgate's poetry in general, they are
not, in fact, an adequate accounting of the evidence in this text.[3]
Certainly the poet selects these pious tales from quite separate
points in the source,[4] but his arrangement and articulation of
them, far from being irrational, or even merely didactic and
ecclesiastical, reveal a notable interest in artistic balance.

(1) The first (848–1106) and last (i.e., seventh, 1314–
1407) miracles involve harassment from the Danes and feature
Ayllewyn, whose devotion to the martyr's remains seems to keep
him constantly en route — at both points through Essex — and
results in successful opposition to tyrant (first) as well as bishop
(seventh).[5] (2) The second (1107–69) and sixth (1240–1313)

Century, trans. A. E. Keep (Berkeley: University of California Press,
1961), p. 165; cf. Hildburg Quistorp, "Studien zu John Lydgates Heiligen-
legenden," Ph.D. diss., University of Bonn, 1951, pp. 150, 164, and,
equally, her damning conclusion: "Man kann diesen Mirakeln in ihrer
Gesamtheit keine künstlerische Funktion im Rahmen der ganzen Legende,
noch im Einzelnen eine poetische Gestaltung zuschreiben" (p. 166). The
"great compilation" referred to by Schirmer is the Latin *vita* and miracles in MS Bodley 240, printed in Carl Horstmann, ed., *Nova Legenda
Anglie . . .* (Oxford, 1901), II, 575ff.; abbrev. *NLA.*

3. Nor is the characterization of them merely as "some miracles of
St. Edmund, such as any monastic life of its patron-saint would tend
to accumulate to itself"; see D. A. Pearsall, *John Lydgate,* Poets of the
Later Middle Ages, John Norton-Smith and Roger Fowler, gen. eds.
(Charlottesville: The University Press of Virginia, 1970), p. 282.

4. Cf. the sequence in Lydgate's poem and the pages (given in paren-
theses) on which the corresponding material appears in Horstmann's
print (*NLA*) of the source: 1 (600–603), 2 (593), 3 (665), 4 (661–
662), 5 (594–595), 6 (608–610), 7 (596–600). For an analysis of this
relationship in the light of chronology, see Quistorp, pp. 150–151.

5. Evidently to heighten pathos, Lydgate himself supplies the details,
in the first miracle, that Ayllewyn had to spend the night in a church-
yard (1000ff.), and in the seventh, that it was almost *eue* (1331) when
he arrived in London (Quistorp, pp. 152, 162n., 165). Rhyme common
to both includes *late/gate* (1000–01; 1331, 1333) and contributes to the
similarity between the two situations in which the traveler finds himself
"destitut . . . off herbergage" (1002) and then later is once again "denyed
herbergage" (1317). On Essex, see 1081, 1316, 1401; the latter two,
which immediately precede and follow the seventh miracle, have no
express counterpart in the source (*NLA,* II, 600). For a recurrence between the first (1042) and second (1161–62) miracles which is not in the
Latin, see Quistorp, p. 153n. Lydgate's lack of "regard for chronological
order" between the first and seventh miracles may also reflect adher-

miracles each involve a Leoffstan[6] — sheriff and abbot, respectively — and have a common theme:

> To heere off hym froward by dysdeyn
> Off his myracles . . .
> To heere hem rad the tyme spent in veyn   (1115–17)[7]

> . . . lyk a wood man ferde
> The myracles off Edmund whan he herde

> Despysed his myracles whan he herde hem reede.
>   (1245–46, 1249)

(3) The third (1170–83), fourth (1184–97), and fifth (1198–1239) miracles, all treating of thieves, begin, respectively, in first lines at two-stanza intervals:

> Knyhtes fyue . . .   (1170)[8]

> Eek oon off Flaundres . . .   (1184)

> Theuys eyhte . . . .   (1198)

This overall structure is reinforced with patterns of common rhyme which give it additional continuity and balance. Thus, rhymes on -*ence,* which are prominent throughout, contribute, on the one hand, to the effect that the several miracles are but variations on a single theme, and, on the other, to verbal clusters

---

ence to sources earlier than MS Bodley 240 which "relate, and evidently conceive of, the Sweyn series of events, as *anterior* to that connected with the translation to London"; see Thomas Arnold, ed., *Memorials of St. Edmund's Abbey,* Rolls Ser. 96 (London, 1890–1896), I, xxv.

6. Lydgate suppresses other proper names in the second miracle (Quistorp, p. 155).

7. Lines 1115, 1117 also illustrate Lydgate's use of verbal balance (*To heere* . . .) within the stanza to reinforce the structure of rhyme.

8. Their number is not given in the source, which does contain the inconvenient date 1267—"tempore discordie inter regem Henricum et barones Anglie"—and other particulars omitted by Lydgate; see *NLA,* II, 665, and Quistorp, pp. 156–157. Further, in the Latin prose these thieves are apprehended after their return to Ely, but in the English poem they experience another kind of seizure "or they passyd the boundis off the gate" (1178), the divine punishment of them thus conforming to that of the thieves in miracles four and five.

which recur with a symmetry corresponding to that seen above.
(1) Successive a-rhymes in the introduction of the first miracle

> . . . was no resistence
>
> . . . oppressid by mortal violence   (876, 878)
>
> . . . was . . . no reuerence
>
> . . . oppressid by sclandrous violence   (883, 885)

have their counterpart in a b-rhyme concluding the seventh
miracle

> . . . no resistence
>
> . . . withoute violence
> . . . with . . . reuerence.   (1367, 1369–70)

(2) Rhyme phrases in consecutive stanzas of the second miracle

> . . . doyng no reuerence
>
> . . . beyng in presence   (1127, 1132)

reappear almost unchanged in the stanza introducing the sixth
miracle

> . . . do reuerence
>
> . . . beyng in presence.   (1241, 1243)[9]

Related to the patterns of this larger symmetry are others from
one miracle to the next. The second and third, for example, are
linked by another development of the same common rhyme

> . . . violence
>
> . . . make resistence   (1126, 1129)

9. While the fifth miracle shows similar, if also distinctive, recurrence
in its last two stanzas — ". . . the gret offence" (1228), ". . . that gret offence" (1238) — another structure unites the third and fourth miracles:
the first and last (fourth) stanzas include rhymes on *vengable* (1174,
1196); the second stanza begins and the third ends with rhyme on *stood*
(1177, 1190), enclosing common rhyme on *-oun*.

> . . . make resistence
> . . . violence.   (1175–76)

More striking is the effect of continuity between them created
by the verbal recurrence in lines such as the following, which
open or close their respective stanzas:

> To seynt Edmund hadde no deuocioun   (1114)
>
> Vnto the seynt doyng no reuerence   (1127)
>
> No reuerence doon to the seyntuarye   (1149)
>
> Hadde to the martir gret deuocioun.   (1183)

Individually, the longer miracles, with which the entire unit
begins and ends — the first and second and the sixth and seventh
— exhibit internal patterns of some interest. The sixth culmi-
nates in an appeal to the saint elaborated in a parallel between
successive final couplets:

> Prayyng . . . off his benygnyte
> On . . . Osgothus forto han pite   (1294–95)
>
> . . . knelyng on . . . kne
> To saue Osgothus off his Infirmyte.   (1301–02)[10]

The rhyme and in part the phrasing have been anticipated by an
earlier pair of lines:

> Off his . . . and . . . dignyte
> Off his . . . and . . . bounte.   (1276, 1279)

The transition to the seventh miracle begins and ends with
rhyme on *blyue/lyue* (1310, 1312; 1336–37), the phrases *al his
lyue* and *al hir lyue* referring to figures in the previous and present miracles, respectively. The action then proceeds to its climax

---

10. For the use of common rhyme and other parallel in successive
final couplets, cf. ". . . joie/. . . I myghte hire sen ayein come into Troie"
and ". . . joie/I may sen hire eft in Troie" (*Troilus and Criseyde,* V.
608–609, 615–616); see F. N. Robinson, ed., *The Works of Geoffrey
Chaucer,* 2nd ed. (Boston: Houghton Mifflin, 1957), p. 466.

in a series of four stanzas (1338–65) with interlocking patterns.
Elaborate parallel between the first two, especially in respective
fourth lines, defines the contest for possession of the remains,
with some effect of wit or irony resulting from a difference in
application of the same words or similar constructions:

> Thre yeer . . .
> Took . . . the Bysshope vpon a day . . .
> To leede kyng Edmund ageyn to Bury toun
> But . . .
> The bysshop . . .
> . . . in-to Powlys cherche   (1338ff.)

> Vpon a day took . . . clerkis thre
> . . . cherche . . .
> To karye the martir fro thenys preuyly
> But . . . the bysshop . . .
> . . . to Poulis . . . .   (1345ff.)

The second and third stanzas conclude with sustained alliterative
and other emphasis on the miracle which prevents the bishop
from stealing the casket:

> Yt stood as fyx as a gret hill off ston   (1351)

> For lik a mount it stood ylyche stable.   (1358)[11]

These final lines are followed, in the third and fourth stanzas, by
common a-rhyme contrasting the wrongful *trauayle* with the fact
that it is of *noon auayle* (1352, 1354); in the latter stanza there
is further parallel: *the bysshop gan meruaylle*[12] when the effort
gan to faylle (1359, 1361).

In the second miracle, the third lines of the first five stanzas
all begin with the same preposition, and four of them[13] con-

---

11. The similes are not in the source (Quistorp, p. 162).
12. For more evidence of the context for this parallel in construction,
cf. "The bysshop . . . gan werche" (1343), ". . . the bysshop gan dys-
deyne" (1355), ". . . the bysshop gan meruaylle" (1359).
13. In the second of these five stanzas, the first line belongs to the
series cited previously (1114, 1127, 1149, 1183) and, together with the

stitute a sequence, at once alternating and progressive, of variation on the theme of the abbey as sacred precinct and inviolable sanctuary:

Off seynt Edmund to breke the franchise   (1109)

Off blyssyd Edmund entred is the place   (1123)

Off hooly chirch diffendyng the ffranchise   (1130)

Off the cherche entred is the boundis.   (1137)

The four verbs or verbals have different subjects, in an overall arrangement — *tirant*[14] in the abstract, the *woman gilty* seeking refuge, the *clerkis* offering it, Sheriff *Leoffstan* in particular — heightening the confrontation. Similarly, the parties to the dispute are introduced with formal parallel in the opening words of three successive stanzas:

A woman gilty . . .   (1121)

The clerkis present . . .   (1128)

The offycerys rauynous . . . .   (1135)

This pattern is then linked with another in the last two of these stanzas and the one that follows:

The clerkis present in deuyn seruyse   (1128)

The clerkis prostrat lay in ther praier   (1138)

The clerkis knelyng in ther orysoun.   (1144)

The latter two stanzas, in turn, together with the next, present the crucial action in a form which is dramatic and yet rigorously structured. The final lines in the first and third of these stanzas

---

third line, shows a relation to the present series: "To seynt Edmund hadde no deuocioun/ . . . Off his myracles ful smal affeccioun" (1114, 1116). Cf., in turn, the third and final lines of the stanza which follows: "Off blyssyd Edmund entred is the place/ . . . Vnto the seynt doyng no reuerence" (1123, 1127).

14. The word occurs three times in second lines (1108, 1143, 1150).

show obvious recurrence and apparent wordplay (*ded/Dempt*):

> The woman crieth . . .
> Help blissid Edmund . . .
> . . . I shal . . . be ded   (1139–41)

> The woman crieth . . .
> Help hooly martir shal I be . . .
> Dempt . . . .   (1153–55)

Enclosed by this parallel is another in the appeal to the saint, first by the woman:

> Keep . . . thy Jurediccioun   (1142),

then by the clerks:

> Keep thy ffredam . . . .   (1145)[15]

Finally, the entire succession of patterns is concluded with emphasis on the theme of this miracle in a form which gives further variation to these last formulas and at the same time makes use of the preposition, a thematically significant rhyme word, and other elements which recur in the first pattern cited:[16]

> Dempt in the boundis this day off thy franchise.   (1155)

As the longest of the miracles, the first has the most extended internal patterns of recurrence. It is introduced and elaborately concluded with rhyme involving or deriving from the name of the saint's antagonist. Thus *Sweyn/certeyn* in the introductory stanza (844–845) recurs at the end in successive a-rhymes (1086, 1088; 1093, 1095), immediately followed by a third stanza which ends the entire unit with other rhyme on *-eyn* (1105–06). Initially, the antagonist is characterized by *disdeyn* (888, 998), but nearby first lines also suggest that any opposition to the saint will be *in veyn* (939, 967); the latter's control

---

15. Only the clerks speak in the source (Quistorp, p. 155, and cf. p. 165).
16. See 1109, 1123, 1130, 1137, above.

of the final movement, restoring proper order, is indicated both by a first line (1023) returning the faithful Ayllewyn and by the final one (1106) sending the lifeless body of the invader *hoom ageyn.*

In the first part of the miracle, stanzas ending *this lond* (833, 861)[17] and later rhymes on *his hond* (899, 1028) give immediacy and concrete imagery to the struggle. The effect of a detailed account succinctly rendered is produced by repetition of a syntactical pattern previously noted at the beginning of successive stanzas,[18] but here compressed into consecutive lines of a single stanza:

> Men slayn . . .
> Wyues oppressid . . .
> Widwes rauesshid . . .
> Maidnes diffouled . . .
> Preesthod despised . . . .   (884–888)

Parallel sixth lines tell of appeal to the patron saint by the faithful:

> Besechyng hym his seruantis to socoure   (923)
>
> Besouhte the martir ther fredam to renewe.   (937)

The latter introduces a further development, with notable use of alliteration, in successive final couplets

> . . . ther fredam to renewe
> . . . on ther wo to rewe   (937–938)
>
> . . . ther trouble to termyne
> . . . ther hertis tenlumyne.   (944–945)

The saint's initial response is a speech to Ayllewyn in which similar imperatives, beginning successive stanzas, are addressed, respectively, to the devotee himself and then through him to Sweyn:

17. This is also the rhyme word, e.g., at 897, a first line.
18. Cf. 1121, 1128, 1135, above; also 1170, 1184, 1198.

> Go forth in haste spille no tyme in veyn   (967)
>
> Vexe nat my peeple suffre hem lyue in pees.   (974)

The corresponding fourth and fifth lines call upon Sweyn, in the
third person and then in the first:

> That off my peeple he axe no truage
> Ther ffranchise is to stonde in auantage   (970–971)
>
> To axe hem trybut yt longith nat to the
> Ther ffredam stablysshed off antiquyte.   (977–978)

With similar progression the second lines of this latter and of a
third stanza warn him:

> Trouble nat the kalm off ther tranquyllite   (975);

it is not his

> ... to trouble me and my franchise.   (982)[19]

Subsequent lines in each stanza give the warning virtually identical form:

> Be war therfore ...
> ... thow ... nat ...   (979–980)
>
> Be war therfore ...
> ... thow nat ....   (984–985)

In the latter part of this miracle, rhymes on *tribut* (1039,
1072, 1099)[20] emphasize what is at issue and are twice accom-
panied by lines which, in relation to each other, seem at once
parallel and contrastive, paradoxical and congruent:

19. Cf. this rhyme word in second miracle, as noted above.
20. Line 1072 begins and 1099 concludes respective stanzas, both
lines ending "fro tribut."

> Geyn goddis wil may be no reffut   (1037)
>
> Thanked god off his gracious refut.   (1098)[21]

Tribut itself is given ironic redefinition — *guerdoun couenable geyn fals tyrannye* (1040) — in a series of lines, each the sixth in its stanza

> ... a sharp spere in his hond   (1028)
>
> He with a spere sharp and keene grounde   (1035)
>
> His victorye with spere swerd or sheeld.   (1049)

Concomitantly, in addition to celebration, there is circumstantial insistence on the factuality of this event in second lines sharing common rhyme:

> At Geynesborugh the silue same nyht   (1024)
>
> That Sweyn was slayn in his chaumbre a-nyht   (1045)
>
> That Sweyn was slayn in his bed a-nyht.   (1059)

Fourth lines attribute the miracle to *his myht/* (i.e.) *goddis myht* (1047, 1061), and fifth lines associate its operation with *cleer ... lyht/cleer lyht* (1027, 1048). The beneficial effect of the saint's having paid Sweyn this kind of *tribut* is reiterated, with an approximation to common rhyme, in respective second and fourth lines

> ... sette the Rewm in pes
>
> ... neuer put them-sylff in pres   (1073, 1075)
>
> ... sette this lond ... in surnesse
>
> ... this lond is brouht in ... gladnesse. (1087, 1089)

Within the individual miracle, then, as between one and another, the evidence is unequivocal: Lydgate clearly planned

21. Cf. "breke the franchise," "diffendyng the ffranchise" (1109, 1130) and "hadde no deuocioun," "Hadde ... gret deuocioun" (1114, 1183) in groups cited above.

this unit of his poem in remarkable detail, taking special pains
to combine parallels in word and position with modifications in
content or context which would advance the presentation. Whatever his disregard for the chronology of history or his interest in
the pious lessons of hagiography, the poet is undeniably and
literally concerned about literary form, about patterns of balance
in the arrangement of phrase and word, even of syllable and
letter. What he achieves is something like the harmony of a
musical refrain, which cannot but be considered in some degree
poetic. It is not my aim at present to evaluate the poetry, though
respect for it may well be apparent throughout this paper.
Rather, I would simply argue that the miracles in the third book
of the *St. Edmund and St. Fremund* testify, not to Lydgate's in-
competence or irrationality in organization, but to his use, as a
conscious literary artist, of considerable skill in design and control. Whether this particular skill is evident in other poems must
surely become a concern of Lydgate studies, for which I hope the
present essay will provide suggestions as well as stimulus.[22]

22. For comments on the essay in draft, I thank my colleague Joseph
Milosh.

ELIZABETH WALSH, RSCJ

John Lydgate and the Proverbial Tiger

In his collection of *Proverbs, Sentences, and Proverbial Phrases*
B. J. Whiting gives fourteen entries having the tiger as the central focus of the expression.[1] The fourteen entries contain fifty-
four citations. In his survey of Scottish proverbs[2] he lists seven
tiger entries which include eight citations, three of which have
been repeated in the larger work. Hence, there are fifty-nine
references in all. Of these, forty are drawn from the works of
John Lydgate, the monk of Bury St. Edmunds. The greater part
are contained in poems which are either translations or medieval
adaptations of classical works.

In all probability, however, the poet had never seen a tiger

1. Bartlett Jere Whiting, *Proverbs, Sentences and Proverbial Phrases
from English Writings Mainly before 1500* (Cambridge, Mass.: Harvard
University Press, 1968). In this study of the proverbial use of the tiger
I have confined myself to and allowed myself to be guided by the work
done by Professor Whiting. In all probability many more examples of
"tiger" passages might be cited. This paper makes no claim to be an
exhaustive survey; however, a glance at Professor Whiting's sources
gives one reason to hope that, if not exhaustive, the samplings are at
least representative.

2. Bartlett Jere Whiting, "Proverbs and Proverbial Sayings from
Scottish Writings before 1600," Part Two, *Mediaeval Studies,* 13 (1951),
87–164.

nor had many of his contemporaries. The illuminators of medieval bestiaries depicted a charming creature with the head of a wolf (dog?), the paws and tail of a lion, the neck of a horse. One of the clearest and most finely delineated is that found in Corpus Christi College Cambridge MS 53. The picture illustrates the traditional legend of the tiger and its cubs. The story, found ultimately in Pliny, Ambrose, and Isidore, was an elaboration of the tiger's famed swiftness. So swift was the tiger that it could overtake a hunter riding the fleetest of horses. If a tiger discovered that some thief on horseback had stolen its cubs, it would pursue and overtake him. The thief, seeing the superior speed of the beast, would cast behind him a glass sphere to distract the animal. The tiger, mistaking its own image in the ball for its cub, would give up the pursuit, but upon realizing its mistake it would renew the chase and again overtake the horseman.[3]

The popularity of the tale is evident from its appearance in art and literature. University Library MS, Cambridge Ii 4 26, a twelfth-century manuscript,[4] contains a miniature similar to that in CCC Cambridge 53. The story appears in the margins of the Queen Mary Psalter and is carved on one of the misericords in Chester Cathedral. The author of *Kyng Alisaunder* recalls the legend in describing the savage intensity of Alexander's army marching to Arabia to attack Darius;[5] Chaucer utilizes the tale to illustrate the ferocity of Arcite;[6] Lydgate refers to the tradition in "Reson and Sensuallyte," a dream vision (c. 1408) attributed to him in the manuscripts of the poem.[7] The poet is in the Garden of Pleasure engaged in a game of chess with a fair Maid. The third of his pawns, Sweetness of Thought, bears a shield upon which is emblazoned a tiger:

3. C. Plinius Secundus, *Natural History,* Book VIII, chap. xxv; Isidorus Hispalensis, *Etymologiarum,* Book XII, *Patrologia Latina,* ed. J. P. Migne, vol. LXXXII; Ambrose, *Hexameron,* VI.4.21 in *Sancti Ambrosi Opera,* ed. Carl Schenkl, 3 vols. (Prague, 1896–1902).

4. Montague Rhodes James, *The Bestiary,* Roxburghe Club (Oxford: Oxford University Press, 1928).

5. *Kyng Alisaunder,* ed. Geoffrey V. Smithers, Earl English Text Society, 227, 237 (London, 1952, 1957), 1881–86.

6. "The Knight's Tale," 2626–29, *The Works of Geoffrey Chaucer,* ed. F. N. Robinson, 2nd ed. (Boston: Houghton Mifflin, 1957).

7. John Lydgate, *Reson and Sensuallyte,* ed. Ernst Sieper, Early English Text Society 84, 89 (London, 1901–1903), II, 1ff.

And in hys shelde he bare a beste,
A Tigre, which that ys so rage
And a best[e] most savage,
Swyfes[t] to renne for his pray.
Whan his fovnes be lad away,
He ys deceyved by merours
Which the hountys for socours
Caste in the way[e] for a treyne.   (6974–81)

Thus Lydgate knew of the tiger from legendary sources. It would be difficult to believe that he had not also encountered *tigris* in classical literature. Horace recalls Orpheus' fabled power to tame "tigris rabidosque leones." [8] Virgil describes Turnus rushing towards Pandarus "immanem veluti pecora inter inertia tigrim." [9] Translated by Gavin Douglas "as ane rageand wyld tygyr onstabill," it is this quality of the tiger which most of Lydgate's proverbs express. What took root in the popular mind was not the image of the tiger as a symbol of paternal fidelity, as suggested by Ambrose, not the symbol of a man seduced by the pleasures of the world as reasoned Pierre de Beauvais,[10] but the simpler and evidently more realistic understanding of the tiger found in classical literature.

Nevertheless it was John Lydgate who crystallized this view in English literature. The tiger, to him, was a mad, raging, fierce old fellow.[11] Although the actual Bengal tiger was not known in

8. "Ars Poetica," 393, *Satires, Epistles and Ars Poetica* (Cambridge, Mass.: Harvard University Press, rev. 1929). See also *Carminum liber* III.xi.13, *Horace, The Odes and Epodes* (London, William Heinemann, 1914).

9. *Aeneid,* IX.728–730, *Opera,* ed. R. A. B. Mynors (Oxford: Clarendon Press, 1969).

10. *Mélanges d'archéologie d'histoire et de littérature,* ed. Charles Cahier and Arthur Martin (Paris, 1847–1856), II, 140–142.

11. The only exception I have noted occurs in Lydgate's translation of Guillaume de Deguileville's *Pélerinage de vie humaine.* In the course of his pilgrimage to the Heavenly City the Pilgrim encounters the goddess of Love, who taunts him and asserts that even if he is "Swyfft as A tygre in rennyng" (13458), he will not escape her as long as he is dominated by her associate Gluttony. In this case Lydgate did translate literally, for the simile was also used by the French poet both in the first and second recensions of his poem. See John Lydgate, *The Pilgrimage of the Life of Man from the French of Guillaume de Deguileville,* ed. F. J. Furnivall, Early English Text Society, Extra Ser. 77, 83, 92

heraldry until the end of the eighteenth century, the notion of the animal's ferocity surpassed that of his swiftness in the later Middle Ages. No doubt Lydgate expressed the colloquial understanding of the beast's attributes current in the fifteenth century. But it may well be, too, that his expression was influential in establishing the reputation of the tiger.

Although most of his tiger images are found in works of classical origin, in most cases the figure seems to have been Lydgate's own contribution. That he attached a certain weight to the tiger metaphor becomes evident when one analyzes the texts and discovers that it marks a distinction between Christian and pagan heroes. A survey of these texts may clarify this point.

Lydgate's *Troy Book,* begun in 1412 and completed eight years later, contains several proverbial tigers. The poet begins his account of the Trojan War by recounting the ancestry of the Myrmidons who were descended from King Peleus. Peleus was hostile to his nephew Jason and plotted to do away with him. The author describes the king as "Dowble as a tygre siȝly to compasse" (I.217).[12] The imagery is not in Guido delle Colonne's version of the story, which was Lydgate's source.[13] Somewhat later Hercules is likened to a tiger. At Jason's request King Peleus and the Greeks have attacked the city of Troy. The Trojan king Lamedon is terrified to see the archetypal hero coming into the field:

> Liche a lyou*n*, wood and dispitous,
> Or a tigre in rage furious.   (I.4283–84)

In Guido (Book IV, p. 41) Hercules is described: " . . . ille vir strenuus tam fortis tam audax Hercules supervenit . . . "

In Book II when Paris and the Trojans have plundered the

(London, 1899–1904); Guillaume de Deguileville, *Le pelerinage de l'homme,* Verard (Paris, 1511), fol. lii. See also the first recension, ed. J. J. Stürzinger, Roxburghe Club (London, 1893), p. 331, 10679–82.

12. John Lydgate, *Lydgate's Troy Book,* ed. Henry Bergen, EETS ES 97, 103, 106, 126 (London, 1906–1935).

13. Guido de Columnis, *Historia Destructionis Troiae,* ed. Nathaniel Edward Griffin (Cambridge, Mass.: Mediaeval Academy of America, 1936), p. 6.

Temple of Venus and carried off Helen as well, the Greek sol-
diers waken and give battle:

> Þei ran I-fere as tigres al vnmylde,
> Liche wode liouns or þis boris wylde.   (3857–58)

The similes are not in Guido (VII, p. 75).

In Book III Troilus, who "By his knyȝthod kylled many
Greke," is described as "a tigre, gredy on his pray," (991).
Guido reads " . . . in qua erat Troylus, qui Grecos mirabiliter
opprimebat . . . " (XV, p. 136). In the same battle Archelaus,
the king of Boetia, "Lik a tigre or a wylde bore," (1142) fights
fiercely against the Trojans. Again the imagery is Lydgate's for
Guido reads: "Contra quos rex Prothenor et rex Archelaus cum
gente sua de regno Boecie exiuerunt. Durum bellum committitur
inter eos" (XV, p. 137). Later in the battle Hector, his horse
having been killed, defends himself "lik a tigre in Ynde"
(1394).[14] Later in Book III the two manly champions Hector
and Ajax encounter one another:

> Eueryche on oþer lik tigers or lyons
> Be-gan to falle, and proudly to assaille.   (2054–55)

Guido: "Committitur ergo durum prelium inter duos tam fortes,
sed . . . " (XV, p. 146). In the following battle Hector and
Achilles meet "in her fiȝt . . . /Like wode tigres, or bores in her
rage," (2468–69). As the story nears its climax and Hector and
Achilles have vowed to fight to the death, everyone begins to
fear for Hector's life. One day as he is about to ride to battle
his father Priam forces him to dismount. The knight obeys but
longs to be in the field. The poet inserts a reference to the tiger
of the bestiaries:

> So inwardly sterid was his blod,
> Þat like a tigre or a lyoun wood,

14. Lydgate may well have borrowed this simile from his acknowl-
edged master. Chaucer, in his response to the Clerk's tale of the patient
Griselda, counsels women to be "egre as is a tygre yond in Ynde"
(1199).

> Þat were deprived newly of hir praye,
> Riȝt so firde he al þat ilke day, —
> Or liche a bore þat his tusshes whette,
> While þe Grekis and þei of Troye mette. (5137–42)

Whereas in Guido: "Qui demum in multa contradiccione iussui patris obtemperans redit invitus . . . " (XXI, p. 173). However, after the death of Margariton, his bastard brother, Hector "More furious þan tigre or lyoun" (5246) dons his armor and goes to his last battle. When Achilles sees the harm Hector is doing to the Greek forces he becomes outraged and waxes "as wood/As boor or tigre in her cruel mood" (5297–98). Guido reads: "Achilles autem furibundus irruit in Hectorem . . . " (XXII, p. 175).

Warriors continue to fight with animallike fierceness in Book IV. Deiphobus, beholding Ajax' slaying of Cecilian, a son of Priam, grows "Woder anon þan tigre or lyoun," (1271). Later Troilus, surrounded by the Greeks, displays his manliness: he "As a tigre stondeth at diffence" (2724). The Queen of the Amazons, too, can fight like a beast. Enraged by the death of Hector, Penthesilea attacks the Greeks in vengeance:

> And like a tigre in his gredinesse,
> Or like, in soth, to a lyounesse,
> Þat day she ferde, ridynge vp & doun
> Among þe Grekis.   (3901–04)

Challenged by the queen, Pyrrhus "wexen gan as wood/As any tigre, boor, or wood lyoun — " (4158–59).

The tiger was also an image of cruelty. Polyxena, condemned to death by the Greeks, prays to the gods for mercy and denounces those who are about to slay her as "more cruel . . . / For lak of pite, þan tigre or lyoun" (6787–88). Pyrrhus, Achilles' son, then slays her, and the author comments on his lack of humanity:

> I am astonid, sothly, whan I rede,
> After hir deth, how it dide hym good,
> Like a tiraunte to cast abroad hir blood,

> Or a tigre, þat can no routhe haue,
> Rounde enviroun aboute his fadris graue.   (6860–64)

This personal comment is not in Guido (XXXI, p. 237).

Book V, which concludes Lydgate's *Troy Book,* deals with the aftermath of the war and the Greeks' homeward journeys, including the fateful return of Agamemnon. In a speech prefatory to describing the death of the king, Lydgate beseeches Almighty God to punish murderers, especially those so bold as to slay a king:

> Suffre non swiche to live vp-on þe grounde —
> Wers þan tigre or Cerberus þe hounde.   (1059–60)

In an ensuing episode Diomedes is as angry as a tiger when King Telephus slays his brother-in-law Assandrus (1264–65). Finally Pyrrhus is again compared to a tiger when he is about to slay King Atastus (2577–78), who is subsequently saved through the pleading of his wife.

The Siege of Thebes (c. 1421), Lydgate's contribution to the *Canterbury Tales,* is the tragic story of Oedipus. According to the editors of the work, his principal source was the medieval French *Roman de Thèbes* written c. 1150; his most immediate source was *Le Roman de edipus,* a prose version of the former.[15] As in the *Troy Book* the use of the tiger simile seems to be the English poet's invention.

Among the guests (all of whom augured ill for the kingdom) at the wedding of Edippus and Iocasta was

> Cruel mars as eny Tygre wood,
> Brennyng Ire of unkynde blood.   (867–868)

These guests are not mentioned in the *Roman de Thèbes.*[16] After the death of Edippus his sons cast his body into a pit.

15. John Lydgate, *The Siege of Thebes,* ed. Axel Erdmann and Eilert Ekwall, EETS ES 108, 125 (London, 1911, 1930), II, 6–7.
16. *Le Roman de Thèbes,* ed. Léopold Constans, 2 vols., Société des Anciens Textes Français (Paris, 1890).

Lydgate comments on their unnatural cruelty: "Wers than serpent or eny tigre wood" (1013). The editors note that this was not in the source nor is it in the *Roman de Thèbes*. Later, when Polyneices and Tydeus have both been driven by a storm to seek shelter on the same porch, a fight between them is described. They draw their swords and rush upon each other "In her fury lik Tygres or lyou*n*s" (1356). The author of the *Roman* used a different simile:

> Al porche sont li dui baron,
> Combatent sei come dragon.   (723–724)

In the continuing description of the battle the simile of a lion is used:

> Ensemble jostent li baron,
> Requierent sei come leon.   (765–766)

Finally the two cursed brothers slay each other in mortal combat. They attack one another "lik two Tygres in her rage wood" (4274). In describing the battle the monk considerably expanded his source.

The Fall of Princes (c. 1439) is Lydgate's paraphrase of Laurence de Premierfait's *Des Cas des nobles hommes et femmes,* a French prose redaction of Boccaccio's *De Casibus virorum illustrium* (1355–1360). Again the poet's free use of his sources can be seen in the tiger images. In recounting the fortunes of King Minos, King of Crete, Lydgate tells of Scylla, the daughter of Nisus, King of Megara. This king aided the Athenians against Minos, but Scylla fell in love with the Cretan king and conspired in her own father's death. The poet takes the occasion to remark on the strange behavior of the young woman:

> But offte it fallith, that creatures sclendre,
> Vnder a face off angelik lokyng,
> Been verrai wolues outward in werkyng.
> Eek vnder colour off ther port femynyne,
> Su*m*me be fou*n*de verray serpentyne,

Lambis in shewyng, shadwid with meeknesse,
Cruel as tigres, who doth to hem offence.   (I.2509–15)[17]

The text of Laurence quoted by Bergen reads simply:

... mais apres ce que Nisus roy des mesgarensoys fut occis mo-
yennant le barat de sa fille cilla.   (IV, p. 148)

In retelling the story of Oedipus Lydgate again uses the tiger
image to describe the ferocity with which his sons fought one
another (I.3732–33). Another woman with tigerlike qualities
was Queen Olympias who, in Lydgate's eyes, becomes a paradigm of the cruelty of all women. Wife of Philip of Macedon
and mother of Alexander the Great, she defamed the body of
her murdered husband and honored that of his murderer. The
monk asserts:

What malis may, yif it be declared,
Vnto the malis of wommen be compared?
I speke of them that be malicious
And list of custum for to be vengable:
Among a thousand oon may be vertuous,
And in too thousand sum oon is merciable;
But when thei been of rancour vntretable,
Ther is no tigre mor cruel dout[e]les,
Record I take off Olympiades.   (II.2499–57)

The commentary on the cruelty of women is contained in
Laurence:

Ie dis certes que il nest chose si cruelle comme est couraige de
femme courroucee. Et qui pis est ainsi comme la maniere des
femmes est plus cruelle que de toutes les bestes sauluaiges ...
(IV, p. 217)

But the tiger is Lydgate's. Cleopatra's second husband was also
known for his cruelty, and Lydgate compares him, too, to a

17. John Lydgate, *Lydgate's Fall of Princes*, ed. Henry Bergen, EETS
ES 121–124 (London, 1924–1927). References are to the EETS volume,
page, and line numbering.

tiger. By his marriage to the queen, Euergetes became lord of Egypt, but his title was no guarantee of virtue, for on the day of his marriage "lik a tigre" he slew her eldest son (II.2905).

Another work of Lydgate's dealing with classical lore is *The Serpent of Division* (1422), the only well-authenticated prose work of the monk. In actuality it is a treatise written shortly after the death of Henry V when, because of the youth of Henry VI, civil war was a real possibility. Lydgate utilizes the history of Julius Caesar to illustrate the dangers of civil dissension. In describing Caesar's conquest of Britain the author tells of fighting between the Roman and the brother of the British king Cassibelan. The two warriors "ferden as Tigres and lions, eueryche wowndinge other full mortally"; but by the perversity of Fortune Caesar killed the Briton and gained sway over the land.[18]

For the most part the tiger similes in the above passages convey some rather unpleasant aspects of human nature: tigers are furious, harsh, greedy, mad, cruel, merciless, deceitful. Yet Lydgate has used the image of the beast to describe both heroes and villains, the honorable and the dishonorable.

These images do not appear only in works dealing with classical subjects. Lydgate also made use of tiger images in his religious poems; in these, however, the tiger image is always used to characterize the enemies of God. Pagan heroes may at times have fought like tigers, but Christian heroes did not. In the year when Henry VI celebrated Christmas at Bury (1433) the Abbot requested the monk to compose a poetic version of the life of St. Edmund, the martyred king of East Anglia and patron saint of the monastery. In the poem the Danish princes who come to Anglia seeking revenge for the death of their father begin to plunder and murder. They are described as "woode prynces," who, contrary to the laws of God and nature:

> Be title of wil, as any tigres fel,
> To moordre and robbe spared no creature.
>
> (311–312)[19]

18. John Lydgate, *The Serpent of Division,* ed. Henry Noble Mac-Cracken (London, H. Frowde, 1911), p. 54, 17–18.

19. John Lydgate, "S. Edmund und Fremund," *Sammlung Altenglischer Legenden,* ed. Carl Horstmann (Heilbronn, 1878), pp. 376–440.

Later in the story one of these sons, Hyngwar, demands that Edmund forsake the Christian faith and yield his kingdom. The saint refuses, and when the messenger returns to Hyngwar the Dane responds "as any tigre wood," proceeding to besiege the king's castle (654–655). But Edmund has learned the price of war and will not take up arms. His reward is the crown of martyrdom.

Two other martyrs eulogized by the poet are Saints Albon and Amphabel. Written in 1439, *St. Albon and Amphabel* is the story of two Britons who were converted and later martyred in the time of Diocletian. The infidels, both Romans and Britons, are likened to tigers. In Book Two Lydgate relates how Albon, converted by Amphabel, is sought in Verolamy (a town in Britain) by the Romans:

> For whiche agaynst hym so obstynate they stode
> Lyke wylde boores or tygyrs in theyr rage,
> Vengeable of herte, furyous and wode . . .   (I.849–851)[20]

When he is about to be slain the people who have come to see his execution begin to suffer from thirst. At the saint's prayer a clear stream of water gushes forth for which the pagans thank the sun. Lydgate admonishes their blindness:

> O most unhappy, o people ungratious,
> Worse than beastis, o voyde of all reason,
> O cruell tygrys, o wolfes furyous,
> O folysshe asses . . .   (II. 1724–27)

Book Three relates the martyrdom of Amphabel. Through the influence of these saints many Britons have been converted. When the pagans learn this they threaten the converts with death unless they worship the pagan gods. The Christians refuse, and the pagans fall upon them "Lyke tygrys fell, vengeable as lyons" (III.276). The same imagery is used to describe the pagans' ferocity in lines 990 and 1131.

20. John Lydgate, *S. Albon und Amphabel,* ed. Carl Horstmann (repr. from *Festschrift der Königstädtischen Realschule*), (Berlin, 1882), p. 41.

The image is used in similar fashion in "The Fifteen Ooes of Christ," a hymn in honor of the sorrows of Christ. The poet compares his Lord's enemies to fierce beasts: "Fersere than Tygrees, woder than lyowns" (130).[21]

In another of his minor poems, "Horns Away," Lydgate picks up the antifeminist theme. He delivers an admonition to women which is just the contrary of Chaucer's exhortation at the end of the *Clerk's Tale.* The monk of St. Edmunds advises women to follow the example of simple maidens such as the Virgin Mary and cast away all horns. The poet laments that some women have not the gentility to do away with their horns, which were given to beasts for defense but are unseemly for ladies:

> But arche wives, egre in ther vyolence,
> Fers as tygre ffor to make affray,
>   They haue despit, and ageyn concyence,
> Lyst nat of pryde, ther hornes cast away.   (37–40)[22]

William Dunbar's "wedo" too seems to take it for granted that women are "terne" (fierce), but she advises the "tua mariit wemen" to learn and practice the art of deception:

> Thought ye be kene, inconstant, and cruell of mynd;
> Thought ye as tygris be terne, be tretable in luf.
>   (260–261)[23]

Dunbar's esteem for Lydgate can be surmised from the honorarium given him in "Lament for the Makaris." The Scottish poet devotes one stanza to mourning the loss of "The noble Chaucer, . . . /The Monk of Bery, and Gower, all thre." [24]

Thus Lydgate's reputation and influence extended beyond the geographic confines of east Anglia, beyond the era to which he

21. John Lydgate, "The Fifteen Ooes of Christ," *Minor Poems of John Lydgate,* ed. Henry Noble MacCracken, EETS ES 107 (London, 1911), pp. 238–249.

22. *Minor Poems of John Lydgate,* ed. Henry Noble MacCracken, EETS 192 (London, 1934), p. 663.

23. *The Poems of William Dunbar,* ed. W. Mackay Mackenzie (Edinburgh: Faber and Faber, 1932), p. 91.

24. *Ibid.,* p. 21, 50–51.

was born. This would seem to be a fitting note upon which to conclude this study of the tiger image in the monk's works. It is interesting to observe, from the study of the preceding texts, that he seems to have discerned three categories of persons comparable to tigers: pagan warriors, enemies of the Church, and women. It seems redundant to say that he did not look upon these tigerlike people very favorably.

And his understanding is, for the most part, our own. Anyone who is "as fierce as a tiger" is to be avoided. Whether Lydgate drew this image from the bestiaries, from seeing or reading of tigers emblazoned on shields, from his study of the classics or of Chaucer, is not evident. What is clear is that he shaped and developed the simile used by his literary predecessor, gave it a greater range of meaning and a wider circulation. He gave expression to the popular understanding of what this fabulous beast — tiger — was. The fact that he seems to have been primarily responsible for the literary establishment of this understanding is significant. Lydgate is generally conceded to have been a minor, though prolific, writer. Yet Professor Whiting's listing of tiger proverbs would indicate that his influence was considerable. This small study may serve to show that the tracking of proverbs, like the tracking of tigers, may prove an adventure wherein one may discover some interesting facts about the course of events — and the coursings of the human mind. It is sometimes the minor figures of literary works and of literary history who play a major role in determining both.

STANLEY J. KAHRL

Teaching Medieval Drama as Theatre

Although Professor Whiting is best known for his teaching of Chaucer, it is appropriate to include in a volume of essays dedicated to his career as teacher and scholar an essay on the teaching of medieval drama. During the fifties, when the study of medieval drama was not pursued with much energy, Professor Whiting offered a graduate seminar on medieval drama. One direct consequence of that seminar has been Robert Longsworth's study, *The Cornish Ordinalia.* Knowledge that the seminar had been given, and that Professor Whiting had an interest in the subject that went beyond his own book on *Proverbs in the Earlier English Drama,* encouraged me to read extensively in the subject while preparing for my oral examination. My own interest and work in the field has stemmed directly from that reading. It therefore gives me real pleasure to be able to offer this study as acknowledgment of the original encouragement, without which a path I much enjoy might not have been taken.

No drama is easy to recreate in the context of the classroom. Be it *Aureng-Zebe* or *The School for Scandal, Tamburlaine* or *As You Like It,* all present the same inherent difficulty to the teacher seeking to involve his class imaginatively in the life of a play. For a play to live fully it must move from the flat plane of the printed page to a three-dimensional world, inhabited by actors moving on a stage which presents through various devices a world for those actors to inhabit other than the world of the audience. Seldom is any student equipped both to set an imaginary stage and to people it with creatures of his imagination who can give life to the lines he reads. When that imaginative task involves the creation of a stage and sets such as a student has never seen, then the teacher's task seems nearly insuperable.

Perhaps that is one reason why discussions of medieval English drama have so often followed critical paths more suitable for use in analyzing literary texts. Sources and analogues, dating, metrics, and, more recently, discussions of moral meaning have more often than not been offered as the model approaches we should follow when seeking to arrive at an appreciation of medieval drama. Such approaches are certainly valuable means to understand the aspects of the plays toward which they are directed, but they all have the same inherent difficulty. None of these approaches sees that essential quality which makes a play something other than a poem or a piece of fiction. A play fully exists only as a theatrical experience. Any approach which does not keep this fact central denies the essential nature of the thing described and falsifies the nature of the play itself. Accordingly, we as teachers must muster our imaginary forces with all the power we possess to recreate for a moment at least, in the imagination, if not on a stage, the theatrical experience of the medieval plays we have chosen to teach.[1]

As an example of how we might proceed I would like to con-

1. Those wishing to develop a clearer understanding of the nature of the medieval theatrical conventions should consult: Allardyce Nicoll, *Masks, Mimes and Miracles* (New York: Harcourt, Brace, 1931), pp. 135–213; Richard Southern, *The Medieval Theatre in the Round* (London: Faber and Faber, 1957); Glynne Wickham, *Early English Stages 1300–1660*, vol. I: *1300–1576* (London: Routledge and Kegan Paul, 1959); Bamber Gascoigne, *World Theatre: An Illustrated History* (London: Ebury Press, 1968); Richard Hosley, "Three Kinds of Outdoor Theatre before Shakespeare," *Theatre Survey*, 12 (1971), 1–33; also Stanley J. Kahrl, *Traditions of Medieval English Drama* (London: Hutchinson, 1974). For further bibliographical information, see Carl J. Stratman, C.S.V., *Bibliography of Medieval Drama*, 2nd ed., rev. and enl. (New York: Ungar, 1972), vol. I.

sider the N-Town play of the *Assumption of the Virgin* in its theatrical context.[2] No one can pretend that an approach which depends on a belief in the doctrine at the heart of this play is likely to appeal to a large proportion of a normal class. Recognition of this fact has undoubtedly led to the play's having virtually been ignored in scholarly discussions of medieval English drama.[3] Yet the very fact that the play's doctrinal message is of so limited an appeal today makes the *Assumption of the Virgin* peculiarly suitable for study as an example of effective theatre, in this case a play making extensive use of the resources of the place-and-scaffold theatre to present the doctrine of the bodily assumption of the Virgin, without for a moment considering the truth of that doctrine. What we learn from studying the theatrical qualities of this play should enable us to demonstrate more persuasively the dramatic strength of those medieval plays whose import finds an easier acceptance but whose theatrical qualities have thus far not received the attention they deserve.

The first thing that should be said is that plays about the Assumption of the Virgin were apparently popular in England in the later Middle Ages precisely for their theatrical effect. At York the incident of Fergus the Jew losing his hand as it sticks to the side of the Virgin's bier was so wild a theatrical effect that it apparently brought about the revision of that particular play.[4] Martin Stevens has demonstrated fairly conclusively that Wakefield at one time had a play on the subject borrowed from York, though whether it was the tamer, late-surviving version we do not know.[5] The Assumption play mentioned in the rec-

2. The text cited is the *Ludus Coventriae*, ed. K. S. Block, Early English Text Society, Extra Ser. 120 (London, 1922), 354–373. Subsequent references appear in the text, by line number.

3. R. T. Davies, in a recently published modernized version of the N-Town cycle otherwise containing many of the Marian plays, includes only a severely truncated version of this play. See *The Corpus Christi Play of the English Middle Ages* (London: Faber and Faber, 1972), pp. 364–367. No study specifically devoted to this play is listed in Stratman's bibliography, cited in n.1, above.

4. See V. A. Kolve, *The Play Called Corpus Christi* (Stanford: Stanford University Press, 1966), pp. 130–131.

5. Martin Stevens, "The Missing Parts of the Towneley Cycle," *Speculum*, 45 (1970), 254–265.

ords of Lincoln cathedral also depended on spectacular theatrical effects for its success. We have records of payments to a series of vicars for their work and "super diligence" for the cathedral Assumption play, a number of the later entries containing references to clockwork.[6] That clockwork may have been machinery of the type discussed by Glynne Wickham, machinery for raising and lowering the cloud for Mary's ascent into Heaven at the play's conclusion, though it is also possible that it moved a splendid Heaven.[7] Two, and possibly three, villages in southern Lincolnshire also had a play on the Assumption involving the use of a mechanical cloud, quite probably in imitation of the theatrical effects achieved in the Cathedral.[8] Thus when we find that the N-Town play of the Assumption includes both the incident of the unbelieving Jew sticking to Mary's bier and a stage direction suggesting that an image of the Virgin is to be transported into and out of Christ's bosom at two points in the play, and that John specifically announces after his "sudden" entry that a cloud brought him, it seems fair to infer that this play may stand as an exemplar for this tradition of theatrical spectacle.

The first step to take in discussing the theatrical dimension of a play is to reconstruct the set for which it was written. No assessment of the theatrical quality of a play is possible if we cannot visualize it in its original setting. Given the fact that the cast for this play consists of twenty-eight speaking parts, almost none of which can be doubled, as they all appear on stage in the grand finale, as well as a chorus of angels and a chorus of

6. See Stanley J. Kahrl, *Medieval Drama in Lincolnshire, 1300–1585*, Malone Society, Collections VIII (Oxford: Clarendon Press, 1974), for Lincoln in the years 1457–1559.

7. I am indebted to Frederick Warner, the illustrator for this article, for this suggestion. Dr. Warner points out that mid-fifteenth-century stage machinery was at a stage of development where a simple windlass could have done the job required for raising and lowering a cloud. The clockwork, then, which persists in use well after the heyday of the city's plays, may have been used for some spectacular effect unrelated to the raising of the Virgin, such as a rotating set of planets for the Heavens. See the circular structure behind the throne in the accompanying diagram.

8. See Kahrl, *Medieval Drama in Lincolnshire*, records for Holbeach, Sleaford, and Sutterton.

martyrs, both of whom sing, and given the two stage directions calling for singing to the music of an organ, it would appear that the play as we have it was written for a large ecclesiastical body, either a monastery or a cathedral. Since we know that the Lincoln cathedral chapter sponsored some sort of theatrical spectacle from 1457 on, and since a number of factors unrelated to this play suggest that Lincoln may have been the home of the N-Town cycle, I shall use the admirably suitable space before the choir screen of Lincoln cathedral as the locale for our reconstruction of the N-Town play of the Assumption.

Let me then set the stage. Stage directions give us quite clear indications of the structures we will need. The council of the Jews, which opens the play following the Doctor's prologue, must take place in a raised scaffold, as the council remains on-stage throughout the whole long first part of the play and then descends to attack Mary's bier as it passes in procession toward the sepulchre. Late in the play two demons carry one of the Jewish princes off to Hell, which I would place under the scaffold for the council of the Jews in the style of the Fouquet miniature.[9] This scaffold would be placed at God's left hand, that is, stage left, as it is in the diagram. We will return to the sepulchre, toward which the bier is carried, in a moment.

Mary is presented "in the temple, praying" ("in templo orans," s.d., 67). This structure should balance the council scaffold, both symbolically and literally. I have therefore placed it on the extreme stage right. Mary's prayer ascends to Wisdom (who is Christ), and He, having noted the prayer, sends an angel, singing to a harp, down to comfort Mary. A Heaven scaffold is most certainly called for. Normally such a structure would be located stage center. As it happens, the choir screen in Lincoln cathedral closes off the choir just at the nave crossing. Were a structure for Heaven to have been built on the top of that screen, ascents and descents could be made by way of a permanent small stair leading down to the south aisle of the choir. The screen is wide enough to support a large organ and would

9. For reproductions of this detail in a contemporary theatrical illustration, the Martyrdom of St. Apollonia, by Jean Fouquet (c. 1455), see Southern, *Medieval Theatre in the Round,* p. 101, pl. 5; also Gascoigne, *World Theatre,* p. 75, fig. 59.

provide an excellent bearing surface on which to have built the structural supports for the Heaven scaffold and the cloud. Were I John Hanson, the first chaplain assigned the task of managing the "Assumption and show put on in the cathedral on the feast of Saint Anne," I would most certainly have so built my Heaven. (And so I have, in the stage diagram.)

As I have already obliquely suggested, use of a cloud seems to be indicated not once but twice in this play, the first time to bring the apostles miraculously to Mary on her deathbed (a standard feature of the apocryphal accounts), the second to take Mary to Heaven. I was at first tempted to use the cloud for the descents and ascents of the heavenly host as well, but I am now convinced that such was not the case. The playwright seems to to have made a distinction between the denizens of Heaven, who can move freely between Heaven and earth, presumably on foot, as in the Norwich roof bosses, and humans, who need help.[10] The point must be made, of course, to underline the fact that Mary *in her bodily form* was taken up into Heaven. The playwright even goes to the length of distinguishing between Mary as we see her acting her part and Mary's soul, which leaves her body after her death, enters Christ's bosom, and is carried up to Heaven, whence it is later returned to reenter Mary's body, visibly, before the Assumption takes place.[11]

Having located Heaven together with the cloud on top of the choir screen, it would seem logical to place Mary's house, to which she goes from the temple, and which the apostles enter from the cloud, near the choir screen to the rear of the playing area. Balancing it, then, on the opposite side of the rear acting area would be the sepulchre, which Mary leaves to enter the

10. See M. D. Anderson, *Drama and Imagery in English Medieval Churches* (Cambridge: Cambridge University Press, 1963), pp. 91–92, for a discussion of walking angels, also plates 10b–10d for illustrations of Gabriel walking to Mary taken from the Norwich roof bosses.

11. Mechanical clouds could be used for the ascents and descents of heavenly figures, of course. Cf. uses of an *araceli* in Assumption plays in Spain, N. D. Shergold, *A History of the Spanish Stage* (Oxford: Clarendon Press, 1967), pp. 76–80. The stage practices in Valencia, Elche, and Castellon are strikingly parallel to those proposed here, including such items as a house for Mary, as well as a sepulchre, an *araceli,* worked mechanically, a palm, and a doll figure for Mary's soul's ascent and return to her body.

cloud for the Assumption. Such an arrangement has the further advantage of giving a long space for the funeral procession to proceed through after the death of the Virgin. Before proceeding to the play itself, I would point out that these five structures could all be accommodated easily in the nave crossing of Lincoln cathedral and that spectators could arrange themselves as they wished in the nave. Because of the stage business required for the movements of Mary's soul, which take place inside Mary's house and inside the sepulchre, I doubt that many spectators would have been put in the arms of the transept where these pieces of stage business, essential to the doctrine of the play, would have been missed. As the diagram suggests, the stage structures would fill the nave crossing.

Let us then turn to the play to see how effectively this stage set was employed and for what purpose. The play's opening establishes quickly and economically the nature of the action that will give the play its focus. Mary, we are told by the Doctor who introduces the play (1–26), was the first pilgrim, spending the last twelve years of her life visiting the places in the Holy Land where the important events in Christ's life occurred.[12] The Council of the Jews, which follows immediately, and which opens the play proper, is concerned with the matter of heresy. Most of the council agree that the death of Jesus has effectively ended most of the threat from that quarter, but the third prince points out that Mary still constitutes a threat to orthodoxy. Killing her as well is suggested, but the Bishop proposes a more politic plan. Since Mary's death would arouse the people were they to accomplish it, better to wait until she is dead and then "We shal brenne here body and the aschis hide/and don here all the dispith we can here devise" (59–60). In the scene which follows immediately, Christ sends an angel to Mary to tell her of her impending death. She accepts the news with equanimity, as might be expected, but does ask that she "se not the fende" (127) when she parts from this world. The action of the play, then, is to answer the common prayer, "Save me from the as-

12. In the plays at Valencia and Elche, Mary's return visit to the Stations of the Cross was acted out, with the actor playing the part of Mary moving from station to station in the cathedral. See Shergold, *Spanish Stage,* pp. 76–79.

saults of my enemies," both terrestrial and spiritual. The reason why the Virgin's body did not remain to be adored by succeeding pilgrims, the reason why her tomb was not one of the places to visit in the Holy Land, was that her body would have been desecrated had it been allowed to remain within the control of the Jewish authorities.

The scene for the Council of the Jews is brief, just sufficient to establish the necessary tension. The language is that of medieval stage tyrants, blustering, crude, vulgar. By contrast, the scene that follows, Mary's prayer to Christ and the descent of the angel to inform her of her coming death, is a study in composure and grace. The angel descends to the music of the harp he is carrying, establishing at once the strong connection between the spiritual composure of the Christians and musical harmony so much a part of this play. The angel brings the traditional heavenly palm guaranteed to protect Mary from the assaults of her enemies, until such time as she is received into Heaven. Mary's one request of the angel, when she learns of her approaching death (other than her wish to avoid seeing the fiend) is that she might once more see "my brether the appostelis . . . or I passe to that lyth" (117–18). However, she realizes that this is not likely to happen, as they are now all scattered in their ministries. To this the angel responds, "A yis lady inpossible to god nothyng trowe ye" (120), and we are ready for the first miracle.

Once the angel has returned to Heaven, either up a ladder to the scaffold or else up the stairway to the top of the screen, Mary leaves the temple to return to her house with her two attending virgins to prepare herself for death.

The ensuing stage direction reads "here suddenly appears saint John the evangelist before the door of Mary" ("hic subito apparet sanctus Iohannes euangelista ante portam marie," 162). How John "suddenly" arrives, as we have said before, is not clear from this direction. However, he almost immediately informs the audience that "In pheso I was prechying a fer contre ryth [. . .]/and by a whyte clowde I was rapt to these hyllys" (164–165). Later, when the other apostles appear, Peter too declares that they were brought by clouds from the place where they were preaching to one cloud which then brought them to

Mary (256–257). Certainly it is possible that John and Peter
say that they came in a cloud precisely because they did *not*
appear to do so. However, given the evidence for use of mechanical gadgets at Lincoln for the Assumption, and given the
adverb "suddenly," indicating some sort of surprise, we will
assume that a cloud descended from Heaven as Mary, in her
house, prays "So wolde god my brether were here me by/To
bere my body that bare jhesu oure savyoure" (160–161).

John steps out of the cloud, then, alone, in answer to Mary's
prayer. Once Mary has explained why he has been wafted to
her home, she gives him the heavenly palm, with instructions
to bear it before her bier to ward off the assaults of the Jews.
She, it seems, knows of their plans to desecrate her body and
wants John to arrange for a secret burial so that this may not
happen. She clearly does not expect the Assumption to take
place. Once Mary's instructions are complete, the remaining
apostles step out of the cloud.[13] Peter and Paul are the only
ones with speaking parts, which are brief, just enough to identify who they are for the audience. John then greets them, tells
them what he has learned about the reasons for their sudden
bodily translations to Mary's house, and they enter the house.

Until this point, Mary has apparently been seated or kneeling,
praying, and she then rises to greet the apostles. However, once
they have all greeted one another, her flesh begins to fail, and
the stage direction reads "here she will be very properly arranged in bed" ("hic erit decenter ornatus in lecto," 276). The
reason for this becomes apparent in a moment. Once Mary is
properly arranged, the apostles begin to light candles in preparation for the funeral procession to Mary's sepulchre. At the
same time, Christ with all the company of Heaven, consisting
of two angels, Michael, and the choruses of angels and martyrs,
descends to Mary. Her modest comment on the appearance of
this host of people, led by Jesus, is one of the most delightful
in the play — "A wolcom gracyous lord Jhesu sone and god of
mercy/an aungyl wold a ssuffysed me hye kyng at this nede"

13. The stage direction at l. 205 reads "Here suddenly let all the
apostles be brought together before the door, wondering" — "hic subito
omnes apostoli congegentur ante portum mirates [*sic*]." The repetition
of *subito* (cf. l. 162) is particularly noteworthy.

(286–287). However, Jesus informs her that he has come to sing her dirge and proceeds to do so.

Once the antiphon is over, the stage direction reads, "here the soul of Mary leaves from her body to the bosom of God" ("hic exiet anima marie de corpore in sinu dei," 301). Now it becomes clear what was involved in arranging Mary "properly" in bed. One of the apostles must have hooked up a doll figure of some sort to a wire strung to the ceiling and thence to a pulley arrangement similar to those used to pull stars across the stage in the Nativity plays. Now the soul of Mary is seen departing from her body, as Jesus unhooks the doll from the wire and places it in his robe. Before leaving to return to Heaven, he orders the apostles to take Mary's body to the vale of Josephat where a sepulchre awaits them and where he will appear to them three days hence. The heavenly court then departs, singing.

The apostles prepare to make up the funeral procession. John is given the palm after it has been offered to Peter. As they raise the body of Mary from the bed, with their candles lit, Peter leads them in singing Psalm 113 (114 in the King James version), "When Israel went out of Egypt, the house of Jacob from a people of strange language;/Judah was his sanctuary and Israel his dominion," a psalm of hope for those persecuted by a false religion.[14] As they chant the psalm, the angelic choir sings an Alleluia in Heaven, and the procession moves off.

One must realize that a great deal has been happening already in this play, all of it motivated naturally by the events that are unfolding. But even more is to come. As the procession winds out of Mary's house across the central acting area toward the sepulchre in the vale of Josephat, the Jews are struck by the sound of the music. Curiously, the third prince looks out, the same member of the Council who most feared the effects on the Law of Mary's continued existence, and is stunned to see Mary's bier passing. Angry shouting erupts, promises of an effective at-

14. The Douai Bible contains the following gloss to the first line of this psalm: "People of false religion counted barbarous, especially such as also persecute the true Religion" (*The Second Tome of the Holie Bible faithfully translated into English, out of the authentical Latin* [Douai, 1610], p. 207).

tack on the procession are made, and the threat promised in the opening scene is realized.

As the Jews descend from their scaffold, one should visualize fully the scene. The funeral procession is arranged as follows: John is leading, carrying the heavenly palm. Peter, Paul, and probably four other disciples are carrying Mary, most probably on the bed on which she died, which serves as her bier. Before and after the bier come the remaining apostles, carrying lighted candles. For those students whose personal experience with a funeral is slight, perhaps the memory of a state funeral, President Kennedy's or Johnson's for example, will serve to recall the solemn nature of a procession of pallbearers. Imagine, then, the shock as the first prince of the Jews runs out of the group of Jews, all of whom are now going frantically mad, toward the bier to wrest it from the pallbearers — and the theatrical effect of his startled discovery that he is stuck fast to the bier!

Unlike the older York version of this incident, there is no tearing loose of a hand in this play. Instead, Peter offers to save the first prince if he will believe Jesus Christ our Savior and "his moder that we bere on bere" (407). When the prince has affirmed his faith, Peter orders him to take the palm to his nation as a sign of God's mercy. The palm, he is told, will function as all relics will, healing all forms of sickness. As he leaves, the apostles continue on to the sepulchre where they place the body of Mary, censing it while they conclude the singing of Mary's dirge. Meanwhile, the first prince has returned to his frantic fellows to cure their madness with the palm. The second prince is converted and healed. The third, he who has always been most upset by the effect of Mary on his Law, violently refuses the offer to repent and be saved and is almost immediately carried off to Hell by two demons. Parenthetically, the stage direction covering the healing suggests that more than the second prince is involved, as the "believers are healed" ("credentes . . . sanati sunt," 441). Similarly, the demons gloat over "tho harlotis" that they will carry off. All this suggests that the cast may be even larger than originally suggested.

Once the stage is cleared of the unbelievers, Christ descends to the waiting apostles, declaring that the Assumption is now to take place. First, however, Mary's soul must return to her body, and so it does. Clearly another set of wires must have been located in the sepulchre, to which Christ attaches the doll figure once he enters the structure. As the soul moves towards its destination, Jesus addresses it affectionately and then orders Mary to arise and follow him. Mary does so and is greeted by Jesus and Michael. They ascend to Heaven while the organ plays ("hic assendent in celum cantantibus organis," 493). The cloud, which had rested between Mary's house and the sepulchre throughout the play, is, in the proposed reconstruction of the set, waiting to accomplish the Assumption, which comes as a fitting climax. Once in Heaven, Christ crowns Mary, Michael calls for "melody," and the play concludes with the *Deo gracias*.

The N-Town Assumption of the Virgin is an excellent play. Every portion is tailored to the whole, every small action supports the main action of the play. Set within the world of pilgrimages and worship of the saints, each detail makes excellent sense and builds toward the spectacular climax. The space within which the action occurs is fully utilized, with each scene progressing naturally to the one that follows. While much of the success of the play depends on spectacular theatrical effects, none of them are introduced solely for their own sake. From the image of Mary's soul to the heavenly palm, each visual effect is fitted to the central action of the play, "Lord, save me from the assaults of my enemies."

Understood in this light, one can understand why the Assumption play was cut from the Wakefield cycle, why so little of the Marian drama of medieval England survives. Every play demands a suspension of disbelief on the part of the audience at its beginning. We are not in the Holy Land as we watch this play any more than we are in Rome to watch Shakespeare recreate the death of Julius Caesar. But once we have made that initial act of acceptance, the powerful world of the theatre has the capacity to persuade us that, at least for the moment of the play, the world it imagines is as real as the world we move back into as the scene fades. And when the play draws so effectively on the habit of mind which made Walsingham a goal for pilgrims, one realizes that for some at least of those who saw the N-Town play of the Assumption, the effect would have been to reaffirm one's faith in the doctrine at the heart of the play, particularly if the events imagined are taking place in a cathedral dedicated to the Virgin herself.

This reading is proposed, finally, not to convince anyone that Mary was assumed bodily into Heaven, but to provide a model approach to the teaching of all medieval drama. Dramatic representations of Abraham and Isaac are, to be sure, excellent instances of medieval typological thinking. But the typology of those plays will only live if they are effective theatre. Of course, a medieval play need not go to the lengths of the N-Town play of the Assumption in its use of theatrical devices to make its point. The York *Nativity* is a stunning, yet very simple play. I have only selected this Assumption play for examination because its theatricality is so rich and because it gives us so much to work with. What I am asking is that, whatever play you choose to teach, seek first to understand it as effective theatre and evaluate it in those terms. To such an understanding all other approaches contribute. Without it, they are as sounding brass to our students.

JOHN B. BESTON

How Much Was Known of the Breton
Lai in Fourteenth-Century England?

When one raises the question how much was known in fourteenth-century England of the Breton lai, one is really asking
how much was known of the French lai. For there is no evidence
that the Bretons were traveling around England then presenting
their lais. The authors of the English lays seem to have been
attracted to the French lais because they saw their potentiality
for minstrel presentation at a single performance lasting about
an hour to an hour and a half. The English authors conceived
of their lays as brief, dramatic minstrel poems and relied for
their appeal mainly on that concept, not on their perpetuation
of an old, distinguished Breton art form.

Between the latest Old French lais and the earliest Middle
English lays of which we have knowledge, there is a lapse of
perhaps a century. The French lais, along with the French romances, were revived in fourteenth-century England during the
fashion for translation. This circumstance suggests that the inspiration for the Middle English lays came from French sources,
not from Bretons who had continued during the thirteenth and
fourteenth centuries to travel throughout England presenting
their lais. Even when it was revived in England, the lay fluc-
tuated in popularity and never matched its vogue or quality in
France.

Despite the century or more nearer to us in time, only nine poems survive in English (as against thirty-four in French[1]) that call themselves lays or could be regarded as lays: *Sir Landevale* and its derivative *Sir Launfal,*[2] *Lay le Freine, Sir Orfeo, Sir Degaré, Sir Gowther, The Erle of Tolous, Emaré,* and Chaucer's *Franklin's Tale.* Four of these were written early in the fourteenth century: *Sir Landevale* and the three lays in the Auchinleck MS, *Lay le Freine, Sir Orfeo,* and *Sir Degaré.*[3] All of these are in four-stress couplets, adapted from the French octosyllabic couplets. Then there is a gap of a quarter century or more (that is, to about 1365) until *Sir Gowther* or *Sir Launfal; The Erle of Tolous* and *Emaré* were written near the end of the century.[4] These four lays are all in tail-rhyme stanzas. The *Franklin's Tale* is in all important ways an anomaly. Written around 1390,[5] it belongs neither with the lays in couplets nor

1. In addition to the lais of Marie de France, there are 22 French poems that could be considered lais: *Desiré, Melion, Graelent, Doon, Guingamor, Tydorel, Tyolet, Haveloc, l'Espine, le Cor, Nabaret, le Trot, l'Ombre, le Conseil, l'Amours, Aristote, le Vair Palefroi, l'Oiselet, l'Espervier, Narcisse, le Lecheor,* and *Ignaure.*

2. As far as the tail-rhyme stanza permits, Chestre follows the wording of *Sir Landevale.* When one excludes the interpolations with which he breaks up *Sir Landevale,* one finds that he takes more than two thirds of his rhymes from it. S. T. Knight, in "The Oral Transmission of *Sir Launfal," Medium Aevum,* 38 (1969), 164–170, argues that Chestre knew *Sir Landevale* in an oral form.

3. The Auchinleck MS was compiled between 1327 and 1340. See L. H. Loomis, "Chaucer and the Breton Lays of the Auchinleck MS," *Studies in Philology,* 38 (1941), 14–33. A. J. Bliss in his edition of *Sir Launfal* (New York: Thomas Nelson, 1960) concludes that *"Landevale* belongs to the beginning of the fourteenth century" (p. 15). In "Thomas Chestre: A Speculation," *Litera,* 5 (1958), 1–6, he suggests that *Landevale* may once have been included in the Auchinleck MS.

4. Both A. M. Trounce, in "The English Tail-Rhyme Romances," *MAE,* 2 (1933), 194–197, and A. J. Bliss in *Sir Launfal* (p. 15) agree that *Sir Launfal* was written late in the fourteenth century. The archaic features in *Sir Launfal,* I suggest, proceed from Chestre's having taken them over unchanged from his sources. Trounce places *Sir Gowther* around the third quarter of the fourteenth century ("The English Tail-Rhyme Romances," *MAE,* 3 [1934], 40), *The Erle of Tolous* at the end of the fourteenth century (*MAE,* 2 [1933], 190), and *Emaré* at the turn of the century (*MAE,* 3 [1934], 45).

5. See F. N. Robinson, *The Works of Geoffrey Chaucer,* 2nd ed. (Boston: Houghton Mifflin, 1957), pp. xxix and 721.

those in taii-rhyme stanzas in verse form or concept.[6] It is not an isolated work in its own right, but is part of a dramatic framework, a tale that reveals more of the personality of the teller than of the genre to which it attaches itself. Its source, moreover, is Italian: Boccaccio's *Filocolo.*

Within the English lays, then, there are two rather clear groups, separate in time and in form from each other. There is also a regional difference between the two groups: the couplet lays were written near London or in the South Midlands, while the tail-rhyme lays were written in East Anglia.[7] The geographical distance between the two areas is not great, but the difference between the cultures that they express is quite marked. Although both groups are minstrel poems, the couplet lays are addressed to a rather sophisticated audience, familiar with the courtly tradition, while the tail-rhyme lays are addressed to a somewhat crude but robust audience. The East Anglian audience was perhaps of a lower social composition; in any case it was more commercially oriented on the one hand, more ecclesiastically on the other.[8] East Anglia was the Bible Belt of fourteenth-century England, so to speak.

6. M. J. Donovan in *The Breton Lay: A Guide to Varieties* (Notre Dame: University of Notre Dame Press, 1969) distinguishes between the couplet lays and the tail-rhyme lays through form, but he does not go on to remark upon the regional and ultimately cultural differences that attend this distinction in form.

7. Margaret Wattie places *le Freine* in London or Middlesex (*The Middle English Lai le Freine,* Smith College Studies in Modern Languages, X, no. 3 [Northampton, Mass., 1929], viii), the same area Bliss proposes for *Sir Orfeo* (*Sir Orfeo* [Oxford: Oxford University Press, 1954], p. xx). *Sir Landevale* is located by Bliss "somewhere in the South Midlands" (*Sir Launfal,* p. 7), the area suggested for *Sir Degaré* by Walter French and Charles Hale (*Middle English Metrical Romances* [New York: Prentice-Hall, 1930], p. 287). For *Sir Launfal,* Trounce suggests a North Essex origin (*MAE* 2 [1933], 194), and for *Sir Gowther,* the border of East Anglia and the Northeast Midlands (*MAE,* 3, 40). *The Erle of Tolous* is in the Northeast Midlands dialect (Trounce, *MAE,* 2, 189–190). *Emaré* is placed by French and Hale in the Northeast Midlands (p. 423), by Trounce more vaguely "somewhere near East Anglia" (*MAE,* 3, 45).

8. In a series of articles in *Medium Aevum* from 1932 to 1934, Trounce presents convincing evidence for the existence of a school of tail-rhyme poems in East Anglia. See also his introduction to his edition of *Athelston* (London: Oxford University Press, 1951).

The tail-rhyme lays form part of a regional school of poetry. They belong as much with the tail-rhyme romances of East Anglia as with the couplet lays of the South — perhaps more so. In East Anglia in the fourteenth century, Trounce has demonstrated, there was a resurgence of local feeling reflected in the tail-rhyme school of poetry: "every condition favourable to poetical activity was present. The land was prosperous from the wool-trade and manufactures, which made Norwich second in importance only to London; a religious revival which covered East Anglia with churches that are still a wonder, furnished spiritual force and inspiration . . . This part of England . . . moulded a society, half feudal, half bourgeois." [9] Along with the vitality of a young culture, East Anglia had the comparative vulgarity, evidenced in the tail-rhyme lays in a fondness for scenes of physical contest (never a preoccupation in the French lais), with much splitting of heads, spilling of blood, and splintering of shafts. The couplet lays are written within a more courtly tradition. Mrs. Loomis would not accept *Sir Orfeo* as a minstrel poem,[10] essentially because it is less blatantly so than *Sir Cleges,* but *Sir Orfeo* does nevertheless bear "the whole character of minstrel poetry, which English literature of the thirteenth and fourteenth centuries possesses in such abundance. The poet works with the complete apparatus of rhetorical formulae." [11] Both groups of lays are minstrel poems, but the Southern authors are more skillful minstrels, writing with the advantage of a more established tradition.

There are two main ways of ascertaining how much the authors of the English lays knew of the French lais: the contents of the lays themselves, and the descriptions of lais in the prologue common to *le Freine* and *Sir Orfeo* and the prologue to the *Franklin's Tale.* To a lesser extent, too, the degree of prestige attaching to a poem in associating itself with the Breton lais provides a measure of how well known the lai was in fourteenth-century England.

9. Trounce, *MAE,* 3, 47–50. .

10. See the sections on *Sir Cleges* and *Sir Orfeo* in her *Medieval Romance in England* (New York: Burt Franklin, 1960). Note especially p. 195 and its footnote.

11. O. Zielke, *Sir Orfeo* (Breslau: Koebner, 1880), p. 6.

In examining the contents of the English lays, we again need to consider the couplet and the tail-rhyme lays separately. The problems involved are simpler with the couplet poems than with the tail-rhyme: the couplet poems are close to translation of French originals, while the tail-rhyme poems are close to romances in general. We have direct knowledge of a French original only with the couplet lays: *Sir Landevale* and *Lay le Freine* are translations from Marie de France, and *Sir Orfeo* is probably rendered from the lost *Lai d'Orfée,* whose existence is attested in the *Lai de l'Espine, Floire et Blanceflor,* and the prose *Lancelot,* and might have been suspected from the un-English use of the singular in "swete is þe note" (600). *Sir Degaré* may come from a French lai, but I am inclined rather to believe that it is an imitation of a lai made up of a number of different stories. Within its compass it "manages to combine an astonishing number of folk-lore and romance motifs," [12] which does suggest composite work. (The French lai which most resembles it in its proliferation of motifs, *Desiré,* may itself be a pastiche.) *Sir Degaré* is not simply a translation in any case, for it borrows ideas and even phrasing from *Lay le Freine,*[13] perhaps one of the earliest and most influential of the couplet lays.

The tail-rhyme lays resemble the tail-rhyme romances generally: the motifs in the lays are the same as the motifs that occur in the longer romances.[14] Because of the extensive imitation among the tail-rhyme poems, it is difficult to determine whether any of the lays had its source in a French lai rather than a romance, either from the tail-rhyme school or from elsewhere. But since the lays are distinguished from the romances by little other

12. L. H. Loomis, *Medieval Romance in England,* pp. 301–302.
13. The chief debts of *Sir Degaré* to *le Freine* are its account of the birth of Degaré and its description of the maiden's journey with him through the winter night.
14. For instance, we find the situation of the pretended lover discovered in the bed (or bedroom) of the chaste wife in both *Octavian* and *Sir Tryamour,* probably earlier than in *The Erle of Tolous.* The false accusation by the mother-in-law occurs in *Octavian* as well as in *Emaré;* and the heroine is exposed with her offspring in these two poems as well as in *Sir Eglamour* and its adaptation, *Torrent of Portyngale.* The judicial ordeal occurs earlier in *Amis and Amiloun* and *Athelston* than in *The Erle of Tolous;* and the three days' tournament is found around the same time in both *Sir Gowther* and *Ipomadon.*

than brevity, we would need good evidence of a French lai similar in name or content to a tail-rhyme lay in order to give ready credence to the claim that the English lay derives from a French one. *Sir Launfal* is little more than a retelling of *Sir Landevale* to suit a different verse-form, swelled out by interpolations from other romances. *Sir Gowther* "cannot *as a whole* derive from a literary Breton lay"; [15] it appears to have used an analogue of *Tydorel* combined with the legend of Robert the Devil. *The Erle of Tolous* does not suggest an underlying French lai; it is simply a brief "romance of the high Middle Ages . . . one of the most complete and most characteristic embodiments of chivalric romance." [16] *Emaré* is an episodic romance.[17] If there is Breton material in the tail-rhyme lays — and *The Erle of Tolous* and *Emaré* do not show evidence of that — it could well have come from French or English romances, not from French lais. We must assume that the authors of the tail-rhyme lays knew some couplet lays, from which they derived their knowledge of the length and general nature of the lay form; but we do not have convincing evidence that they knew the French lais.

Chaucer, writing late in the century, may have known only couplet lays. He seems to have known the lays in the Auchinleck MS,[18] but he gives no evidence of having known any of the French lais. The *Franklin's Tale* is not Celtic in its main story, and the names of the characters are unlikely to have come from a lai[19] — a genre which the Franklin, at least, and perhaps Chaucer himself, knew imperfectly. The Franklin's brief summary of the Breton lais, we will see, is vague and inaccurate.

15. G. V. Smithers, "Story-Patterns in Some Breton Lays," *MAE,* 22 (1953), 78.

16. G. Paris, "Le Roman du Comte de Toulouse," *Annales du Midi,* 12 (1900), 6.

17. N. D. Isaacs, "Constance in Fourteenth Century England," *NeuMit,* 59 (1958), 276.

18. See L. H. Loomis, "Chaucer and the Breton Lays of the Auchinleck MS."

19. J. W. Archer, in "On Chaucer's Source for 'Arveragus' in the Franklin's Tale," *PMLA,* 55 (1950), 318–322, maintains that Chaucer's source for the names of his personages was not Geoffrey of Monmouth, but a source associating an Arviragus and his wife with a happy marriage and fidelity to a pledge. That association exists in Layamon's *Brut* (which was not necessarily Chaucer's source, however).

The English lay-writers, then, knew at least two of Marie's lais. They do not explicitly name her, so it is possible that separate lais by her had survived outside her series. Marie's name apparently brought no automatic prestige in fourteenth-century England, and she may even have been quite forgotten; her fame seems to have been short-lived. Apart from their apparently partial knowledge of Marie, the English lay-writers seem to have known the *Lai d'Orfée* and perhaps an analogue of *Tydorel*. The author of *Sir Degaré* knew something of the French lais and was acquainted with romances relating Breton material, but we cannot be sure that he translated a French lai rather than created a composite. A creative writer is more prone to composite work than to scholarly reproduction anyway. The English lay-writers show no acquaintance with the group of French lais that are concerned with love rather than narrative and that do not deal with Celtic material: the lais of *l'Ombre, le Conseil, l'Amours, Aristote, le Vair Palefroi, l'Oiselet, l'Espervier, Narcisse, le Lecheor,* and *Ignaure.* The English authors, unlike those of *l'Ombre* or *le Conseil* or *l'Amours,* are never interested in courtly love. There is no counterpart in their lays of the "bourdes & ribaudy" in *Aristote, l'Espervier, le Lecheor,* or *Ignaure.* While it is true that one would hardly expect parody of the form during a revival of it in England, one may also suspect that not enough was known of the French lai to make an *Ignaure* or *le Lecheor* even theoretically possible. The total range of themes in the English lays is not wide, for the audience itself was limited.

The information about lais that is contained in the *le Freine-Sir Orfeo* prologue and the prologue to the *Franklin's Tale* does not point to much knowledge on the part of the author of the genre in France, let alone the Breton lai behind the French lai. On close inspection, the *le Freine-Sir Orfeo* prologue turns out to be less accurate and informed about lais than at first appears. For convenience, I will refer henceforth to the common prologue as the *le Freine* prologue, since it is rather more likely to belong originally to that poem;[20] and I will use the *le Freine* prologue

20. *Le Freine* seems to have been popular early in the fourteenth century. At the least, it provided *Sir Degaré* with some incidents and

as the basic text, taking account of evidence of some corruption
in it. I supply the text from the Auchinleck MS, folios 261–262,
in the Advocates' Library in Edinburgh:

> We redeþ oft & findeþ ywrite
> & þis clerkes wele it wite,
> layes þat ben in harping
> ben yfounde of ferli þing.
> Sum beþe of wer & sum of wo
> & sum of ioie & mirþe also
> & sum of trecherie & of gile,
> of old auentours þat fel while,
> & sum of bourdes & ribaudy
> & mani þer beþ of fairy.
> Of al þinge[s] þat men seþ
> mest o loue for soþe þai beþ.
>   In Breteyne bi hold time
> þis layes were wrouȝt so seiþ þis rime,
> when kinges miȝt our yhere
> of ani meruailes þat þer were
> þai token an harp in gle & game
> & maked a lay & ȝaf it name.
> Now of þis auentours þat weren yfalle
> y can tel sum ac nouȝt alle.[21]

Although this prologue contains the most detailed account that
we have in English of the lai, it is limited in its knowledge of the
French lais and at times even inaccurate. Its account of the subject matter of the French lais, for all the apparent detail, hardly
says more than that they dealt with all kinds of things (5–10).

---

phrases. And there may have been at its conclusion, which is missing
from the Auchinleck MS, a prayer that supplied the model for the
prayers that conclude both *Sir Degaré* and *Sir Orfeo*. The Rawlinson *MS*
of *Sir Degaré* and the Auchinleck *Sir Orfeo* end almost identically. If
my speculation is correct, *le Freine* would have ended something like
this: "Þus com le Freine out of hire care./God graunt ous eke wele to
fare!"
    21. In line 1 of the MS, the first four letters of *ywrite* are blurred;
and in line 11, the MS has *þingeþ* in error for *þinges*. I have expanded
contractions in the MS. I use a minimal punctuation, for overpunctua-
tion tends to impose a modern syntax upon a medieval poem.

We have no reason to assume that the English authors had a wider knowledge of the French lais than modern scholars do; indeed, the English authors may not know as much. Even the claim implicit in "of þis auentours þat weren yfalle/y can tel sum ac nouȝt alle" seems to be only a minstrel bid for attention, not a promise to present a number of lays. The author may even be saying, "Out of this attractive repertoire, I am going to choose a particular one (*sum*) especially worth listening to, so

> 'herkneþ lordinges soþe to sain,
> ichil ȝou telle Lay le Frayn.' "

I do not see these lines as a literal statement that the author intends to tell other lays; in any case, I do not believe that he is the author of *Sir Orfeo*.[22]

The description in the *le Freine* prologue of the contents of the French lais is not satisfactory. While there are many lais dealing with woe ending in weal, only *Les Deus Amanz* tells a tale of utter woe. None of the surviving French lais is much concerned with "wer" (if that is the correct reading, the Ashmole MS of *Sir Orfeo* agreeing with it as against "wele" in the Harleian MS of *Sir Orfeo*).[23] Although "mirþe" associated with "bourdes & ribaudy" is found in seven extant French lais — *le Cor, Nabaret, le Trot, Aristote, l'Espervier, le Lecheor,* and *Ignaure* — there are no surviving comic lays in English to testify to a definite knowledge of them. We have no instance "of trecherie & of gile" as a main theme in any lai, French or English; the appearance of treachery in *Bisclavret* and *Melion, Haveloc, The Erle of Tolous,* and *Emaré* is secondary, merely setting the principal action into motion. If the *le Freine* poet is describing the lais as "mest o loue" (so also the Ashmole MS, but "moost to lowe" in the Harleian MS of *Sir Orfeo*), then he is referring almost exclusively to Marie, since love as a main theme appears only incidentally elsewhere, except in that group of lais

22. See my article, "The Case against Common Authorship of *Lay le Freine* and *Sir Orfeo*," forthcoming in *Medium Aevum*.

23. The prologue to *Sir Orfeo* is missing from the Auchinleck MS, but is found in two later manuscripts, the Harleian and the Ashmole.

that the English lay-writers do not seem to have known (see discussion above); but even Marie's interest tends to waver between love and adventure. If the *le Freine* poet knew Marie's lais well, then it is surprising that he omits her mention (in *Guigemar*) of the rote along with the harp as instruments accompanying the Breton lais. His account of the composition of lais at the instigation of the king also differs from hers, agreeing rather with the situation described in *Guingamor* (675–676):[24]

> In Breteyne bi hold time
> þis layes were wrouȝt so seiþ þis rime,
> when kinges miȝt our yhere
> of ani meruailes þat þer were
> þai token an harp in gle & game
> & maked a lay & ȝaf it name.   (13–18)

There is a textual problem involved here, however. The reading of the Ashmole *Sir Orfeo* —

> Off aventours þat fell som-deys
> The Bretonys þer-of made leys,
> Off kyngys þat be-fore vs were;
> When þei myȝt any woundres here
> They lete them wryte as it were do   (21–25) —

suggests that the original version may have been

> In Breteyne bi hold time
> þis layes were wrouȝt so seiþ þis rime,
> of kinges þat þer were.
> When þai meruailes miȝt ourhere,
> þai token an harp in gle & game
> & maked a lay & ȝaf it name.

The *le Freine* poet did stress one important characteristic of the French lais, their concern with "ferli þing" ("many þer beþ of fairy"); but interest in the faery is much more marked in the English lays than in the French. The entire *le Freine* prologue

24. See *Lais inédits de Tyolet, de Guingamor, de Doon, du Lecheor et de Tydorel,* ed. G. Paris, *Romania,* 8 (1879), 29–72.

could be written from a limited knowledge of the French lais supplemented by guesswork. If guesswork was involved, the reference to "bourdes & ribaudy" was a lucky guess, the references to "wer," "trecherie," and "gile" unlucky.

Chaucer, writing more than sixty years later, was not in a good position to know much about the Breton lais. The Franklin's five-line summary in his prologue is, like the *le Freine* prologue, vague and inaccurate:

> Thise olde gentil Britouns in hir dayes
> Of diverse aventures maden layes,
> Rymeyed in hir firste Briton tonge;
> Whiche layes with hir instrumentz they songe,
> Or elles redden hem for hir plesaunce.[25]

That the Bretons composed lais of "diverse aventures" is a safe but uninformative statement, saying in two words essentially what the *le Freine* author says in eight lines (5–12). It is an equally safe assumption that the Bretons composed their lais "in hir firste Briton tonge"; precision enters only when we ask in what language they presented these lais to a non-Breton audience. The Franklin's one precise statement, that the Bretons sang their lais "with hir instrumentz" (either a wider or vaguer word than "harpes"), is undermined by the alternative, "Or elles redden hem for hir plesaunce." While some Breton contes may not have had a musical lai attached to them, the evidence suggests that most did, and that the conte-lai relationship was ordinarily too close to allow the free choice of performance that the Franklin describes. The Franklin is enamored of the old world of romance even as he has his feet planted in the world of fourteenth-century realities. When he portrays the world of the "olde gentil Britouns," he constantly injects his own common sense into it, thereby continually deflating the romantic atmosphere he strives for. His description of the Bretons in his prologue, first as singing their lais to the accompaniment of their instruments, then as reading out their lais to their audience, is only one instance of his habit of first presenting a romantic pic-

25. *The Works of Geoffrey Chaucer,* ed. F. N. Robinson, V (F) 709–713.

ture, then following it by a realistic one that diminishes it. The former picture of the Bretons has a romantic glow about it, while the latter portrays a commonplace method of delivery in the fourteenth century. Likewise, in his tale proper, the Franklin shows Aurelius racked by "torment furyus" for more than two years, then shows his brother rejoicing that Dorigen will have to keep her promise and so cure Aurelius, or else Aurelius will "shame hire atte leeste." A frustrated suitor in real life may derive some satisfaction from his lady's disgrace, but a frustrated suitor in romance can only linger in anguish or die; the notion that a tormented suitor could find some consolation in his lady's shame deflates the concept of romantic passion. Typically, when he offers an alternative, the Franklin undercuts a point he is making or diminishes an effect he is seeking.

Neither prologue nor tale offers any evidence that Chaucer had more than a slight acquaintance with French lais. Within the tale itself Chaucer uses the word "lay" to mean a kind of song: Aurelius, we are told, found an outlet for his unsatisfied love in composing

> many layes,
> Songes, compleintes, roundels, virelayes,
> How that he dorste nat his sorwe telle,
> But langwissheth as a furye dooth in helle.   (947–950)

The tale does not necessarily gain in authenticity by being one of only two English lays to be set in Brittany, for the setting in Brittany is as natural a notion as that the Bretons composed originally in Breton, all the more natural because of the famous cliffs of nearby Brittany. An examination of the prologue to the *Franklin's Tale* corroborates what we gauge from the other lays: that not much was known about the Breton lai in England, and that it was never there the popular and vital form that it had been in France.

Marie de France, in her prologues and epilogues, and in *Chaitivel* and *Chevrefoil,* had devoted considerable space, while still remaining finally vague, to the circumstances of composition of the original Breton lais. Few French lais outside hers tell us much about the Bretons and their habits of composition. Her picture of Breton society is probably her own. The other French lai-writers usually draw upon her for their information about the Bretons and their lais, but they are hindered by her vagueness; hence, in order to account for their originals, they fall back upon their own inspiration or else borrow ideas from the romances (as the author of *l'Espine* does from *Cligés*). They contradict Marie occasionally, and even contradict themselves. *L'Espine,* for instance, is discrepant within itself, telling an aventure "Qui lonc tens a esté oscure," but which is one of a number "en Bretaingne conneües/Et en plusors leus . . . veües." [26] If the authors of the French lais did not know much about the origin and nature of the Breton lais, how much less did the English lay-writers of the fourteenth century!

The degree of prestige that attached to a poem's calling itself a lay is another way of determining how much was known of the lai in fourteenth-century England. One should point out at the outset that not all the English lays explicitly call themselves lays. Neither *Sir Landevale* nor *Sir Degaré* claims to be a lay (although *Sir Landevale* is, being a translation of Marie's *Lanval*). Yet these two poems were written early in the century, when one would expect them to take advantage of any great prestige associated with the claim that they were lays. Only *le Freine* and *Sir Orfeo,* which share the same prologue, and the first two tail-rhyme lays, *Sir Launfal* and *Sir Gowther,* stress their membership in the genre. *Sir Launfal,* however, is content to call itself a "ley" without invoking the Bretons; and *Sir Gowther,* for all its styling itself a lay at its beginning and its end, also refers to its original as a "romans" (470, 543) and "þo testamentys" (309). [27] *The Erle of Tolous* and *Emaré* mention only at the end that they derive from a Breton lay — surely the position of least emphasis, the least likely to dispose the audience of these minstrel poems to attention. The impression that emerges from

26. *Le Lai de l'Epine,* ed. R. Zenker, *Zeitschrift für romanische Philologie,* 17 (1893), 232–255.

27. For *Sir Gowther,* I have used the edition by K. Breul (Oppeln: Franck, 1886). For *The Erle of Tolous* and *Emaré,* I have used French and Hale, *Middle English Metrical Romances,* my basic text for the English lays. Thomas Rumble's *The Breton Lays in Middle English* (Detroit: Wayne State University Press, 1965) conveniently prints the lays in one volume, but lacks a well considered editorial viewpoint.

a survey of the lays that survive to us is that most lays do not seem to care much what genre they are thought to belong to. The tail-rhyme lays in particular lack a definite concept of the genre and refer to their originals quite variously. Both *The Erle of Tolous* and *Emaré* allude to an original "story" (*ET* 810, 1070; *Em* 115, 162 — a "tale" 405, 465) or "romans" (*ET* 1203, *Em* 216). *The Erle of Tolous* uses "geste" and "lay" interchangeably at its conclusion: "Yn Rome thys geste cronyculyd ywys;/A lay of Bretayne callyd hyt ys" (1219–20). *Emaré* in the same place possibly interchanges "lay" and "plaint": "Thys ys on of Brytayne layes ... Men callys 'Playn þe Garye'" (1030–32). The Franklin does not identify his source, but refers vaguely and somewhat discrepantly to "the book" and "thise bookes" (812 and 1243). Late in the fourteenth century the lay seems to have lost prestige and to have been loosely conceived of as a genre. The four tail-rhyme poems appear to have thought of the lay largely in terms of romance (Chestre inserts and acknowledges interpolations from French romance), with the advantage of brevity. The audience of the tail-rhyme lays for their part cared less for the genre than for the story told. It is difficult to say whether the sophisticated audience of the *Franklin's Tale* was as attracted to the notion of a Breton lay as was the old-fashioned Franklin; but even he cannot successfully revitalize an outdated concept of courtliness. His tale ends with no further mention of Breton provenance, but with a question that overshadows it: which of the three main characters acted the most "gentilly."

Not only did the lay sink in prestige in fourteenth-century England; it also underwent considerable changes in concept. Gone, for instance, except for the prologues to *le Freine-Sir Orfeo* and to the *Franklin's Tale,* is the typical French prologue that attached the poem to the Bretons, to Brittany or Britain, and to a former time (especially the time of Arthur). The English lays are not much concerned with locality or time of occurrence and derive no atmospheric value from them. Only two lays are set in Brittany, *Sir Degaré* and the *Franklin's Tale*. The *Franklin's Tale* was written too late in the century to gain from the former association of Brittany with marvels; it tells in fact of magic brought to Brittany from Orleans. *Lay le Freine* is set in "þe west cuntre" of "Breteyne," meaning England, for we are told

> Bi þat hye was of .xii. winter eld
> in al Inglond þer nas non
> a fairer maiden þan hye was on.   (238–240)

Sir Orfeo is likewise translated to England, Thrace being explained as the old name for Winchester. *Sir Launfal* is set in Britain, which was "vncuth londe" in *Sir Landevale*. *Lay le Freine, Sir Orfeo,* and *Sir Launfal* are almost as bent on appropriating the personages and happenings of their originals to England as on asserting their Breton provenance.

The tail-rhyme lays prefer an attachment to Rome to a connection with Brittany, no doubt because of their ecclesiastical orientation. *The Erle of Tolous* is chronicled in Rome (1219), much of *Emaré* is set there (notably the final reunion), and *Sir Gowther* has its hero seek forgiveness from the Pope there. The tail-rhyme lays are further from the French lais than are the couplet lays. To whatever they took over of the themes of French romance they gave an ecclesiastical cast. (The prayers at beginning and end are only the most immediate indication of that.) Their themes, like those of the tail-rhyme poems generally, are concerned with vindication after false accusation, with the expiation of transgression, and with the punishment of falseness. Launfal, the Empress of Almayn, and Emaré come to mind as illustrations of the first theme; Launfal, Gowther, and Emaré's father as illustrations of the second; and Guinevere and the mayor in *Sir Launfal,* the false knights in *The Erle of Tolous,* and the wicked queen in *Emaré* as illustrations of the third. The tail-rhyme lays are also preoccupied with the notion of compliance with the will of God, and God's intervention is often evident in them. In *Emaré* the will of God is elevated into a major theme. There events are forced into a Christian mold: the heroine's sufferings are blithely attributed to "wederus yll" (336) or "chawnses ylle" (684), but her coming to land is

> Thorow þe grace of God yn trone,
> That all þyng may fulfylle.   (680–681)

When Emaré is represented at the end of the poem as recovered from her afflictions "Thorow grace of God in Trinité" (944), we find the reunion story, which also underlies the couplet lays le Freine and Sir Degaré, submitted to what Mrs. Loomis calls "the grey influence of ecclesiastical thought." [28]

Also gone in the English lays is the notion of commemorating an "aventure," a notion that is important in Marie's lais and the narrative French lais that followed her, like, say, Melion or Guingamor or l'Espine. The word aventure itself does not often appear in the English lays and rarely keeps its French meaning of a marvelous happening. Sir Launfal promises to tell of "a wondyre cas," which is the equivalent of an aventure, but it dissipates its account of Launfal's aventure with the fée by interpolations: the confused Launfal-Guinevere relationship[29] and the tournaments. Sir Orfeo narrates an aventure in the French sense, the abduction and rewinning of Herodis; but it adds the episode of the faithful steward and leaves us contemplating that story rather than the marvelous aventure. If the faithful steward appeared in the lost Lai d'Orfée, then that was a lai that departed from Marie's unified concept. Sir Degaré uses aventure more frequently than any other lay, but its author does not appear to have understood the French connotation of the word and is inconsistent in his usage. The aventures that knights are said in the opening lines to seek by night and day are concerned with "Hou ȝhe miȝte here strengthe asai," a mundane concept of an aventure. The hero's marriage with his mother and contest with his father are likewise described as aventures, the first with some probably unintended humor. Only when Degaré announces his intention to leave his lady to seek "More of hauentours" (979) does the word retain its association with the winning of "pris," a sense that could come from a French romance rather than a

28. Medieval Romance in England, p. 54.
29. See M. Mills, "The Composition and Style of the 'Southern' Octavian, Sir Launfal and Libeaus Desconus," MAE, 31 (1962), 88–109: "enough evidence is available to show that whether Chestre used one source or several, in English or in French, his treatment is consistently inept and careless." B. K. Martin, however, argues that "many of the features of Sir Launfal which critics find most disagreeable may be explained as the conventions of a specific style, the style of the folklore" ("Sir Launfal and the Folktale," MAE, 35 [1966], 199–210).

French lai. *Sir Degaré* itself is confused in purpose, wavering
between the theme of successive quests (for the hero's mother,
then his father) and the theme of the formation of a perfect
knight.[30] *Aventures* means happenings in the late *Franklin's
Tale* (710) and news or incidents in *Emaré* (754). The word
had broadened its meaning from its French sense and was used
less often. When the English lays wanted to convey the sense
of a marvelous adventure, they used a phrase, like the "wondyre cas" of *Sir Launfal,* or "ferli þing" of *le Freine,* or the
"selcowgh thyng" of *Sir Gowther.* The English lays do not strive
to commemorate an aventure; they simply want to tell a good
tale. Accordingly, they sometimes announce the subject of the
tale with an eye to audience appeal rather than accuracy. Thus
The Erle of Tolous is not primarily about

> How a lady had grete myschefe,
> And how sche couyrd of hur grefe;

nor is *Sir Gowther* essentially about "a warlocke greytt" who
brought sorrow to his mother; still less is *Emaré* a story of "my-
kyll myrght" mixed with mourning.

Their lack of knowledge of the lai is no doubt one reason
why the English lay-writers did not create a major genre.[31]
They were separated, after all, by a time gap of about a century
from the latest French lais, which had already at least fifty
years' tradition behind them. Hence they were not able to go
on like the authors of *l'Ombre, le Conseil, l'Amours,* and *Aristote* and extend the genre in notable original achievements. And
then, perhaps fourteenth-century England was too late for either

30. The confusion is most evident when Degaré leaves his lady, not
to continue his search for his father, but to seek further aventures. See,
however, Henry Kozicki, "Critical Methods in the Literary Evaluation of
Sir Degaré," Modern Language Quarterly, 29 (1968), 3–14.

31. The situation is not as open as Baader suggests in *Die Lais*
(Frankfurt: Klostermann, 1966) when he says we have to consider "ob
die mancherlei Variationen, welche die 'Lai' genannte epische Kurzform
aufweist, nicht fälschlich für die Folge eines Mangels an Genrebewusst-
sein der mittelalterlichen Dichter gehalten wurden, sondern in Wahrheit
Konsequenz einer historischen Entwicklung sind" (p. 225). Baader's
discussion of the English lays is perhaps the weakest section of his
otherwise definitive study of the lai.

the faery or the courtly elements of the French lais to thrive. There was not, in even the traditional culture of southern England, the right audience for the lai; in East Anglia it could hardly survive the stifling influence of ecclesiastical thinking. The one great lay, Chaucer's, is not really a Breton lai, and it is great for its portraiture of the Franklin rather than for its essentially thin story. Some of the English lays are skillfully told, some are merely competent; but it is broadly true that the English lay did not achieve a great deal beyond translation in the couplet lays and retelling in romance style in the tail-rhyme poems. Considering all the factors acting against a vital revival of the lai in England, one of which is the sheer lack of knowledge of the lai, we can hardly wonder that it failed to achieve literary distinction there.

MORTIMER J. DONOVAN

Middle English *Emare* and the
Cloth Worthily Wrought

This essay describes the relationship of a central object — a
Sicilian monarch's gift of cloth — to Emare, the leading character and daughter of the Emperor, in what might be called a
moral narrative.[1] This is framed as a Breton lay, but is set in
the Mediterranean world with few or no ties to Great or Little
Britain, except possibly for old or feeble ones collected along
Norman routes of travel or conquest and discovered in faraway
places: [2]

> Thys ys on of Brytayne layes,
> That was vsed by olde dayes:
> Men callys "Playn þe Garye."   (ll. 1030–32)

1. Available editions include: Edith Rickert, ed., *The Romance of
Emare,* Early English Text Society, Extra Ser. 99 (London, 1906): W.
H. French and C. B. Hale, eds., in *Middle English Metrical Romances*
(New York: Prentice-Hall, 1930), pp. 423–455; T. C. Rumble, ed.,
The Breton Lays in Middle English (Detroit: Wayne State University
Press, 1965). I have used French and Hale from longstanding affection,
but the two other editions are equally useful.
2. For discussion and bibliography on Breton lays, see J. Burke
Severs, gen. ed., *A Manual of the Writings in Middle English: 1050–
1500* (New Haven: The Connecticut Academy of Arts and Sciences,
1967), fasc. 1, pp. 133–143, 292–297.

No sooner is *Emare* recognized as a Breton lay than the reader meets a well-known problem: what should be done with a description extending for 98 lines (82–180) in a narrative itself lasting just over a thousand lines (1,035 to be exact)? There seems to be a problem in proportion, to say the least. Unfortunately there is only one manuscript to be guided by, one recording *Emare,* Cotton Caligula A ii of the British Museum (Rickert, pp. ix–xi), but more than a few analogues exist, whatever their particular value.[3] Analogous descriptions in Marie de France, to mention a few "long" ones, include *Guigemar* (ll. 154–189) and *Lanval* (39–106). Short descriptions are common.

A fresh reading of *Emare,* lines 82–180 in particular, might support the view that, whatever the inadequacies of the manuscript reading, the long descriptive passage might be intended to stand as it is. Dieter Mehl (p. 139) finds it easier to accept this "elaborate piece of descriptive writing" than not and so goes along with his contemporary, Hanspeter Schelp, who calls the poem unified in the cloth references, even as it is later on, when the cloth becomes a robe.[4] Two parts of *Emare* are thus involved in the division of the cloth: first, lines 82–180, with attendant questions, mostly about proportion; second, all subsequent lines, which serve to enhance Emare's beauty whenever *cloth* or *robe* is mentioned.

Lines 82–180, I would maintain here, follow a pattern observable in certain lays of Marie de France; according to a study of *Lai du Chievrefueil,* Anna Granville Hatcher concludes[5] that there is in the lays a "procedure of choosing a specific, concrete object as the centre of her *lai* which shall develop, within the poem, new varieties of symbolic content" (p. 339). To turn to the text, the lays which Hatcher chooses to characterize build on such objects: *Equitan* (a scalding bath), *Le Fraisne* (a pre-

3. A. Ewert, ed., *Marie de France, Lais* (Oxford: Blackwell, 1947).

4. For two recent studies of the Middle English romances, see Hanspeter Schelp, *Exemplarische Romanzen im Mittelenglischen,* Palaestra 246 (Göttingen, 1967); and Dieter Mehl, *The Middle English Romances of the Thirteenth and Fourteenth Centuries* (New York: Barnes and Noble, 1969).

5. *Romania,* "Lai du Chievrefueil, 61–78 and 107–113," 71 (1950), 330–344.

cious cloth robe), *Les Deus Amanz* (magic potion). Whatever the explanation, the prominence given the various objects is undeniable. Among the didactic lays *Trot* (an equine term), *Oiselet* (small bird), and *Ombre* (shadow), all show how the poet goes to the basic narrative for a central object and title.

Despite its limited space, *Emare* dramatizes many varieties of theme and does so with a versatility which is remarkable. Such varieties are: love of the Deity for errant man, and man for the Deity; love for human offspring; even incest; and at the same time we notice faint traces of other genres: legend, fabliau, and exemplum. The familiar lovers occur together (82–180): Ydoyne and Amadas, Trystram and Isowde, Florys and Blawncheflour, and the Son of the Sowdan of Babylon and the Amerayles Dowghtyr; no effort is needed to make out pairs of lovers named in the corners of the cloth — by what process isn't made clear, but possibly by embroidery. It is important, however, to recognize here that the effect is somewhat mechanical: four corners, four opportunities to set down a pair of lovers — eight in all, no more and no fewer. It is, so far as one can see, difficult to contrast in quality the love of each pair, but plainly the gallery of ideals which Emare takes with her on her travels reflects no need for explication here or there.

When examining *Emare,* lines 82–180, one would do well to recollect that allusions to precious stones, flowers, birds, probably do not appear in literature for the first time in the poem under study: the imagery developing repetitioulsy in the 98 lines of verse is traditional. Included in the long description are four separable stanzas of twelve lines each; each stanza develops in parallel fashion with the three other stanzas treating the three pairs of lovers and opening with a kind of formula:

> In þat on korner made was
> Idoyne and Amadas,
> > Wyth love that was so trewe:
> For þey loveden hem wyth honour,
> Portrayed þer wer wyþ trewe-love-flour,
> > Of stones bryght of hewe
> Wyth carbunkull and safere,
> Kassydonys and onyx so clere,
> > Sette in golde newe;

Deamondes and rubyes,
And oþer stones of mychyll pryse
And menstrellys wyth her glew.   (121–132)

Then, mechanically, just as this stanza names Ydoyne and
Amadas as the characters of the first stanza, so the second
stanza in the series names Trystram and Isowde (133–144);
the third names Florys and Blawncheflour (145–156); and the
fourth names the Son of the Sowdan of Babylone and the Amerayles Dowghtyr (157–168). Each pair of lovers has in common a reputation in medieval fiction, French and English alike,
which is well known. Each pair has that reputation here, and
the wearer of the cloth — or cloth turned into robe — will share
in the timeless life. But what else does the cloth having four corners reveal?

When the Emperor examines the embroidery so prominent in
the story and questions his guest, the King of Sicily, one wonders
whether the cloth is the work of fairies, which he suspects. For
unlike the robe in *Lai le Freine* this one has powers surpassing
those merely human, and by some margin. Perhaps the most important part assigned the robe, itself a beautiful object, is to
reflect beauty. Mehl is right when he finds that the robe aids
Emare as it "serves to set off her beauty to even better effect,
because her robe is always mentioned whenever her beauty impresses the beholders" (p. 139).

So far in the poem the discussion of the cloth, begun pages
back, has moved over such alluring topics as the minstrel's prologue,[6] the presentation of courtly characters, including an emperor and a king, and the quality of their lives; then follows the
description of the four-cornered cloth, later converted into a
robe. Then comes the action, and so through movement, from
line 181 on to the end, the cloth remains prominent. Although
the cloth still loses none of its beauty (it is almost a character),
not until the ending of the poem is the power of the human experience it represents completed in clear, vivid terms. In the

6. I pass up with regrets A. C. Baugh, "The Authorship of the Middle
English Romances," *Annual Bulletin of the Modern Humanities Research Association,* 22 (1960), 21, where the sentiments of the medieval
author are examined.

description of the first corner of the cloth (121–132), certain precious stones are observed: *carbunkull, safere, kassydonys, deamondes, rubyes;* in the second corner (133–144), *topase, rubyes, crapawtes, nakette;* in the third corner (145–156), *ememerawdes, deamoundes, koralle, perydotes, crystall, garnettes;* in the fourth corner (157–168), *vnykern,* plus conventional flowers, birds, and precious stones. So the fourth part of the cloth is finished off — in the poet's words "Stuffed wyth ymagerye," nothing compromised (168).

In the page or so which follows, discussion of the cloth continues beyond line 181 and through 312, which treats Emare's first exile. A complication comes about when the Emperor weakens on sight of the cloth, now recognizable as magical in its effect, clearly so when it is changed into a robe and given to Emare to wear. At the time this effect is felt, the Emperor becomes enamoured of his own daughter, and what seems to be incest becomes that with complications. The incest becomes ironic when the same robe that complicated the Emperor's offense serves to soften and render bearable Emare's fortune, which the speaker reads as "Goddys wylle" (327). At the time of the Emperor's rejection and of Emare's exile there is no other comfort aboard her light craft.

Besides comforting Emare, the robe serves to identify her on landing in Galys (Galicia?) as "non erdly þyng." She instructs in silken work — how to sew and mark, a combination which serves her well against future needs and failing resources. She sees the occasion and before long becomes Queen, despite open and covert opposition from the Queen Mother. But, as long as the jewels continue to brighten the robe Emare wears, her attire identifies her as by birth courtly, or as such by seeming; and the Queen Mother, ever conniving, lets appearances stand, however untruthful they are and diabolical.

During the King's prolonged absence fighting the Saracens, and during the Queen Mother's freedom to pursue her plot against Emare, the second exile comes off easily and sees Emare betrayed again. The robe is the source of comfort, status, and direction, and the speaker says (679) that Emare is driven toward Rome by the Grace of God. By the time Emperor as well as King reaches Rome for purposes penitential, the heaviest demand attaching to the magic cloth has already been made, and Emare has already assumed the position of witness, helper, and guide to the new life for seekers after order. But the poem in its final two hundred or so lines traces its appeal to the joy of family reunion and the recovery of a state of grace, which with resolutions made publicly would create a lasting and solid morality for all to witness and be guided by. Of the various dramatic devices conceived or drawn on from the common store, the cloth turned into robe should indeed be mentioned.

ANNE THOMPSON LEE

Le Bone Florence of Rome: A Middle English Adaptation of a French Romance

It has long been a critical commonplace to make certain general distinctions between the French and English versions of a given medieval story, with reference to such familiar romances as *Ywain and Gawain* or *Sir Launfal.* Dieter Mehl, in his *Middle English Romances of the Thirteenth and Fourteenth Centuries,* deplores the prevailing tendency to "allow the English romances a certain freshness, charming simplicity and native vigour, but to dismiss most of them as inferior translations or imitations." [1] Like Mehl, I feel that many English romances are worthy of acclaim as original artifacts. I maintain nonetheless that much can also be learned by studying the precise relationship between a French source and its English redaction, as we see, for instance, in B. J. Whiting's comparison of the proverbial material in French and English romance. [2]

The purpose of this article is to illustrate the radical alterations in descriptive technique, narrative order, and dramatic fo-

1. (New York: Barnes and Noble, 1969), pp. 1–2.
2. B. J. Whiting, "Proverbs in Certain Middle English Romances in Relation to Their French Sources," *Harvard Studies and Notes in Philology and Literature,* 15 (1933), 75–126.

cus which have occurred in one little-known Middle English romance and to comment on the artistic rationale behind these alterations. *Le Bone Florence of Rome,* a late-fourteenth-century poem in tail rhyme stanza, is a reworking of an early-thirteenth-century French romance in *vers alexandrins* (*Florence de Rome*).[3] Mehl describes this English romance as showing "a remarkable degree of independence" (p. 140) but offers no detailed analysis of the methodology or reasoning which lies behind the author's divergence from his source.

The nature of most of the major changes can be summarized in a few sentences. The French poem, which runs to over 6,000 lines, proceeds in a leisurely, often rambling and disconnected manner, but shows simultaneously a concern for the preservation of logical consistency in very small details. The English adaptation, some 4,000 lines shorter, moves forward with a breathtaking speed which sometimes creates a momentary confusion but seldom affects the overall dramatic coherence of the story. The greater length of the French source goes hand in hand with a dry and humorless style that nonetheless allows for some subtlety in the portrayal of character. The tone and style of the English romance, accurately described as "pious but merry," is lively and seldom dull, but affords smaller scope for anything beyond the stereotypes of character. The French *Florence* demonstrates further a highly specific knowledge of social and military background as well as a great interest in astrology and magic, but the English author has little interest in either of these areas. The French poem also contains frequent and exhaustive reference to biblical material which the English eliminates almost entirely.

Several episodes have been chosen to illustrate these changes, but first a brief outline of the plot is in order:

3. *Le Bone Florence of Rome* is preserved only in a large fifteenth-century folio manuscript in the Cambridge University Library (Ff 2.38). The French text is found in a manuscript of the fourteenth century, Nouv. acq. franc., 4192, Bibliotheque Nationale. A. Wallensköld has made a detailed study of the many versions of the Florence story and their relationship to each other: *Le Conte de la femme chaste convoitée par son beau-frère* (Helsinki: Societatis 1, Herariae fennicae, 1907), pp. 28–32).

Garcy, the aging king of Constantinople, wishes to marry Florence, daughter of Otes, the emperor of Rome. During the course of the war which follows Florence's rejection of Garcy, the heroine is abducted by the treacherous brother of her newly chosen husband. After further persecution at the hands of many villains, the virtuous Florence is reunited with her husband, and the villains receive their due punishment.[4]

The initial presentation of Florence's aged suitor, Garcy, points up the differing descriptive techniques of the two versions. In the French poem Garcy's great age, his white hair, long beard, and clothing all draw comment before we learn that he has called his men together to address them on the subject of marriage. Having heard of Florence's beauty, he has resolved to have his men fetch her back to be his wife in spite of the fact that, as he admits: " 'Tot me tramble li cors, car forment sui lassez/Par moi n'iert mes ma lance ne mes escus portez' " (laisse III).[5] The whole scene is filled with elaborate formal detail, but is largely static. Garcy's age is mentioned on three separate occasions but always in a totally nondramatic context: "Mes mout fut viaus et frelles et chenuz et usez" (laisse III).

The fourth laisse (twenty lines) repeats Garcy's command to his men and then adds a list of the rich treasures Otes will be offered. Not until the fifth laisse does this scene dissolve into action, when the messengers prepare for the journey and even then the poet lingers fondly over the details of the ship loading:

> Une nef ont chargie, comme cil qui sont sage,
> De besquit et de vin, de pain et de fromage,
> D'eisil et d'eue froide et de poison maraige;

4. The basic story goes back to an Oriental original in all probability. It has many different forms, some of which were widely diffused during the Middle Ages in the *Gesta Romanorum* and the *Miracles of the Virgin*. Chaucer's *Man of Law's Tale*, or the story of Constance, also has certain affinities with the tale. For a discussion and summary of the whole complex see Wallensköld, *Le Conte*.

5. *Florence de Rome*, ed. A. Wallensköld (Paris Firmin-Didot, 1907). All quotations are to be found in the second volume of this edtion.

Tant i mistrent avoir et poipres de Quartage
Et mules et chameus, mainte beste savage,
Destriers et pallefrois, con lor vint en corage.   (V)

This is all highly absorbing, but it diminishes the effectiveness
of the rare moments when the narrative actually moves forward,
moments which make a rather meager and unmemorable filling
sandwiched between layers of bread, wine, and fish on the one
side, and tag phrases like "comme cil qui sont sage" on the
other.

The tail-rhyme stanza puts a similar pressure on the English
poet to fill in with tag lines, but because the tags habitually fall
in the six-syllable lines and are hence very short, and because
the poet remains, at all costs, firmly committed to a rapid advance in the action, we never lose our sense of what is happening, nor our suspense as we wait to hear what will happen next.
The scene between Garcy and the messengers develops quite
differently. Instead of pointing out the emperor's age and in-
firmity, the poet speaks first of Garcy's passion for Florence,
how "he waxe hasty as the fyre." This colorful simile is followed
by a very direct six-line speech in which Garcy reveals his intention to win Florence, willy-nilly. His age is mentioned, but without editorial comment, and his clothing is dismissed in two lines.
When the French Garcy notes politely at the end of his long
speech that if Otes does not send Florence "mar i perdra encore
tote sa Lombardie," we do not feel that Otes will be much wor-
ried by this threat. Garcy, however, cannot be bothered to couch
his threats in such courteous language, and he says baldly:

And yf he any gruchyng make,
Many a crowne y schall gare crake
And bodyes to drowpe and dare.   (St. 8) [6]

The full extent of Garcy's antiquity is revealed only *after* his
obsessive desire and threatened violence have been described:

6. *Le Bone Florence of Rome,* ed. Wilhelm Vietor (Marburg, 1899).
All references are to this edition of the poem.

> Hys flesche trembylde for grete elde,
> Hys blode colde, hys body vnwelde,
>   Hys lyppes blo forthy;
> He had more mystyr of a gode fyre,
> Of bryght brondys brennyng schyre
>   To beyke hys boones by;
> A softe bath, a warme bedd,
> Then any maydyn for to wedd,
>   And gode encheson why.   (9)

The ironic contrast between the limitless aspiration of Garcy's lust: "Sche schall me boþe hodur and happe [cuddle and embrace]/And in hur louely armes me lappe" and the grotesque reality of his senescence gives an entirely different emphasis to this scene. In spite of the fact that the French poet uses many more words to describe both the appearance and activity of his protagonists, we have a more vivid sense of these same people in the English poem because relatively less time is given to peripheral detail, and because there is a more direct and exclusive focusing on the protagonists and their action.

A later episode illustrates not only the ways in which the English poet compresses his source and omits references to supernatural prophecy, but also his significant restructuring of narrative order. During the course of a banquet Florence and her father are introduced to Emere, her future champion, and his wicked brother Mylys. This scene then shifts, in the French poem to Garcy's pavilion where one of his retainers is trying to dissuade him from battle. Garcy's enraged negative is duly reported to Otes, at which point Mylys offers the emperor some tactical advice: lock the city gates and defend from within. Emere counters this by urging Otes to send his men out bravely onto the battlefield and conquer Garcy once and for all.

There are some curious differences in the timing of these events in the two poems. In *Florence de Rome* Emere and Mylys speak after dinner and after the spy's report, but the English author has the two brothers speak out during dinner and before the spy has brought back the news of Garcy's unquenched thirst for revenge. Logically the French version makes more sense. There is better motivation for the brothers to offer a plan of action after the alarming news from Garcy. On the other hand, the scene seems to have been differently ordered in the English version for dramatic reasons. Coming at the dinner table and therefore in Florence's near presence, these speeches provide her with a direct revelation of the brothers' nature. The French poet has already made several direct statements in his own person regarding the relative propensities for good and evil (or caution) of the two brothers, but since the English poet has not forewarned us in any way, Emere and Mylys reveal themselves here for the first time, through their own words.

Furthermore, the English poem actually clarifies a confusion in timing which is found at the end of this sequence in the French poem. From the moment when the knights sit down to eat up to the beginning of the next day's battle, we never actually hear from the French poet that a night has passed. There is no explicit transition between the point when Emere and Mylys go back to their lodging after the feast and that when Otes dons his hauberk to begin the new day's combat. The English author seems to have been aware of this telescoping in his source: because he has transposed the spy's report from the middle to the end of the evening's activities, he is able to utilize it in a transitional passage, for when Otes hears the report that Garcy is still determined to do battle:

> He lepe on hys stede Bandynere,
> And in hys honde he hent a spere
>   And rode abowte all nyght;
> To the lordys of the towne
> And bad þey schulde be redy bowne,
>   Tymely to the fyght.   (50)

As the time for battle draws near in the French poem, we must once again curb our impatience and listen to a lengthy and admiring list of everyone and everything which pertains to the battle. We learn not only the names of many valiant knights, but also the names of their horses. The glorious standard is described. Garcy's armour is described. Indeed, the poet is so overwhelmed by all the splendid pomp and circumstance that he pauses to draw a wistful breath and tell us:

Seignor, iceste estoire n'est pas d'ui ne d'ier,
Ains est vielle et antive dou tens anciennier.   (XLVI)

With great relish he also treats us to extensive accounts of the
various individual combats, whereas the English poet tends to
epitomize the action in a few striking images and exclamations:

Hedys hopped vndur hors fete
As hayle-stones done in þe strete.   (54)

or:

Gode olde fyghtyng was there.   (57)

Late in the day the emperor Otes is killed by the Greeks and
Emere is taken prisoner by them, but the French poet would
have us take comfort from the fact that Florence's servant Awdegone:

... en a son sort gité
Et el cors des estoile veü et esgardé
Qu'il [Emere] seroit empereres de Romme la cité:
Encore avra Florence, si l'a Deus destiné.   (LXII)

As we might expect, the English poet ignores this prophecy and
similarly makes no reference to Florence's dream, which follows
shortly thereafter. Florence reveals this dream as, without knowing that her father is on it, she watches a bier being brought in
at the city gates. First, she says, it seemed that she saw lightning
strike a high tower and crumble the whole city of Rome with
fire. Then she watched her father fall into a deep sleep from
which she could not wake him. Finally she dreamed she had
gone hunting taking her favorite sparrow-hawk, and when the
bird settled on a laurel, his jets became so firmly attached to the
tree that Florence was forced to abandon him there, which last
foretells a long separation from Emere.

In omitting this sequence the English poet has once more
made clear his preference for letting a situation declare itself

dramatically, rather than prejudging character, or, as here, revealing future events through prophecy. In the French poem, Florence's swooning over the realization of her father's death seems forced in the wake of the dream she has just recounted, whereas the English poet lets his heroine receive the full shock of knowledge without any prior warning.

> Then can feyre Florence sayne,
> "ʒondur ys begonne an euyll bargayn,
>   Y see men brynge a bere,
> And a knyght in handys leede
> Bondynowre my Fadurs stede,"
>   Then all chawngyd hur chere.
> Sche and hur maystres Awdygon
> Went into þe halle allone,
>   Allone wythowten fere;
> And caste vp þe cloþe, þen was hyt so,
> The lady swowned and was full woo,
>   There myght no man hur stere.   (69)

The Greeks lay siege to Rome after Otes' death, and Florence is anxious to find a deliverer. Awdegone, who is rather an opportunistic seer, considering that her last prophecy foretold success for Emere, now says the stars show that either Emere or Mylys will be Florence's champion, but she is not sure which: since a rumor of Emere's death has reached Rome the two women decide on Mylys. The English poem omits the prophecy and more plausibly has Florence act on the advice of all her barons.

In the French *Florence* Awdegone now brings Mylys before Florence, who offers herself in return for his agreement to defend the kingdom. Mylys, cautious fellow, asks for time to think it over, and Florence's caustic rejoinder heaps him with scorn: " 'Comment,' ce dist Florence, 'respit me demandez?/Est ce marchiez a fere, que respit en volez?' " (LXXVI). Before hearing this proposal, however, we have already learned, through a transitional passage, of Emere's release from captivity. The English version reorders the scene so that Florence's proposal and Mylys' equivocation both come before the freeing of Emere, which gives their confrontation more tension, since we do not yet know that Emere, whom she prefers, is already on his way back to solve all her problems. On the other hand, in fairness we must note on this occasion that the English poet adds some confusion of his own, chiefly because he is, as usual, speeding up the action. Instead of having Florence send Awdegone to fetch Mylys, the servant goes to Mylys and makes the proposal herself. Then when Mylys says, "Y schall avyse me" (76), Florence reproaches him and we are never told how she came to be present for this dialogue.

The added coherence and realism of the English version, which are gained through the deliberate suppression of supernatural elements, emerge with particular clarity in a later episode: when Mylys abducts Florence, he tries to seduce her, and in the French version she is protected by a magic clasp encircling her neck:

> La belle ot a son col une noche fermee
> Que fu de riches pierres porprise et aornee,
> De jaspes, de safirs par leus enluminee;
> En l'or ot une pierre enz ou milieu plantee
> Que fu dedans la teste d'une sarpent trouvee.
> Il n'a malaide ou siecle, ce est choze esprovee,
> Se l'en avoit la pierre a sa char adesee,
> Que la ou tocheroit ne fust sempres senee;
> Ne femme que la porte n'iert ja desvirginee
> Ne outre son voloir par nul home adesee,
> Por ce qu'elle ait o lui compaignie privee.   (CXXX)

Since the Pope gave this clasp to Florence, its marvelous properties are presumably of Christian, not infernal, origin, but the English author, whose distaste extends to magic clasps as well as to astrology and dreams, omits any mention of it. It turns out that the magic clasp is used to protect Florence only from Mylys, the first of her many persecutors, and our practical author may well have felt that there was little point in retaining an item of such limited value.

There are several major divergences in the two versions in the episodes following Florence's abduction. In the French poem the couple ride all day and all night, finally alighting to rest by a fountain. Mylys is attacked by a lion which he kills after a long struggle, but it then transpires, to our amusement and Florence's delight, that he is now too exhausted to attempt seduction. When he tries to rest, however, two apes attack him. Terrified and convinced that they are devils which the girl has conjured, he flees once more with his captive, and they ride throughout the entire next day. Florence says incorrectly here and elsewhere that she has not eaten for three days: it is only the second since her departure. The English poet tallies the days correctly, perhaps because there are fewer events and hence less confusion.

The English poet leaves out the lion and the apes. Instead, this Mylys, whose energies have not been sapped by fighting, does try to ravish Florence at the end of the first day. She offers a special prayer to God and to Mary, whereupon, wondrous to report, "hys lykyng vanysched all away" (121).

The elimination of the animal sequences (there are several more in the French poem, involving serpents and other wildlife) has enabled the English poet to focus more directly on the human aspects of lust. When the villains in the French romance assault the heroine it often appears to be only an afterthought, whereas the English poet creates a connecting thread which runs from Garcy through Mylys and the later persecutors. Mylys' persistence also casts Florence's struggles into greater dramatic relief, for no minor skirmishes distract our attention from the conflict between her and Mylys.

The French poet's fondness for biblical history often betrays him into allowing long digressions which have an attenuating effect on his narrative. The last passage to be discussed shows the English poet's awareness of this weakness and his different handling of the same situation.

After valiantly enduring the sufferings imposed by her many persecutors, Florence at last finds refuge in a convent. When one of the sisters there falls ill, Florence offers up a prayer which takes the whole Bible as its province, ranging from Adam and Abraham to Judas (though not in consecutive order), and binding the whole together very loosely indeed with the theme of folk whom in one way or another God has helped:

Les trois enfens gardastes en la fornesse lee,
Que estoit de charbon et de feu enbrasee,
Susaine dou grant crime dont elle iert escusee,
Daniel dou leon, que la goule ot baee,
Jonas en la balenne, que ot la pance lee . . .
Ici comme jel croie par veraie pencee,
Garissiez ceste dame, que est envenimee,
Qui de mal et d'angoise a si la char criblee.   (CXC)

The miraculous cure which follows this prayer in the French
poet's presentation is a major focal point. Almost a hundred
lines are devoted to it, the greatest proportion being taken up
by Florence's prayer. The entire narrative has been leading up
to this moment where the power of the heroine's Christian piety
(and learning) is finally made manifest to everyone. The English poet, on the other hand, uses the episode simply as the vehicle for setting in motion the conclusion of the story. Less than
a stanza is given up to the miracle:

A systur of þe hows was seke
Of the gowte and odur euyls eke,
   Sche myȝt not speke nor goon;
Florence vysyted hur on a day
And helyd hur or sche went away,
   Sche wolde þer had wytten þerof none.   (161)

No doubt something is lost here in terms of the ability or desire
to center upon the religious nature of this critical moment, but
the inferior knowledge of biblical history which the English heroine displays actually makes her more rather than less appealing,
and the engaging humility of her wish to keep the miracle quiet
is quite absent in the French version. Moreover, the English poet
unifies his story here, as throughout, by keeping our attention
directed toward Florence herself and on the suspenseful progression towards the denouement, where she will triumphantly pre-
side over the villains who have mistreated her. Thus, while Florence remains a pious and in some ways exemplary heroine, it is
her human aspects which the poet emphasizes and which draw
the story together.

The evidence of these passages does, I think, point to an English adapter who has made certain deliberate choices about the material he was working with. Without pretending to a complex or sophisticated style, he has shown a definite concern for organizing and focusing his source so as to give it a tighter narrative structure and a dramatic realism which are almost completely lacking in the French romance. In this respect, at least, he appears to cater more nearly to the tastes of the modern reader, as well as to those of his own time.

J. B. BESSINGER, JR.

The Gest of Robin Hood Revisited

Returning to *The Gest of Robin Hood*[1] after a reasonable interval is not an unsettling experience. It is not like coming back for a tour of duty or pleasure in the *Brut* or in Malory's *Tale of the Sankgreal* or the *Arcadia*. In these ampler books one may be newly moved or amused or challenged by surprise, as if the literary work had room to accommodate more than one stage of perception in a given reader. The *Gest* is a minor work that maintains an affectionately remembered stasis. It is perhaps not so good a poem as its near-twin *Gamelyn* or a few of the other Robin Hood pieces, but it is enjoyable to read again; its good things still gratify.

We willingly rediscover the greenwood setting, whether perfunctory (3), or realistically ironic (196), or heroic-arcadian (445–449); the *Gawain*-like beginning, with Robin as a restless, wild-brained monarch uncertain (but it may be only the

1. The normalized title is cited from William Hall Clawson's monograph *The Gest of Robin Hood* (Toronto: University of Toronto Library, 1909), but the text is quoted, always by stanza number and without editorial diereses, from Francis James Child, "A Gest of Robyn Hode," in *The English and Scottish Popular Ballads* (Boston, 1883–1898), III, 39–89, where the collation of the seven early printed texts (of various titles) is to be found.

poet's uncertainty) whether to delay dinner for "som vnkouth gest" (6) or for three masses in worship of the Father, the Holy Ghost, and Our Lady (8–9); the distracted entrance of the Knight, who does nothing in the rest of the poem so interesting as to ride into the scene with one foot dangling beside a stirrup (22); the religious comedy ("Our Lady hath doubled your cast," 248); and so on through a series of feasts and mock-feasts (forced entertainments, 68, 247, or occasions when a visitor is not fed, 102ff., 156ff.) that punctuate or dramatize the chief encounters of the story, Robin Hood and the Knight, the Sheriff, and the King, a series paralleled and supplemented by a heroic repertory of combats and mock-combats (archery matches, wrestling, Little John's brawl with the Sheriff's steward and cook, 158–168, an ambush and escape, 296–308, a siege and rescue in force, 319–350, and a game of buffets in which Robin is downed by the King himself, 398–409), until Robin's return from the court to the forest stirs deeper chords in resonance with *As You Like It* (I.i):

> They say hee is already in the Forrest of *Arden,* and a many merry men with him; and there they live like the old *Robin Hood of England*: they say many yong Gentlemen flocke to him every day, and fleet the time carelesly as they did in the golden world.

With this passage we may recall Thoreau's essay "Walking" [2] and its primitivistic quotation from the end of the *Gest:*

> Whan he came to grene wode,
>   In a mery mornynge,
> There he herde the notes small
>   Of brydes mery syngynge.
> 'It is ferre gone,' sayd Robyn,
>   'That I was last here;

---

2. "Walking" in *Excursions* (Boston, 1880), and often reprinted. These primitivist versions of a tamed but ennobled hero associated with a Renaissance golden age apparently had their origin in the work of fifteenth-century Scottish chroniclers who were folklorists in spite of themselves. They have had a potent modern influence; Child himself was affected. See J. B. Bessinger, Jr., "Robin Hood: Folklore and Historiography, 1377–1500," *Tennessee Studies in Literature,* 11 (1966), 61–69.

> Me lyste a lytell for to shote
>   At the donne dere.'
> Robyn slewe a full grete harte;
>   His horne than gan he blow
> That all the outlawes of that forest
>   That horne coud they knowe,
> And gadred them togyder,
>   In a lytell throwe.
> Seuen score of wyght yonge men
>   Came redy on a rowe,
> And fayre dyde of theyr hodes,
>   And set them on theyr kne:
> 'Welcome,' they sayd, 'our [dere] mayster,
>   Under this grene-wode tre.'   (445–449)

The *Gest* remains what it was, one surmises gratefully; age has not withered it nor custom staled its somewhat limited variety. But the world moves, the last monograph on the *Gest* was published in 1909,[3] and some modern scholarly contributions and critical theories, a few of them quite recent and some already gone over the hill, seem at first glance to call for some application to this short epic or long ballad — 456 ballad quatrains, but what kind of poem is it? — about the English outlaw. This is no place for a roll call of current critical events, but it is true that Robin Hood can be tracked through almost any random selection of them, or dragged into almost any arrangement of them. We shall mention some of them here briefly and in no special order, but starting with international studies technically exterior to the *Gest* and concluding with some unorthodox remarks on the structure of the poem itself.

Biblical exegesis has left the *Gest* strictly alone, probably because the exegetes have more pressing things to do. Still, the religious or ecclesiastical elements in the poem are noteworthy at various levels. A devout rebel, the king of the forest, at war with the establishments of church and state, plays Good Samaritan to a member of the other side. Robin Hood and Little John are another David and Jonathan. (It is true that they are

3. Clawson, who cites and discusses Richard Fricke, *Die Robin-Hood-Balladen* (Braunschweig, 1883), and W. M. Hart, *Ballad and Epic: A Study in the Development of the Narrative Art* (Boston: Ginn, 1907).

equally another Gilgamesh and Enkidu, and so on through a
list of heroic bonded males, not all of them with Christian associations.) The Knight confronts a good prior and a bad abbot; in another structural balance, Robin (like outlaws in the
Legenda Aurea and similar collections[4]) worships Mary but is
murdered by a prioress who loves another knight. The legend
of Eustace the Monk (forest renegade, outlawed nobleman, and
trickster; one of his disguises is that of a potter, cf. Child 121)
is sometimes cited as an analogue to the Robin Hood ballads,
and a number of motif-analogues in early exempla and miracles
of Mary link his story to Robin Hood's.[5] The miraculous return
of a loan (*Gest* 248) reflects Proverbs 19:17 ("He that hath
pity upon the poor lendeth unto the Lord; and that which he
hath given will he pay him again") as paraphrased in *Piers
Plowman* B VIII 82–83 and elsewhere.[6] It would seem that as
a Christian poem the *Gest* is a more crowded hunting-ground
than some other late-medieval pieces that have been more dili-
gently searched for game. We are not complaining of the neglect,
but noticing an emptiness that might some day be filled.

The motif-analogues just mentioned are a reminder that international folklore science made contributions to Robin Hood
studies even in advance of Stith Thompson's *Motif-Index to
Folk Literature,*[7] which omits the ballads and metrical romances
as a source of research, while of course including numerous
overlapping sources — e.g., in the chapter on "Deceptions" motif K 385, "Host robs guest [cf. *Gest* 234ff.]," which is cited
only from India. Child's headnote and Clawson's monograph
contain the partly organized materials for an extensive analysis
of certain motifs in the *Gest*. Clawson is particularly impressive
when he lays out (pp. 26–40) the varieties of the motif "Deity
repays a loan" in two major branches (sober miracle, jocular

4. Child, III, 51.
5. Child, III, 53, 109; Clawson, pp. 15ff.; Maurice Keen, *The Outlaws of Medieval Legend* (Toronto: University of Toronto Press, 1961),
pp. 53–63.
6. Child, III, 52n.; Clawson, p. 25.
7. Rev. and enl. ed. (Bloomington: Indiana University Press, 1955–
1958). There is no such index to the ballads, but see Gerald Bordman,
Motif Index of the English Metrical Romances, FF Communications 190
(Helsinki: Academia Scientarium Fennica, 1963).

imitation of a miracle), located in Arabic, Latin, French, Anglo-French, Provençal, Spanish, Russian, Norse, and Middle English sources. I cannot find that anyone has taken the matter further since 1909.

Robin Hood's international connections are a legitimate concern of comparative mythologists as well as folklorists, but the loose theorizing of some myth critics has provided fair game to critics of other persuasions at least since Child (III, 47–48) demolished Kuhn's equation of Robin Hood and the Hobby-Horse. Students of myth, however, not disposed to accept refutation as an argument, continue to present Robin Hood as myth, mythic ritual, and mythic archetype in works of very different value. Lord Raglan's *The Hero* (1936, 1949) maintains that ritual drama generates all traditional narrative and uses Joseph Ritson's *Robin Hood* (1795) as authority for treating the English hero as a mythic-heroic criterion.[8] Robert Graves' *The White Goddess: A Historical Grammar of Poetic Myth* (1948), an engrossing if deeply subjective work, relates Robin Hood to ancient and modern mythic cults. From white goddesses to green men is an easy step, and John Speirs took it a year after the book by Graves,[9] but it remained for Northrop Frye to adopt the identification of Robin Hood and the Green Man into an elegant and cohesive archetypal theory,[10] one which incidentally explains the "resonance" mentioned at the beginning of this es-

8. See my review in *Speculum,* 28 (1953), 606–611. I was probably wrong to attack Raglan on the grounds of documentary error and historical misunderstandings. A few centuries mean nothing to a myth, and a Robin Hood of the late May Games is as legitimately mythic or folkloristic as a Robin Hood of the early ballads.

9. "Sir Gawain and the Green Knight," *Scrutiny,* 16 (1949), 247 and n.; cf. his *Middle English Poetry* (London: Faber and Faber, 1957), p. 289.

10. *Anatomy of Criticism* (Princeton: Princeton University Press, 1957), p. 144: "The identity of the human body and the vegetable world gives us the archetype of Arcadian imagery, of Marvell's green world, of Shakespeare's forest comedies, of the world of Robin Hood and other green men who lurk in the forests of romance, these last the counterparts in romance of the metaphorical myth of the tree-god." Cf. Thoreau's "Walking," pp. 193–194: "English literature . . . is an essentially tame and civilized literature, reflecting Greece and Rome. Her wilderness is a green wood, — her wild man a Robin Hood." Thoreau had quoted from the *Gest,* p. 164.

say between the *Gest,* a Shakespearean pastoral comedy, and an American visionary of the last century.

Folklore and myth studies may deal with Robin Hood as archetypes of genesis; oral-formular and comparative heroic studies provide frameworks within which to consider archetypes of heroic diction and heroic action. To date, these latter branches of current scholarship have all but ignored Robin Hood and his *Gest.* A good close study of its diction, motifs, and themes, in a formulary analysis that embraced also the other early outlaw ballads, would make the *Gest* eligible for inclusion in some unwritten chapter resembling Albert B. Lord's "Some Notes on Medieval Epic" in *The Singer of Tales.*[11] Studies as early as W. M. Hart's *Ballad and Epic* and Clawson's *Gest of Robin Hood* (pp. 9ff.) and as recent as David C. Fowler's *A Literary History of the Popular Ballad,*[12] call attention to the "symmetry" and "elaborate repetition" of certain stanzas in the *Gest.* These are symmetrical and repetitive either as the result of authorial composition or as a result of the strictures of oral-traditional composition, or both, but in any case they exhibit formular metrical language and the interchangeable variables of formulaic systems, and so deserve a special treatment from formular criticism. The stanzaic analyses just mentioned are essentially structural, not lexical, metrical, and formulaic. For Fowler, "formulaic" is a synonym for "perfunctory" (p. 10). While it goes without saying that "formulaic" is no longer properly a synonym for "oral,"[13] some examination of the *Gest* as a transitional (oral to written) text might well carry further Fowler's interesting thesis that the *Gest* was the product of a new fifteenth-century minstrelsy, an original but transitional

11. Cambridge, Mass.: Harvard University Press, 1960. Cf. his pertinent chapter on "Writing and Oral Tradition," which wrestles with the categorical difficulties for the oral-formular critic inherent in transitional texts, of which the *Gest* is an excellent example.

12. Durham, N.C.: Duke University Press, 1968, pp. 77ff. Fowler does not mention Clawson.

13. Ann Chalmers Watts, *The Lyre and the Harp* (New Haven: Yale University Press, 1969), pp. 195–197 and passim; Larry D. Benson, "The Literary Character of Anglo-Saxon Formulaic Poetry," *PMLA,* 81 (1966), 334–341.

poem, not the reorganized detritus of earlier ballads (p. 79 and passim).

As for the identification of Robin Hood among the archetypes of heroic action in orally based traditional narrative poetry, that is, for the comparative study of themes in the *Gest,* the world is all before us where to choose. H. M. Chadwick's *The Heroic Age* (1912) considered but two cultures (Greek and Teutonic) and their typical poetry, whereas C. M. Bowra's *Heroic Poetry* (1952) considers dozens, among them the formulaic Homer and the oral-formular singers of modern Yugoslavia. Neither comparativist mentions the *Gest,* which exists apparently in a limbo somewhere just outside the heroic mode, in a cloud of ambiguous and conflicting definitions.

The word "epic" has caused some of the confusion. The larger term "heroic" easily contains epic forms plus a number of related nonepic or partly epic forms: the *Iliad,* a heroic epic; *Beowulf,* an "epic-elegy" perhaps, after Tolkien; *Maldon,* a heroic lay; *Brunanburg,* a heroic panegyric, and so on. With such reasonable nomenclature there would be no difficulty in thinking of the *Gest* as, say, a heroic ballad. We could then send the term "epic" on vacation until some of the confusion died down and was forgotten:

> Gummere: *"The Gest of Robin Hood* is an epic poem." [14]
> Child: "The Gest is a popular epic." [15]
> Leach: "This poem is a kind of popular epic." [16]
> Gerould: "The *Gest* . . . is not an epic at all." [17]

Nor need one consider it less than an epic, that is, a spoiled epic or an unachieved epic, to see that the *Gest* is more than what Karl Brunner called it, "just a conglomeration of bal-

14. F. B. Gummere, *The Popular Ballad* (Boston: Houghton Mifflin, 1907), p. 270.

15. Child, III, 49.

16. MacEdward Leach, ed., *The Ballad Book* (New York: Harper and Brothers, 1955), p. 14.

17. Gordon Hall Gerould, *The Ballad of Tradition* (Oxford: Clarendon Press, 1932), pp. 102–103.

lads." [18] It is no more a conglomeration of ballads than the *Iliad* is a conglomeration of songs, but both are heroic poems: the *Gest* is a minor heroic poem, with affinities also to the romance (it being like the *Odyssey* in this).

If we paraphrase and summarize Bowra's first chapter in *Heroic Poetry,* the *Gest* will respond to almost every one of Bowra's touchstones. In the main, heroic poetry is international and archetypal (not local; often not national), anthropocentric or humanistic (not deistic or theocentric), objective (not sentimental or didactic), narrative (not lyric), linear (not stanzaic), lengthy (not brief), and is in origin oral, musical, and anonymous (not literary); it can be distinguished from earlier shamanistic poetry (the hero as magician), and it often absorbs panegyric and elegy into narrative; the heroic concern with honor is supposed to entertain us and enlarge our imaginations. It is possible to quibble about a few of these criteria as applied to the *Gest* — Robin of Barnsdale is arguably a more local hero than Odysseus of Ithaka; the *Gest,* like the vastly heroic but stanzaic *Poetic Edda,* fails the linear test — but on the whole the *Gest,* whatever its epic status, is more heroic than not. It also has strong ties with the heroic subgenres of praise and lament. Remarkably, in so humorous a poem, one of its chief themes is elegaic, in the heroic tradition of the outlaw-exile. Robin Hood is a late-English *wrecca,*[19] deserted toward the end by all but a pair of his *comitatus:*

> By than the yere was all agone
>   He had no man but twayne,
> Lytell Johan and good Scathelocke,
>   With hym all for to gone.
> Robyn sawe yonge men shote
>   Full fayre vpon a day;
> 'Alas!' than sayd good Robyn,
>   'My welthe is went away.

18. In MacEdward Leach, ed., *Studies in Medieval Literature in Honor of Professor Albert Croll Baugh* (Philadelphia: University of Pennsylvania Press, 1961), pp. 219–220.

19. Cf. Stanley B. Greenfield, "The Formulaic Expression of the Theme of Exile in Anglo-Saxon Poetry," *Speculum,* 30 (1955), 200–206.

'Somtyme I was an archere good,
  A styffe and eke a stronge;
I was compted the best archere
  That was in mery Englonde.
'Alas!' then sayd good Robyn,
  'Alas and well a woo!
Yf I dwele lenger with the kynge,
  Sorowe wyll me sloo.'   (435–438)

The paradoxes of his outlawed state make for a curious pathos. Robin is exiled in the forest, where he is in effect a king; when he joins the real king at court, he is in exile from his proper kingdom, but when he returns to his own forest he is killed — though not promptly enough for a tragic effect (twenty-two years! — which however pass in a single stanza, 450).

The farther we press the *Gest's* heroic affinities, and they should clearly not be pressed all the way, the more we find it suspended not only between two related genres, ballad and epic, but also between these and a third, romance; and here too the *Gest* remains either an unacknowledged orphan or the object of hesitation and dispute. Among the romances its close kin are found in the Matter of England, especially in *Havelok* and *Gamelyn.* Indeed, authorities on romance often notice this kinship, but without admitting the *Gest* to the canon of noncyclic legendary English romances.[20] Rather strangely, the most impressive witness for the *Gest* as a product of romance-related minstrelsy, David C. Fowler, omits any reference to *Havelok* and *Gamelyn.* With the latter poem the *Gest's* ties are particularly close; *Gamelyn's* plot was even reworked into a later Robin Hood ballad, "Robin Hood Newly Revived" (Child 128). Whatever their possible backgrounds in oral tradition, both poems come down to us as minstrel products, blocked (in the case of *Gamelyn,* very roughly) in "fits" and addressed to a bourgeois or proletarian audience. They share themes of outlawry and forest exile, of wrestling and rescue, of inheritance

20. Laura A. Hibbard [Loomis], *Mediaeval Romance in England* (New York: Oxford University Press, 1924), pp. 158–161; Charles W. Dunn in J. Burke Severs, gen. ed., *A Manual of the Writings in Middle English* (New Haven: The Connecticut Academy of Arts and Sciences, 1967), Fascicule 1, p. 32.

and legalized injustice. They exemplify the class-conscious, anti-ecclesiastical social protest of the age,[21] and so they seem political to us, though Child pronounced that Robin Hood had "no sort of political character, in the Gest or any other ballad" (III, 43). Fowler has suggested that songs of radical protest in the 1960s may have helped to bring this aspect of the *Gest* closer to us,[22] and there is a startlingly topical evocation of the Watergate era toward the end of *Gamelyn*:[23]

> The justice and the sherreve   bothe honged hie
> To waiven with ropes   and with the wind drie.
>   (879–880)

The themes of political revenge and of corruption in high places through bribery and conspiracy are prominent in the *Gest* also, in the episode of the Knight and the Abbot. The Abbot has retained (that is, bribed) the Chief Justice "both with cloth and fee" (*Gest* 107) to help him victimize the Knight. Social historians therefore correctly treat the *Gest* and *Gamelyn* with other English romances of outlawry as symptoms of political unrest,[24] thereby revising Child's opinion; but it is irrelevant to this argument whether there was a real historical Robin Hood whose story generated a ballad, a romance, or a heroic ballad-romance. It is enough for the present to conclude that the *Gest* should properly be associated with such genres.

If the *Gest* may then legitimately be grouped with the romances through theme and content, I should like to conclude this short survey with some observations about the form of this unusual poem. We have been noticing contributions (or the lack

21. Dunn in *A Manual of the Writings in Middle English,* p. 32. The language of *Gamelyn* is "Ca. 1350–70, Northeast Midland" (*Manual,* p. 14). The *Gest* "may have been put together as early as 1400, or before. There are no firm grounds on which to base an opinion" (Child, III, 40).

22. Fowler, p. 332, who takes politics in the Robin Hood ballads for granted.

23. Donald B. Sands, ed., *Middle English Verse Romances* (New York: Holt, Rinehart and Winston, 1966), p. 180.

24. Keen, pp. 188, 213–214 and passim; David Parker, "Popular Protest in 'A Gest of Robyn Hode,'" *Modern Language Quarterly,* 32 (1971), 3–20.

of them) to the understanding of genesis and genre, which have only incidentally (as in our glance at oral-formular theory) touched on structure. In recent years, however, the structure of narrative in many genres has seemed to demand increasing attention. We shall limit our remarks about the structure of romance to two roughly contemporary and at first sight radically different examples, the *Gest* and Malory's Arthuriad.

They are alike in one compositional aspect. Each was put together serially and with certain additions and modifications from preexisting materials (in Malory's case from identifiable French and English romances in verse and prose, in the case of the *Gest* perhaps from earlier ballads and other tales that have not survived). The nature of the resulting design in Malory's great prose cycle had better remain beyond the scope of this article, but we may say pretty certainly of the *Gest* that if a selection of preexisting Robin Hood materials of any sort had been joined in a loose cycle and stitched together by an indifferently skillful minstrel or literary poet, the result would not be like the *Gest,* for the *Gest* has a striking design. Child (III, 50) called it a "three-ply web" plus a "mere epilogue." He "decomposed" it in a dense prose summary that may be outlined thus:

I. Robin Hood, the Knight, and the Abbot: fits 1, 2, 4.
II. Robin Hood, Little John, and the Sheriff: fit 3.
    Robin Hood, the Knight, and the Sheriff: fits 5, 6.
III. Robin Hood, the Knight, and the King: fits 7, 8.

We note first that this outline takes us only to *Gest* 450, omitting the "mere epilogue," 451–456. Next, this unparticularized analysis gives a disjointed appearance to the "three-ply web," there being a real awkwardness about the epilogue and an apparent incongruity in the location of fit 3 in Child's section II, where, however, it certainly belongs in terms of thematic content. Child's section II is, so to speak, the Sheriff's section, so fit 3 would be out of place in the first section, which is monopolized by Robin Hood and the Knight.

Let us make a different structural analysis, borrowing diagrammatic devices and supporting ideas from Albert B. Lord's alphabetical schema — the simple episodic interlocking structure

of a song in *The Singer of Tales*;[25] from a similar device in
Eugène Vinaver's commentary on "The Book of Sir Launcelot
and Queen Guinevere";[26] from the central theme of the same
author's "The Poetry of Interlace";[27] and from the elaborate
chart in Morton W. Bloomfield's "Episodic Motivation and
Marvels in Epic and Romance." [28] The reader may be glad to
learn that our composite analysis will be simpler than the sum of
its parts, but he must exert his imagination to think of the vertical outline below as somehow horizontal and linear (to show
this would take a fold-out page) so as to suggest a narrative
time-sequence as well as an interweaving or "interlocking of
episodes." [29] If we properly utilized Bloomfield's sigla to show
episodic *motivation,* we should be able in a chart like the one
following to trace minutely the leaping and lingering course of
the narrative within each of the episodes shown here *en bloc*.
Instead, our outline follows Child's in showing only the sequence
and relation of episodes. But the *Gest* is now seen as an episodic
interlaced structure containing three plots and a structurally
cogent epilogue, in nine episodes distributed through eight fits;
the "epilogue" is in effect the ninth fit. The three plots are (A)

25. P. 96, in analysis of the "Song of Bagdad." "The structure could
be schematized as follows: a (council), b¹ (letter), c (conversation), d¹
(letter), d² (answer), b² (answer). Theme b is interrupted by themes c
and d, which are counterparts of a and b."

26. *The Works of Sir Thomas Malory* (Oxford: Clarendon Press,
1947), III, 1573–75.

27. In *The Rise of Romance* (New York: Oxford University Press,
1971), with citations (pp. 79, 92nn.) of John Leyerle, "The Interlace
Structure of *Beowulf*," *University of Toronto Quarterly,* 37 (1967), 1–
17, and Rosemond Tuve, *Allegorical Imagery: Some Medieval Books
and their Posterity* (Princeton: Princeton University Press, 1966), who
discusses *entrelacement* and special qualities of "web-structure," pp. 363–
364.

28. In his *Essays and Explorations* (Cambridge, Mass.: Harvard University Press, 1970). See also Bloomfield's joint review of Vinaver's *The
Rise of Romance* and William W. Ryding's *Structure in Medieval Narrative* (The Hague: Mouton, 1971) in *Speculum,* 48 (1973), 584–587. I
have not yet been able to see Ryding's book.

29. Bloomfield, "Episodic Motivation," p. 101. I intend no reference
to Bloomfield's different uses of the terms "horizontal" and "vertical,"
p. 108. Cf. his caveat in *Speculum,* 586, that "narrative moves in time
and cannot be kept in mind at one time," and his reminder on the following page that "dividing a narrative into divisions is a very subjective
activity."

Robin Hood, Knight, and Abbot; (B) Robin Hood, Little John, Sheriff, and Knight; (C) Robin Hood, Knight, and King. The epilogue is (D) and now ought to be called the Morte of Robin Hood.

Relations	Fit	Episode	Stanzas
AB: 3+1	1	A₁: Robin Hood & Knight	1–81
	2	A₂: Knight & Abbot	82–143
	3	B₁: Robin Hood, Little John, & Sheriff	144–204
BA: 3+1	4	A₃: Robin Hood & Abbot	205–280
	5	B₂: Robin Hood & Sheriff	281–316
	6	B₃: Robin Hood, Sheriff, & Knight	317–353
CD: 2+1	7	C₁: Robin Hood, Knight, & King	354–417
	8	C₂: Robin Hood & King	418–449
	[9]	D : Morte	450–456

This outline, which may seem already pretentiously complicated, attempts to show the *Gest* as a reasonably well-articulated structure, but supplementary outlines could be imposed upon it to make its articulation appear somewhat more remarkable — the reader with a curious mind and a pencil is invited to make improvements. We might wish to show, for example, that plot (C) is linked reversely to (A) and (B) by the King's disguise as an Abbot (372ff.) and by his disguise as an outlaw in Lincoln green to ride upon Nottingham (418ff.), the structural point being that this stronghold was that of the late Sheriff. The King's disguises in (C) point back to majority stockholders in episodes (A) and (B).

The motivation of episodes in the *Gest* proves to be less sequential than that of the episodes in *Beowulf* as analyzed by Bloomfield,[30] which is perhaps the proper mode of epic, and resembles instead the blocking and interlocking of some of Malory's sources, like for instance the *Suite du Merlin*.[31] This interlocking or interlaced process Malory used himself to a much

30. "Episodic Motivation," pp. 125–128.
31. Vinaver, *The Works of Sir Thomas Malory,* III, 1266–73.

smaller degree; it was a process he progressively attempted to
undo in the pursuit of a more linear — in structural terms we
might have to say a more epic — design.[32] The author of the
Gest wove where Malory unwove. In effect, the Robin Hood
poem is structurally conservative and francophile in orientation,
and the interlace structure (if it is not an optical illusion, which
I think entirely possible) is of a type that Malory strove with
increasing skill to remove from his narrative.

What Malory added to his narrative was "a greater appearance of design and a greater sense of necessity" as he moved
toward the Morte of Balin or of Arthur;[33] but the *remanieur* of
the heroic ballad evidently wove his structure too tightly, motivating the Morte of Robin Hood only in the most rudimentary
way. The hero's death does not arise from his character or that
of any of his *comitatus* or out of the action of his return to the
forest. If the *Gest* poet was attempting a tragic culminating design, it eluded him, but some readers may think he almost
achieved something different, namely a suggestive structure. One
would like to know where he learned such a technique. One
wonders if he was aware that Robin Hood's charmed life and
ironic death (in a nunnery, of all places, as the victim of a
woman to whom he had entrusted himself) in some ways resem-
bled that other trickster Merlin's, at least in "the irony of his
death at the hands of the woman to whom he had recklessly
entrusted the secret of his 'subtle crafts.' " [34]

Our structural analysis, at any rate, suggests that this narrator
intended by the death stanzas more than "a mere epilogue" and
just possibly was striving for a rational (not, of course, a numer-
ological) relation of weight and balance. Some readers will think
that he achieved instead a bad structure, with a false ending like
that of the *Odyssey*. "Surely," writes G. S. Kirk of the structural
anomalies in that heroic romance or epic song, "those are right
who believe that the whole ending of the *Odyssey* [i.e., from
23.296], and at least the final book, is a patchwork which reveals
the taste, the capacity and some of the language of declining
exponents of the epic . . . , whether over-ambitious reciters or

32. Vinaver, III, 1273.
33. Vinaver, III, 1276.
34. Vinaver, III, 1277.

decaying singers and minor cyclical poets." [35] Was the maker of the *Gest* an overly ambitious minstrel, a failing ballad-singer, or a compiler of some skill?

"I shall proffer you large proffers," said Lancelot, ready to fight Meliagrance with one hand tied behind him. It is likewise good sport to try to show that *The Gest of Robin Hood* curiously resembles a French prose romance of the sort that Malory and his contemporaries knew, when it more obviously resembles an English metrical romance, and resembles even more some uncommon blend of ballad and epic. Its composer would have been puzzled at our categories, but might well have preferred lively disputes over his poem to an indifferent audience or a reading public in stasis, however well disposed.

> 'Smyte on boldely,' sayd Robyn,
> 'I giue the large leue.'

35. *The Songs of Homer* (Cambridge: Cambridge University Press, 1962), p. 251.

ALICE B. MORGAN

"Honour & Right" in *Arthur of Little Britain**

John Bourchier, Lord Berners (c. 1467–1533), a translator in
the tradition of Caxton, seems to have had no ideological axe to
grind, but to have responded simply to his own taste and that of
his intimates in determining to translate certain works into English. Unlike Caxton, he did not have to be primarily concerned
with what would sell, and unlike Malory he does not seem to
have been captivated by any major literary cloth whose elements
could be unraveled and rewoven. The range of his work is especially significant in its movement, in a manner almost too good
to be true, from *Huon of Bordeux* (1515)[1] and the medieval
chronicle of Froissart (1523–1525) through the late French
romance *Arthur of Little Britain,* to two brief but influential

* I am grateful to the American Association of University Women
which awarded me a grant for research in sixteenth-century English literature.

1. *Huon of Bordeux* (STC 13998.5, J. Notary) is now dated c. 1515
on the basis of its woodcuts. Sidney Lee edited the poem (Early English
Text Society, Extra Ser. vols. 40, 41, 43, 50; 1882, 1883, 1884, 1887).
The first edition of *Arthur of Little Britain* is now dated 1560? and was
printed by Redburn. There are four copies extant (STC 807). It was
again printed by T. East (1582). Dates are due to Katherine Pantzer
of the Houghton Library.

Spanish pieces, both of which have been credited with introducing Euphuism into English.[2] *The Castle of Love,* from the Spanish (via French) of Diego de San Pedro, is a striking mixture of love allegory, rhetoric (for the most part in lengthy letters), and social nicety, where reputation is all. The whole is presented through the eyes of a consoling and assisting narrator, whose role and presence contrast sharply with the transparence of narration in the two romances. Guevara's *Golden Book of Marcus Aurelius* is nearly all sententious rhetoric. Berners relied on a French version printed in 1531, and this was his last work of translation. He died shortly after the date of completion given in the colophon (1533), and it was published in 1535.[3]

Such a sequence encourages the literary historian, rightly or wrongly, to speak of the period's changing taste, as the audience moved from a ready acceptance of chivalric encounters with men and magic, culminating in the union of the hero with his golden princess, to a static tale of the anguish caused by the psychological effects of love and the social state of shame, culminating in separation and sentimental despair (as in *The Castle of Love*).[4] In this context, *Arthur of Little Britain* is of particular interest. Its author was at home in his chosen genre, and the story can serve as an encyclopedia of romance motifs. Most critics have accordingly thought of the book in terms of its action, especially since R. S. Loomis discerned important Celtic elements in two of the major encounters. It is ironic and also highly significant that while Loomis believes *Arthur of Little Britain* to embody most fully and accurately the story of the Perilous Bed and other Grail material, C. S. Lewis contends that it lacks "those roots in legend and folk-lore without which it is

2. See Lee, *Huon,* EETS ES 50, 985–988; C. S. Lewis, *English Literature in the Sixteenth Century Excluding Drama* (Oxford: Clarendon Press, 1954), pp. 150–151; Diego de San Pedro, *The Castle of Love,* ed. William G. Crane (Gainesville, Fla.: Scholars' Facsimiles and Reprints, 1950), Introduction.

3. Guevara, *The golden boke of Marcus Aurelius.* T. Berthelet, 1535. N. F. Blake, in "Lord Berners: A Survey" (*Medievalia et Humanistica,* 2, 1971) dates this 1531–32, rather than 1532–33 (p. 128).

4. See Blake, "Berners," 130, for a conjecture about this progression. Even if Berners encountered a change in taste in his own circle, however, the larger audience of his works apparently read both types well into the sixteenth century: see Lee, *Huon,* EETS ES 40, xlvii–xlviii.

hard for romance to have the necessary solidity." [5] W. P. Ker's assessment is even harsher. In his introduction to Berners' *Froissart,* he speaks of *Arthur of Little Britain* as "one of the mechanical rearrangements of the common matter that repeated the old stock incidents and sentiments wearily, a book that one would save, more for the honour of its ancestry and for the noble language, than for any merit in the author's imagination." [6]

The force of these strictures is enhanced by the fact that the first to voice them in print was Berners himself, in a rare personal statement[7] apologizing for the frivolity of his material:

> Wherfore, after that I had begon this sayd processe [of translation], I haue determined to haue left and gyuen vp my laboure, for I thoughte it sholde haue be reputed but a folye in me to translate be seming suche a fayned mater, wherin semeth to be so many vnpossybylytees: how be it than I called agayne to my remembraunce, that I had redde and seen many a sondrye volume of dyuerse noble hystoryes, wherin were contayned the redoubted dedes of the auncyent inuynsyble conquerours, & of other ryght famous knightes, who acheued many a straunge and wonderfull aduenture, the whyche, by playne letter as to our vnderstandynge, sholde seme in a maner to be supernaturall;

5. Lewis, p. 152; Loomis, *Celtic Myth and Arthurian Romance* (New York: Columbia University Press, 1927) pp. 172, 302–305. In *Arthurian Tradition and Chrétien de Troyes* (New York: Columbia University Press, 1949) he asserts that *Arthur of Little Britain* embodies the earliest version of the perilous bed motif (pp. 42, 206–208). But cf. E. Vinaver's discussion of this sort of reasoning in *The Rise of Romance* (New York: Oxford University Press, 1971), pp. 53–67. See also M. Schlauch, "The *Rémundar Saga Keisarasoner* as an Analogue of *Arthur of Little Britain,*" *Scandinavian Studies,* 10 (1929), 189–202, where she stresses the mythological import of Arthur's adventures (esp. 195–196).

6. *The Chronicle of Froissart,* ed. W. E. Henley, in *The Tudor Translations* XXVII (London, 1901), I, xvii.

7. This is apparently Berners' only entirely original preface. W. G. Crane, "Lord Berners' Translation of Diego de San Pedro's *Carcel de Amor,*" *PMLA,* 49 (1934), 1032–35, shows that Berners' prologue was taken from the French version of this work, while S. K. Workman, "Versions by Skelton, Caxton, and Berners of a Prologue by Diodorus Siculus," *Modern Language Notes,* 56 (1941), 252–258, notes that the prologue to Berners' *Froissart* is largely a translation of Diodorus. There is no translator's prologue to Berners' Guevara. Blake, "Berners" (note 3 above), notes parallels between the prologue to *Arthur* and some of Caxton's prologues, pp. 125–126.

wherfore I thought that this present treatyse myght as well be reputed for trouth as some of those . . . [8]

Berners not only offers a sound criticism of the romance, but suggests, in his justification, where the true problem lies. While we give many fantastic tales credence within their conventions, the events of *Arthur of Little Britain* are audaciously unconvincing. The numerous military engagements are recounted with detail and verve, but they always result in Arthur's triumph, sometimes with the aid of a master magician. The hero's friends are occasionally taken prisoner, but their ultimate rescue is never in doubt. The first and only significant death in his party occurs in chapter 107 (out of 117), producing a paroxysm of grief, although the character is quite minor. In addition to sheer implausibility, the romance offers repeated situations which eventually take on a parodic cast: one critic finds six incidents using Grail material! [9] But more important is the superficiality of the conflict. Good opposes evil, and although its total triumph is delayed, individual encounters always reflect that larger opposition and ultimate victory. One may compare the frequent occurrences in Malory (based on his sources) of conflicts between persons and principles neither wholly good nor wholly bad. Such potentially tragic motifs as divided loyalty, mistaken identity, inaccurate information, or temporary mental breakdown, all of which Malory uses to good advantage, are entirely absent from *Arthur of Little Britain*.[10]

8. E. V. Utterson, ed., *The History of the Valiant Knight Arthur of Little Britain* (London, 1814) iii–iv. Citations are to this edition, which follows Redburn closely but adds punctuation. Berners translates the French with little variation: I have compared the edition in the New York Public Library, *Le preux chevalier Artus de bretagne,* Paris, Michel Le Noir, 1509.

9. S. Michie, "*The Faerie Queene* and *Arthur of Little Britain,*" *Studies in Philology,* 36 (1939), 106.

10. It is not necessary to take Malory as the basis for comparison. Romances of far lesser stature than his, with events quite as extraordinary as those of *Arthur of Little Britain,* avoid this oversimplification. The other romance Berners translated, *Huon,* offers a hero who, like Arthur, has magic on his side — in this case Oberon, King of the Fairies. But Huon's over-confidence and stubbornness lose him Oberon's support (pp. 80, 97), as does an accidental lie (115–116), and later an intentional one. Gerames, one of Huon's supporters, opposes him in battle, by

The absence of meaning and complication in the external battles has its inner counterpart: Arthur is never assailed by doubt, inclined to disloyalty, or prone to despair. His single moment of indecision, noteworthy for its isolation, will be discussed below, but in general he is as impervious spiritually as he is physically. At his moment of supreme trial, at Porte Noyre for example, the description generates a powerful picture of the marvelous and the intimidating, but never transfers the quality of struggle to the protagonist himself:

> Than was Arthur so wery, & so sore trauayled, and his woundes bledde so fast, that he had much payne to sustain himselfe on his fete . . . out of [the] window there yssued suche a smoke & fume so blacke, that it made al the hous so darke that Arthur coude se nothing; the which fume stanke so abominably, that Arthur therby was nye dead: than there arose suche a wynde so grete & feruent, that it brast the glasse windowes & latesses, so that the tyles & stones flew all about the hous lyke hayle; . . . and the paleys trembled like to haue gone all to peces; and at the last he perceyued a brennynge spere al of fyre, the whiche . . . fell on a knyght as he lay a bedde, and so brent hym clene thrugh: and the fyre descended thrughout bedde and chambre and al, & sanke depe in to the erth: . . . and than al the hole palays began to tourne aboute lyke a whele . . . And so than at the last the tournynge of thys palays began to sece, and the derkenes began to avoyde & to waxe fayre and clere, and the ayre peasyble: than Arthur sate hym downe vpon the ryche beddes syde, ryght feble & faynt . . . than the voyce sayd agayne twyse: It is ended! it ys ended!   (143–144)

The high quality of this section is considerably undercut when, only a bit further on, Arthur runs another supernatural gamut at the Toure Tenebrous. The action here, like the name, is too

---

accident — and wins (192–199). Huon encounters some opponents who show qualities which are not purely evil: the giant's courtesy is ill rewarded by Huon (105), and when the Admiral learns that Huon is not dead in his dungeon, as he has been told, but instead is being cared for by his own daughter, he finds it a very good joke (143–144). *Paris and Vienne* and *Blanchardyn and Eglantine,* both translated by Caxton, offer other such instances in romances with similar overall situations.

similar to the earlier sequence to do more than sabotage its effect on the reader. More seriously, there is a failure of signification: the portentousness of the encounter is given no thematic justification. There is no principle of evil involved; Arthur's triumph shows him worthy to marry Florence but does not save a suffering land or defeat a force of disorder or malice. In the several such confrontations, there is only once an association between the enchantment and Arthur's human foes, and only once between the enchantment and forces opposing Christianity. We have only intimations divorced from meaning: this is the mystery without its heart. It will require a Spenser to reconstitute the kernel of significance for which the inexplicable and threatening shell is truly appropriate (as in the House of Busirane, at the end of *The Faerie Queene,* Book III).[11]

Despite its comprehensiveness and its artful construction, the plot of *Arthur of Little Britain* carries no great burden of meaning. The author's serious commitment seems rather to lie elsewhere, in his delicate presentation of the social environment. We see this most clearly in the first, and most striking, episode, the affair of Arthur and Jehannet, occupying only fifteen chapters, or roughly one tenth of the book.

Jehannet is the daughter of a bankrupt knight, now dead; she subsists in poverty with her mother. When Arthur first meets her, on a hunting expedition, Governor, his tutor, admonishes him: "remember how grete a lorde ye be, both of lygnage, honour, and of frendes; and thinke how that she is but a poore gentylwoman as to your knowlege. And if ye do her ony vylony to her body, as in takynge from her that he can not render agayne, syr, it were to you a grete synne, and ye ought therein to be more blamed than a nother meane persone" (10–11). Arthur's response and subsequent behavior show him to be a perfect gentleman, but his attraction to Jehannet is made clear. Now he becomes engaged to a lady with a dubious reputation, whose mother is anxious to cover up her daughter's deviation from virtue. To this end she offers Jehannet £500 to substitute

11. See Michie for a comparison of this episode and others in *FQ* with *Arthur*. *Huon* once again offers a contrast: one senses Oberon's association with the mystery of Christian sacrifice, and the romance treats seriously the opposition of Christian to Saracen.

for the bride. Jehannet's mother objects, but Jehannet herself agrees, refusing, however, any reward. When the trick has been turned, she reveals all to Arthur, who repudiates his bride, Perron. The latter soon dies of shame. Even before the substitution has been suggested, Jehannet teases Arthur about his approaching marriage, saying she is to be married the same day, at the same hour, to one who resembles him in all things. He is perplexed, but she refuses to be more forthright. And yet when Arthur is at last free of his entanglement, through Jehannet's sacrificial agency, he does not marry her, but rather embarks on five years of travel, with Florence as part of his goal. It is clear that Jehannet is unhappy at his action, for she weeps at his departure, although she says it is because she, a "poore orphelyne," is losing "her good lord and chief father" (38). Characteristically, we are told, concerning the dowry given to Jehannet when she was in bed with Arthur, pretending to be his wife, that "she kepte it tyl suche season as Arthur caused her to be crowned a quene, and gaue her Gouernar in mariage, as it is more playnely conteyned in this present boke" (36).

Several points must be considered in this matter. First, the affair, bringing the two together in marriage and yet not in marriage, is inconclusive despite its aura of predestination. It is not resumed, no child is born of it, and it does not culminate, ultimately, in marriage. (One may compare, in this regard, *Sir Degaré, Sir Torrent of Portyngale, Sir Eglamour of Artois,* and *Partonope of Blois,* in all of which an interrupted affair terminates in marriage.) Second, the narrator is willing to tell us the final end of Jehannet, even though that end is one hundred chapters distant, and even though it is an alliance suggested by Florence herself, as yet unknown to us (and to Arthur). Like the unorthodox treatment of this whole relationship, this suggests that the events are not central, but that the emotions and situation are. Arthur is unquestionably fond of Jehannet. Although he resists the fairy Proserpine when she tries to deflect his affection from Florence, he has some trouble resisting Jehannet, who is not seriously trying anything. His first message on his return to Brittany after his five-year absence is, to his squire: "Frende, ye muste go to my lorde and fader, and to my lady my moder, and to Jehannet, and salute me ryght humbly vnto them" (457) — five years, four hundred pages, and a fiancée have not erased Jehannet from Arthur's memory or affections. Indeed, when he does see her, and she weeps in welcoming him, Arthur "could not kepe his eyen fro dystyllyng of salte teares for her sake: for he loued so the damosel, that he was sore tempted to haue repented him in that he had fyaunced Florence" (460). Steven, Florence's magician companion, who is with Arthur on this visit, is afraid Arthur will not want to return to his engagements in the East.

On her part, Jehannet is very frank. When she hears of the approach of Florence, a paragon of beauty, virtue, and wealth, she declares, "I woulde gladly se her, and shal serue and loue her wyth a good herte: yet, notwythstandyng, I had rather haue had Arthur to haue bene my louer than hers" (523). Such sturdy independence is noteworthy in a romance in which, Lewis asserts, "there are no characters" (151). Certainly there are not many, but Jehannet is, equally certainly, an exception. Moreover, Florence, given only the usual rather dim characterization of a heroine, comes alive when she and Jehannet finally meet. Florence has descended from her chariot, and the duchess, Arthur's mother, who has ridden out of town to meet her, has alighted from her palfrey. The two embrace, and the duchess makes an enthusiastic speech of praise and welcome, to which Florence responds in kind. Jehannet is one of the party, and we are told:

Whan she sawe Florence come so richly, and that she was of so gret beuty, she wisshed in her hert that Florence had bene xxiiii. yeres elder than she was, for it greued her hert right sore, thassurance of her & of Arthur: how be it, she held her selfe contente, because of the gret honor and profyt of Arthur: & therewith she wente to Florence & enbraced her, and sayde: Madame, ryght hye honoured quene! of you wyl I make myne own dere loue the floure of al other, the gentil Arthur. And whan Florence herd her, she demaunded of the duches what she was? & what she ment by her saying? Than Florence and the duches sate downe togider, and there the duches recounted to Florence all the hole mater as it was of Arthurs fyrst wife, & how that Jehannet was sent for into the forest, & how that she had alwaies loued Arthur, & called him euer her lord and dere loue, and kept her self true to him. (524)

Despite the space accorded to them, it is not Arthur's many battles that one remembers most vividly in this romance, or even the supernatural encounters, fraught with mystery though they be, but such scenes as this of the two women discussing Jehannet and her devotion and marveling at it.

Florence proves herself equal to Jehannet, for the decision to marry her to Governor comes from her. And lest we fail to understand it, we are allowed to overhear another conversation, this time among three noblewomen:

> Than the countesse of Neruers sayd to the Countesse of Foreste: Madam, this noble lady Florence hath done right wysely & nobly to make these mariages. That is true, quod the lady Forest; she hath done it to thentent that Arthur shoulde not resorte to Jehannet, otherwise than reason & honour wolde. Than the lady Rossillon sayd, Ye, now Florence wil suffre theyr company in al honour & right. (527–528)[12]

There is further interest in this framing matter of Arthur and Jehannet. Here we have a love affair that goes awry, although the parties remain friends, and despite its consummation in some sort of good faith. There are few comparable situations. One occurs in another of Berners' translations, *The Castell of Loue,* by Diego de San Pedro. Although its sources are quite different, it shares with this example its explicitly social motivation. In a narrative which vacillates between allegory and social realism, Leriano and Laureola engage in courtly dialogue, an affair, and finally a chivalric rescue in which Leriano saves Laureola from the consequences of their passion. But after this she refuses to have anything more to do with him, preferring not to risk such dangers again. He despairs and dies. Laureola is grieved but considers her attitude justified. It is not clear why a marriage here was impossible, but Laureola is the daughter of a king. It seems likely, then, that Leriano was not sufficiently well-born to address her as a formal suitor. Such a social difference is common in romance, of course, where it can be overcome by valiant deeds or, occasionally, by the revelation of an unsuspected high

---

12. A similar ruse occurs in Caxton's *Blanchardyn and Eglantine,* ed. Leon Kellner, EETS ES 58 (1890, rpt. 1962), p. 73.

birth. (Indeed, it comes up in *Arthur of Little Britain,* since Arthur conceals his identity, leading Florence and her family to wonder if he is sufficiently noble to marry her.) The trouble with Jehannet, too, seems to be one of degree. Although romances offer numerous instances of a high-born lady ultimately accepting a knight of lower birth, there are few in which the process is reversed. (The sole example known to me is *Floris and Blanchefleur.*)[13] Thus the key words in the quotations above are "gret honor and profyt" and "honour & right." These sum up the goals of Arthur, Florence, Jehannet, and their friends and relations. In marrying Jehannet to Arthur's companion, Florence recognizes her merit, and the pair are awarded a kingdom, so that they can participate as equals in the social life of Arthur and his bride. At the same time, potential embarrassment is avoided for all concerned.

Nor is this the only part of the romance which displays the author's overwhelming interest in issues of honor and status. Governor's caution to Arthur about Jehannet has been cited above; in an early encounter Hector expresses interest in his hostess, and he and Governor have a debate on illicit love, ending in a joust, which Arthur must terminate by overcoming both participants (66–67). With this should be contrasted Governor's apparently inconsistent behavior later on, when he himself sleeps with a different hostess (289). The two cases are distinguished, however, in a very important way. In the first case, the host is old, with a wife of twenty-one. They are already in bed when Arthur and his friends, weary with travel and fighting, arrive. Yet this host tells his servants to make them welcome and sends his wife to do them honor. In the second instance, the Earl of Yle Perdue has refused, out of jealousy, to provide hospitality to any of the knights who are in town for a tournament. When he finally allows Governor in, it is only after ordering his wife to address no conversation to him and to answer none of his remarks. She is furious at being forced to be so discourteous, and the cuckolding is but one part of her revenge, for the next day Governor defeats the Earl roundly in the tournament. In the

13. See the analysis of love and degree in M. A. Gist, *Love and War in the Middle English Romances* (Philadelphia: University of Pennsylvania Press, 1947), pp. 65–71.

first case Hector would be effecting a breach of courtesy, for he has been hospitably received, while in the second, Governor is merely answering one discourtesy with another.

Serious love, of course, must be pure; it would not do for Arthur and Florence to dally. This is one of the charges her father brings against Florence, when she has again avoided marriage with the emperor: "she hath done me shame and despyte: for she hath gone awaye fro me with a straunge knyght, and she is come to hyde herself in this castel, & ther folyshely she kepeth company with this straunge knight; the which is a shame to her for euermore" (416) — he goes on in this vein for three pages. When he finds himself in his daughter's company, his conversation is only slightly more temperate, and they engage in one of numerous debates on the qualities of love:

> And whan the king perceiued that it was she, he sayd: Who hath brought the in to thys place wher as I am, syth thou haste shamed thy selfe with a fugityue knyght? A! syr, sayd Florence, for Goddes sake saye ye so no more: for, by the holy baptism that I receyued at the fonte stone, & on the dampnacion of my soule, my body was neuer by hym, nor by none other, enpayred, neyther in word nor in dede. Certaynly, said the kynge, fole as thou arte, I byleue the not: why hast thou elles ben so moche in his company without doyng of any other thing? for loke, where as the hert is, there is the body habandoned, for the body enclyneth to the herte. Why, sayde Florence, it nedeth not alwayes to accomplysshe al the wylle of the herte, but such as are honourable & good. (436)

Arthur comes to aid her argument, but Emendus is convinced only after much further discussion. Beside the problems of honor, those of simple physical triumph pale into insignificance.

We see this especially in the delineation of Arthur's character. His physical prowess is so great that it has no distinguishing features, and the author allows him not only a magic shield and sword, which are virtually impervious, but also the help of Steven's necromancy. This last on diverse occasions produces an imaginary army; storms of wind, rain, and mist; the removal of Arthur's sleeping enemies to his stronghold; and the transformation of Arthur and his friends to blacks to enable them to pass through the Emperor's lines. In his individual encounters, although he is always invincible, Arthur is also a model of courtesy. This is manifest in his treatment of women, of those lower in station than himself, and of those he has defeated: in general, then, in his attitude toward those over whom he has an advantage. Arthur praises loyalty, even to his enemies (123, 337). When possible, he refuses to kill, preferring to grant mercy. In the case of his arch-enemy Isembarte, nephew to the Duke of Bygor, Arthur leaves his fate to the lady Isembarte has most offended. "And whan the commen people of the countrey saw the duke desyre the ladye to pardon hys neuewe, they were in greate feare leaste that she would haue granted hys request; therfore a great company of them rusht into the prese, tyll they came there as syr Isembarte laye styll, and they all at ones layd on hym in suche wise, that they left no ioynt together wyth other" (272–273). In this way the aristocrats' chivalry is left untainted, but Isembarte does not escape his well-deserved death.

Arthur's courtesy is apparent when he refuses to wash with Steven "because he [Steven] was son vnto a kynge" (150), just as it is apparent when he, having overcome Governor in battle, finds a string of excuses for him. In a more striking instance of this same trait, we have the near debacle of the book's final tournament. This occurs when Arthur has conquered his enemies and is at last married to Florence. A tournament is proposed, wherein the knights of Soroloys will battle their recent allies, the knights of France. Arthur recognizes that this is likely to lead to trouble, and he and Governor disguise themselves and assist the French who are outnumbered ten to one. Despite the fantastic prowess of these two, the French are being beaten, but their pride does not permit them to yield. A friendly tournament is about to turn into a blood-letting, when Steven realizes what is happening, and says, "A! gentyl knyght! that cannest not fayle thy frendes! I cannot suffre any lenger that you shold endure more trauayle. Than the mayster blewe such a blast, that there rose sodenlye in the tourney such a myst, that one could scant se an other" (538). In this way, tragedy is averted, but the demands of both chivalry and courtesy are satisfied.

It is in their delicacy of response to the situations of love and war that the leading characters in this romance prove to deserve each other. And it is in the exploration of these situations that the author of *Arthur of Little Britain* seems most involved. To provide the necessary sense of courtly society for his readers, the narrator uses extensive sequences of conversation, both formal and informal. Frequently, major elements of his fantastic plot are recounted in the course of dialogue, or re-recounted. An example is the substitution of Jehannet for Arthur's affianced Perron, early in the book. First we are given the scene itself: "And whan that Arthur was thus a bedde, he beganne to draw nere to his wyfe as to his knowlege." And Jehannet, before permitting the nuptial rite, demands her dowry (26–27). This leads to the moment when Arthur is shown the dowry contract and ring, which he believes he gave to Perron, in Jehannet's possession. "A mercy God! quod Arthur, swete loue Jehannet, where hadde you this rynge and charter? Syr, ye delyuered it to me out of your owne hands in to myn. Of my delyueraunce! quod Arthur: I praye you, fayre lady, where was that? Certainly, syr, in your bedde. In my bed, fayre loue! and whan was that? As God helpe me, syr, this same nyghte paste . . ." (28–29). This teasing but courteous exchange leads to the moment when Governor makes his formal accusation of Perron, who has been unable to produce the dowry contract Arthur insists he has given her:

> She hath defouled her bodi with a nother knight: and therfore this night she caused an other damoysell, who was a true mayde, to lye by my lorde Arthur . . . How be it she was not so folish but or she wold suffre my lorde to touche her, she demaunded of him her dowrye: and so my lorde Arthur delyuered to her the charter and the ringe, as he thought none yll. And in dede, syr, to certefye this thinge, sende for the damoysell; and than shal ye know, by her owne mouthe, all the trouth how my lorde was betrayed. (32)

The differentiated levels of discourse ring true, and give the romance its social locale, which is very strong. The concern with love, honor, and status, together with the delicately conveyed milieu, fully justify Schlauch's treatment of *Arthur of Little Britain* as a "society romance." [14]

14. M. Schlauch, *Antecedents of the English Novel, 1400–1600* (Warsaw: Polish Scientific Publishers, 1963), pp. 69–75. She focuses almost exclusively on the episode involving Jehannet.

The tale thus offers a contrast in techniques. On the one hand are the broad strokes of its plot, its comprehensive romance motifs, and the simplicity of Arthur's physical heroism. On the other, we find precise and delicate delineations of social situations: romantic extravagance is here employed as a vehicle for social realism. Whether or not this combination accounts for Berners' decision to translate *Arthur of Little Britain,* it probably helped keep it popular in the latter half of the sixteenth century. Readers could respond either to its vigorous romance plot or to its more realistic treatment of social, moral, and psychological issues.

WILLIAM ALFRED

A Deliberate Analogue of Fitt I of *Thomas of Erceldoune* in the Thornton MS (1430–1440)

Committed in Honor of B. J. Whiting for Grateful Collation
by Scholars to Come

When, dazed with longing, alone he lay
   Underneath a fledging tree,
Thomas saw her make her way
   Through short grass green as the shallowing sea.

Her palfrey was a dappled grey
   Huge as a great moss-freckled stone;
And as the sun on an August day
   Her grey eyes warmed him to the bone.

His blood lurched up like a fountain spray.
   He ran where the mountain touched the sky;
And first, if it is as the stories say,
   At Eldon Tree they met eye to eye.

He threw himself upon one knee,
   Underneath the greenwood spray:
"Beautiful lady, be good to me
   Upon this puzzling April day.

Beautiful lady, be good to me,
   For I, I swear, am prepared to dwell
With you for life, or eternity,
   Either in Heaven or in Hell."

"Your flesh is earth; you will do me harm."
   She said. "But do with me what you will.
I must warn you, though: you will break the charm;
   And when you break the charm, you kill."

She sank to the grass, as soft as the light
   That played upon the greenwood spray;
And, if the story we have is right,
   Seven times with her he lay.

Thomas got up from their grassy bed
   And looked at her. Night was fondling day.—
Her hair hung like fly-clogged webs from her head;
   Her eyes seemed blind, they were so grey.

All her rich clothes had shredded away
   Like rotting damask on bones long dead.
One leg was black, the other, grey;
   And her flesh was as bruised as tarnished lead.

"What is it that I have brought to pass?"
   Said Thomas, crippled by that sight;
"Where is the August in your face,
   The dazzle that glazed your flesh with light?"

"Thomas, take leave of the sun and the moon.
   Take one long look at the leaves on that tree.
Deep under the earth, and under the stone,
   Your fate is to spend twelve months with me."

She led him in at Eldon Hill
   Through a ravine half-blocked with scree,
Dark as it is when the moon goes dark.
   The water rode up his shin to the knee.

One day he waded, then two, then three;
   And heard but the wash of the numbing flood.
At last, he said: "All is up with me.
   I am almost dead for lack of food."

She led him in to a pretty arbor
   Where rich fruit starred each heavy tree.
Sweetness bled through pears as salt through a harbor,
   And apples smelled sweet as a loaded bee.

He reached for the fruit with one shaking hand,
   That famished man about to faint.

She said: "Don't, Thomas. Let things stand.
   That fruit is sapped with the devil's taint.

If you pluck that, mark what I say,
   Your soul will sink in the fire of Hell,
And not float up before Doomsday,
   But drown in such pain as no tongue can tell.

When we reach my castle, I beg and pray,
   Do not fail in courtesy;
But whatever anyone may say,
   Make sure you answer none but me."

Thomas reached (and lived in) that fair place
   In such joy as no man's words can say,
Till one bright morning—God give us grace!—
   That lady told him: "Go away.

Hurry, Thomas. Go back again.
   You must. You can no longer stay.
Hurry with all your might and main.
   I will lead you back to Eldon Tree."

Thomas's grief was sharp as fear.
   "Beautiful lady, let me stay.
I know for a fact I have been here
   Two days at most, or perhaps, three."

"Listen, Thomas, and listen well:
   You have been here three years and more.
Longer than that no man may dwell
   Behind the shelter of this door.

Tomorrow, from hell, the filthy fiend
   Comes among us for his pay,
To choose the soul he can worst offend.
   He will choose you, Thomas. Go away.

For all the gold they could promise to pay,
   In this rich place where all mines end,
You will never be betrayed by me.
   I love you, Thomas. I am your friend."

She led him back to Eldon Tree,
   Underneath the greenwood spray.
As he stumbled through the rattling scree,
   The fiend caught her hand and took his pay.

She fell with her fingers stretched towards where he
   Had burst from the cave. She was bones and clay.
As he drank down the air, the birds flew free,
   And flooded with song both night and day.

The Writings of Bartlett Jere Whiting

1924

Poems of Carew, Suckling, Lovelace and Herbert, with Biographical Introductions, Haldeman-Julius Little Blue Book (Girard, Kansas: Haldeman-Julius).

Review

M. A. DeWolfe Howe, *Barrett Wendell and His Letters,* in *Harvard Advocate,* 111, 155–156.

1925

Review

Wilbur Cortez Abbott, *Conflicts with Oblivion,* in *Harvard Advocate,* 111, 203.

1926

"The Ballad of Lord Randal," *Journal of American Folklore,* 39, 81–82.

1931

"The Origin of the Proverb," *Harvard Studies and Notes in Philology and Literature,* 13, 47–80.

Review

Aus Mittelenglischen Medizintexten: Die Prosarezepte des Stockholmer Miszellankodex X.90, ed. G. Müller, in *Speculum,* 6, 488–489.

1932

"The Nature of the Proverb," *Harvard Studies and Notes in Philology and Literature,* 14, 273–307.

"A Further Note on Old English Tree Climbing: *Christ,* vv. 678–79," *Journal of English and Germanic Philology,* 31, 256–257. [Original title: "An Anglo-Saxon up a Tree."]

"Lieutenant Governor Thomas Oliver in Bristol," Publications of the Colonial Society of Massachusetts 28 (1935), *Transactions,* 1930–1933, 305–306.

"An Analogue to the Mak Story," *Speculum,* 7, 552.

Review

Helen Pennock South, *The Proverbs of Alfred Studied in the Light of the Recently Discovered Maidstone Manuscript,* in *Modern Language Notes,* 47, 263–264.

1933

"Proverbs in Certain Middle English Romances in Relation to Their French Sources," *Harvard Studies and Notes in Philology and Literature,* 15, 75–126.

"The *House of Fame* and Renaud de Beaujeu's *Le Biaus Desconeüs,*" *Modern Philology,* 31, 196–198.

Reviews

Kathryn Huganir, *The Owl and the Nightingale: Sources, Date, Author,* in *Speculum,* 8, 282–283.

Russell Krauss, Haldeen Braddy, and C. Robert Kase, *Three Chaucer Studies,* in *Speculum,* 8, 531–538.

1934

Chaucer's Use of Proverbs, Harvard Studies in Comparative Literature 11 (Cambridge, Mass.: Harvard University Press).

"Ac he kan hongi bi þe boȝe: Owl and Nightingale, v. 816," *Anglia,* 58, 368–373.

"Some Current Meanings of 'Proverbial'," *Harvard Studies and Notes in Philology and Literature,* 16, 229–252.

"Proverbial Material in the Popular Ballad," *Journal of American Folklore,* 47, 22–44.

"Scott and Wyntoun," *Philological Quarterly,* 13, 296.

Reviews

English Lyrics of the Thirteenth Century, ed. Carleton Brown, in *Speculum,* 9, 219–225.

Eugen Schnell, *Die Traktate des Richard Rolle von Hampole "Incendium Amoris" und "Emendatio Vitae" und deren Übersetzung durch Richard Misyn,* in *Modern Language Notes,* 49, 272–273.

1935

"Proverbial Material in the Old-French Poems on Reynard the Fox," *Harvard Studies and Notes in Philology and Literature,* 18, 235–270.

"Proverbs in the *Ancren Riwle* and the 'Recluse'," *Modern Language Review,* 30, 502–505.

"Proverbs in the Writings of Jean Froissart," *Speculum,* 10, 291–321.

Review

G. R. Owst, *Literature and Pulpit in Medieval England,* in *Modern Language Notes,* 50, 338–341.

1936

"A Handful of Recent Wellerisms," *Archiv für das Studium der neuern Sprachen und Literaturen,* 169, 71–75.

"Old Maids Lead Apes in Hell," *Englische Studien,* 70, 337–351.

"More on Chaucer's Pardoner's Prologue (*CT* VI (C) 377–90)," *Modern Language Notes,* 51, 322–327.

"The Earliest Recorded English Wellerism," *Philological Quarterly,* 15, 310.

"Proverbial Material in the Poems of Baudouin and Jean de Condé," *Romanic Review,* 27, 204–228.

1937

"Reynard Climbs (*Owl and Nightingale* 816)," *Anglia,* 61, 126–128.

"The Miller's Head," *Modern Language Notes,* 52, 417–419.

Reviews

R. H. Hodgkin, *A History of the Anglo-Saxons,* in *Speculum,* 12, 122–124.

William George Smith, *The Oxford Dictionary of English Proverbs,* in *Modern Language Notes,* 52, 433–434.

1938

Proverbs in the Earlier English Drama, with Illustrations from Contemporary French Plays, Harvard Studies in Comparative Literature 14 (Cambridge, Mass.: Harvard University Press).

"The Devil and Hell in Current English Literary Idiom," *Harvard Studies and Notes in Philology and Literature,* 20, 201–247.

Review

Sister Mary Ernestine Whitmore, *Medieval Domestic Life and Amusements in the Works of Chaucer,* in *Speculum,* 13, 370–372.

1939

With Frances W. Bradley, Richard Jente, Archer Taylor, and M. P. Tilley, "The Study of Proverbs," *Modern Language Forum,* 24, 57–83.

1941

"The Wife of Bath's Prologue and Tale," in *Sources and Analogues of Chaucer's* Canterbury Tales, ed. W. F. Bryan and Germaine Dempster (Chicago: University of Chicago Press), pp. 207–268.

1942

"The Early Period," in *The College Survey of English Literature,* ed. B. J. Whiting, Fred B. Millett, Alexander M. Witherspoon, et al. (New York: Harcourt, Brace).

1944

"A Dramatic Clyster," *Bulletin of the History of Medicine,* 16, 511–515.

"A New-England Dialogue," *American Speech,* 19, 227–228.

"The Pronunciation of the Latin Language in America and Hungary," *The Classical Journal,* 40, 104–106.

"Some Chaucer Allusions, 1923–42," *Notes and Queries,* 187, 288–291.

"Guyuscutus, Royal Nonesuch and Other Hoaxes," *Southern Folklore Quarterly,* 8, 251–275.

1945

"Emerson, Chaucer, and Thomas Warton," *American Literature,* 17, 75–78.

"American Wellerisms of the Golden Age," *American Speech,* 20, 3–11.

"Canoodle," *American Speech,* 20, 178–183.

" 'Mossyback' and 'Carpetbagger'," *American Speech,* 20, 236–237.

"Pepys, Fuller and an Archbishop," *Harvard Theological Review,* 38, 71–73.

" 'By My Fader Soule,' *CT* II (B) 1178," *Journal of English and Germanic Philology,* 44, 1–8.

"The Wee Ghaist and Oral Transmission," *Journal of American Folklore,* 58, 48–50.

"A Fifteenth-Century English Chaucerian: The Translator of Partonope of Blois," *Mediaeval Studies,* 7, 40–54.

"Troilus and Pilgrims in War Time," *Modern Language Notes,* 60, 47–49.

"A Probable Allusion to Henryson's *Testament of Cresseid,*" *Modern Language Review,* 40, 46–47.

"Óhthere (Óttar) and *Egil's Saga,*" *Philological Quarterly,* 24, 218–226.

"English Proverbs of Stéphane Mallarmé," *Romanic Review,* 36, 134–141.

"The Vows of the Heron," *Speculum,* 20, 261–278.

"Diccon's French Cousin," *Studies in Philology,* 42, 31–40.

Review

Joanna Carver Colcord, *Sea Language Comes Ashore,* in *New England Quarterly,* 18, 516–520.

1946

"Froissart as Poet," *Mediaeval Studies,* 8, 189–216.

"Words from *A Glossary of Virginia Words* Current in Maine," *Publication of the American Dialect Society,* no. 6, pp. 44–46.

1947

" 'By My Fader Soule,' *CT* II (B) 1178," *Journal of English and Germanic Philology,* 46, 297.

"Canoodle-Kidoodle," *American Speech,* 22, 75–76.

"Independent Origins: Maine and Morogoro," *Journal of American Folklore,* 60, 85–86.

"Gawain: His Reputation, His Courtesy and His Appearance in Chaucer's *Squire's Tale,*" *Mediaeval Studies,* 9, 189–234.

"Incident at Quantabacook, March 1764," *The New England Quarterly,* 20, 169–196.

"Proverbial Sayings from Fisher's River, North Carolina," *Southern Folklore Quarterly,* 11, 173–185.

"Partial Immersion in Georgia and Maine," *Southern Folklore Quarterly,* 11, 261–262.

Review

"Folklore in Recent Maine Books," *Southern Folklore Quarterly,* 11, 149–157.

1948

"A Word List from Morrill, Maine (c. 1887)," *American Speech,* 23, 111–116.

"Apperson's *English Proverbs and Proverbial Phrases:* Some Additions and Corrections," *Journal of American Folklore,* 61, 44–48.

"Notes on the Fragmentary Fairfax Version of the *Disticha Catonis*," *Mediaeval Studies,* 10, 209–215.

"A Colt's Tooth," *Mediaeval Studies in Honor of Jeremiah Denis Matthias Ford,* ed. U. T. Holmes and A. J. Denomy (Cambridge, Mass.: Harvard University Press), pp. 319–331.

"John Maxwell's *Sum Reasownes and Prowerbes*," *Modern Language Notes,* 63, 534–536.

"Report of Delegates to the American Council of Learned Societies," *Speculum,* 23, 535–537.

Reviews

"Folklore in Recent Maine Books II," *Southern Folklore Quarterly,* 12, 211–223.

A Treasury of New England Folklore: Stories, Ballads, and Traditions of the Yankee People, ed. B. A. Botkin, in *Western Folklore,* 7, 396–406.

1949

"Lowland Scots and Celtic Proverbs in North Carolina," *Journal of Celtic Studies,* 1, 116–127.

"Proverbs and Proverbial Sayings from Scottish Writings before 1600. Part One. A–L.," *Mediaeval Studies,* 11, 123–205.

"The Rime of King William," *Philologica: The Malone Anniversary Studies,* ed. Thomas A. Kirby and Henry Bosley Woolf (Baltimore: Johns Hopkins Press), pp. 89–96.

"Emerson and Merlin's 'Dungeon Made of Air'," *PMLA,* 64, 598–599.

"A Maine Word-List from David Barker's 'My First Courtship' (c. 1869)," *Publication of the American Dialect Society,* no. 11, pp. 28–37.

Reviews

The Good Wife Taught Her Daughter. The Good Wyf Wold a Pylgremage. The Thewes of Gud Women, ed. Tauno F. Mustanoja, in *Speculum,* 24, 606–607.

Proverbia Communia: A Fifteenth Century Collection of Dutch Proverbs Together with the Low German Version, ed. Richard Jente, in *Western Folklore,* 8, 87–90.

"Recent Historical Novels," *Speculum,* 24, 95–106.

George R. Stewart, "Men's Names in Plymouth and Massachusetts in the Seventeenth Century," in *New England Quarterly,* 22, 125–126.

1950

"Report of the Delegate to the American Council of Learned Societies," *Speculum,* 25, 411–413.

Reviews

"Historical Novels (1948–1949)," *Speculum,* 25, 104–122.

William George Smith, *The Oxford Dictionary of English Proverbs,* second ed. rev. Sir Paul Harvey, in *Western Folklore,* 9, 93–96.

1951

"The Early Period," in *The College Survey of English Literature,* Shorter Version, rev. (New York: Harcourt, Brace). [See 1942: all changes were made by the publisher without consulting Whiting.]

"Proverbs and Proverbial Sayings from Scottish Writings before 1600 (Part Two, M-Y)," *Mediaeval Studies,* 13, 87–164.

"Report of the Delegate to the American Council of Learned Societies," *Speculum,* 26, 569–572.

Review

"Historical Novels, 1949–1950," *Speculum,* 26, 337–367.

1952

"Proverbs and Proverbial Sayings," in *The Frank C. Brown Collection of North Carolina Folklore,* ed. N. I. White and Paull F. Baum (Durham, N.C.: Duke University Press), 1, 331–501.

"Report of the Delegate to the American Council of Learned Societies," *Speculum,* 27, 441–445.

"William Johnson of Natchez: Free Negro," *Southern Folklore Quarterly,* 16, 145–153.

Reviews

Randle Cotgrave, *A Dictionarie of the French and English Tongues,* reproduced from the first edition, London 1611, with an introduction by William S. Woods, in *Speculum,* 27, 94–96.

Standard Dictionary of Folklore, Mythology, and Legend, ed. Maria Leach, in *Speculum,* 27, 228–234.

"Historical Novels, 1950–1951," *Speculum,* 27, 507–530.

1953

"Report of the Delegate to the American Council of Learned Societies," *Speculum,* 28, 631–635.

"Tilley's Dictionary of Proverbs," *Western Folklore,* 12, 30–43 and 105–113.

Reviews

Selwyn Gurney Champion, *Racial Proverbs: A Selection of the World's Proverbs Arranged Linguistically,* in *Journal of American Folklore,* 66, 185–187.

"Historical Novels (1951)," *Speculum,* 28, 527–554.

1954

"Miller's Head Revisited," *Modern Language Notes,* 69, 309–310.

"Report of the Delegate to the American Council of Learned Societies," *Speculum,* 29, 639–642.

1955

Traditional British Ballads (New York: Appleton-Century-Crofts).

"Report of the Delegate to the American Council of Learned Societies," *Speculum,* 30, 502–508.

1956

"Report of the Delegate to the American Council of Learned Societies," *Speculum,* 31, 557–562.

1957

"Report of the Delegate to the American Council of Learned Societies," *Speculum,* 32, 629–633.

Review

"Thirteen Historical Novels," *Speculum,* 32, 118–142.

1958

With Archer Taylor, *A Dictionary of American Proverbs and Proverbial Phrases, 1820–1880* (Cambridge, Mass.: Harvard University Press).

"Report of the Delegate to the American Council of Learned Societies," *Speculum,* 33, 447–452.

With Urban T. Holmes and Taylor Starck, "Alexander Joseph Denomy," *Speculum,* 33, 461–462.

Review

Scottish Poetry: A Critical Survey, ed. James Kinsley, in *Journal of English and Germanic Philology,* 57, 108–112.

1959

"Report of the Delegate to the American Council of Learned Societies," *Speculum,* 34, 518–523.

With Urban T. Holmes and Charles R. D. Miller, "Jeremiah Denis Matthias Ford," *Speculum,* 34, 531–532.

1960

"Sir Richard Baker's *Cato Variegatus* (1636)," in *Humaniora: Essays in Literature, Folklore, Bibliography Honoring Archer Taylor on His Seventieth Birthday,* ed. Wayland D. Hand and Gustave O. Arit (Locust Valley, N.Y.: Augustin), pp. 8–16.

"Report of the Delegate to the American Council of Learned Societies," *Speculum,* 35, 507–512.

1961

"Vignette LXV: 'Fred Norris Robinson'," *PMLA,* 76 (June), ii–iii.

"Report of the Delegate to the American Council of Learned Societies," *Speculum,* 36, 522–527.

1962

Respectfully Submitted: Reports to the Mediaeval Academy by Its Delegate to the ACLS (New York: American Council of Learned Societies). [Reports 1948–1961]

"Report of the Delegate to the American Council of Learned Societies," *Speculum,* 37, 476–482.

1963

A Selection of Scottish Verse of the Fourteenth, Fifteenth, and Sixteenth Centuries (Cambridge, Mass.: Harvard University Department of English).

"Report of the Delegate to the American Council of Learned Societies," *Speculum,* 38, 515–520.

With F. P. Magoun, Jr., and H. M. Smyser, "Howard Rollin Patch," *Speculum,* 38, 530–531.

1964

"Report of the Delegate," *Speculum,* 39, 581–588.

1965

"A Collection of Proverbs in BM Additional MS. 37075," in *Franciplegius: Medieval and Linguistic Studies in Honor of Francis Peabody Magoun, Jr.,* ed. Jess B. Bessinger and Robert P. Creed (New York: New York University Press), pp. 274–289.

"Report of the Delegate," *Speculum,* 40, 569–575.

With H. M. Smyser and Taylor Starck, "Charles Roger Donohue Miller," *Speculum,* 40, 585.

1966

"Fred Norris Robinson," *Chaucer Review,* 1, iii.

"Report of the Delegate," *Speculum,* 41, 580–585.

1967

With F. P. Magoun, Jr., and H. M. Smyser, "Fred Norris Robinson," *Speculum,* 42, 591–592.

1968

Proverbs, Sentences, and Proverbial Phrases from English Writings Mainly before 1500, with the collaboration of Helen Wescott Whiting (Cambridge, Mass.: Harvard University Press).

"Report of the Delegate to the American Council of Learned Societies," *Speculum,* 43, 559–564.

1969

"Report of the Delegate to the American Council of Learned Societies," *Speculum,* 44, 513–518.

1970

"Introduction," in George Lyman Kittredge, *Chaucer and His Poetry,* Fifty-fifth Anniversary Edition (Cambridge, Mass.: Harvard University Press), pp. vii–xxxvi, reprinted as "George Lyman Kittredge," *Harvard Library Bulletin,* 18, 382–394.

"Report of the Delegate to the American Council of Learned Societies," *Speculum,* 45, 505–511.

1971

"Report of the Delegate to the American Council of Learned Societies," *Speculum,* 46, 556–563.

1972

"Proverbs in Cotton Mather's 'Magnalia Christi Americana'," *Neuphilologische Mitteilungen,* 73, 477–484.

"Report of the Delegate to the American Council of Learned Societies," *Speculum,* 47, 584–591.

1973

"George Lyman Kittredge," in *Dictionary of American Biography,* Supplement Three 1941–1945, ed. Edward T. James (New York: Scribner's), pp. 422–424.

"Report of the Delegate to the American Council of Learned Societies," *Speculum,* 48, 607–613.

Contributors

WILLIAM ALFRED, Ph.D. '57
  Department of English
  Harvard University
  Cambridge, Massachusetts

J. B. BESSINGER, JR., Ph.D. '52
  Department of English
  New York University
  New York, New York

JOHN B. BESTON, Ph.D. '66
  University of Western Australia
  Nedlands, Australia

KENNETH A. BLEETH, Ph.D. '70
  Department of English
  Boston University
  Boston, Massachusetts

CHRISTOPHER BROOKHOUSE, Ph.D. '64
  Department of English
  University of North Carolina
  Chapel Hill, North Carolina

LEGER BROSNAHAN, Ph.D. '58
  Department of English
  Illinois State University
  Normal, Illinois

ALFRED DAVID, Ph.D. '57
  Department of English
  Indiana University
  Bloomington, Indiana

MORTIMER J. DONOVAN, Ph.D. '51
  Department of English
  University of Notre Dame
  South Bend, Indiana

ANTHONY E. FARNHAM, Ph.D. '64
  Department of English
  Mount Holyoke College
  South Hadley, Massachusetts

ALBERT B. FRIEDMAN, Ph.D. '52
  Department of English
  Claremont Graduate School
  Claremont, California

JOSEPH HARRIS, Ph.D. '69
  Department of English
  Stanford University
  Stanford, California

STANLEY J. KAHRL, Ph.D. '62
  Center for Medieval and Renaissance Studies
  Ohio State University
  Columbus, Ohio

ANNE THOMPSON LEE, Ph.D. '74
  Department of English
  Bates College
  Lewiston, Maine

R. T. LENAGHAN, Ph.D. '57
  Department of English
  University of Michigan
  Ann Arbor, Michigan

JOHN LEYERLE
  Centre of Medieval Studies
  University of Toronto
  Toronto, Canada

ROBERT LONGSWORTH, Ph.D. '65
  Department of English
  Oberlin College
  Oberlin, Ohio

JAMES I. MILLER, Ph.D. '67
  Department of English
  Northern Illinois University
  DeKalb, Illinois

ALICE B. MORGAN, Ph.D. '67
  Brookline, Massachusetts

GEORGE F. REINECKE, Ph.D. '60
  Department of English
  Louisiana State University, New Orleans
  New Orleans, Louisiana

EDMUND REISS, Ph.D. '60
  Department of English
  Duke University
  Durham, North Carolina

ALAIN RENOIR, Ph.D. '55
  Department of English and Comparative Literature
  University of California at Berkeley
  Berkeley, California

JAMES REPPERT, Ph.D. '53
Department of English
Albright College
Reading, Pennsylvania

FLORENCE H. RIDLEY, Ph.D. '57
Department of English
University of California at Los Angeles
Los Angeles, California

DONALD B. SANDS, Ph.D. '53
Department of English
University of Michigan
Ann Arbor, Michigan

DAVID STAINES, Ph.D. '73
Department of English
Harvard University
Cambridge, Massachusetts

MCKAY SUNDWALL, Ph.D. '72
Department of English
Columbia University
New York, New York

PAUL THEINER, Ph.D. '62
Department of English
Syracuse University
Syracuse, New York

ELIZABETH WALSH, RSCJ, Ph.D. '74
Department of English
Louisiana State University
Baton Rouge, Louisiana

The sixth volume in this series, *The Worlds of Victorian Fiction,* will be edited by Jerome H. Buckley; the seventh will deal with the influence of Shakespeare in the western tradition, especially Anglo-Saxon-speaking countries.

Morton W. Bloomfield
Jerome H. Buckley
Reuben A. Brower
Harry Levin

— Editorial Board